SWAMP THING

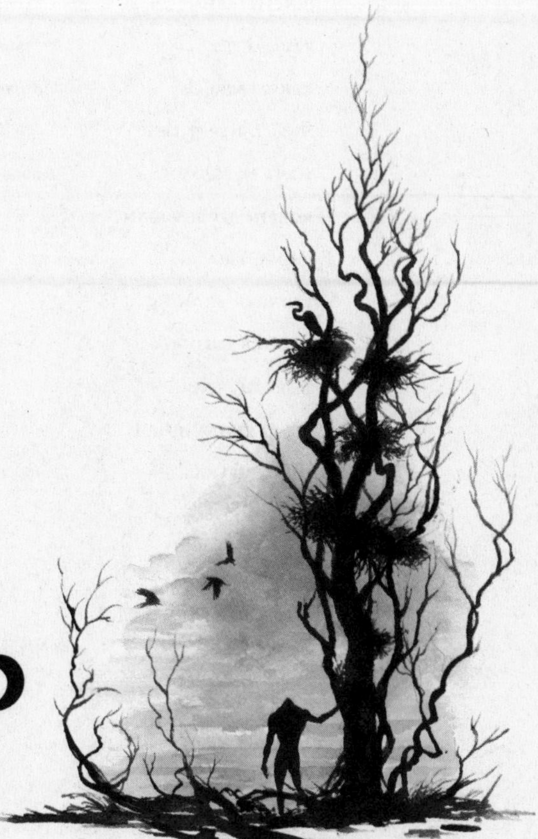

earth to earth

ALAN MOORE   RICK VEITCH
JOHN TOTLEBEN   ALFREDO ALCALA

TATJANA WOOD
COLORIST

JOHN COSTANZA
LETTERER

STEPHEN BISSETTE
ORIGINAL COVERS

SWAMP THING CREATED BY LEN WEIN & BERNI WRIGHTSON

SWAMP THING: EARTH TO EARTH PUBLISHED BY DC COMICS. COVER
AND COMPILATION COPYRIGHT © 2002 DC COMICS. ALL RIGHTS
RESERVED. ORIGINALLY PUBLISHED IN SINGLE MAGAZINE FORM AS
SWAMP THING 51-56. COPYRIGHT © 1986, 1987 DC COMICS. ALL
RIGHTS RESERVED. ALL CHARACTERS, THEIR DISTINCTIVE LIKENESSES
AND RELATED ELEMENTS FEATURED IN THIS PUBLICATION ARE
TRADEMARKS OF DC COMICS. THE STORIES, CHARACTERS AND
INCIDENTS FEATURED IN THIS PUBLICATION ARE ENTIRELY FICTIONAL.
DC COMICS DOES NOT READ OR ACCEPT UNSOLICITED SUBMISSIONS
OF IDEAS, STORIES OR ARTWORK. DC COMICS, 1700 BROADWAY,
NEW YORK, NY 10019. A WARNER BROS. ENTERTAINMENT COMPANY.
PRINTED IN CANADA. SECOND PRINTING. ISBN: 1-56389-804-7.
ISBN 13: 978-1-56389-804-4. COVER ART BY JOHN TOTLEBEN.
PUBLICATION DESIGN BY LOUIS PRANDI.

table of contents

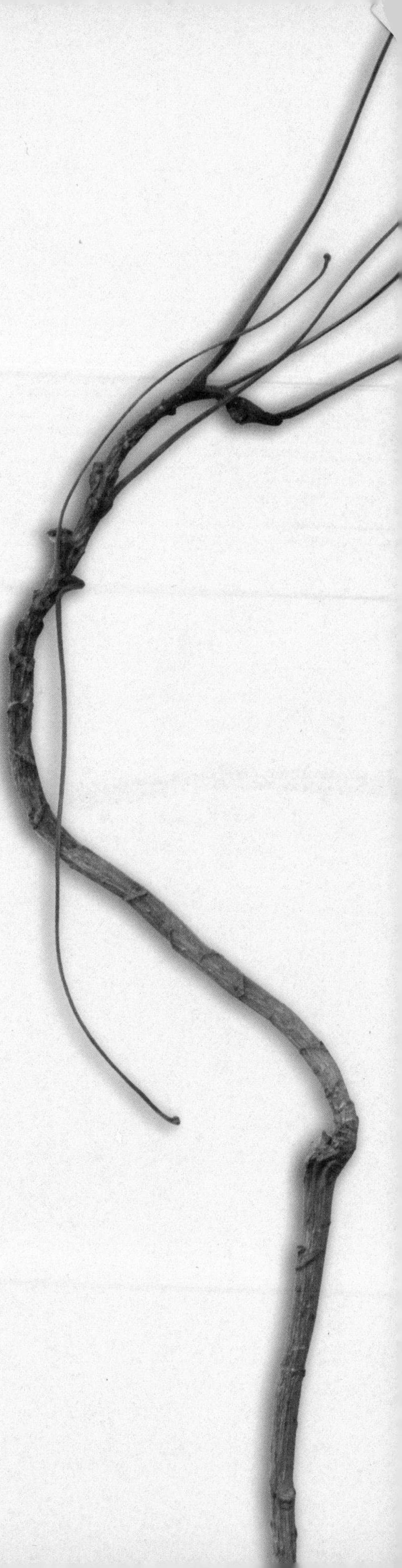

SWAMP THING
earth to earth

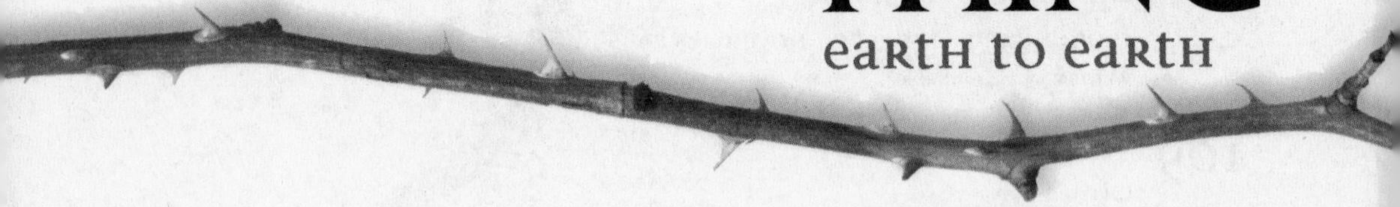

CHAPTER 1

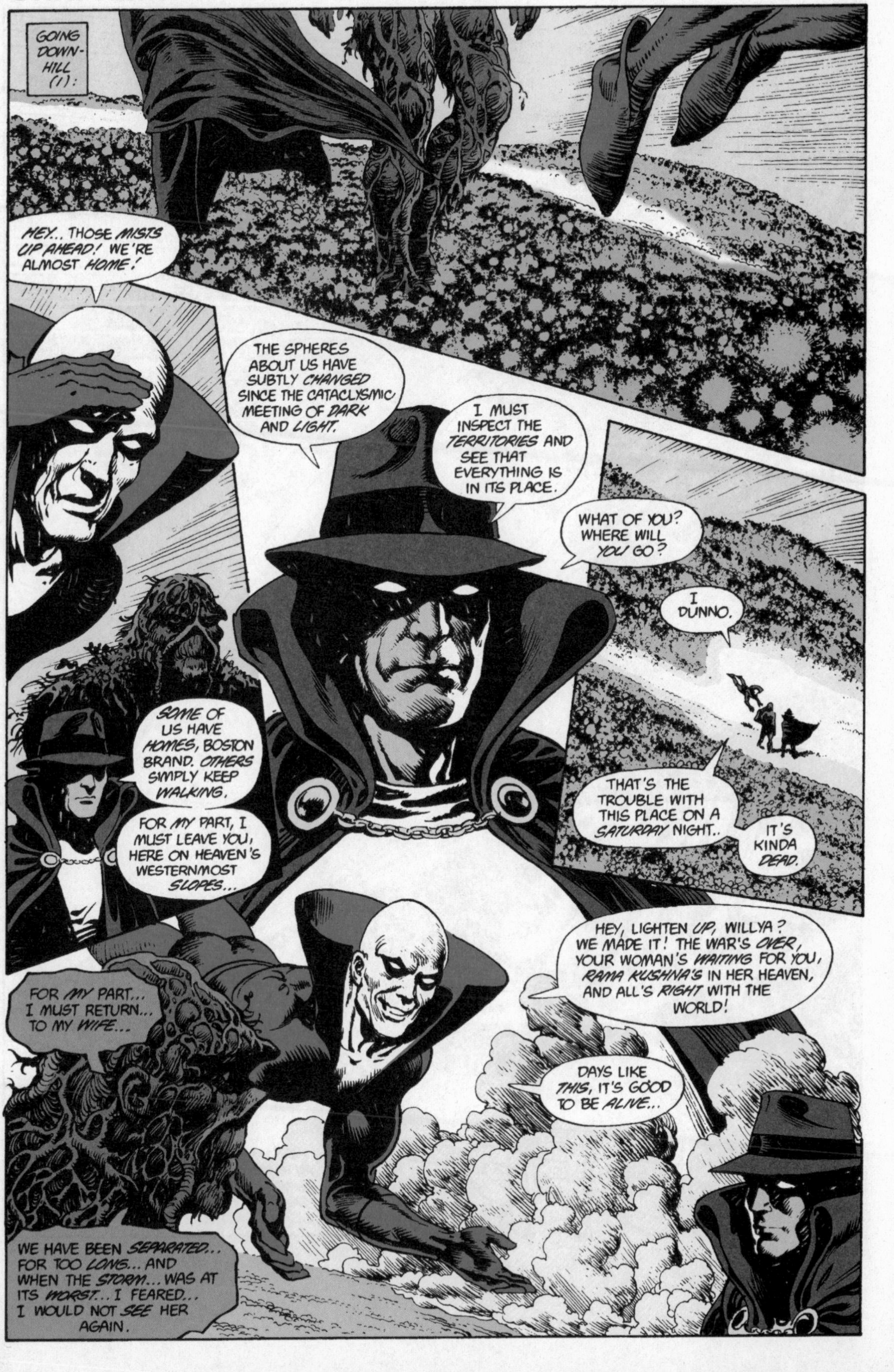
GOING DOWN-HILL (1):
HEY... THOSE MISTS UP AHEAD! WE'RE ALMOST HOME!
THE SPHERES ABOUT US HAVE SUBTLY CHANGED SINCE THE CATACLYSMIC MEETING OF DARK AND LIGHT.
I MUST INSPECT THE TERRITORIES AND SEE THAT EVERYTHING IS IN ITS PLACE.
WHAT OF YOU? WHERE WILL YOU GO?
I DUNNO.
THAT'S THE TROUBLE WITH THIS PLACE ON A SATURDAY NIGHT..
IT'S KINDA DEAD.
SOME OF US HAVE HOMES, BOSTON BRAND. OTHERS SIMPLY KEEP WALKING.
FOR MY PART, I MUST LEAVE YOU, HERE ON HEAVEN'S WESTERNMOST SLOPES...
HEY, LIGHTEN UP, WILLYA? WE MADE IT! THE WAR'S OVER, YOUR WOMAN'S WAITING FOR YOU, RAMA KUSHNA'S IN HER HEAVEN, AND ALL'S RIGHT WITH THE WORLD!
FOR MY PART... I MUST RETURN... TO MY WIFE...
DAYS LIKE THIS, IT'S GOOD TO BE ALIVE...
WE HAVE BEEN SEPARATED... FOR TOO LONG... AND WHEN THE STORM... WAS AT ITS WORST... I FEARED... I WOULD NOT SEE HER AGAIN.

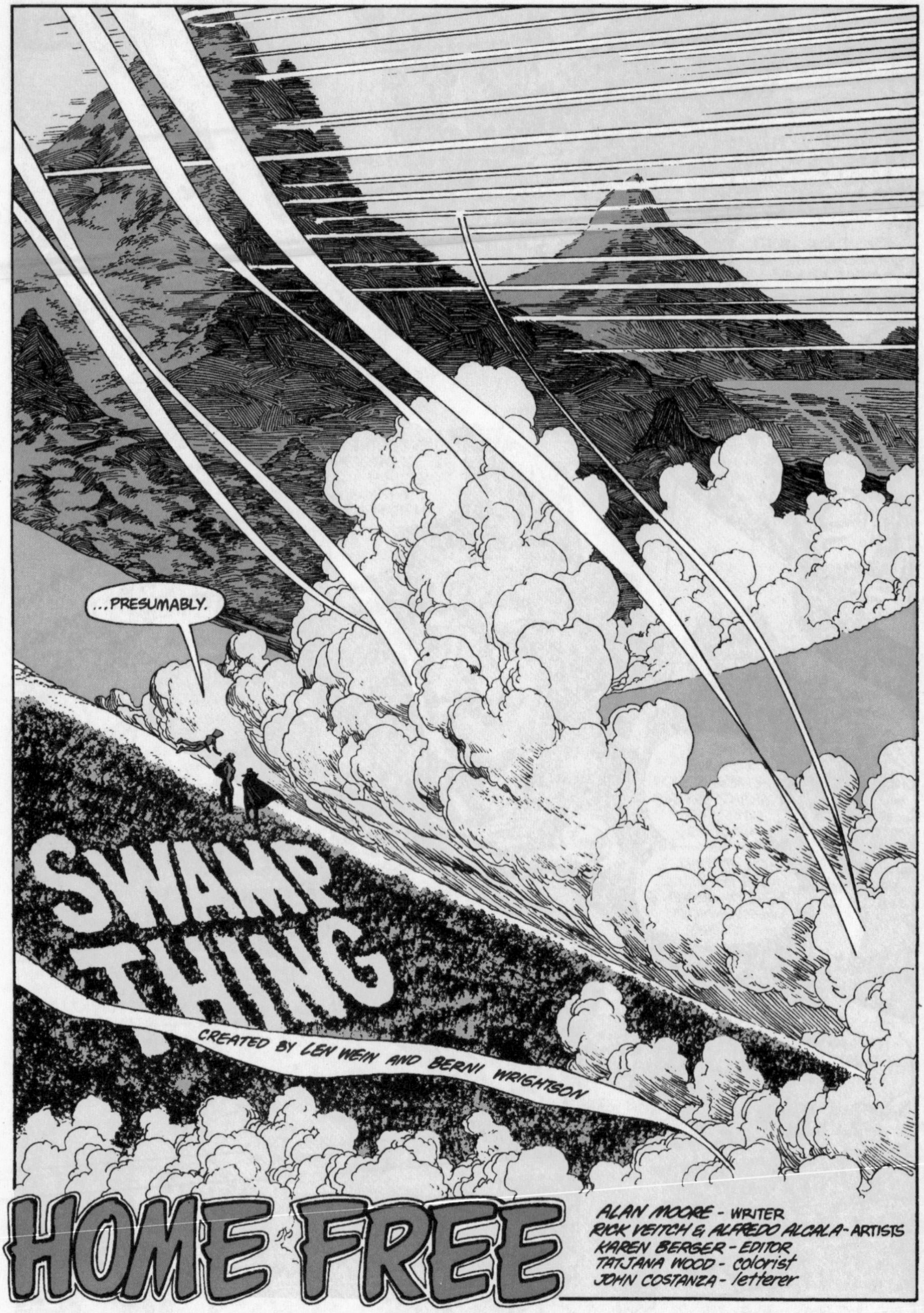
...PRESUMABLY.
SWAMP THING
CREATED BY LEN WEIN AND BERNI WRIGHTSON
HOME FREE
ALAN MOORE - WRITER
RICK VEITCH & ALFREDO ALCALA - ARTISTS
KAREN BERGER - EDITOR
TATJANA WOOD - colorist
JOHN COSTANZA - letterer

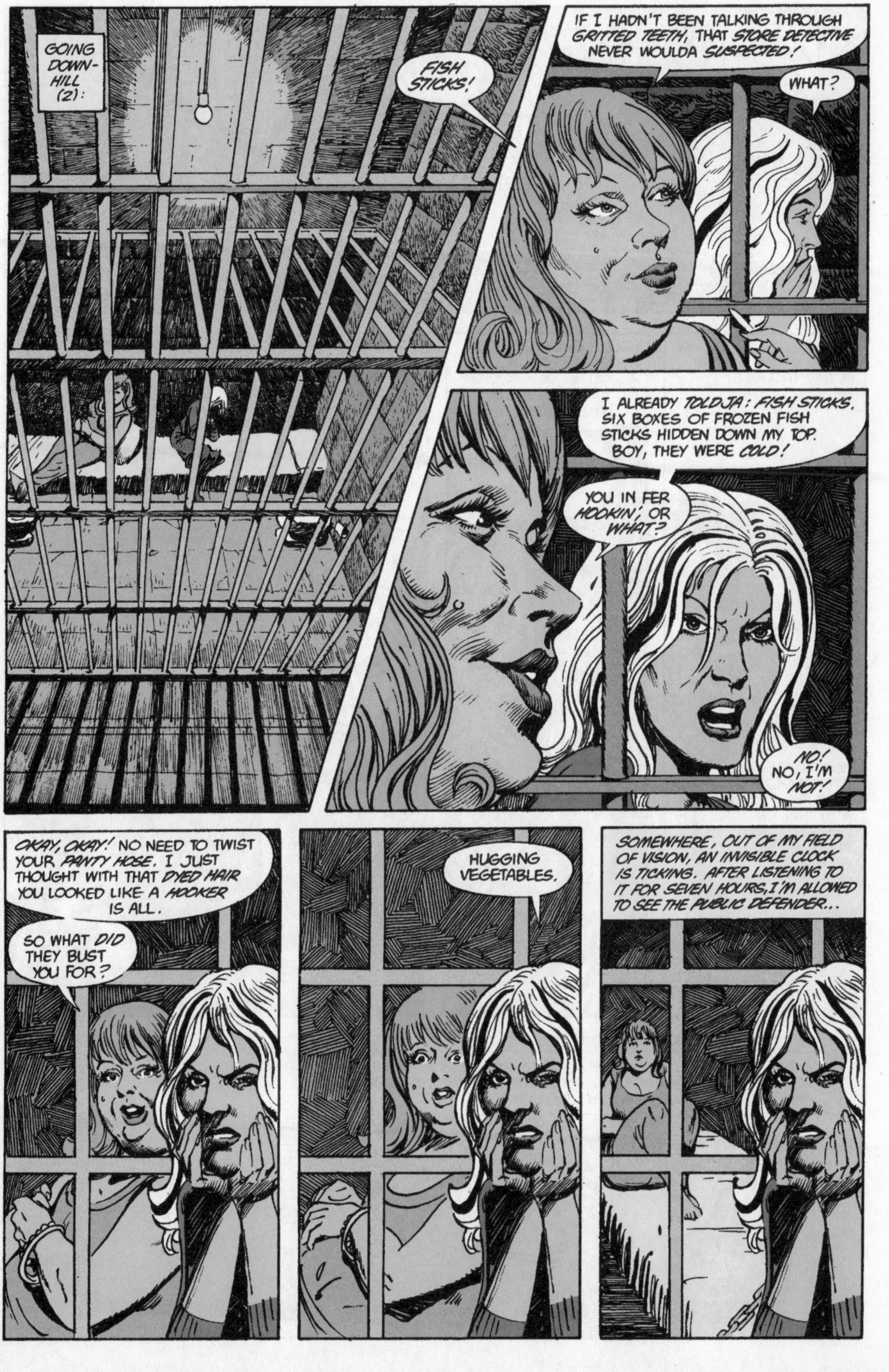
GOING DOWN-HILL (2):
FISH STICKS!
IF I HADN'T BEEN TALKING THROUGH GRITTED TEETH, THAT STORE DETECTIVE NEVER WOULDA SUSPECTED!
WHAT?
I ALREADY TOLDJA: FISH STICKS. SIX BOXES OF FROZEN FISH STICKS HIDDEN DOWN MY TOP. BOY, THEY WERE COLD!
YOU IN FER HOOKIN', OR WHAT?
NO! NO, I'M NOT!
OKAY, OKAY! NO NEED TO TWIST YOUR PANTY HOSE. I JUST THOUGHT WITH THAT DYED HAIR YOU LOOKED LIKE A HOOKER IS ALL.
SO WHAT DID THEY BUST YOU FOR?
HUGGING VEGETABLES.
SOMEWHERE, OUT OF MY FIELD OF VISION, AN INVISIBLE CLOCK IS TICKING. AFTER LISTENING TO IT FOR SEVEN HOURS, I'M ALLOWED TO SEE THE PUBLIC DEFENDER...

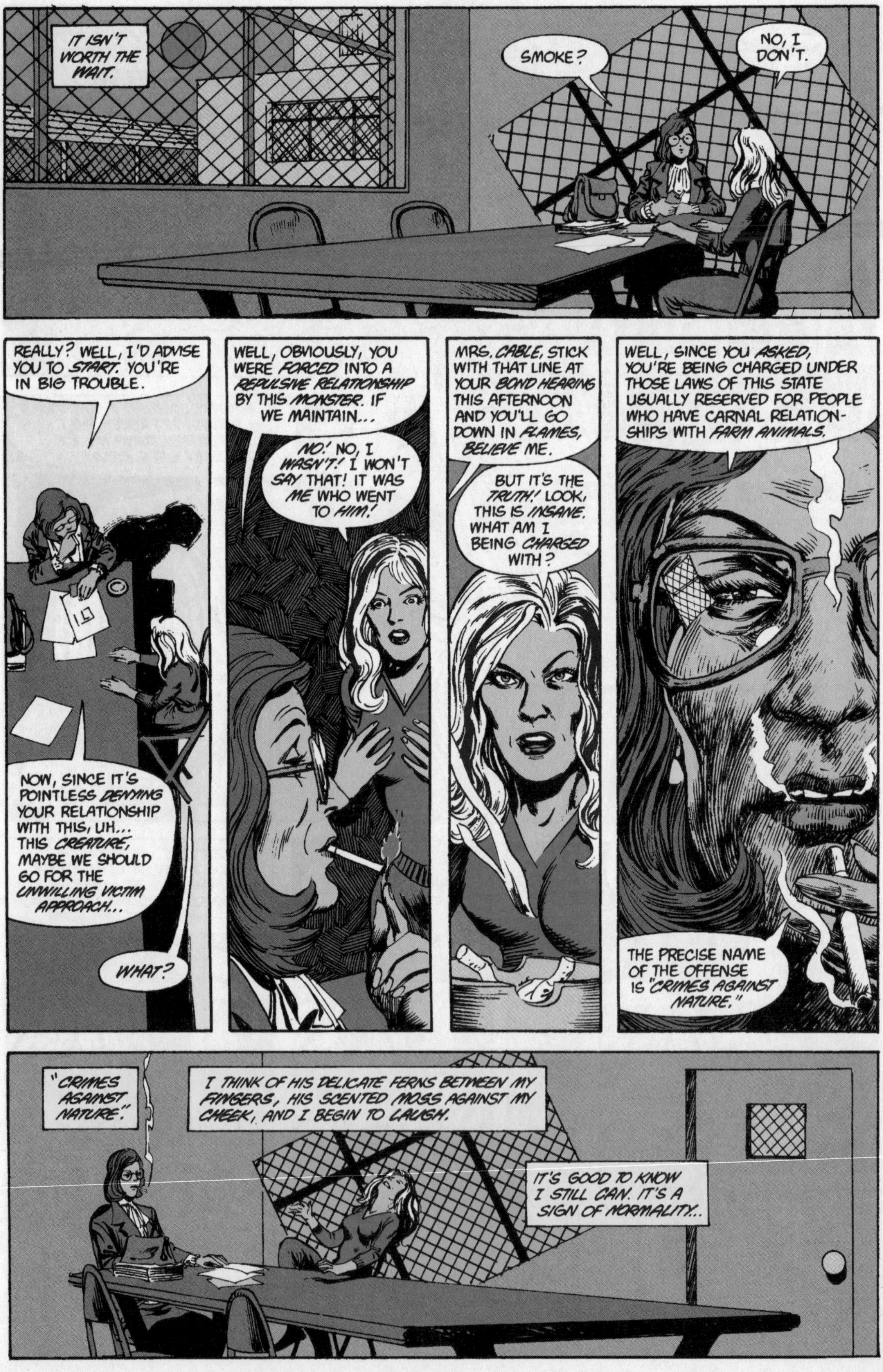
IT ISN'T WORTH THE WAIT.
SMOKE?
NO, I DON'T.
REALLY? WELL, I'D ADVISE YOU TO START. YOU'RE IN BIG TROUBLE.
NOW, SINCE IT'S POINTLESS DENYING YOUR RELATIONSHIP WITH THIS, UH... THIS CREATURE, MAYBE WE SHOULD GO FOR THE UNWILLING VICTIM APPROACH...
WHAT?
WELL, OBVIOUSLY, YOU WERE FORCED INTO A REPULSIVE RELATIONSHIP BY THIS MONSTER. IF WE MAINTAIN...
NO! NO, I WASN'T! I WON'T SAY THAT! IT WAS ME WHO WENT TO HIM!
MRS. CABLE, STICK WITH THAT LINE AT YOUR BOND HEARING THIS AFTERNOON AND YOU'LL GO DOWN IN FLAMES, BELIEVE ME.
BUT IT'S THE TRUTH! LOOK, THIS IS INSANE. WHAT AM I BEING CHARGED WITH?
WELL, SINCE YOU ASKED, YOU'RE BEING CHARGED UNDER THOSE LAWS OF THIS STATE USUALLY RESERVED FOR PEOPLE WHO HAVE CARNAL RELATIONSHIPS WITH FARM ANIMALS.
THE PRECISE NAME OF THE OFFENSE IS "CRIMES AGAINST NATURE."
"CRIMES AGAINST NATURE".
I THINK OF HIS DELICATE FERNS BETWEEN MY FINGERS, HIS SCENTED MOSS AGAINST MY CHEEK, AND I BEGIN TO LAUGH.
IT'S GOOD TO KNOW I STILL CAN. IT'S A SIGN OF NORMALITY...

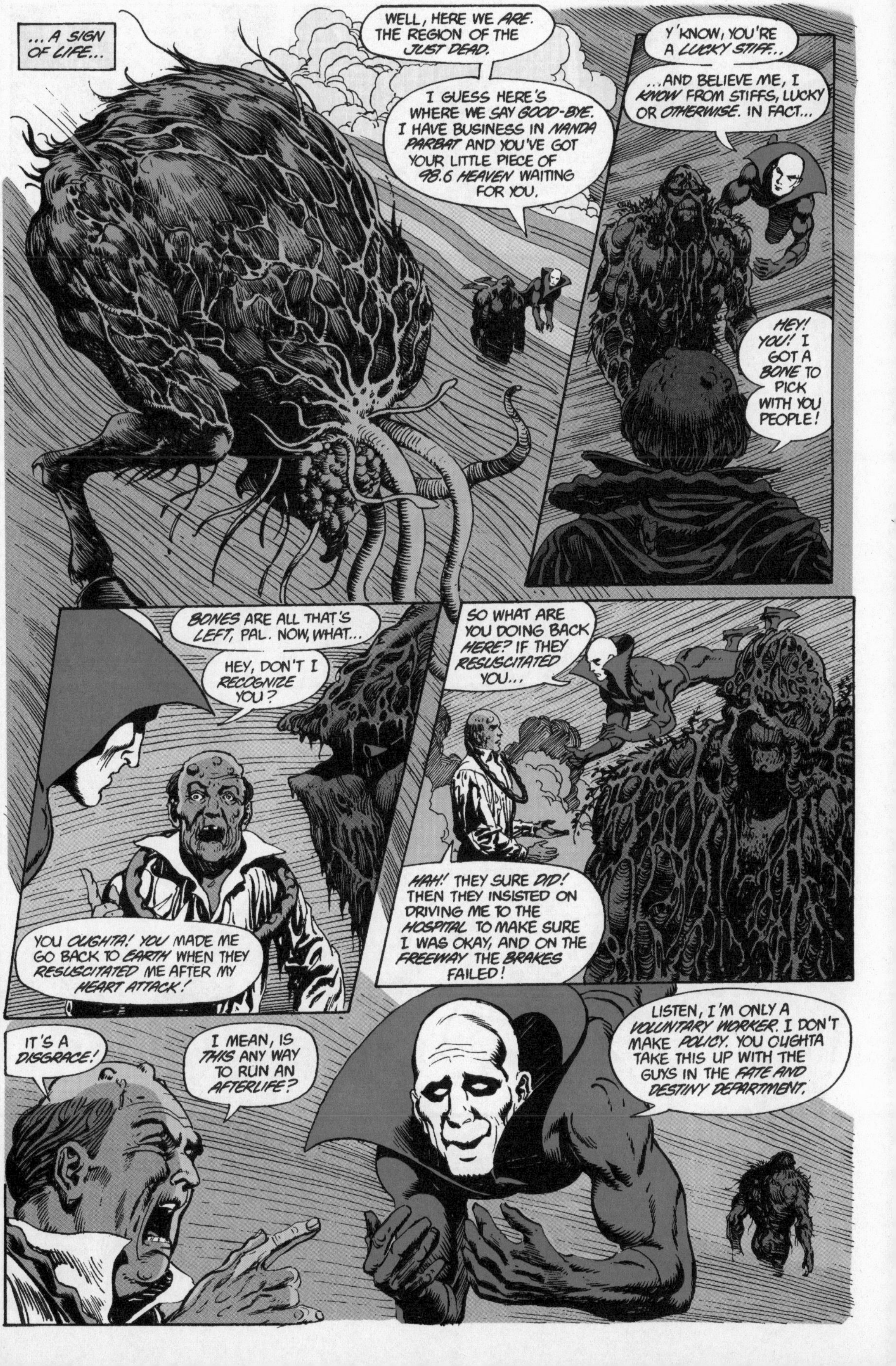
... A SIGN OF LIFE...
WELL, HERE WE ARE. THE REGION OF THE JUST DEAD.
I GUESS HERE'S WHERE WE SAY GOOD-BYE. I HAVE BUSINESS IN NANDA PARBAT AND YOU'VE GOT YOUR LITTLE PIECE OF 98.6 HEAVEN WAITING FOR YOU.
Y'KNOW, YOU'RE A LUCKY STIFF...
...AND BELIEVE ME, I KNOW FROM STIFFS, LUCKY OR OTHERWISE. IN FACT...
HEY! YOU! I GOT A BONE TO PICK WITH YOU PEOPLE!
BONES ARE ALL THAT'S LEFT, PAL. NOW, WHAT...
HEY, DON'T I RECOGNIZE YOU?
YOU OUGHTA! YOU MADE ME GO BACK TO EARTH WHEN THEY RESUSCITATED ME AFTER MY HEART ATTACK!
SO WHAT ARE YOU DOING BACK HERE? IF THEY RESUSCITATED YOU...
HAH! THEY SURE DID! THEN THEY INSISTED ON DRIVING ME TO THE HOSPITAL TO MAKE SURE I WAS OKAY, AND ON THE FREEWAY THE BRAKES FAILED!
IT'S A DISGRACE!
I MEAN, IS THIS ANY WAY TO RUN AN AFTERLIFE?
LISTEN, I'M ONLY A VOLUNTARY WORKER. I DON'T MAKE POLICY. YOU OUGHTA TAKE THIS UP WITH THE GUYS IN THE FATE AND DESTINY DEPARTMENT.

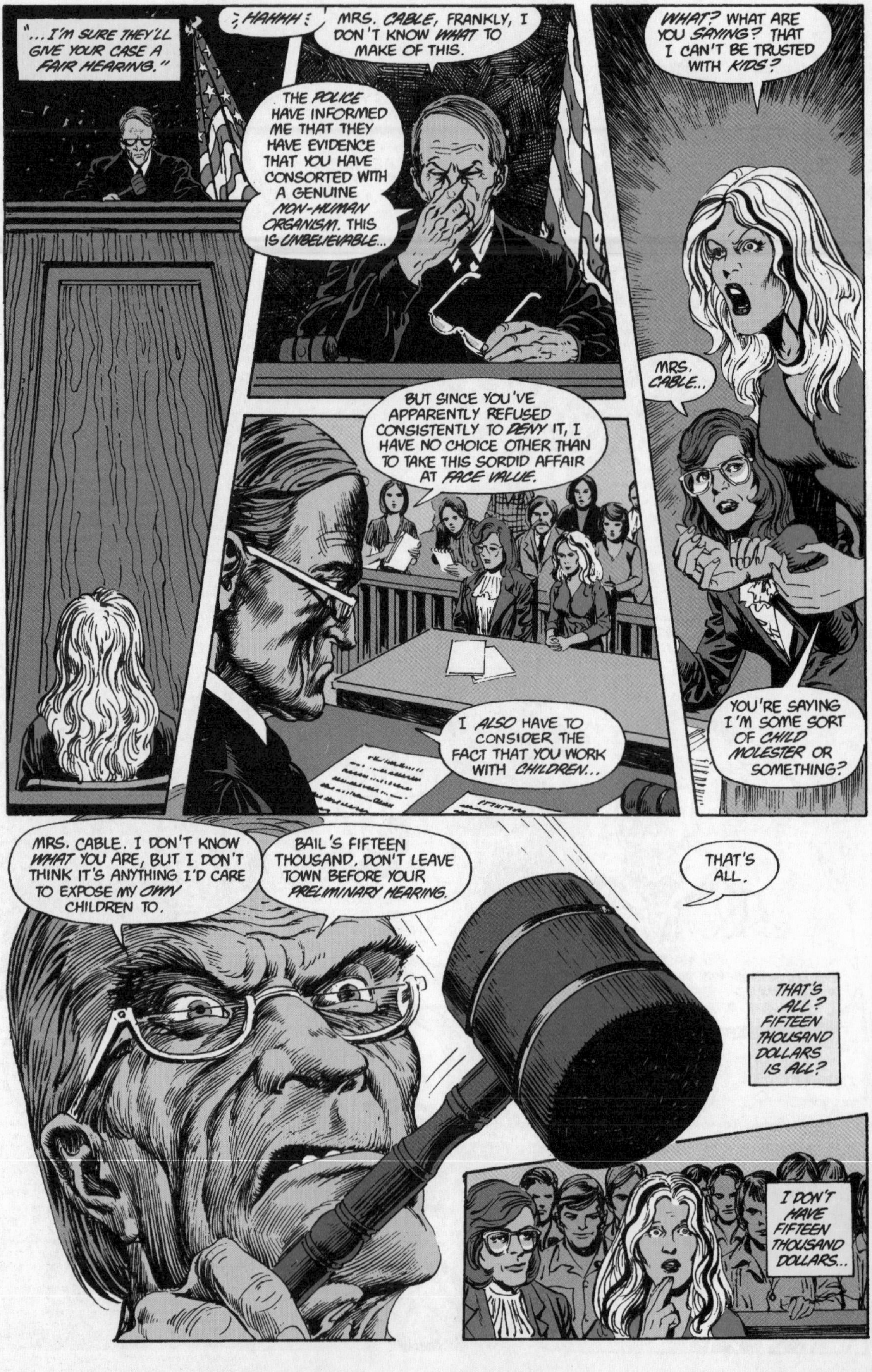
"...I'M SURE THEY'LL GIVE YOUR CASE A FAIR HEARING."
HAHHH
MRS. CABLE, FRANKLY, I DON'T KNOW WHAT TO MAKE OF THIS.
THE POLICE HAVE INFORMED ME THAT THEY HAVE EVIDENCE THAT YOU HAVE CONSORTED WITH A GENUINE NON-HUMAN ORGANISM. THIS IS UNBELIEVABLE...
WHAT? WHAT ARE YOU SAYING? THAT I CAN'T BE TRUSTED WITH KIDS?
BUT SINCE YOU'VE APPARENTLY REFUSED CONSISTENTLY TO DENY IT, I HAVE NO CHOICE OTHER THAN TO TAKE THIS SORDID AFFAIR AT FACE VALUE.
MRS. CABLE...
I ALSO HAVE TO CONSIDER THE FACT THAT YOU WORK WITH CHILDREN...
YOU'RE SAYING I'M SOME SORT OF CHILD MOLESTER OR SOMETHING?
MRS. CABLE. I DON'T KNOW WHAT YOU ARE, BUT I DON'T THINK IT'S ANYTHING I'D CARE TO EXPOSE MY OWN CHILDREN TO.
BAIL'S FIFTEEN THOUSAND. DON'T LEAVE TOWN BEFORE YOUR PRELIMINARY HEARING.
THAT'S ALL.
THAT'S ALL? FIFTEEN THOUSAND DOLLARS IS ALL?
I DON'T HAVE FIFTEEN THOUSAND DOLLARS...

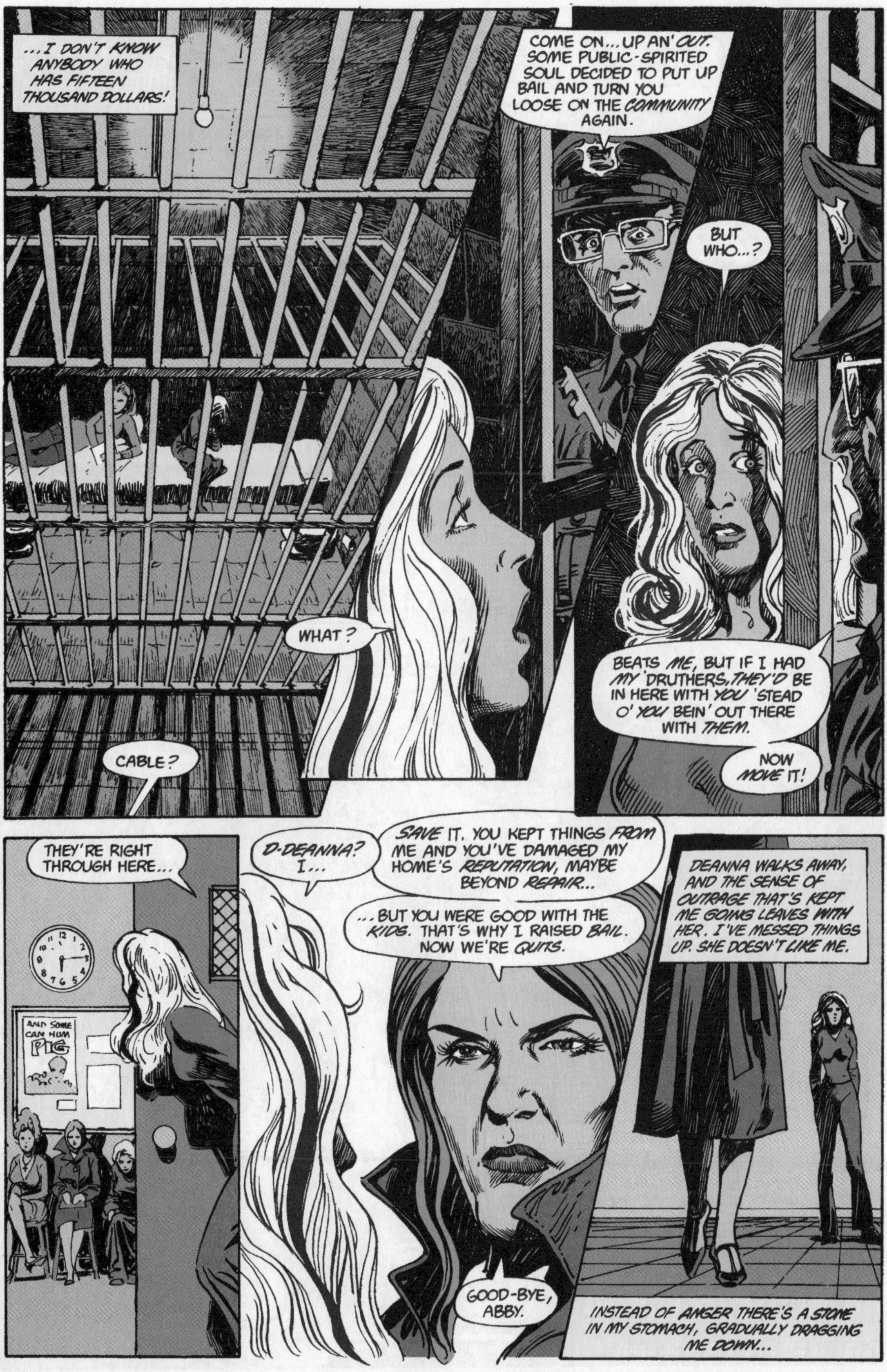
...I DON'T KNOW ANYBODY WHO HAS FIFTEEN THOUSAND DOLLARS!
WHAT?
CABLE?
COME ON... UP AN' OUT. SOME PUBLIC-SPIRITED SOUL DECIDED TO PUT UP BAIL AND TURN YOU LOOSE ON THE COMMUNITY AGAIN.
BUT WHO...?
BEATS ME, BUT IF I HAD MY 'DRUTHERS, THEY'D BE IN HERE WITH YOU 'STEAD O' YOU BEIN' OUT THERE WITH THEM.
NOW MOVE IT!
THEY'RE RIGHT THROUGH HERE...
AND SOME CAN HUM
PIG
D-DEANNA? I...
SAVE IT. YOU KEPT THINGS FROM ME AND YOU'VE DAMAGED MY HOME'S REPUTATION, MAYBE BEYOND REPAIR...
...BUT YOU WERE GOOD WITH THE KIDS. THAT'S WHY I RAISED BAIL. NOW WE'RE QUITS.
GOOD-BYE, ABBY.
DEANNA WALKS AWAY, AND THE SENSE OF OUTRAGE THAT'S KEPT ME GOING LEAVES WITH HER. I'VE MESSED THINGS UP. SHE DOESN'T LIKE ME.
INSTEAD OF ANGER THERE'S A STONE IN MY STOMACH, GRADUALLY DRAGGING ME DOWN...

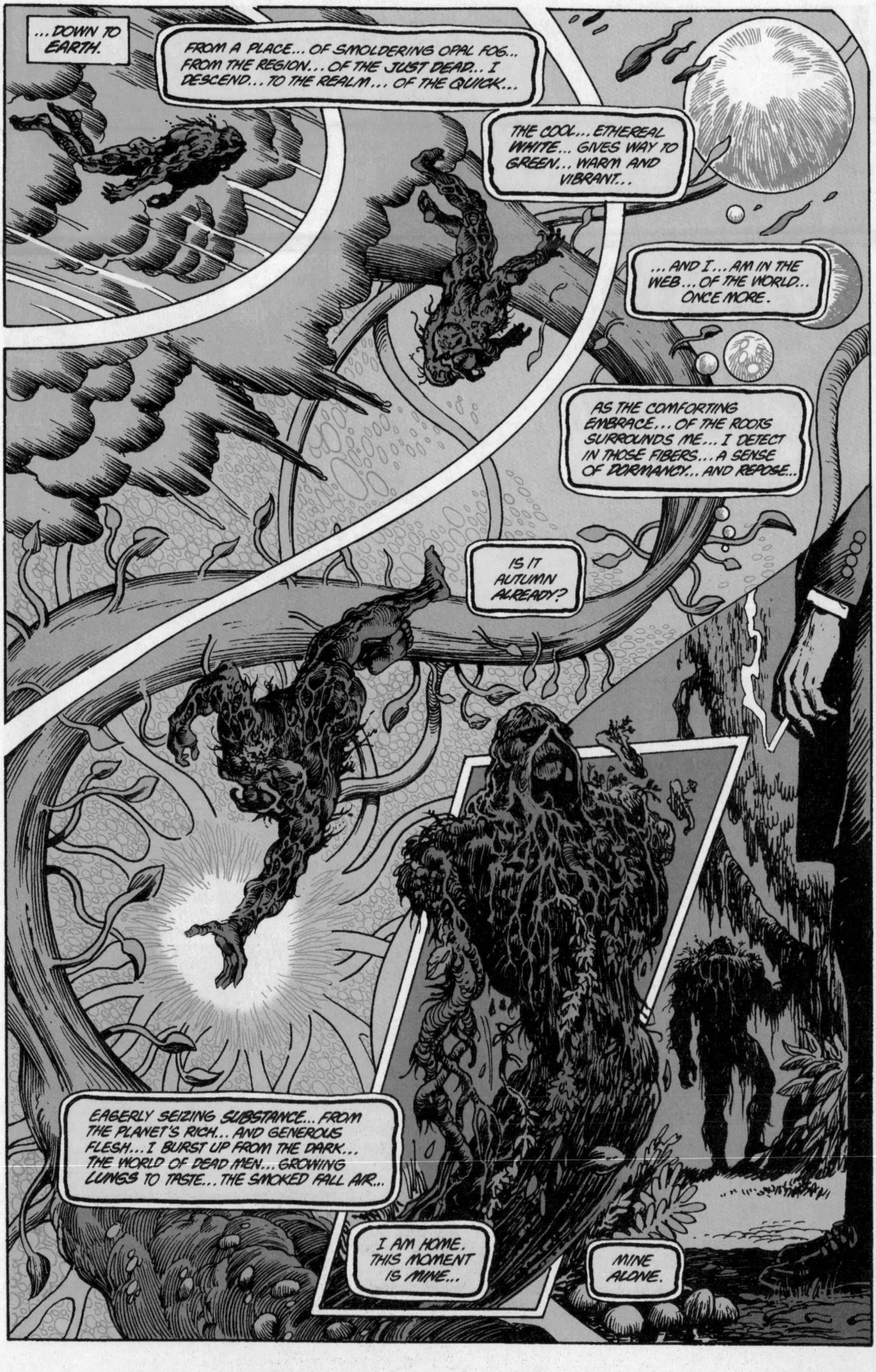
...DOWN TO EARTH.
FROM A PLACE... OF SMOLDERING OPAL FOG... FROM THE REGION... OF THE JUST DEAD... I DESCEND... TO THE REALM... OF THE QUICK...
THE COOL... ETHEREAL WHITE... GIVES WAY TO GREEN... WARM AND VIBRANT...
...AND I... AM IN THE WEB... OF THE WORLD... ONCE MORE.
AS THE COMFORTING EMBRACE... OF THE ROOTS SURROUNDS ME... I DETECT IN THOSE FIBERS... A SENSE OF DORMANCY... AND REPOSE...
IS IT AUTUMN ALREADY?
EAGERLY SEIZING SUBSTANCE... FROM THE PLANET'S RICH... AND GENEROUS FLESH... I BURST UP FROM THE DARK... THE WORLD OF DEAD MEN... GROWING LUNGS TO TASTE... THE SMOKED FALL AIR...
I AM HOME. THIS MOMENT IS MINE...
MINE ALONE.

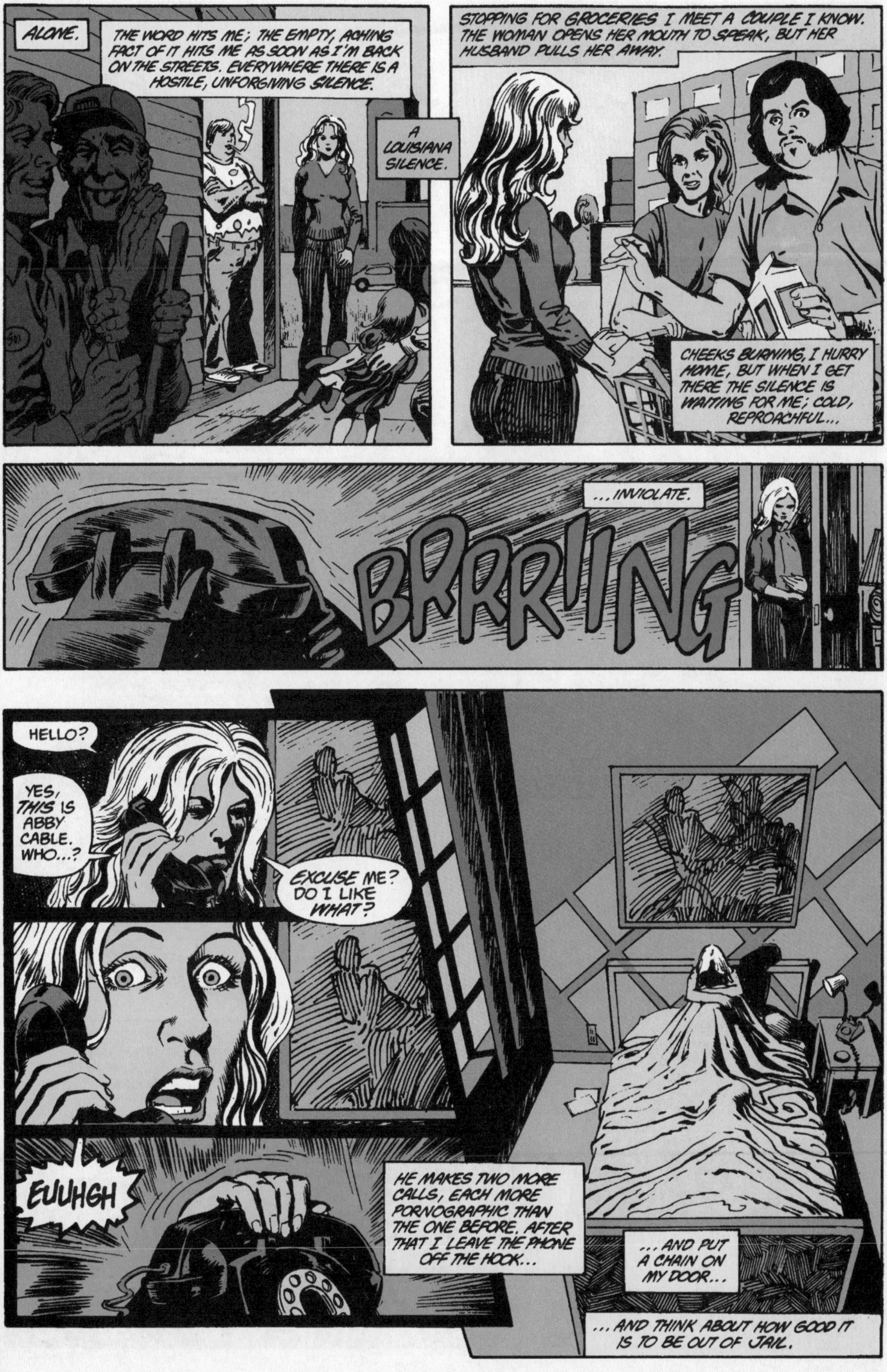
ALONE.
THE WORD HITS ME; THE EMPTY, ACHING FACT OF IT HITS ME AS SOON AS I'M BACK ON THE STREETS. EVERYWHERE THERE IS A HOSTILE, UNFORGIVING SILENCE.
A LOUISIANA SILENCE.
STOPPING FOR GROCERIES I MEET A COUPLE I KNOW. THE WOMAN OPENS HER MOUTH TO SPEAK, BUT HER HUSBAND PULLS HER AWAY.
CHEEKS BURNING, I HURRY HOME, BUT WHEN I GET THERE THE SILENCE IS WAITING FOR ME; COLD, REPROACHFUL...
...INVIOLATE.
BRRRIING
HELLO?
YES, THIS IS ABBY CABLE. WHO...?
EXCUSE ME? DO I LIKE WHAT?
EUUHGH
HE MAKES TWO MORE CALLS, EACH MORE PORNOGRAPHIC THAN THE ONE BEFORE. AFTER THAT I LEAVE THE PHONE OFF THE HOOK...
...AND PUT A CHAIN ON MY DOOR...
...AND THINK ABOUT HOW GOOD IT IS TO BE OUT OF JAIL.

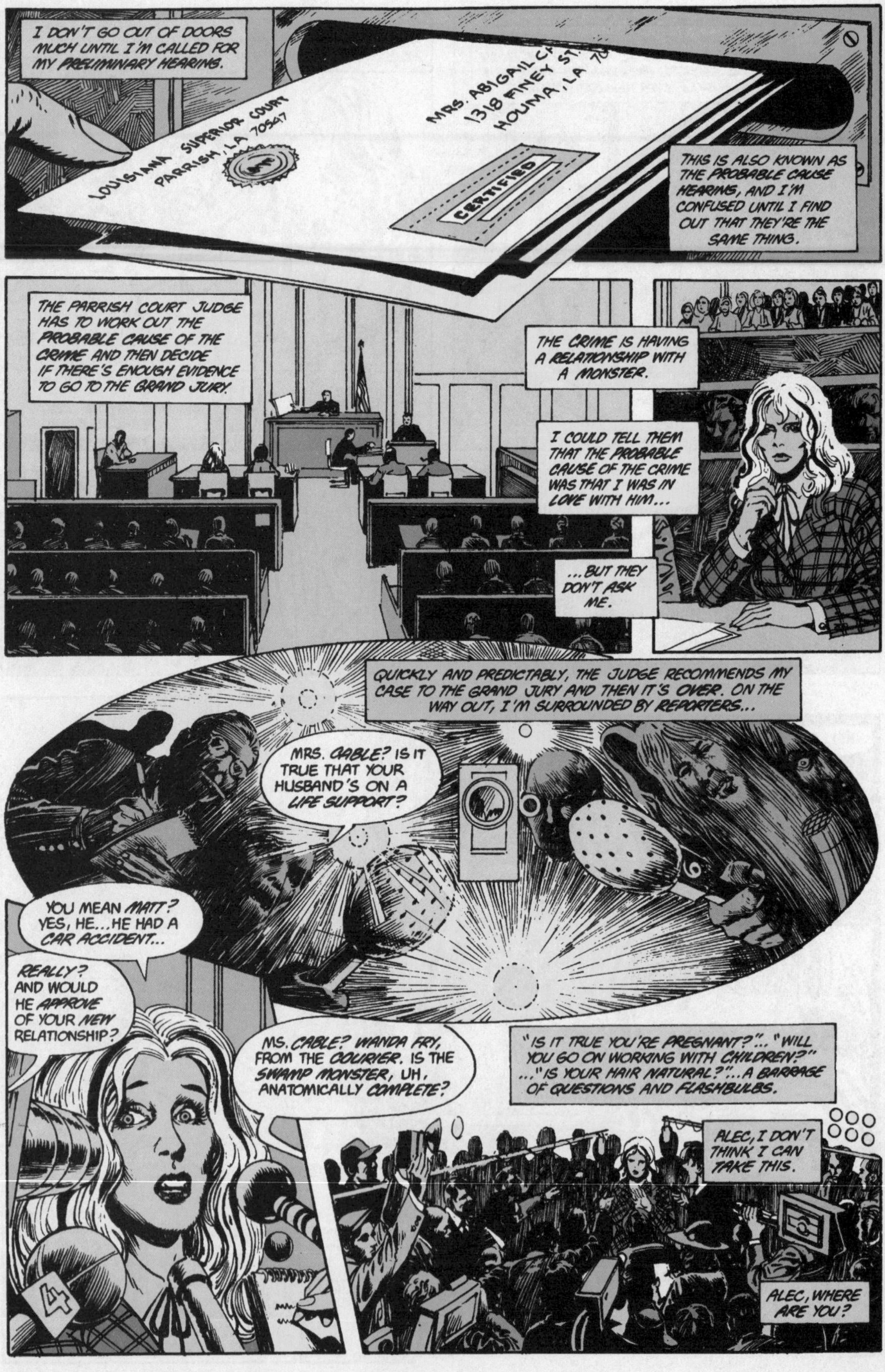
I DON'T GO OUT OF DOORS MUCH UNTIL I'M CALLED FOR MY PRELIMINARY HEARINGS.
LOUISIANA SUPERIOR COURT
PARRISH, LA 70547
MRS. ABIGAIL C
1318 FINEY ST.
HOUMA, LA 70
CERTIFIED
THIS IS ALSO KNOWN AS THE PROBABLE CAUSE HEARINGS, AND I'M CONFUSED UNTIL I FIND OUT THAT THEY'RE THE SAME THING.
THE PARRISH COURT JUDGE HAS TO WORK OUT THE PROBABLE CAUSE OF THE CRIME AND THEN DECIDE IF THERE'S ENOUGH EVIDENCE TO GO TO THE GRAND JURY.
THE CRIME IS HAVING A RELATIONSHIP WITH A MONSTER.
I COULD TELL THEM THAT THE PROBABLE CAUSE OF THE CRIME WAS THAT I WAS IN LOVE WITH HIM...
...BUT THEY DON'T ASK ME.
QUICKLY AND PREDICTABLY, THE JUDGE RECOMMENDS MY CASE TO THE GRAND JURY AND THEN IT'S OVER. ON THE WAY OUT, I'M SURROUNDED BY REPORTERS...
MRS. CABLE? IS IT TRUE THAT YOUR HUSBAND'S ON A LIFE SUPPORT?
YOU MEAN MATT? YES, HE...HE HAD A CAR ACCIDENT...
REALLY? AND WOULD HE APPROVE OF YOUR NEW RELATIONSHIP?
MS. CABLE? WANDA FRY, FROM THE COURIER. IS THE SWAMP MONSTER, UH, ANATOMICALLY COMPLETE?
"IS IT TRUE YOU'RE PREGNANT?"..."WILL YOU GO ON WORKING WITH CHILDREN?" ..."IS YOUR HAIR NATURAL?"...A BARRAGE OF QUESTIONS AND FLASHBULBS.
ALEC, I DON'T THINK I CAN TAKE THIS.
4
ALEC, WHERE ARE YOU?

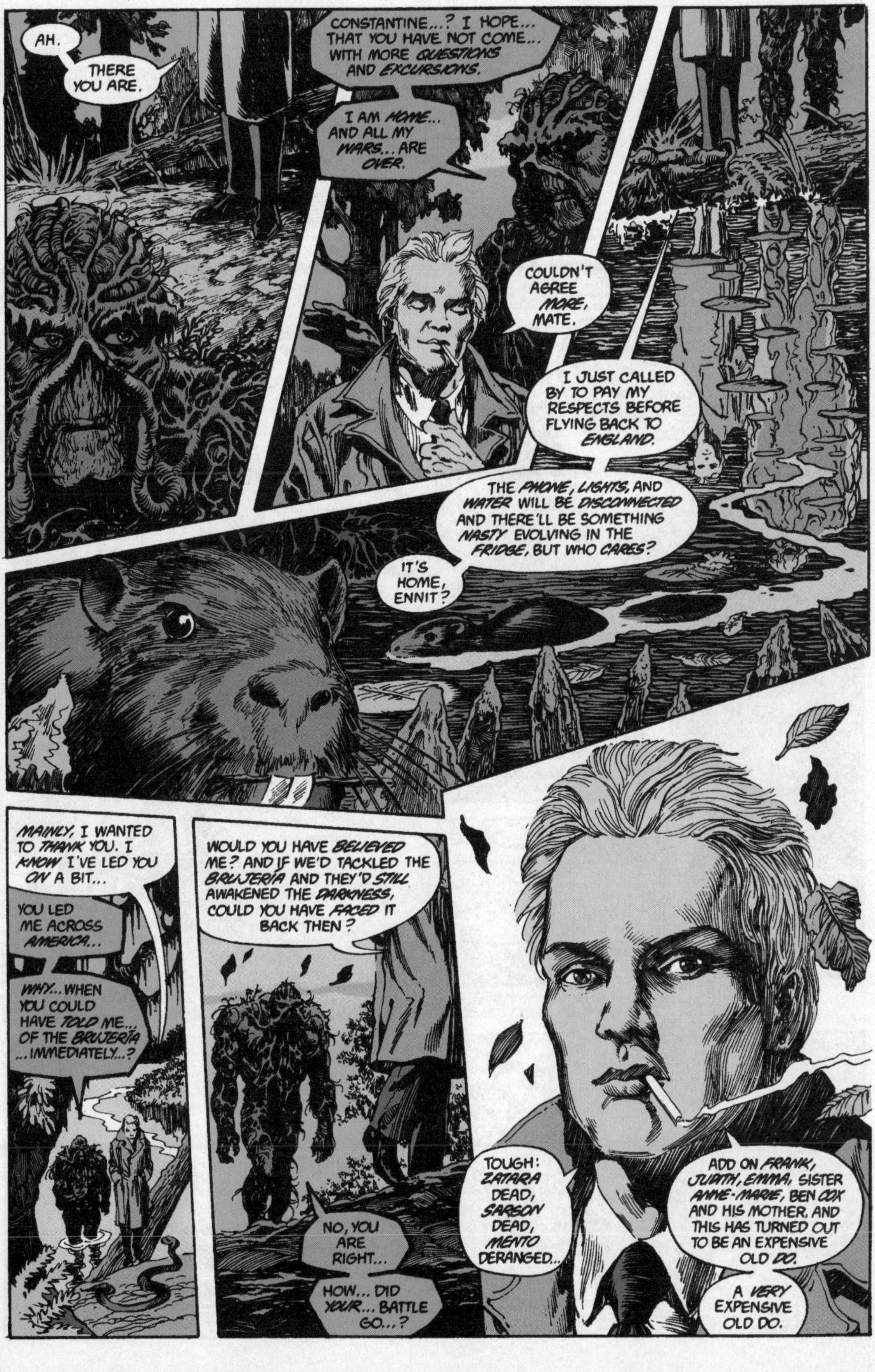
AH.
THERE YOU ARE.
CONSTANTINE...? I HOPE... THAT YOU HAVE NOT COME... WITH MORE QUESTIONS AND EXCURSIONS.
I AM HOME... AND ALL MY WARS... ARE OVER.
COULDN'T AGREE MORE, MATE.
I JUST CALLED BY TO PAY MY RESPECTS BEFORE FLYING BACK TO ENGLAND.
THE PHONE, LIGHTS, AND WATER WILL BE DISCONNECTED AND THERE'LL BE SOMETHING NASTY EVOLVING IN THE FRIDGE, BUT WHO CARES?
IT'S HOME, ENNIT?
MAINLY, I WANTED TO THANK YOU. I KNOW I'VE LED YOU ON A BIT...
YOU LED ME ACROSS AMERICA...
WHY... WHEN YOU COULD HAVE TOLD ME... OF THE BRUJERIA ...IMMEDIATELY...?
WOULD YOU HAVE BELIEVED ME? AND IF WE'D TACKLED THE BRUJERIA AND THEY'D STILL AWAKENED THE DARKNESS, COULD YOU HAVE FACED IT BACK THEN?
NO, YOU ARE RIGHT...
HOW... DID YOUR... BATTLE GO...?
TOUGH: ZATARA DEAD, SARGON DEAD, MENTO DERANGED...
ADD ON FRANK, JUDITH, EMMA, SISTER ANNE-MARIE, BEN COX AND HIS MOTHER, AND THIS HAS TURNED OUT TO BE AN EXPENSIVE OLD DO.
A VERY EXPENSIVE OLD DO.

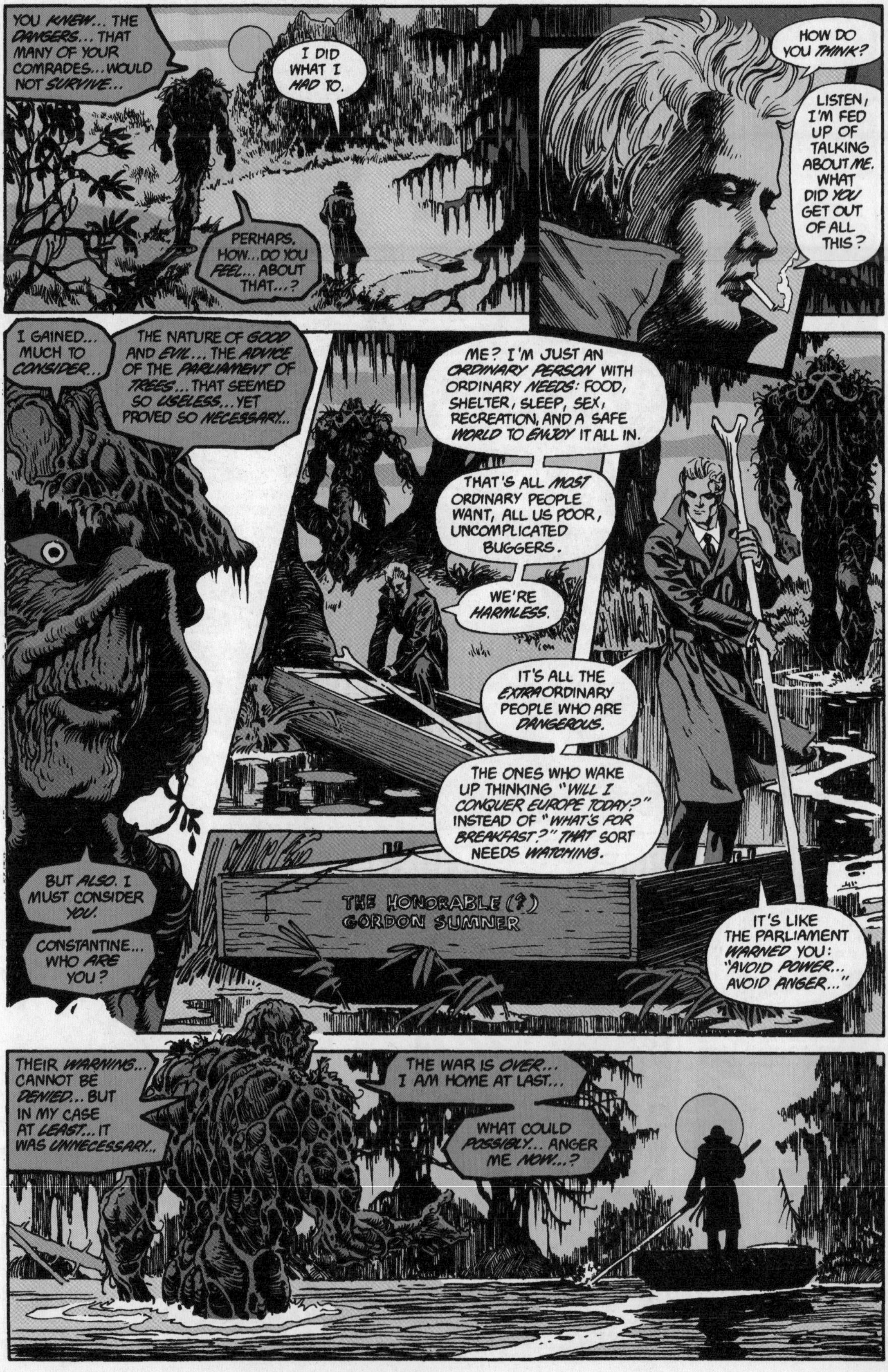
YOU KNEW... THE DANGERS... THAT MANY OF YOUR COMRADES...WOULD NOT SURVIVE...
I DID WHAT I HAD TO.
PERHAPS. HOW...DO YOU FEEL... ABOUT THAT...?
HOW DO YOU THINK?
LISTEN, I'M FED UP OF TALKING ABOUT ME. WHAT DID YOU GET OUT OF ALL THIS?
I GAINED... MUCH TO CONSIDER...
THE NATURE OF GOOD AND EVIL... THE ADVICE OF THE PARLIAMENT OF TREES... THAT SEEMED SO USELESS...YET PROVED SO NECESSARY...
BUT ALSO. I MUST CONSIDER YOU.
CONSTANTINE... WHO ARE YOU?
ME? I'M JUST AN ORDINARY PERSON WITH ORDINARY NEEDS: FOOD, SHELTER, SLEEP, SEX, RECREATION, AND A SAFE WORLD TO ENJOY IT ALL IN.
THAT'S ALL MOST ORDINARY PEOPLE WANT, ALL US POOR, UNCOMPLICATED BUGGERS.
WE'RE HARMLESS.
IT'S ALL THE EXTRAORDINARY PEOPLE WHO ARE DANGEROUS.
THE ONES WHO WAKE UP THINKING "WILL I CONQUER EUROPE TODAY?" INSTEAD OF "WHAT'S FOR BREAKFAST?" THAT SORT NEEDS WATCHING.
THE HONORABLE (?) GORDON SUMNER
IT'S LIKE THE PARLIAMENT WARNED YOU: "AVOID POWER... AVOID ANGER..."
THEIR WARNING... CANNOT BE DENIED... BUT IN MY CASE AT LEAST... IT WAS UNNECESSARY...
THE WAR IS OVER... I AM HOME AT LAST...
WHAT COULD POSSIBLY... ANGER ME NOW...?

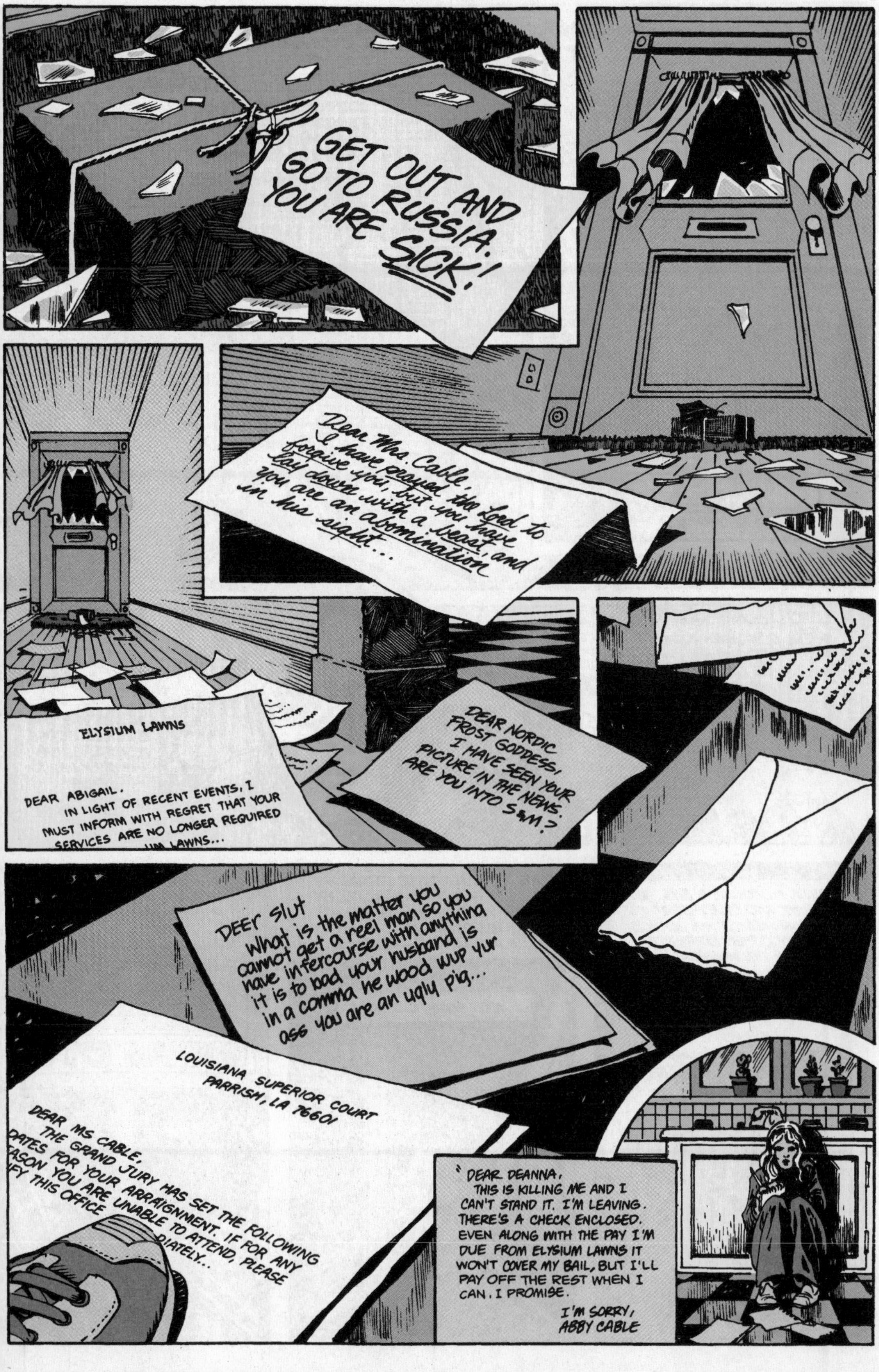
GET OUT AND GO TO RUSSIA. YOU ARE SICK!
Dear Mrs. Cable, I have prayed the Lord to forgive you, but you have lay down with a beast, and you are an abomination in his sight...
ELYSIUM LAWNS
DEAR ABIGAIL. IN LIGHT OF RECENT EVENTS, I MUST INFORM WITH REGRET THAT YOUR SERVICES ARE NO LONGER REQUIRED
UM LAWNS...
DEAR NORDIC FROST GODDESS, I HAVE SEEN YOUR PICTURE IN THE NEWS. ARE YOU INTO S&M?
DEER Slut What is the matter you cannot get a reel man so you have intercourse with anything it is to bad your husband is in a comma he wood wup yur ass you are an ugly pig...
LOUISIANA SUPERIOR COURT PARRISH, LA 76601
DEAR MS CABLE,
THE GRAND JURY HAS SET THE FOLLOWING
DATES FOR YOUR ARRAIGNMENT. IF FOR ANY
EASON YOU ARE UNABLE TO ATTEND, PLEASE
IFY THIS OFFICE
DIATELY...
"DEAR DEANNA, THIS IS KILLING ME AND I CAN'T STAND IT. I'M LEAVING. THERE'S A CHECK ENCLOSED. EVEN ALONG WITH THE PAY I'M DUE FROM ELYSIUM LAWNS IT WON'T COVER MY BAIL, BUT I'LL PAY OFF THE REST WHEN I CAN. I PROMISE.
I'M SORRY, ABBY CABLE

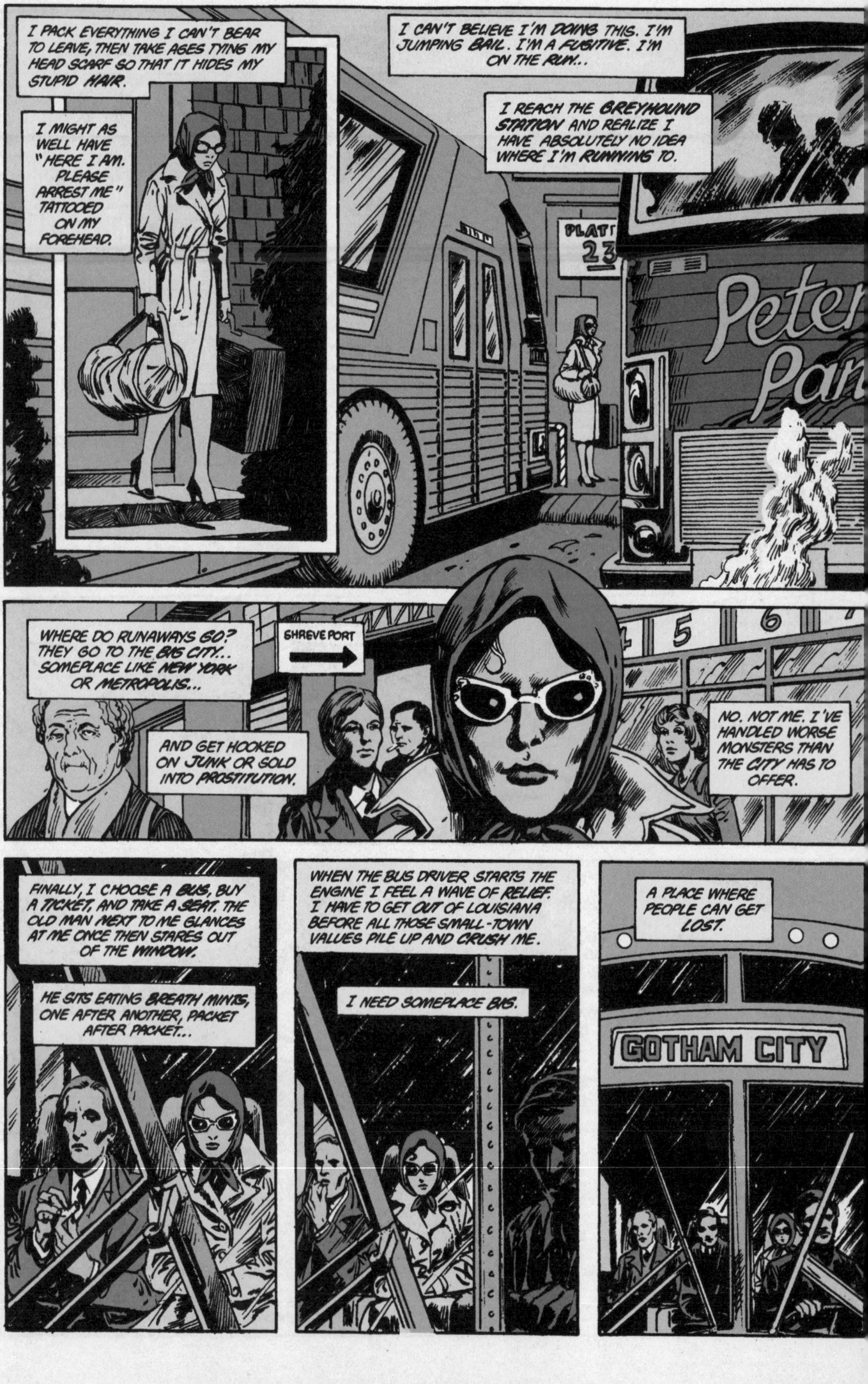
I PACK EVERYTHING I CAN'T BEAR TO LEAVE, THEN TAKE AGES TYING MY HEAD SCARF SO THAT IT HIDES MY STUPID HAIR.
I MIGHT AS WELL HAVE "HERE I AM. PLEASE ARREST ME" TATTOOED ON MY FOREHEAD.
I CAN'T BELIEVE I'M DOING THIS. I'M JUMPING BAIL. I'M A FUGITIVE. I'M ON THE RUN..
I REACH THE GREYHOUND STATION AND REALIZE I HAVE ABSOLUTELY NO IDEA WHERE I'M RUNNING TO.
PLATF
23
WHERE DO RUNAWAYS GO? THEY GO TO THE BIG CITY... SOMEPLACE LIKE NEW YORK OR METROPOLIS...
SHREVE PORT
AND GET HOOKED ON JUNK OR SOLD INTO PROSTITUTION.
NO. NOT ME. I'VE HANDLED WORSE MONSTERS THAN THE CITY HAS TO OFFER.
FINALLY, I CHOOSE A BUS, BUY A TICKET, AND TAKE A SEAT. THE OLD MAN NEXT TO ME GLANCES AT ME ONCE THEN STARES OUT OF THE WINDOW.
HE SITS EATING BREATH MINTS, ONE AFTER ANOTHER, PACKET AFTER PACKET...
WHEN THE BUS DRIVER STARTS THE ENGINE I FEEL A WAVE OF RELIEF. I HAVE TO GET OUT OF LOUISIANA BEFORE ALL THOSE SMALL-TOWN VALUES PILE UP AND CRUSH ME.
I NEED SOMEPLACE BIG.
A PLACE WHERE PEOPLE CAN GET LOST.
GOTHAM CITY

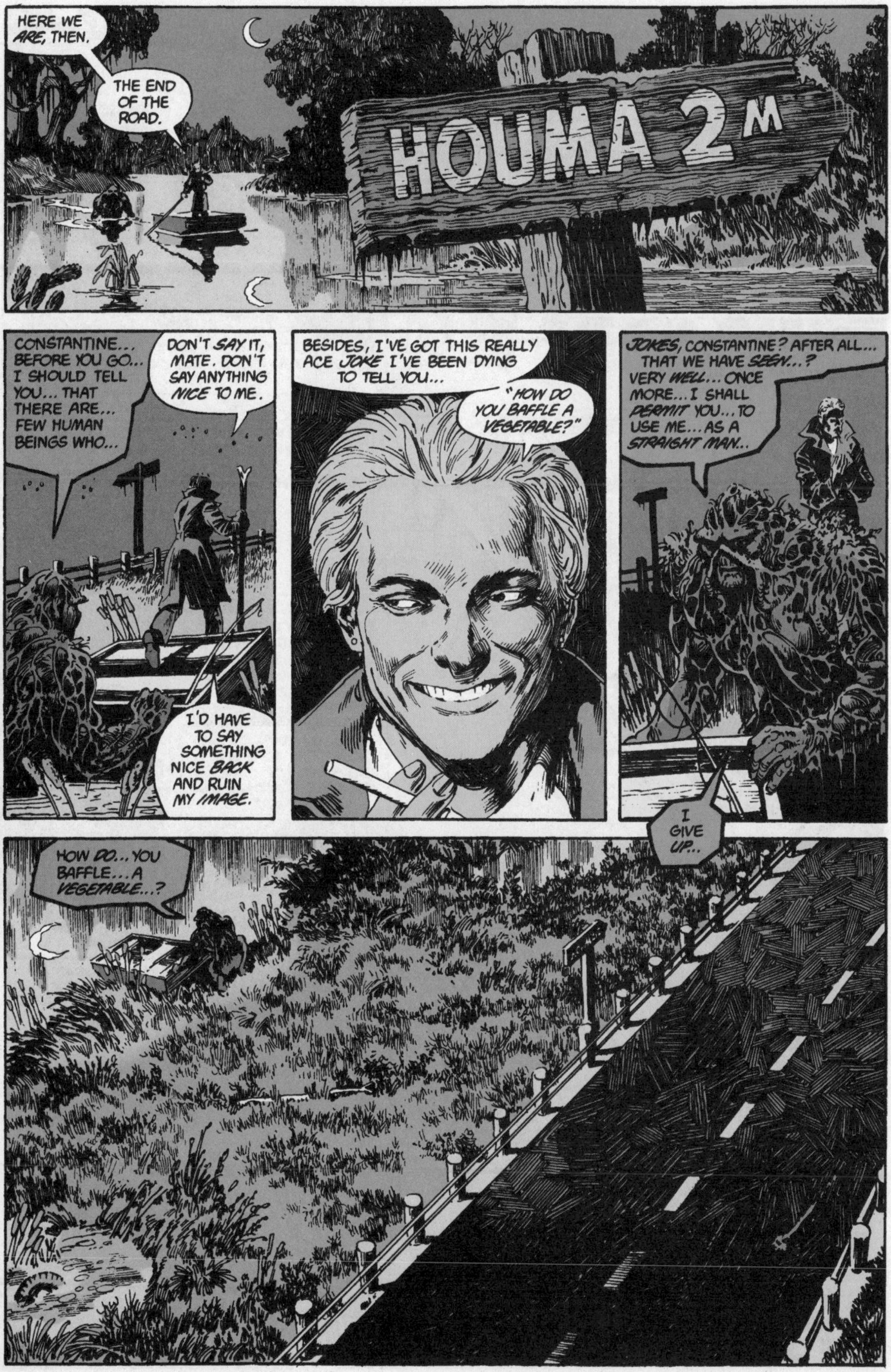
HERE WE ARE, THEN.
THE END OF THE ROAD.
HOUMA 2 M
CONSTANTINE... BEFORE YOU GO... I SHOULD TELL YOU... THAT THERE ARE... FEW HUMAN BEINGS WHO...
DON'T SAY IT, MATE. DON'T SAY ANYTHING NICE TO ME.
I'D HAVE TO SAY SOMETHING NICE BACK AND RUIN MY IMAGE.
BESIDES, I'VE GOT THIS REALLY ACE JOKE I'VE BEEN DYING TO TELL YOU...
"HOW DO YOU BAFFLE A VEGETABLE?"
JOKES, CONSTANTINE? AFTER ALL... THAT WE HAVE SEEN...? VERY WELL... ONCE MORE... I SHALL PERMIT YOU... TO USE ME... AS A STRAIGHT MAN...
I GIVE UP...
HOW DO... YOU BAFFLE... A VEGETABLE...?

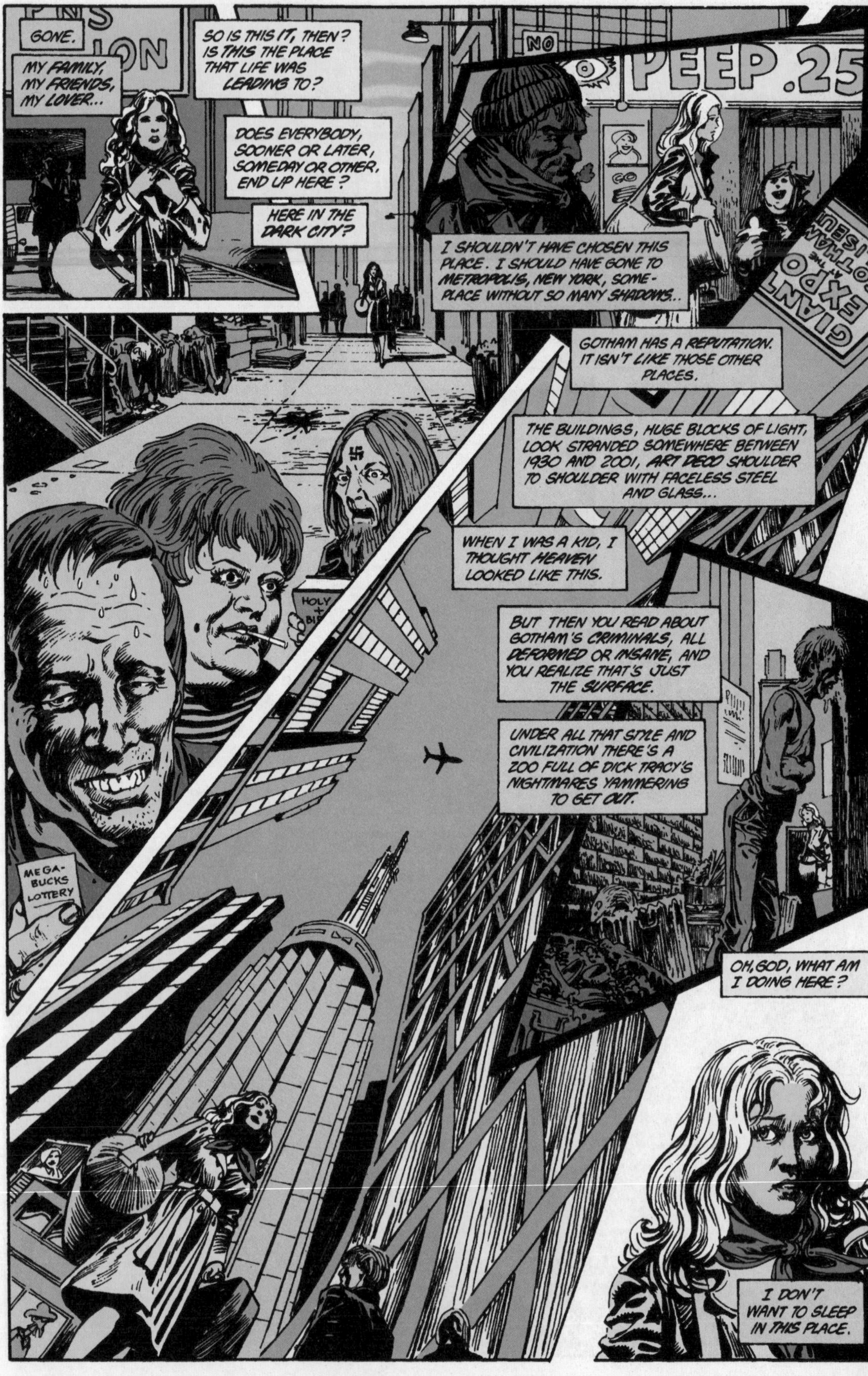
GONE.
MY FAMILY, MY FRIENDS, MY LOVER...
SO IS THIS IT, THEN? IS THIS THE PLACE THAT LIFE WAS LEADING TO?
DOES EVERYBODY, SOONER OR LATER, SOMEDAY OR OTHER, END UP HERE?
HERE IN THE DARK CITY?
NO
PEEP .25
I SHOULDN'T HAVE CHOSEN THIS PLACE. I SHOULD HAVE GONE TO METROPOLIS, NEW YORK, SOME-PLACE WITHOUT SO MANY SHADOWS...
GOTHAM HAS A REPUTATION. IT ISN'T LIKE THOSE OTHER PLACES.
THE BUILDINGS, HUGE BLOCKS OF LIGHT, LOOK STRANDED SOMEWHERE BETWEEN 1930 AND 2001, ART DECO SHOULDER TO SHOULDER WITH FACELESS STEEL AND GLASS...
WHEN I WAS A KID, I THOUGHT HEAVEN LOOKED LIKE THIS.
BUT THEN YOU READ ABOUT GOTHAM'S CRIMINALS, ALL DEFORMED OR INSANE, AND YOU REALIZE THAT'S JUST THE SURFACE.
UNDER ALL THAT STYLE AND CIVILIZATION THERE'S A ZOO FULL OF DICK TRACY'S NIGHTMARES YAMMERING TO GET OUT.
MEGA-BUCKS LOTTERY
OH, GOD, WHAT AM I DOING HERE?
I DON'T WANT TO SLEEP IN THIS PLACE.

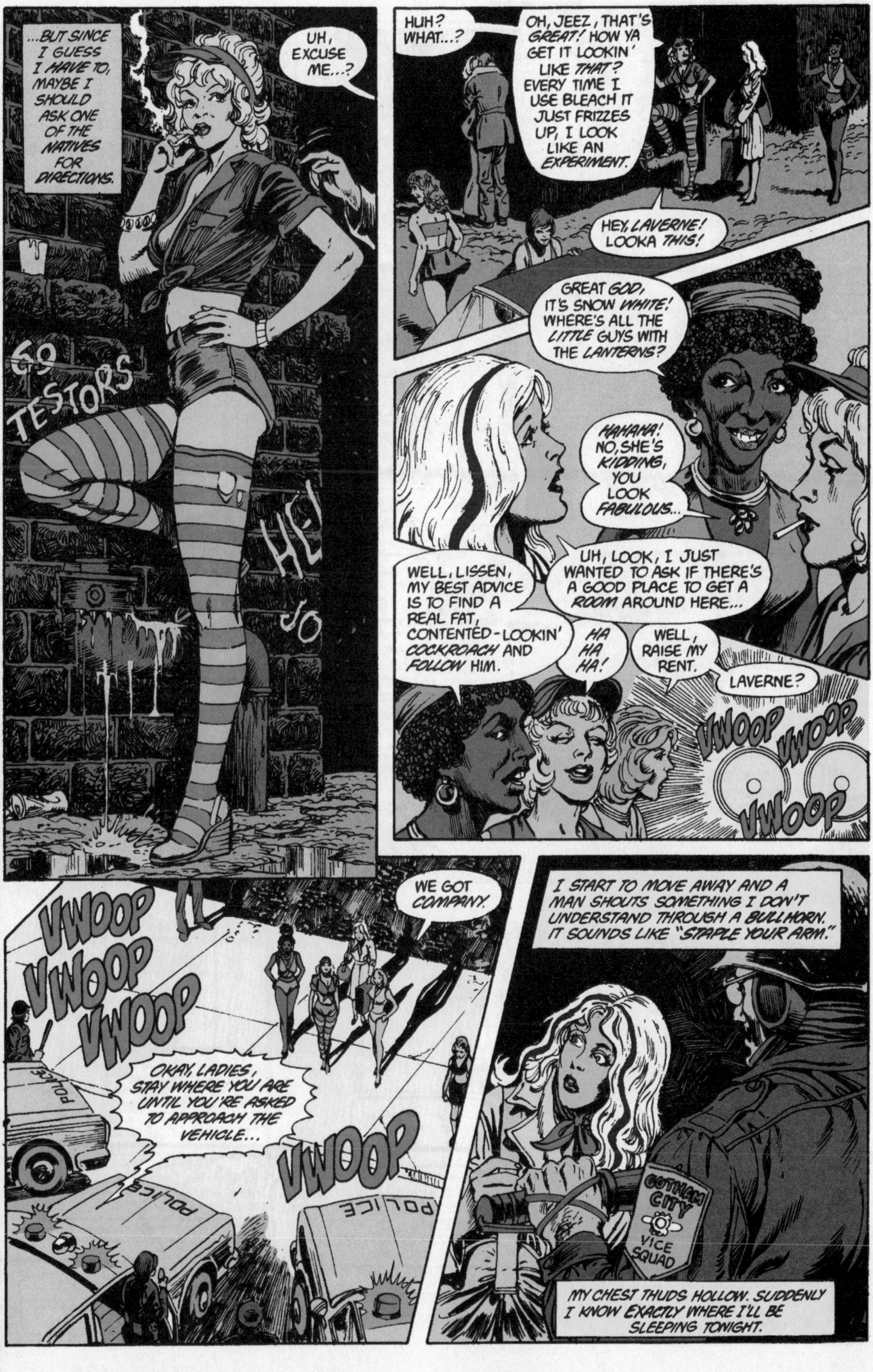
...BUT SINCE I GUESS I HAVE TO, MAYBE I SHOULD ASK ONE OF THE NATIVES FOR DIRECTIONS.
UH, EXCUSE ME...?
GO TESTORS
HUH? WHAT...?
OH, JEEZ, THAT'S GREAT! HOW YA GET IT LOOKIN' LIKE THAT? EVERY TIME I USE BLEACH IT JUST FRIZZES UP, I LOOK LIKE AN EXPERIMENT.
HEY, LAVERNE! LOOKA THIS!
GREAT GOD, IT'S SNOW WHITE! WHERE'S ALL THE LITTLE GUYS WITH THE LANTERNS?
HAHAHA! NO, SHE'S KIDDING, YOU LOOK FABULOUS...
UH, LOOK, I JUST WANTED TO ASK IF THERE'S A GOOD PLACE TO GET A ROOM AROUND HERE...
WELL, LISSEN, MY BEST ADVICE IS TO FIND A REAL FAT, CONTENTED-LOOKIN' COCKROACH AND FOLLOW HIM.
HA HA HA!
WELL, RAISE MY RENT.
LAVERNE?
VWOOP VWOOP VWOOP
VWOOP VWOOP VWOOP
WE GOT COMPANY.
OKAY, LADIES, STAY WHERE YOU ARE UNTIL YOU'RE ASKED TO APPROACH THE VEHICLE...
VWOOP
POLICE
I START TO MOVE AWAY AND A MAN SHOUTS SOMETHING I DON'T UNDERSTAND THROUGH A BULLHORN. IT SOUNDS LIKE "STAPLE YOUR ARM."
GOTHAM CITY VICE SQUAD
MY CHEST THUDS HOLLOW. SUDDENLY I KNOW EXACTLY WHERE I'LL BE SLEEPING TONIGHT.

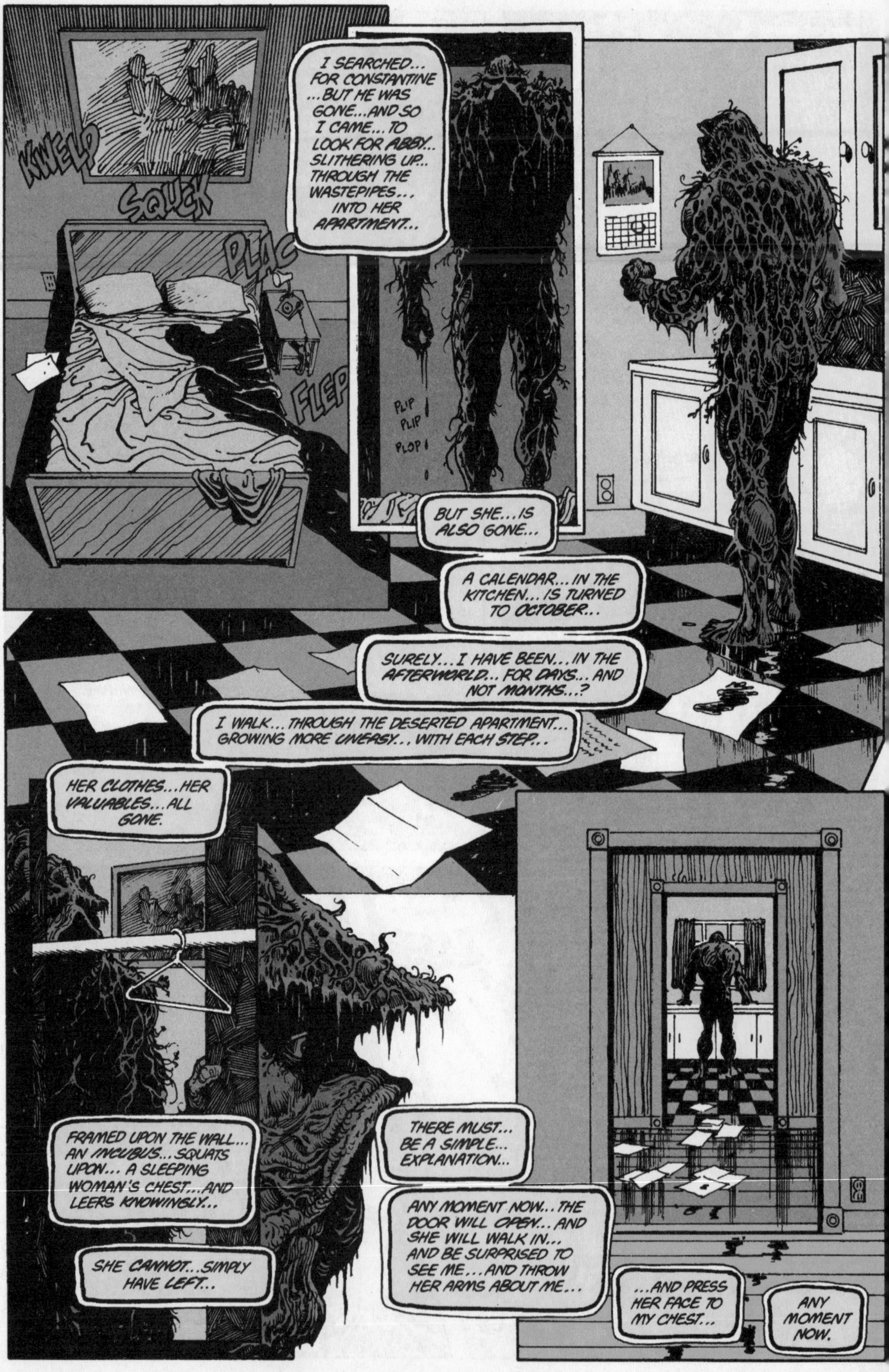
I SEARCHED... FOR CONSTANTINE ...BUT HE WAS GONE...AND SO I CAME... TO LOOK FOR ABBY... SLITHERING UP... THROUGH THE WASTEPIPES... INTO HER APARTMENT...
KWELP
SQUCK
PLAC
FLEP
PLIP
PLIP
PLOP
BUT SHE...IS ALSO GONE...
A CALENDAR...IN THE KITCHEN...IS TURNED TO OCTOBER...
SURELY...I HAVE BEEN...IN THE AFTERWORLD... FOR DAYS... AND NOT MONTHS...?
I WALK...THROUGH THE DESERTED APARTMENT... GROWING MORE UNEASY... WITH EACH STEP...
HER CLOTHES...HER VALUABLES...ALL GONE.
FRAMED UPON THE WALL... AN INCUBUS...SQUATS UPON... A SLEEPING WOMAN'S CHEST...AND LEERS KNOWINGLY...
SHE CANNOT...SIMPLY HAVE LEFT...
THERE MUST... BE A SIMPLE... EXPLANATION...
ANY MOMENT NOW...THE DOOR WILL OPEN... AND SHE WILL WALK IN... AND BE SURPRISED TO SEE ME...AND THROW HER ARMS ABOUT ME...
...AND PRESS HER FACE TO MY CHEST...
ANY MOMENT NOW.

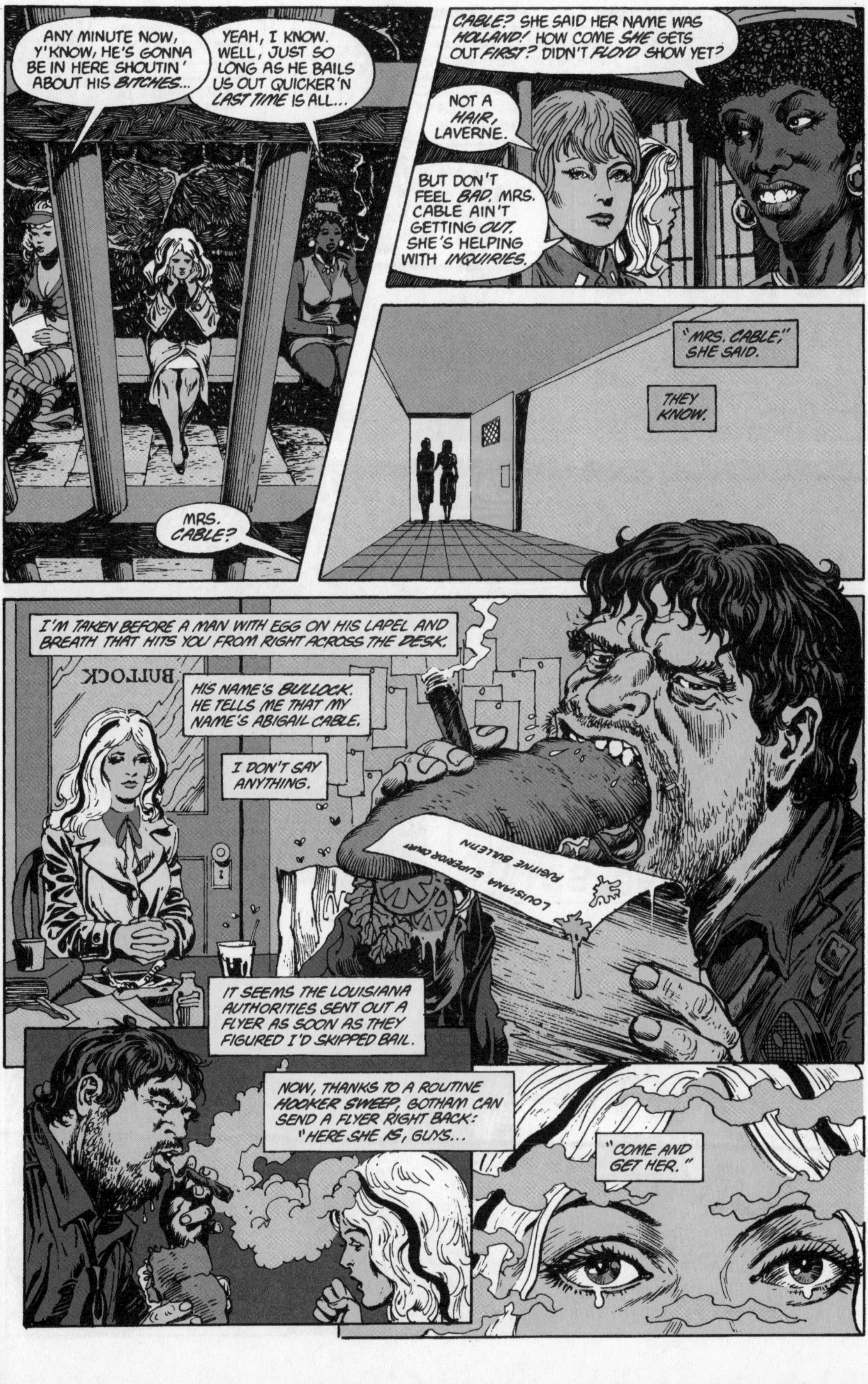
ANY MINUTE NOW, Y'KNOW, HE'S GONNA BE IN HERE SHOUTIN' ABOUT HIS BITCHES...
YEAH, I KNOW. WELL, JUST SO LONG AS HE BAILS US OUT QUICKER'N LAST TIME IS ALL...
MRS. CABLE?
CABLE? SHE SAID HER NAME WAS HOLLAND! HOW COME SHE GETS OUT FIRST? DIDN'T FLOYD SHOW YET?
NOT A HAIR, LAVERNE.
BUT DON'T FEEL BAD. MRS. CABLE AIN'T GETTING OUT. SHE'S HELPING WITH INQUIRIES.
"MRS. CABLE," SHE SAID.
THEY KNOW.
I'M TAKEN BEFORE A MAN WITH EGG ON HIS LAPEL AND BREATH THAT HITS YOU FROM RIGHT ACROSS THE DESK.
BULLOCK
HIS NAME'S BULLOCK. HE TELLS ME THAT MY NAME'S ABIGAIL CABLE.
I DON'T SAY ANYTHING.
LOUISIANA SUPERIOR COURT
FUGITIVE BULLETIN
IT SEEMS THE LOUISIANA AUTHORITIES SENT OUT A FLYER AS SOON AS THEY FIGURED I'D SKIPPED BAIL.
NOW, THANKS TO A ROUTINE HOOKER SWEEP, GOTHAM CAN SEND A FLYER RIGHT BACK: "HERE SHE IS, GUYS...
"COME AND GET HER."

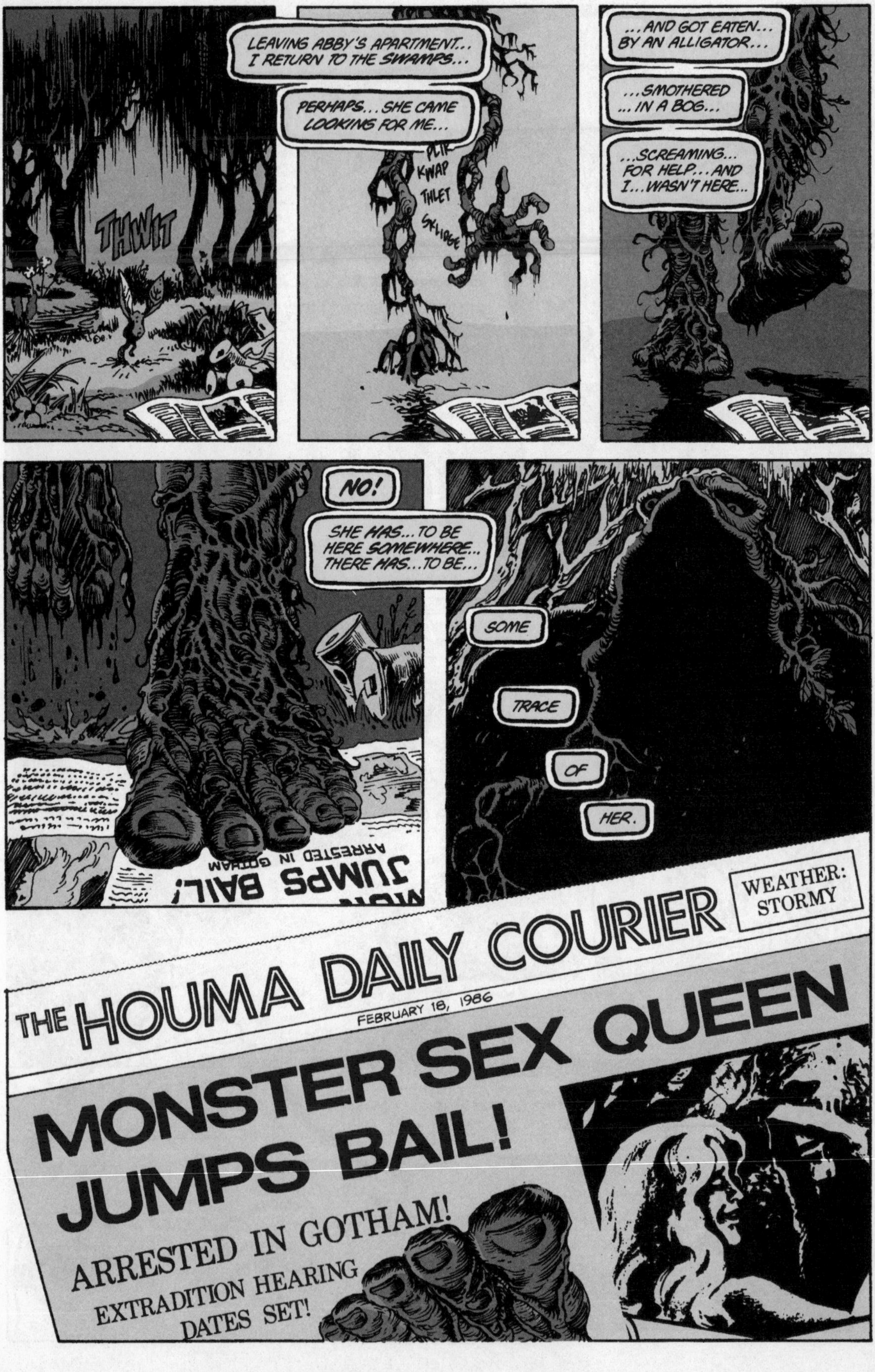
LEAVING ABBY'S APARTMENT... I RETURN TO THE SWAMPS...
THWIT
PERHAPS... SHE CAME LOOKING FOR ME...
PLIK
KWAP
THLET
SKLIDGE
...AND GOT EATEN... BY AN ALLIGATOR...
...SMOTHERED ... IN A BOG...
...SCREAMING... FOR HELP... AND I... WASN'T HERE...
NO!
SHE HAS... TO BE HERE SOMEWHERE... THERE HAS... TO BE...
JUMPS BAIL!
ARRESTED IN GOTHAM
SOME
TRACE
OF
HER.
THE HOUMA DAILY COURIER
WEATHER: STORMY
FEBRUARY 18, 1986
MONSTER SEX QUEEN JUMPS BAIL!
ARRESTED IN GOTHAM!
EXTRADITION HEARING DATES SET!

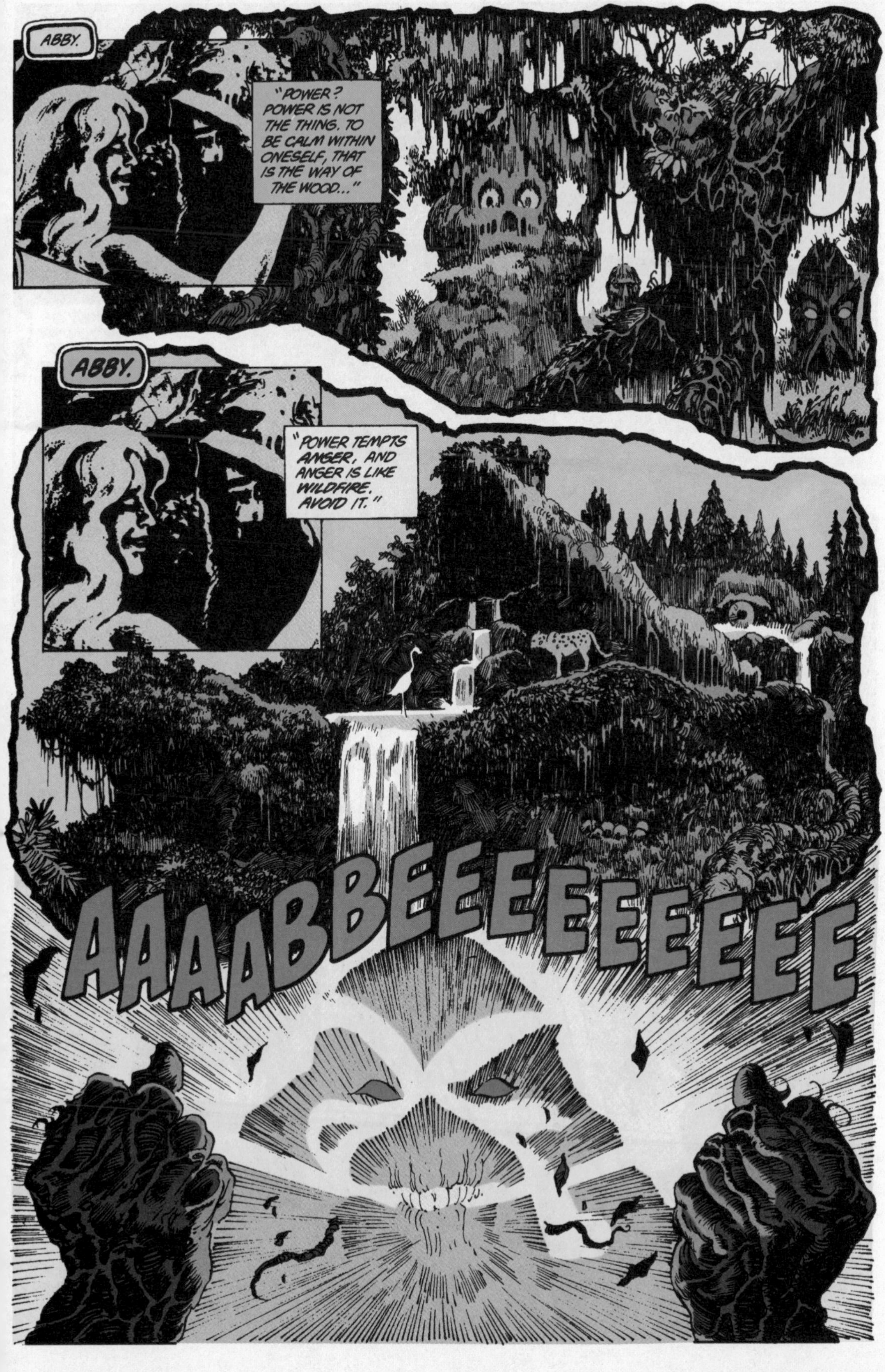
ABBY.
"POWER? POWER IS NOT THE THING. TO BE CALM WITHIN ONESELF, THAT IS THE WAY OF THE WOOD..."
ABBY.
"POWER TEMPTS ANGER, AND ANGER IS LIKE WILDFIRE. AVOID IT."
AAAABBEEEEEEEEEE

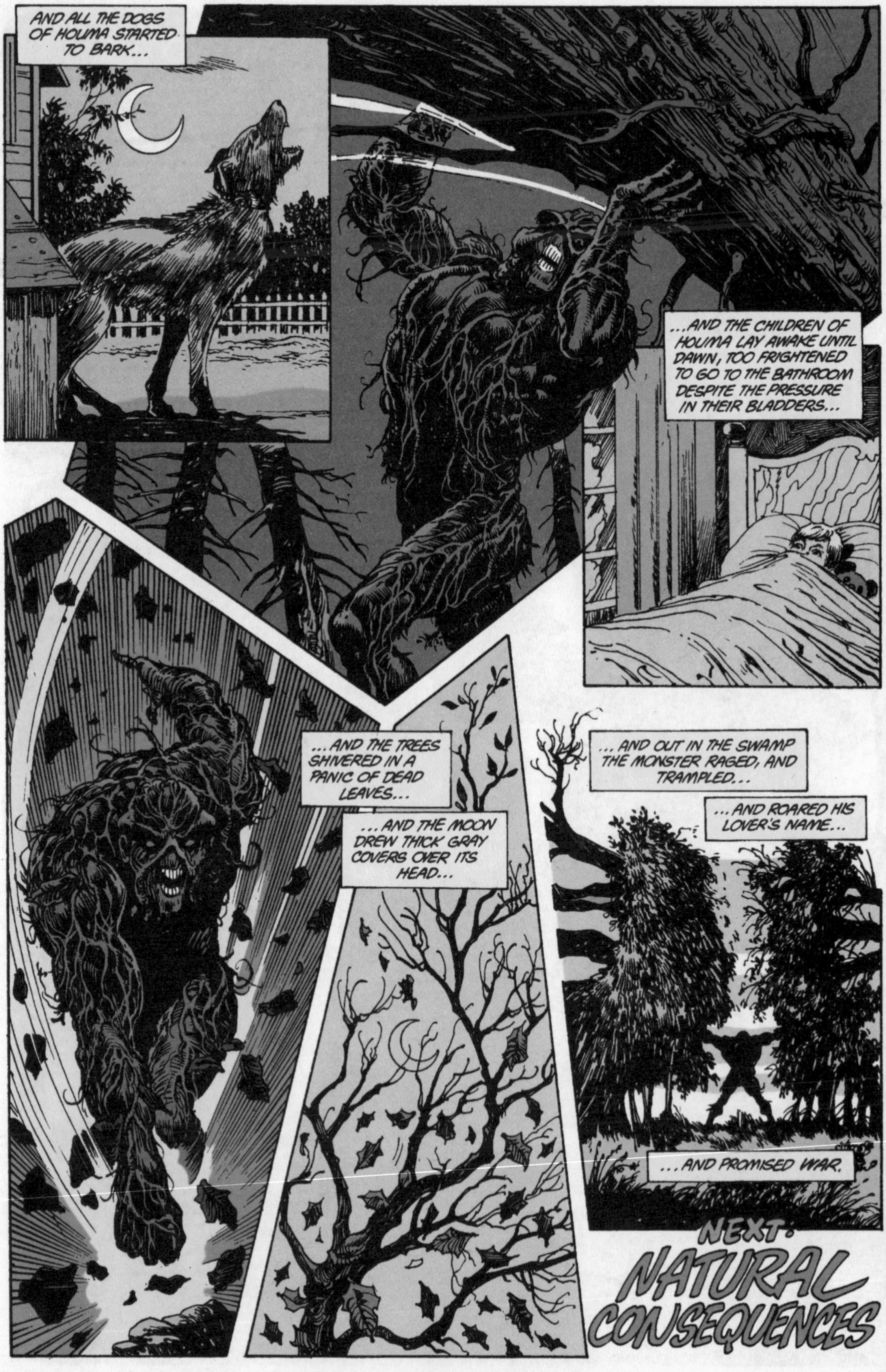
AND ALL THE DOGS OF HOUMA STARTED TO BARK...
...AND THE CHILDREN OF HOUMA LAY AWAKE UNTIL DAWN, TOO FRIGHTENED TO GO TO THE BATHROOM DESPITE THE PRESSURE IN THEIR BLADDERS...
...AND THE TREES SHIVERED IN A PANIC OF DEAD LEAVES...
...AND THE MOON DREW THICK GRAY COVERS OVER ITS HEAD...
...AND OUT IN THE SWAMP THE MONSTER RAGED, AND TRAMPLED...
...AND ROARED HIS LOVER'S NAME...
...AND PROMISED WAR.
NEXT:
NATURAL CONSEQUENCES

CHAPTER 2

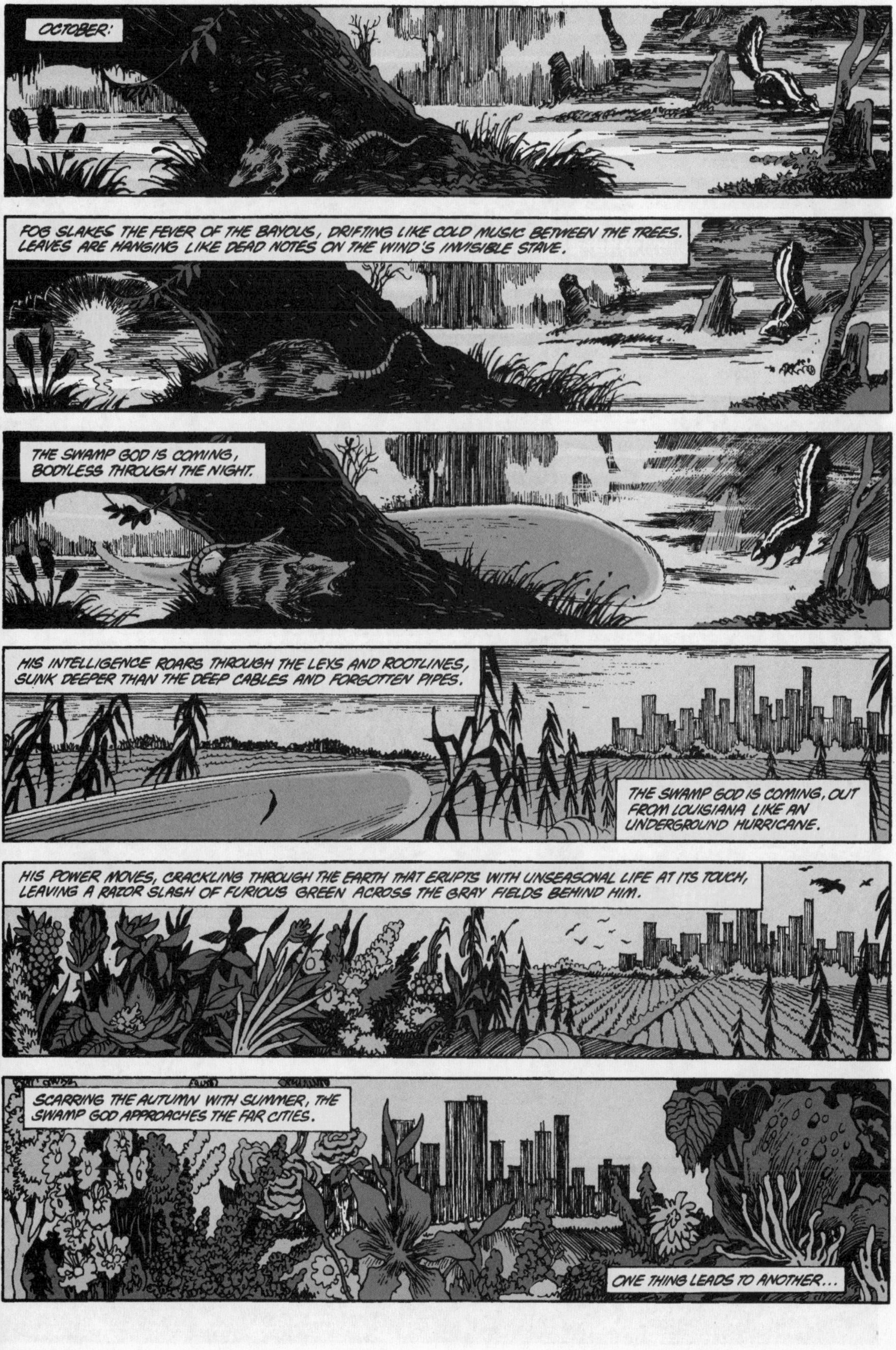
OCTOBER:
FOG SLAKES THE FEVER OF THE BAYOUS, DRIFTING LIKE COLD MUSIC BETWEEN THE TREES. LEAVES ARE HANGING LIKE DEAD NOTES ON THE WIND'S INVISIBLE STAVE.
THE SWAMP GOD IS COMING, BODILESS THROUGH THE NIGHT.
HIS INTELLIGENCE ROARS THROUGH THE LEXS AND ROOTLINES, SUNK DEEPER THAN THE DEEP CABLES AND FORGOTTEN PIPES.
THE SWAMP GOD IS COMING, OUT FROM LOUISIANA LIKE AN UNDERGROUND HURRICANE.
HIS POWER MOVES, CRACKLING THROUGH THE EARTH THAT ERUPTS WITH UNSEASONAL LIFE AT ITS TOUCH, LEAVING A RAZOR SLASH OF FURIOUS GREEN ACROSS THE GRAY FIELDS BEHIND HIM.
SCARRING THE AUTUMN WITH SUMMER, THE SWAMP GOD APPROACHES THE FAR CITIES.
ONE THING LEADS TO ANOTHER...

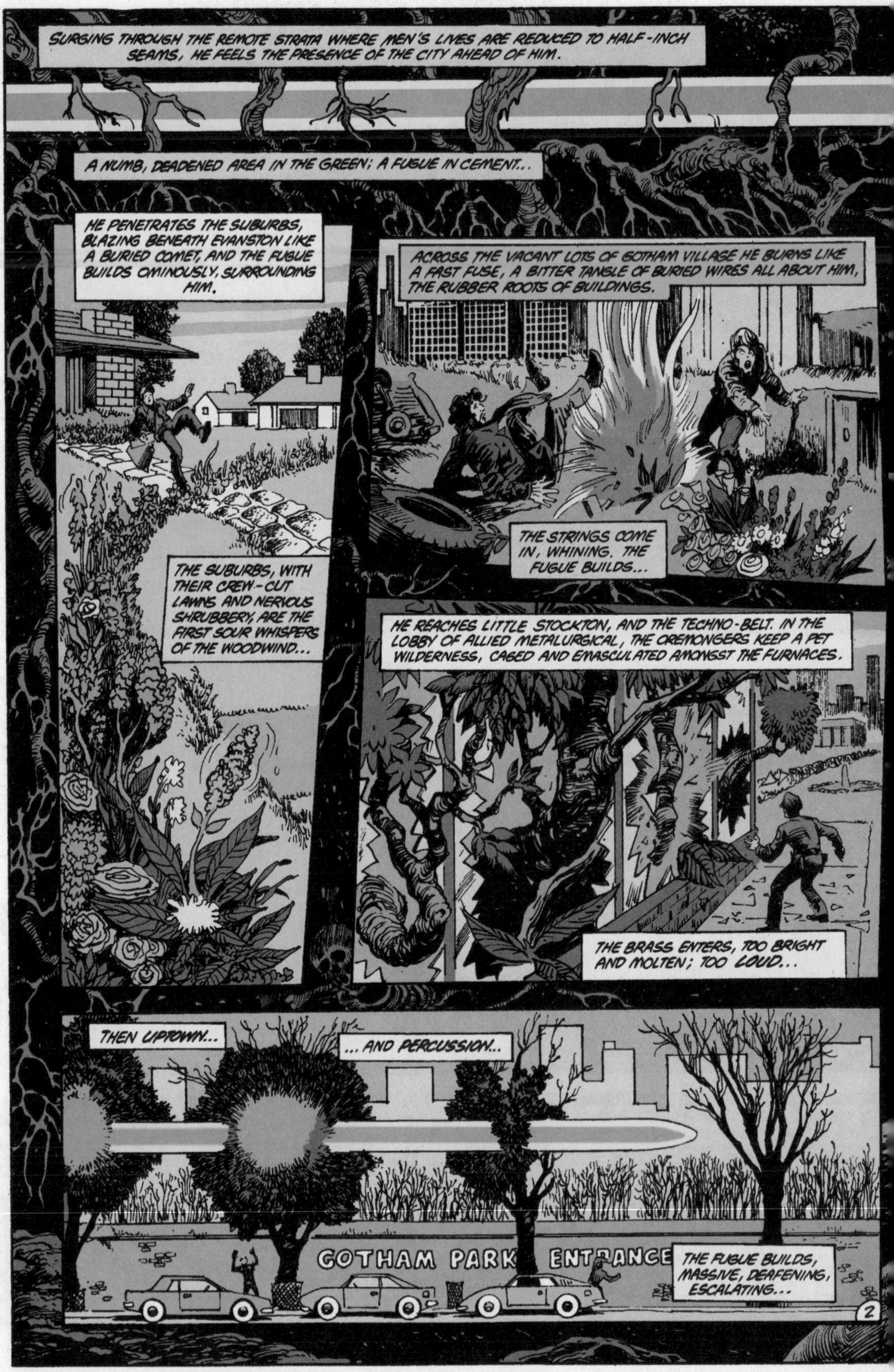
SURGING THROUGH THE REMOTE STRATA WHERE MEN'S LIVES ARE REDUCED TO HALF-INCH SEAMS, HE FEELS THE PRESENCE OF THE CITY AHEAD OF HIM.
A NUMB, DEADENED AREA IN THE GREEN; A FUGUE IN CEMENT...
HE PENETRATES THE SUBURBS, BLAZING BENEATH EVANSTON LIKE A BURIED COMET, AND THE FUGUE BUILDS OMINOUSLY, SURROUNDING HIM.
THE SUBURBS, WITH THEIR CREW-CUT LAWNS AND NERVOUS SHRUBBERY, ARE THE FIRST SOUR WHISPERS OF THE WOODWIND...
ACROSS THE VACANT LOTS OF GOTHAM VILLAGE HE BURNS LIKE A FAST FUSE, A BITTER TANGLE OF BURIED WIRES ALL ABOUT HIM, THE RUBBER ROOTS OF BUILDINGS.
THE STRINGS COME IN, WHINING. THE FUGUE BUILDS...
HE REACHES LITTLE STOCKTON, AND THE TECHNO-BELT. IN THE LOBBY OF ALLIED METALURGICAL, THE OREMONGERS KEEP A PET WILDERNESS, CAGED AND EMASCULATED AMONGST THE FURNACES.
THE BRASS ENTERS, TOO BRIGHT AND MOLTEN; TOO LOUD...
THEN UPTOWN...
...AND PERCUSSION...
GOTHAM PARK ENTRANCE
THE FUGUE BUILDS, MASSIVE, DEAFENING, ESCALATING...
2

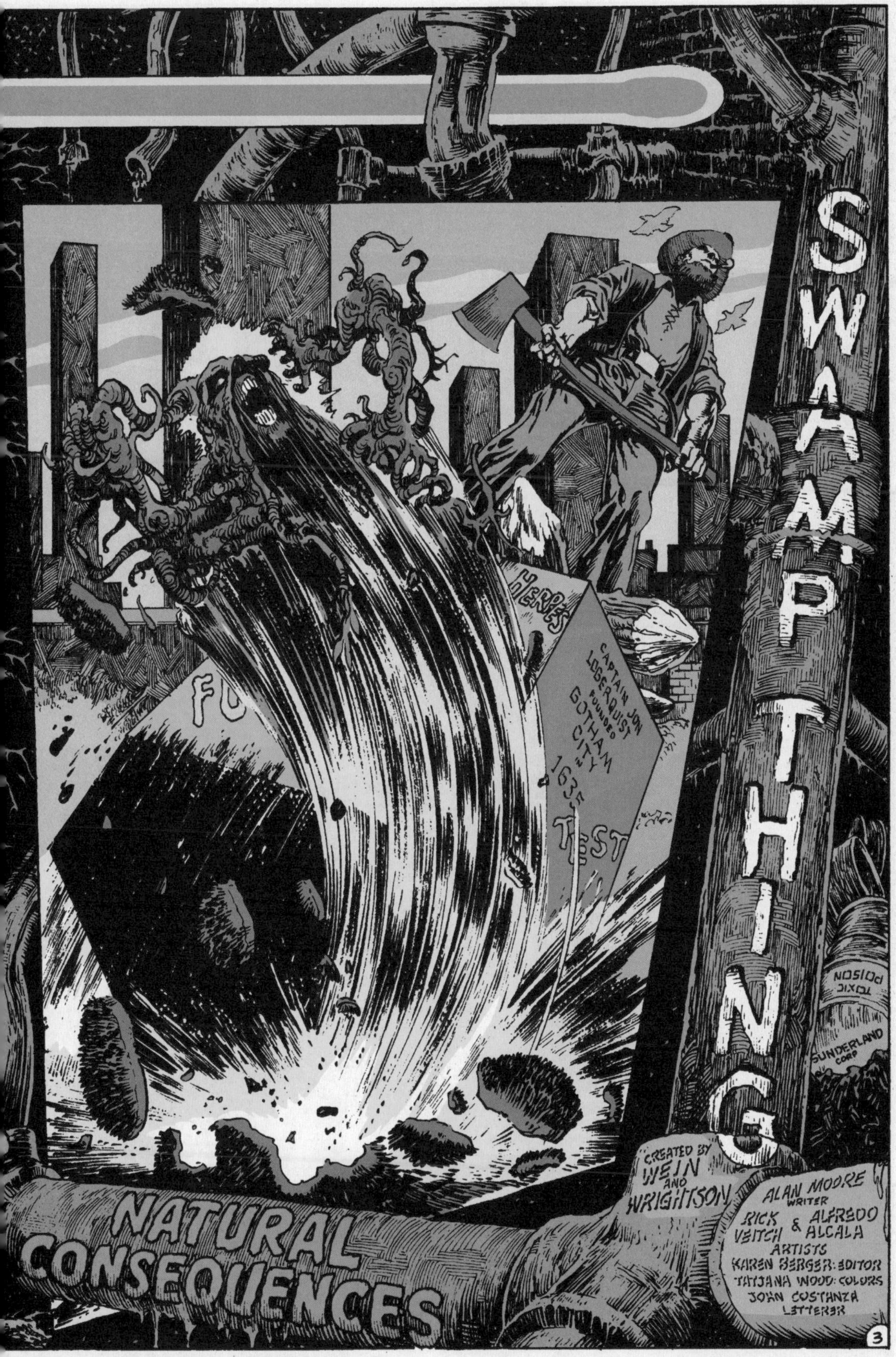
SWAMP THING
HEROES
FU
CAPTAIN JON LOGERQUIST FOUNDED GOTHAM CITY IN 1635
TEST
TOXIC POISON
SUNDERLAND CORP
NATURAL CONSEQUENCES
CREATED BY WEIN AND WRIGHTSON
ALAN MOORE WRITER
RICK VEITCH & ALFREDO ALCALA ARTISTS
KAREN BERGER: EDITOR
TATJANA WOOD: COLORS
JOHN COSTANZA LETTERER
3

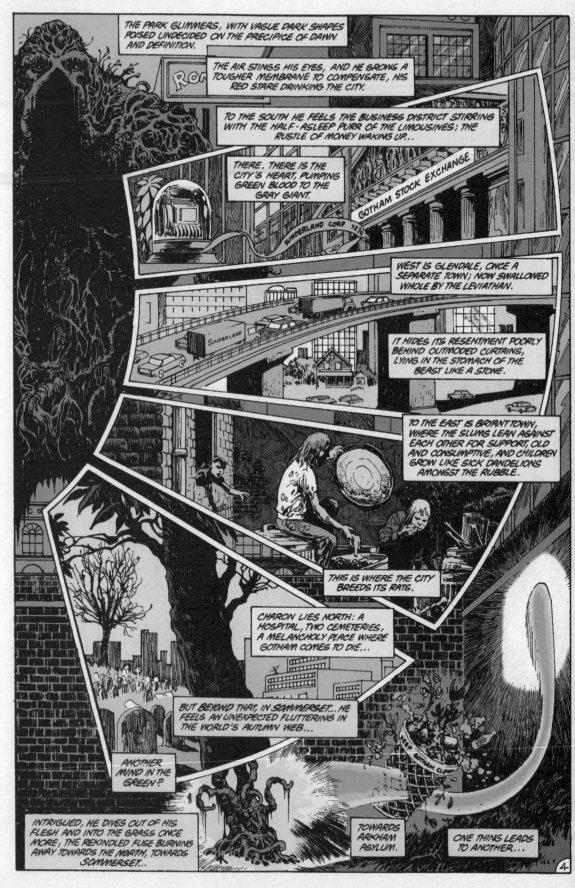

THE PARK GLIMMERS, WITH VAGUE DARK SHAPES POISED UNDECIDED ON THE PRECIPICE OF DAWN AND DEFINITION.

THE AIR STINGS HIS EYES, AND HE GROWS A TOUGHER MEMBRANE TO COMPENSATE, HIS RED STARE DRINKING THE CITY.

TO THE SOUTH HE FEELS THE BUSINESS DISTRICT STIRRING WITH THE HALF-ASLEEP PURR OF THE LIMOUSINES; THE RUSTLE OF MONEY WAKING UP...

THERE, THERE IS THE CITY'S HEART, PUMPING GREEN BLOOD TO THE GRAY GIANT.

GOTHAM STOCK EXCHANGE

SUNDERLAND CORP '73

WEST IS GLENDALE, ONCE A SEPARATE TOWN; NOW SWALLOWED WHOLE BY THE LEVIATHAN.

SUNDERLAND

IT HIDES ITS RESENTMENT POORLY BEHIND OUTMODED CURTAINS, LYING IN THE STOMACH OF THE BEAST LIKE A STONE.

TO THE EAST IS BRYANT TOWN, WHERE THE SLUMS LEAN AGAINST EACH OTHER FOR SUPPORT, OLD AND CONSUMPTIVE, AND CHILDREN GROW LIKE SICK DANDELIONS AMONGST THE RUBBLE.

THIS IS WHERE THE CITY BREEDS ITS RATS.

CHARON LIES NORTH: A HOSPITAL, TWO CEMETERIES, A MELANCHOLY PLACE WHERE GOTHAM COMES TO DIE...

BUT BEYOND THAT, IN SOMMERSET... HE FEELS AN UNEXPECTED FLUTTERING IN THE WORLD'S AUTUMN WEB...

ANOTHER MIND IN THE GREEN?

KEEP GOTHAM CLEAN

INTRIGUED, HE DIVES OUT OF HIS FLESH AND INTO THE GRASS ONCE MORE, THE REKINDLED FUSE BURNING AWAY TOWARDS THE NORTH, TOWARDS SOMMERSET...

TOWARDS ARKHAM ASYLUM.

ONE THING LEADS TO ANOTHER...

4

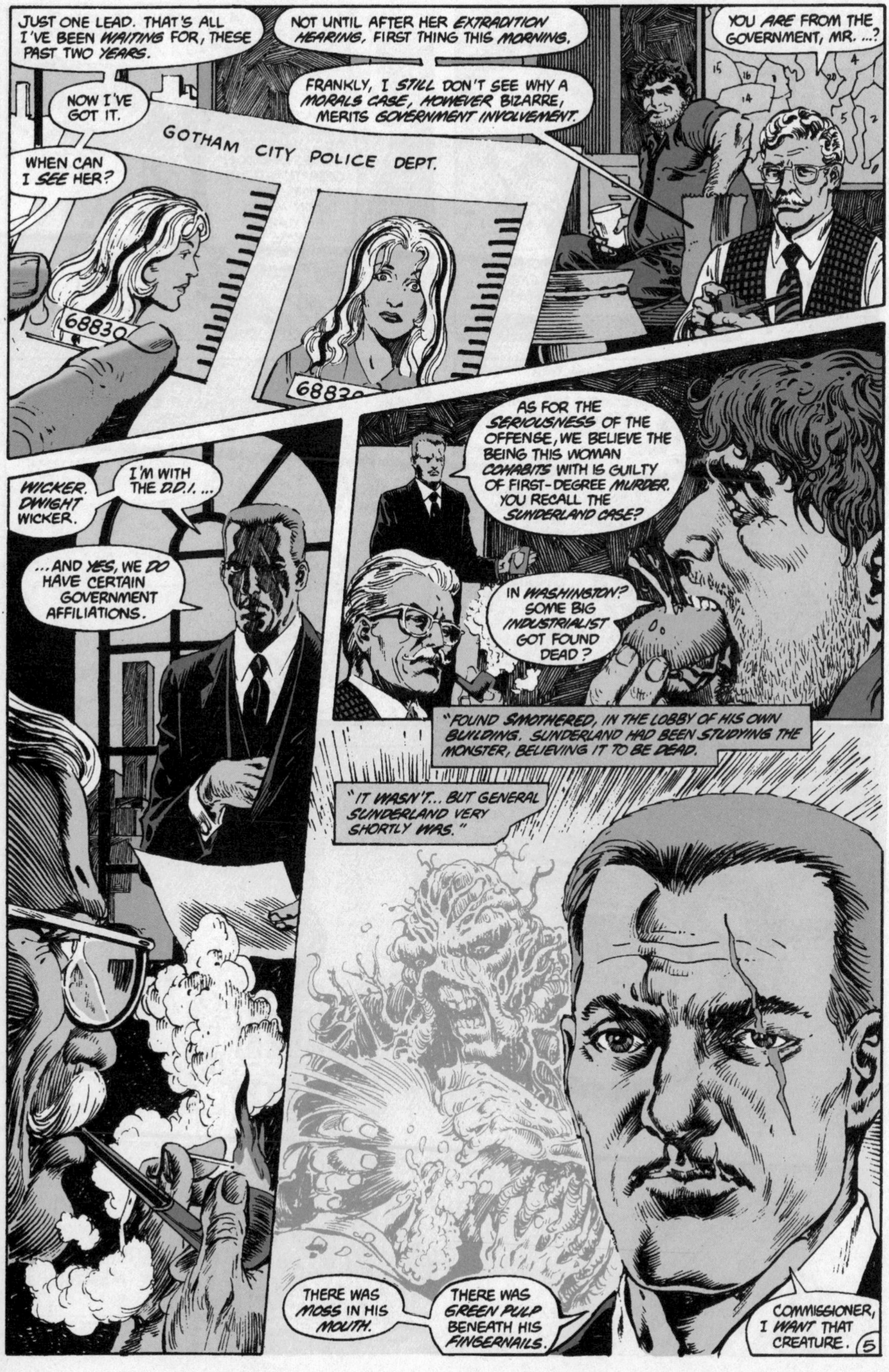
JUST ONE LEAD. THAT'S ALL I'VE BEEN WAITING FOR, THESE PAST TWO YEARS.
NOW I'VE GOT IT.
WHEN CAN I SEE HER?
NOT UNTIL AFTER HER EXTRADITION HEARING, FIRST THING THIS MORNING.
FRANKLY, I STILL DON'T SEE WHY A MORALS CASE, HOWEVER BIZARRE, MERITS GOVERNMENT INVOLVEMENT.
YOU ARE FROM THE GOVERNMENT, MR. ...?
GOTHAM CITY POLICE DEPT.
68830
68830
WICKER. DWIGHT WICKER.
I'M WITH THE D.D.I. ...
...AND YES, WE DO HAVE CERTAIN GOVERNMENT AFFILIATIONS.
AS FOR THE SERIOUSNESS OF THE OFFENSE, WE BELIEVE THE BEING THIS WOMAN COHABITS WITH IS GUILTY OF FIRST-DEGREE MURDER. YOU RECALL THE SUNDERLAND CASE?
IN WASHINGTON? SOME BIG INDUSTRIALIST GOT FOUND DEAD?
"FOUND SMOTHERED, IN THE LOBBY OF HIS OWN BUILDING. SUNDERLAND HAD BEEN STUDYING THE MONSTER, BELIEVING IT TO BE DEAD.
"IT WASN'T... BUT GENERAL SUNDERLAND VERY SHORTLY WAS."
THERE WAS MOSS IN HIS MOUTH.
THERE WAS GREEN PULP BENEATH HIS FINGERNAILS.
COMMISSIONER, I WANT THAT CREATURE.
5

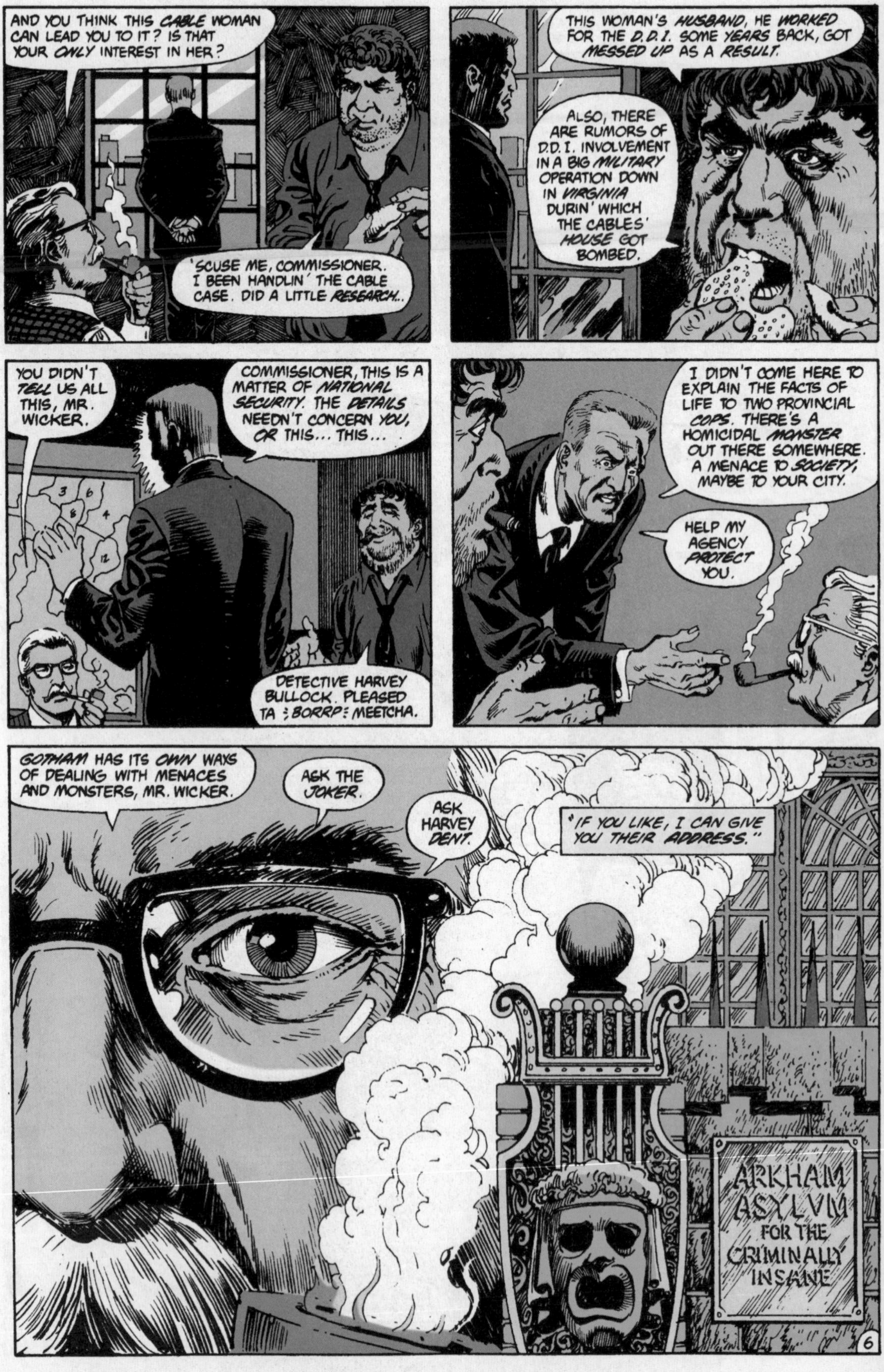
AND YOU THINK THIS CABLE WOMAN CAN LEAD YOU TO IT? IS THAT YOUR ONLY INTEREST IN HER?
'SCUSE ME, COMMISSIONER. I BEEN HANDLIN' THE CABLE CASE. DID A LITTLE RESEARCH..
THIS WOMAN'S HUSBAND, HE WORKED FOR THE D.D.I. SOME YEARS BACK, GOT MESSED UP AS A RESULT.
ALSO, THERE ARE RUMORS OF D.D.I. INVOLVEMENT IN A BIG MILITARY OPERATION DOWN IN VIRGINIA DURIN' WHICH THE CABLES' HOUSE GOT BOMBED.
YOU DIDN'T TELL US ALL THIS, MR. WICKER.
COMMISSIONER, THIS IS A MATTER OF NATIONAL SECURITY. THE DETAILS NEEDN'T CONCERN YOU, OR THIS... THIS...
DETECTIVE HARVEY BULLOCK. PLEASED TA :BORRP: MEETCHA.
I DIDN'T COME HERE TO EXPLAIN THE FACTS OF LIFE TO TWO PROVINCIAL COPS. THERE'S A HOMICIDAL MONSTER OUT THERE SOMEWHERE. A MENACE TO SOCIETY, MAYBE TO YOUR CITY.
HELP MY AGENCY PROTECT YOU.
GOTHAM HAS ITS OWN WAYS OF DEALING WITH MENACES AND MONSTERS, MR. WICKER.
ASK THE JOKER.
ASK HARVEY DENT.
"IF YOU LIKE, I CAN GIVE YOU THEIR ADDRESS."
ARKHAM ASYLUM FOR THE CRIMINALLY INSANE
6

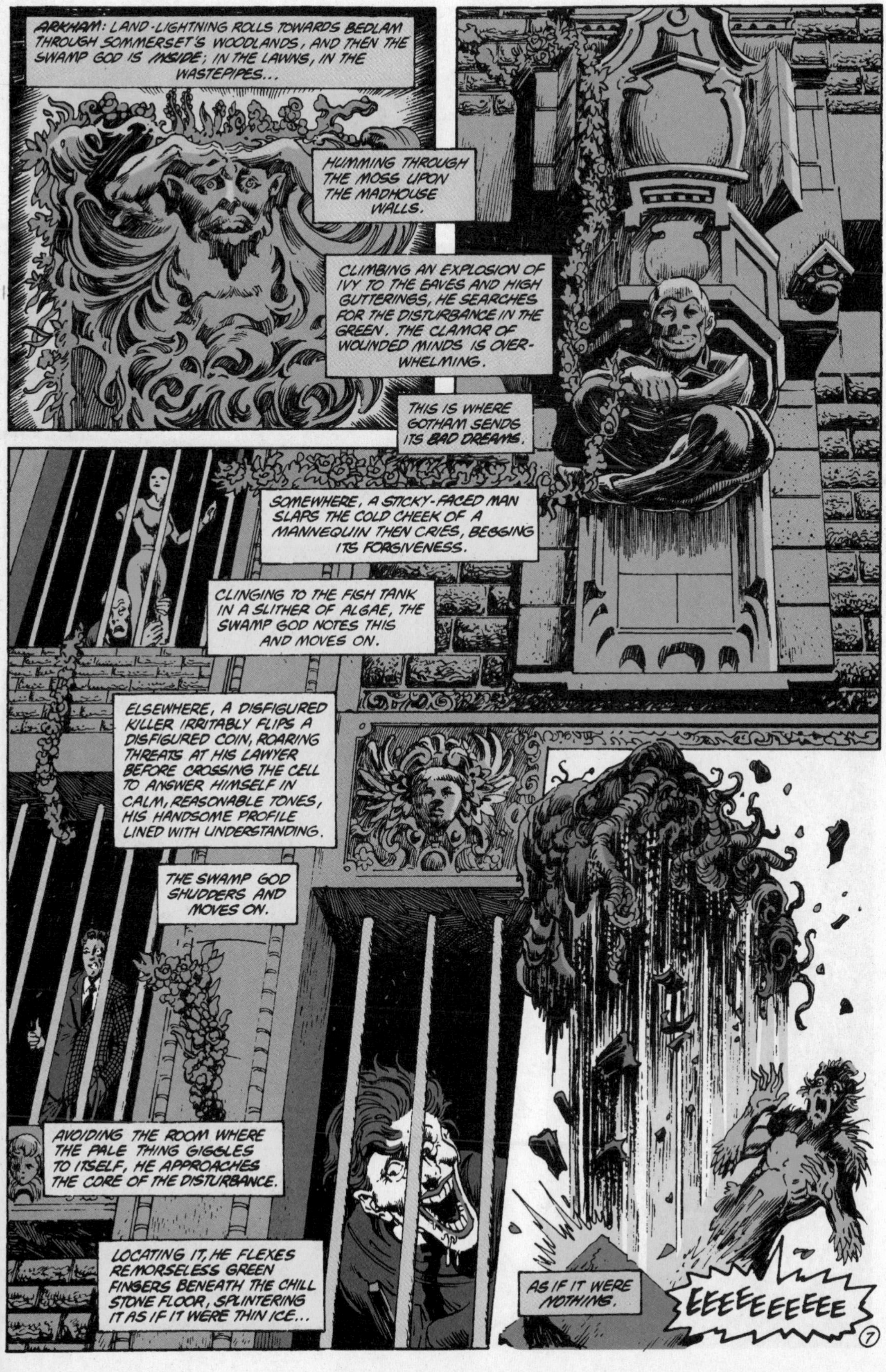
ARKHAM: LAND-LIGHTNING ROLLS TOWARDS BEDLAM THROUGH SOMMERSET'S WOODLANDS, AND THEN THE SWAMP GOD IS INSIDE; IN THE LAWNS, IN THE WASTEPIPES...
HUMMING THROUGH THE MOSS UPON THE MADHOUSE WALLS.
CLIMBING AN EXPLOSION OF IVY TO THE EAVES AND HIGH GUTTERINGS, HE SEARCHES FOR THE DISTURBANCE IN THE GREEN. THE CLAMOR OF WOUNDED MINDS IS OVER-WHELMING.
THIS IS WHERE GOTHAM SENDS ITS BAD DREAMS.
SOMEWHERE, A STICKY-FACED MAN SLAPS THE COLD CHEEK OF A MANNEQUIN THEN CRIES, BEGGING ITS FORGIVENESS.
CLINGING TO THE FISH TANK IN A SLITHER OF ALGAE, THE SWAMP GOD NOTES THIS AND MOVES ON.
ELSEWHERE, A DISFIGURED KILLER IRRITABLY FLIPS A DISFIGURED COIN, ROARING THREATS AT HIS LAWYER BEFORE CROSSING THE CELL TO ANSWER HIMSELF IN CALM, REASONABLE TONES, HIS HANDSOME PROFILE LINED WITH UNDERSTANDING.
THE SWAMP GOD SHUDDERS AND MOVES ON.
AVOIDING THE ROOM WHERE THE PALE THING GIGGLES TO ITSELF, HE APPROACHES THE CORE OF THE DISTURBANCE.
LOCATING IT, HE FLEXES REMORSELESS GREEN FINGERS BENEATH THE CHILL STONE FLOOR, SPLINTERING IT AS IF IT WERE THIN ICE...
AS IF IT WERE NOTHING.
EEEEEEEEEE
7

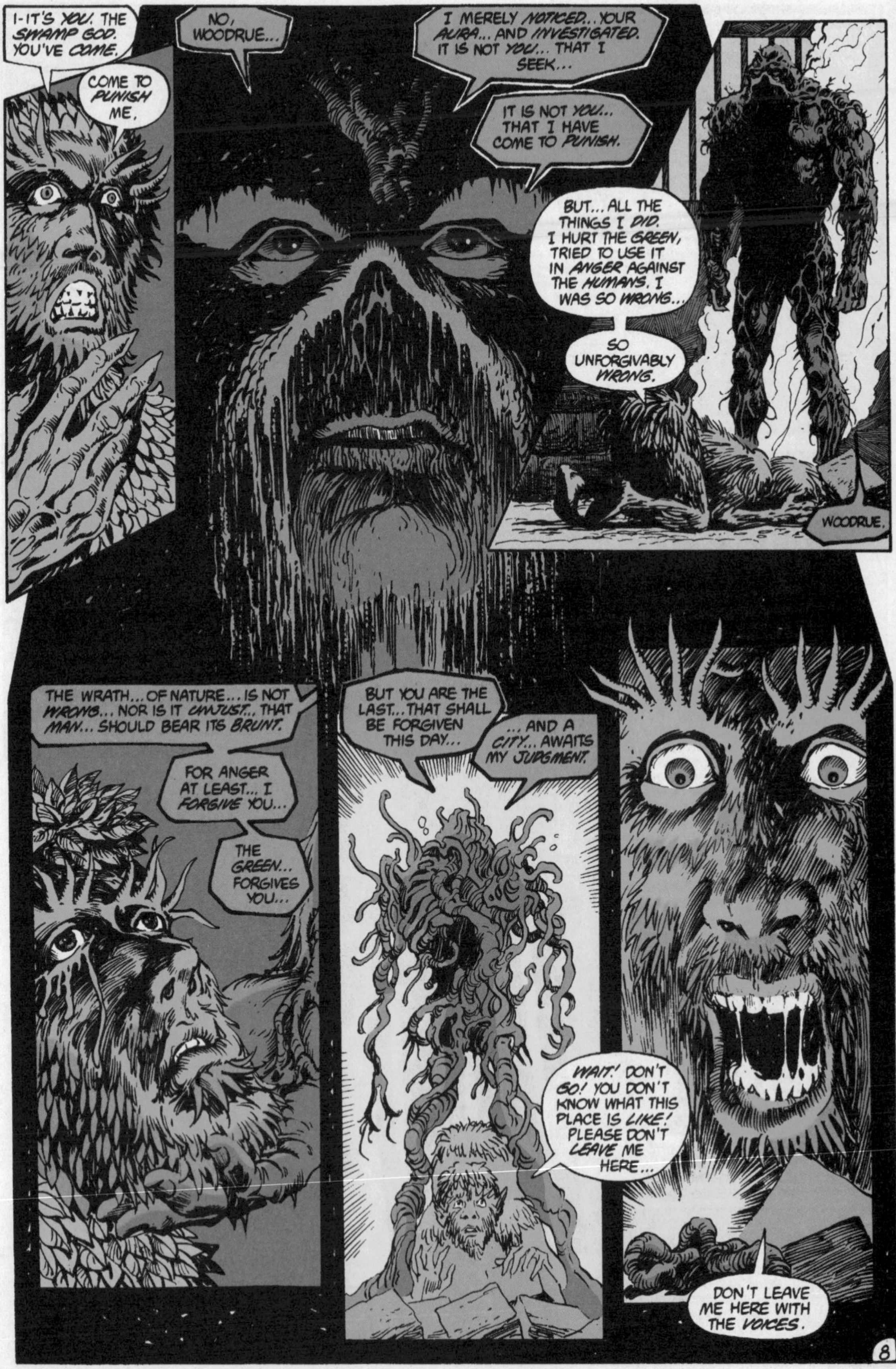
I-IT'S YOU. THE SWAMP GOD. YOU'VE COME.
COME TO PUNISH ME.
NO, WOODRUE...
I MERELY NOTICED... YOUR AURA... AND INVESTIGATED. IT IS NOT YOU... THAT I SEEK...
IT IS NOT YOU... THAT I HAVE COME TO PUNISH.
BUT... ALL THE THINGS I DID. I HURT THE GREEN, TRIED TO USE IT IN ANGER AGAINST THE HUMANS. I WAS SO WRONG...
SO UNFORGIVABLY WRONG.
WOODRUE.
THE WRATH... OF NATURE... IS NOT WRONG... NOR IS IT UNJUST... THAT MAN... SHOULD BEAR ITS BRUNT.
FOR ANGER AT LEAST... I FORGIVE YOU...
THE GREEN... FORGIVES YOU...
BUT YOU ARE THE LAST... THAT SHALL BE FORGIVEN THIS DAY...
...AND A CITY... AWAITS MY JUDGMENT.
WAIT! DON'T GO! YOU DON'T KNOW WHAT THIS PLACE IS LIKE! PLEASE DON'T LEAVE ME HERE...
DON'T LEAVE ME HERE WITH THE VOICES.
8

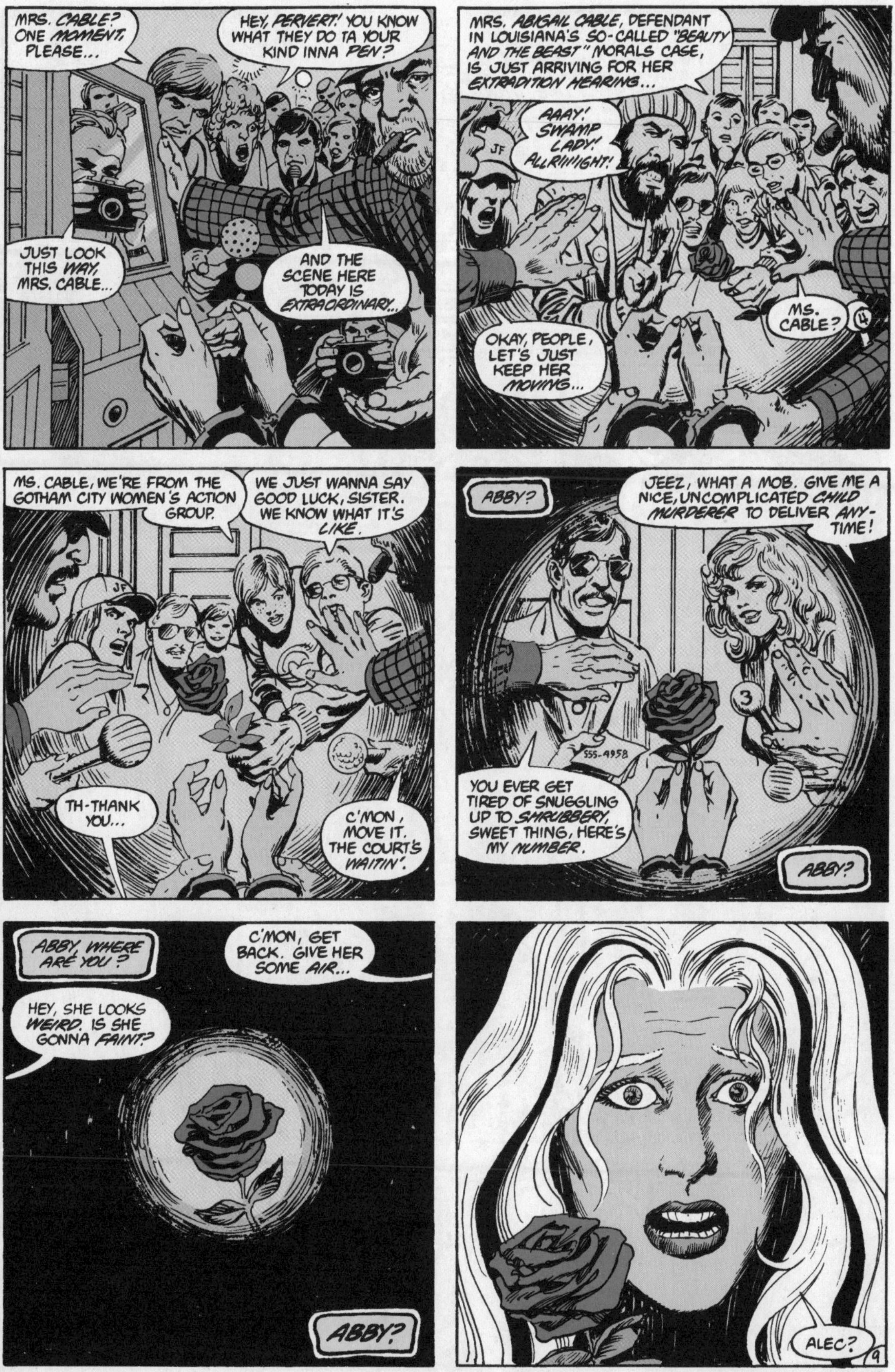
MRS. CABLE? ONE MOMENT, PLEASE...
HEY, PERVERT! YOU KNOW WHAT THEY DO TA YOUR KIND INNA PEN?
JUST LOOK THIS WAY, MRS. CABLE...
AND THE SCENE HERE TODAY IS EXTRAORDINARY...
MRS. ABIGAIL CABLE, DEFENDANT IN LOUISIANA'S SO-CALLED "BEAUTY AND THE BEAST" MORALS CASE, IS JUST ARRIVING FOR HER EXTRADITION HEARING...
AAAY! SWAMP LADY! ALLRIIIIGHT!
OKAY, PEOPLE, LET'S JUST KEEP HER MOVING...
MS. CABLE?
MS. CABLE, WE'RE FROM THE GOTHAM CITY WOMEN'S ACTION GROUP.
WE JUST WANNA SAY GOOD LUCK, SISTER. WE KNOW WHAT IT'S LIKE.
TH-THANK YOU...
C'MON, MOVE IT. THE COURT'S WAITIN'.
ABBY?
JEEZ, WHAT A MOB. GIVE ME A NICE, UNCOMPLICATED CHILD MURDERER TO DELIVER ANY-TIME!
555-4958
YOU EVER GET TIRED OF SNUGGLING UP TO SHRUBBERY, SWEET THING, HERE'S MY NUMBER.
ABBY?
ABBY, WHERE ARE YOU?
C'MON, GET BACK. GIVE HER SOME AIR...
HEY, SHE LOOKS WEIRD. IS SHE GONNA FAINT?
ABBY?
ALEC?

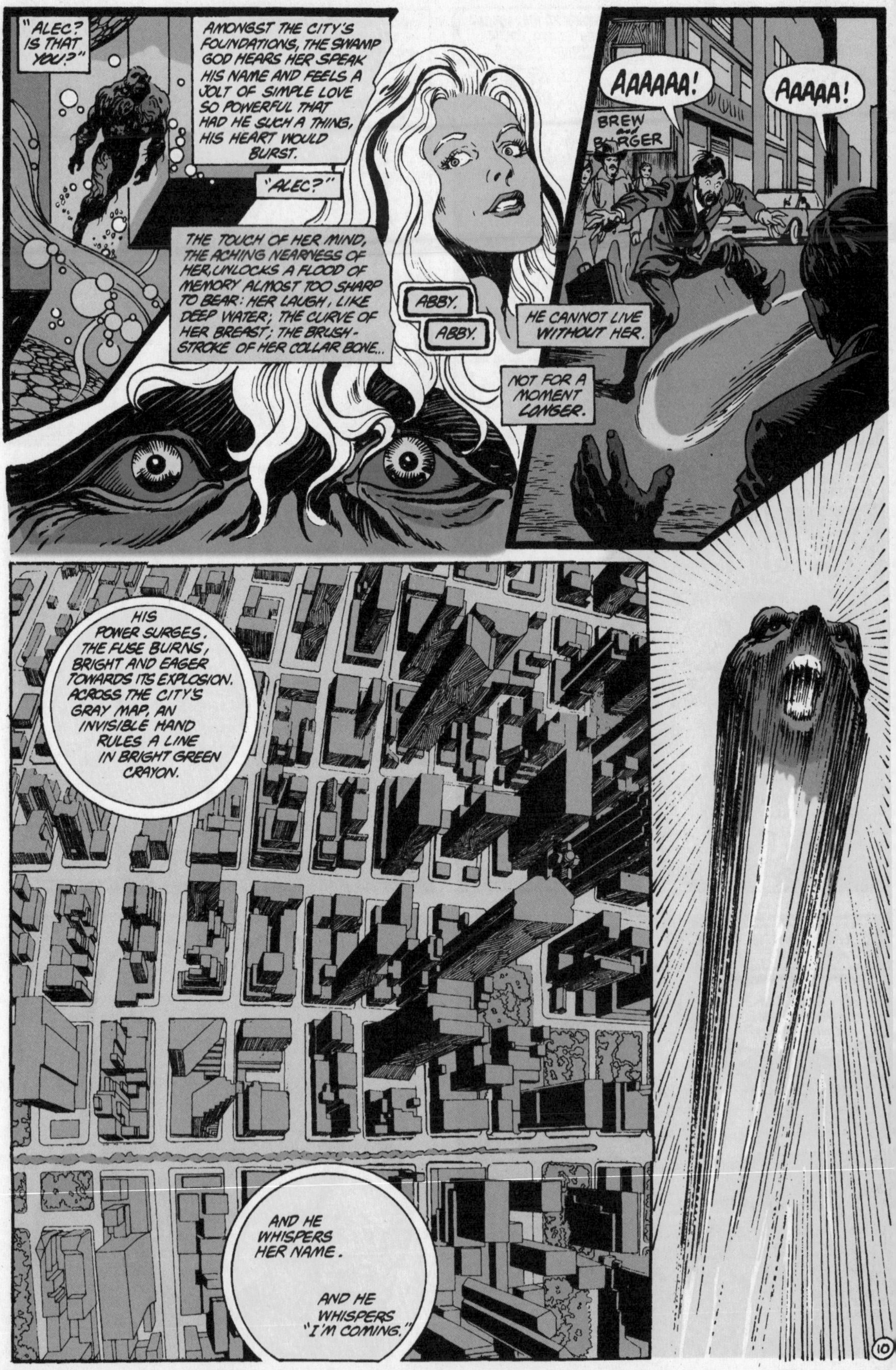
"ALEC? IS THAT YOU?"
AMONGST THE CITY'S FOUNDATIONS, THE SWAMP GOD HEARS HER SPEAK HIS NAME AND FEELS A JOLT OF SIMPLE LOVE SO POWERFUL THAT HAD HE SUCH A THING, HIS HEART WOULD BURST.
"ALEC?"
THE TOUCH OF HER MIND, THE ACHING NEARNESS OF HER, UNLOCKS A FLOOD OF MEMORY ALMOST TOO SHARP TO BEAR: HER LAUGH, LIKE DEEP WATER; THE CURVE OF HER BREAST; THE BRUSH-STROKE OF HER COLLAR BONE...
ABBY.
ABBY.
AAAAAA!
AAAAA!
BREW and BURGER
HE CANNOT LIVE WITHOUT HER.
NOT FOR A MOMENT LONGER.
HIS POWER SURGES. THE FUSE BURNS, BRIGHT AND EAGER TOWARDS ITS EXPLOSION. ACROSS THE CITY'S GRAY MAP, AN INVISIBLE HAND RULES A LINE IN BRIGHT GREEN CRAYON.
AND HE WHISPERS HER NAME.
AND HE WHISPERS "I'M COMING."
10

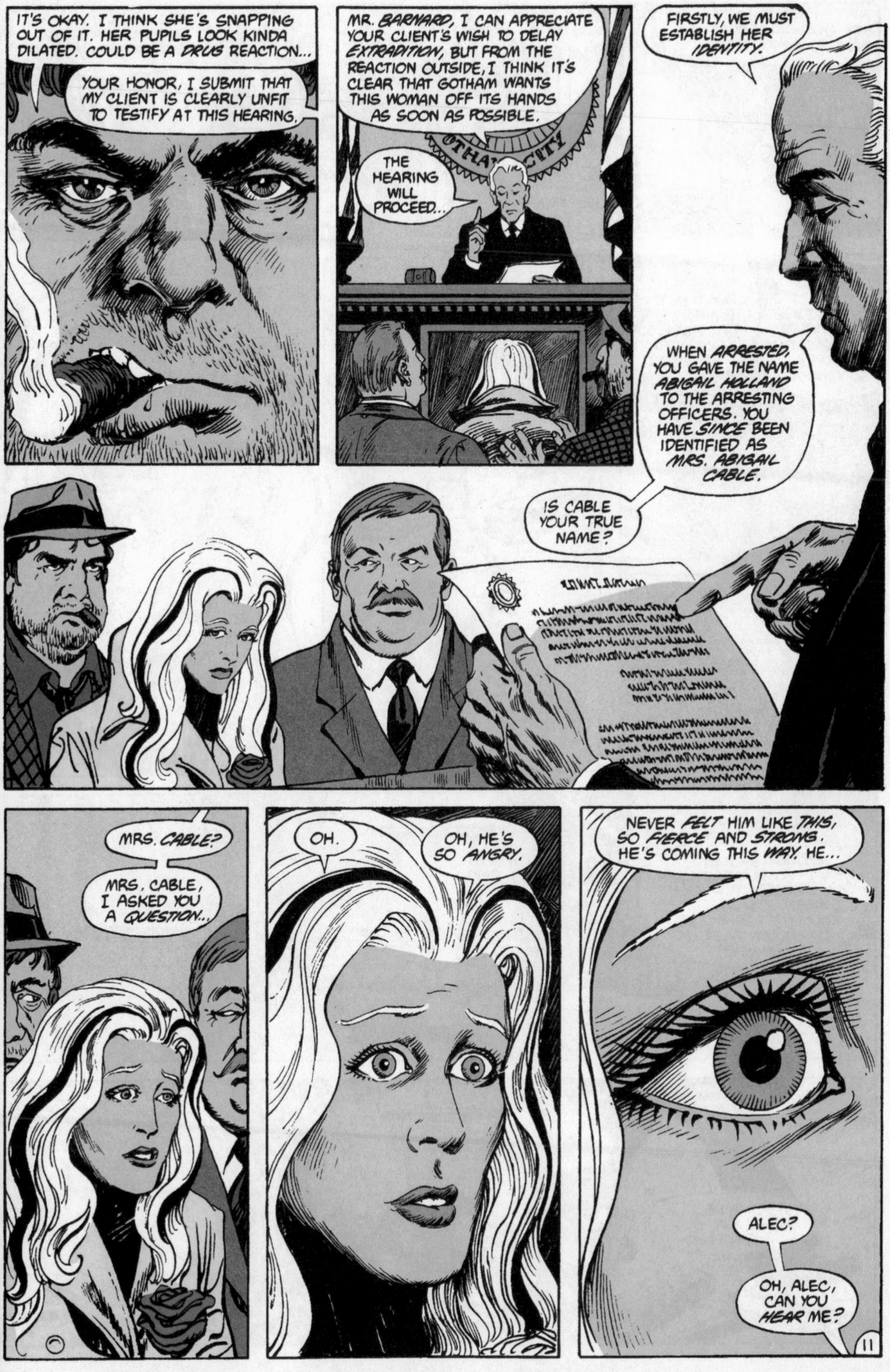
IT'S OKAY. I THINK SHE'S SNAPPING OUT OF IT. HER PUPILS LOOK KINDA DILATED. COULD BE A DRUG REACTION...
YOUR HONOR, I SUBMIT THAT MY CLIENT IS CLEARLY UNFIT TO TESTIFY AT THIS HEARING.
MR. BARNARD, I CAN APPRECIATE YOUR CLIENT'S WISH TO DELAY EXTRADITION, BUT FROM THE REACTION OUTSIDE, I THINK IT'S CLEAR THAT GOTHAM WANTS THIS WOMAN OFF ITS HANDS AS SOON AS POSSIBLE.
THE HEARING WILL PROCEED...
FIRSTLY, WE MUST ESTABLISH HER IDENTITY.
WHEN ARRESTED, YOU GAVE THE NAME ABIGAIL HOLLAND TO THE ARRESTING OFFICERS. YOU HAVE SINCE BEEN IDENTIFIED AS MRS. ABIGAIL CABLE.
IS CABLE YOUR TRUE NAME?
MRS. CABLE?
MRS. CABLE, I ASKED YOU A QUESTION...
OH.
OH, HE'S SO ANGRY.
NEVER FELT HIM LIKE THIS, SO FIERCE AND STRONG. HE'S COMING THIS WAY. HE...
ALEC?
OH, ALEC, CAN YOU HEAR ME?
11

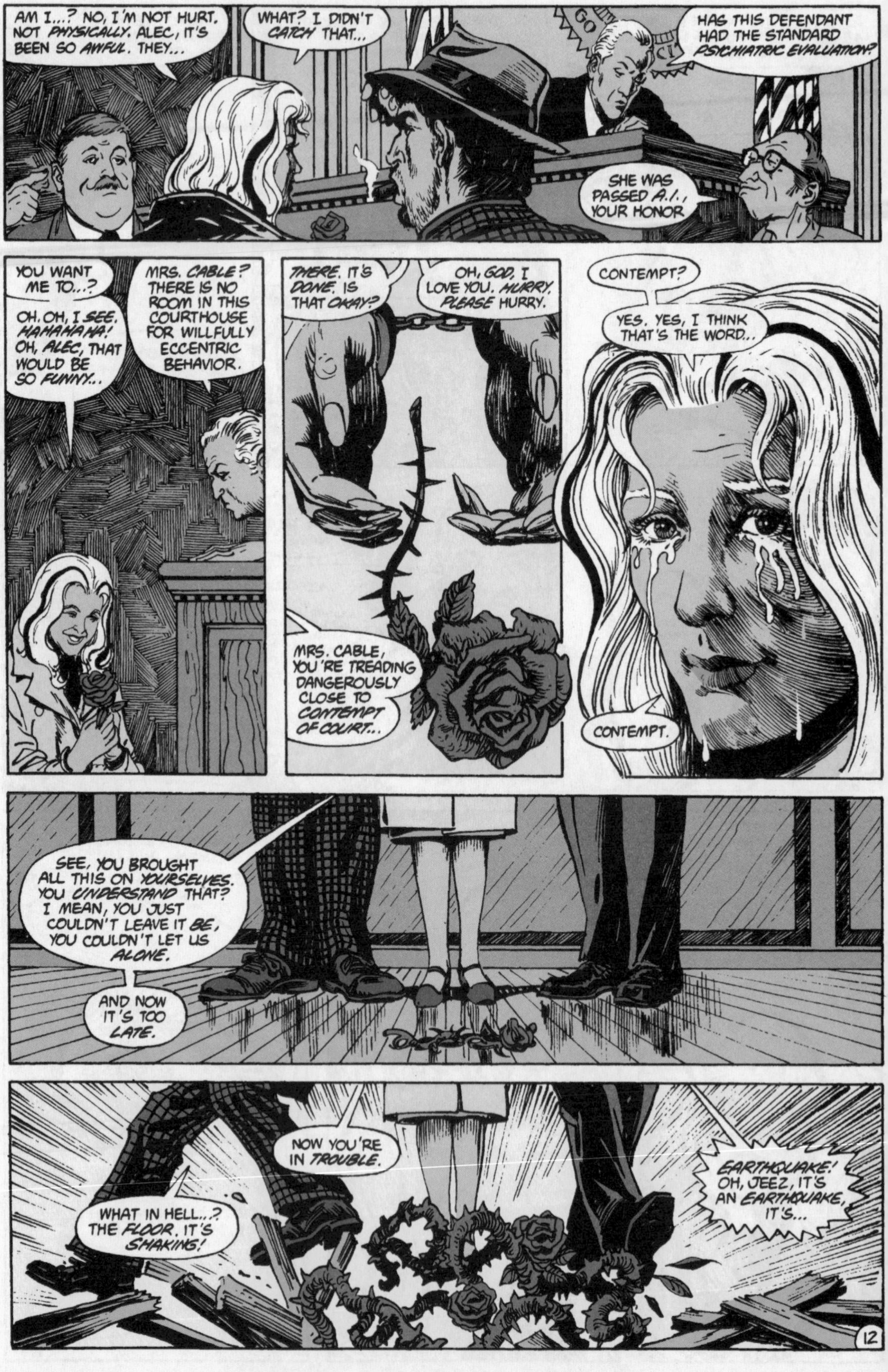
AM I...? NO, I'M NOT HURT. NOT PHYSICALLY. ALEC, IT'S BEEN SO AWFUL. THEY...
WHAT? I DIDN'T CATCH THAT...
HAS THIS DEFENDANT HAD THE STANDARD PSYCHIATRIC EVALUATION?
SHE WAS PASSED A.I., YOUR HONOR
YOU WANT ME TO...?
OH. OH, I SEE. HAHAHAHA! OH, ALEC, THAT WOULD BE SO FUNNY...
MRS. CABLE? THERE IS NO ROOM IN THIS COURTHOUSE FOR WILLFULLY ECCENTRIC BEHAVIOR.
THERE. IT'S DONE. IS THAT OKAY?
OH, GOD, I LOVE YOU. HURRY, PLEASE HURRY.
MRS. CABLE, YOU'RE TREADING DANGEROUSLY CLOSE TO CONTEMPT OF COURT...
CONTEMPT?
YES. YES, I THINK THAT'S THE WORD...
CONTEMPT.
SEE, YOU BROUGHT ALL THIS ON YOURSELVES. YOU UNDERSTAND THAT? I MEAN, YOU JUST COULDN'T LEAVE IT BE, YOU COULDN'T LET US ALONE.
AND NOW IT'S TOO LATE.
NOW YOU'RE IN TROUBLE.
WHAT IN HELL...? THE FLOOR. IT'S SHAKING!
EARTHQUAKE! OH, JEEZ, IT'S AN EARTHQUAKE, IT'S...
12

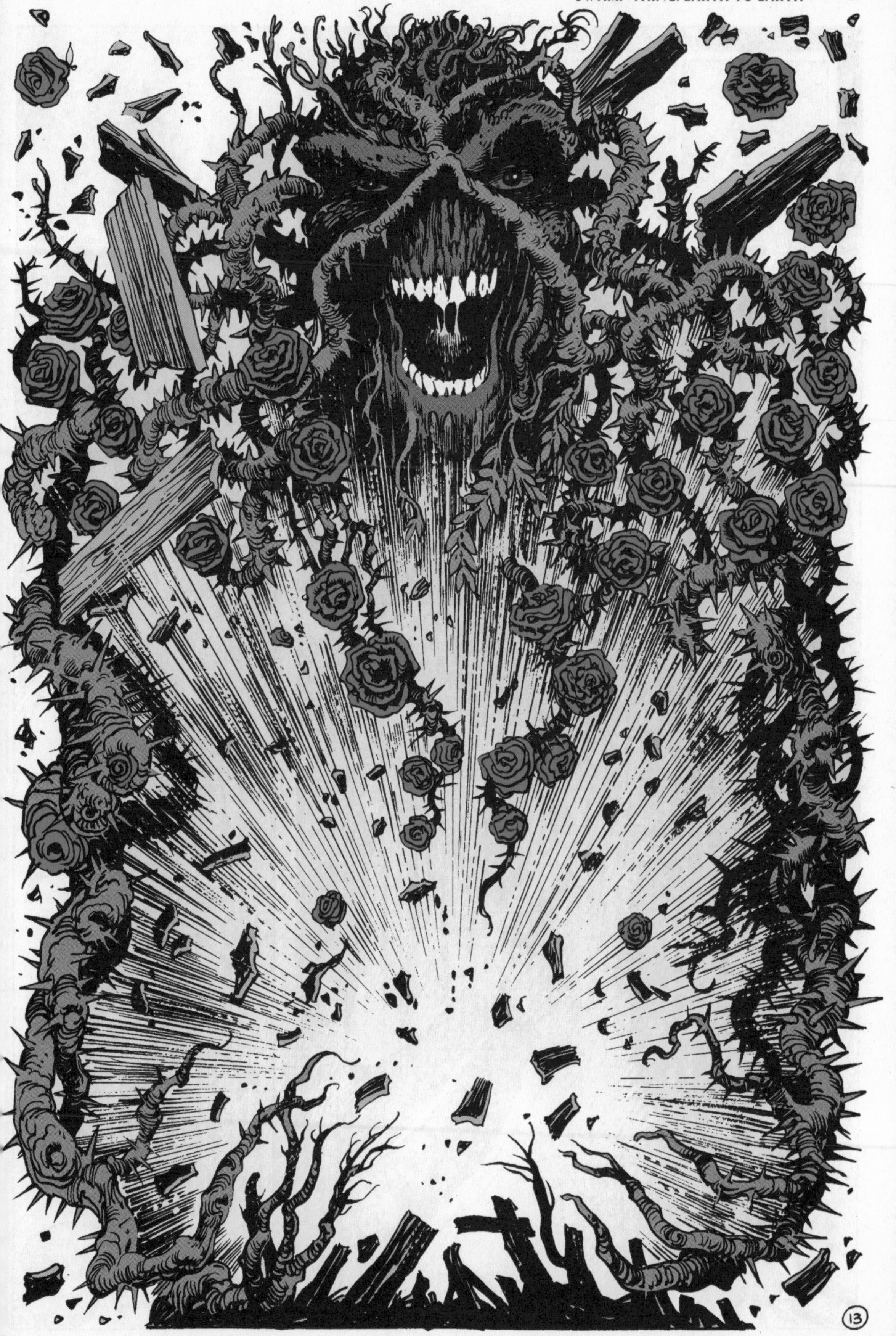
13

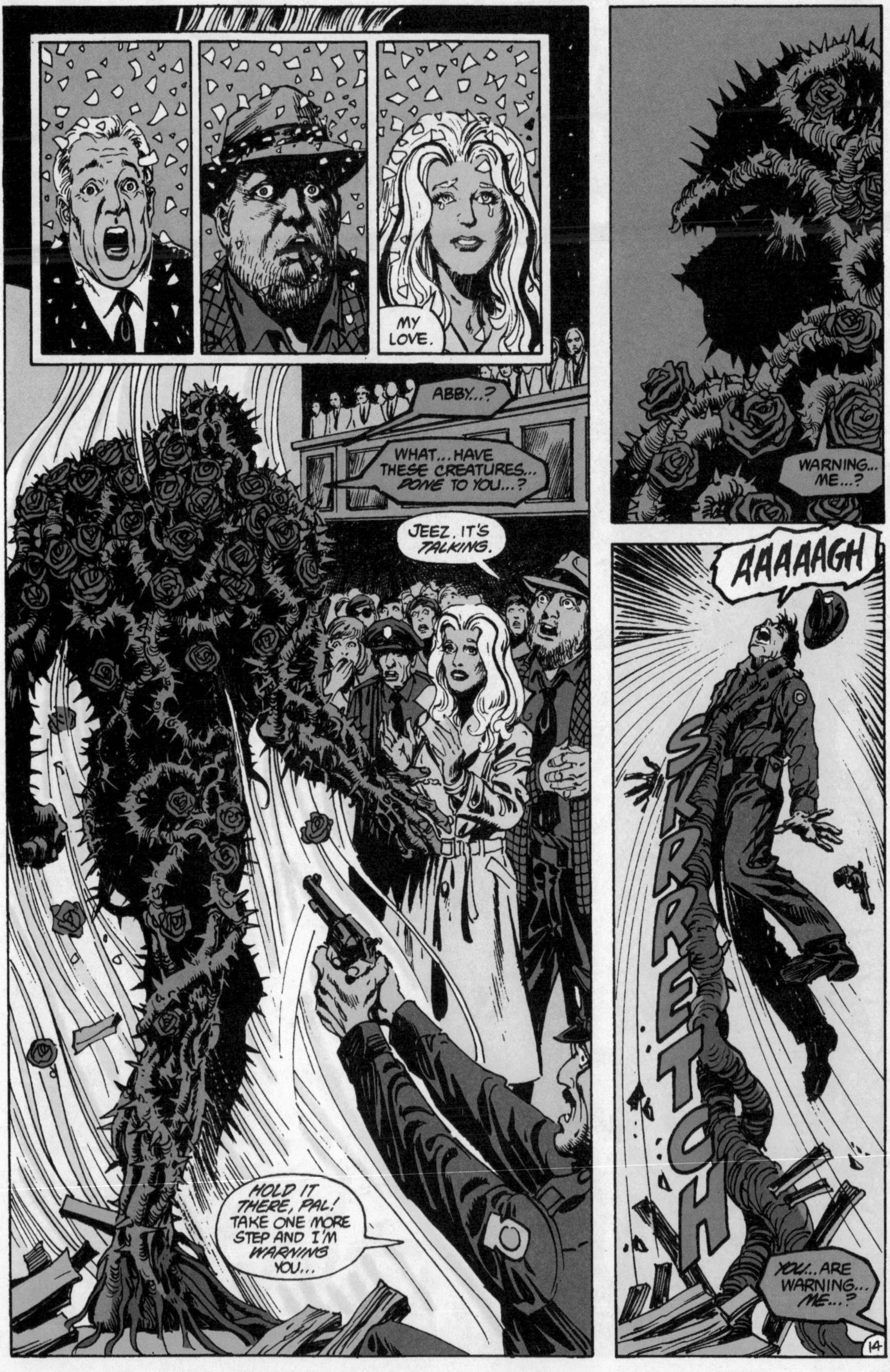
MY LOVE.
ABBY...?
WHAT... HAVE THESE CREATURES... DONE TO YOU...?
JEEZ, IT'S TALKING.
HOLD IT THERE, PAL! TAKE ONE MORE STEP AND I'M WARNING YOU...
WARNING... ME...?
AAAAAGH
SKRRETCH
YOU... ARE WARNING... ME...?
14

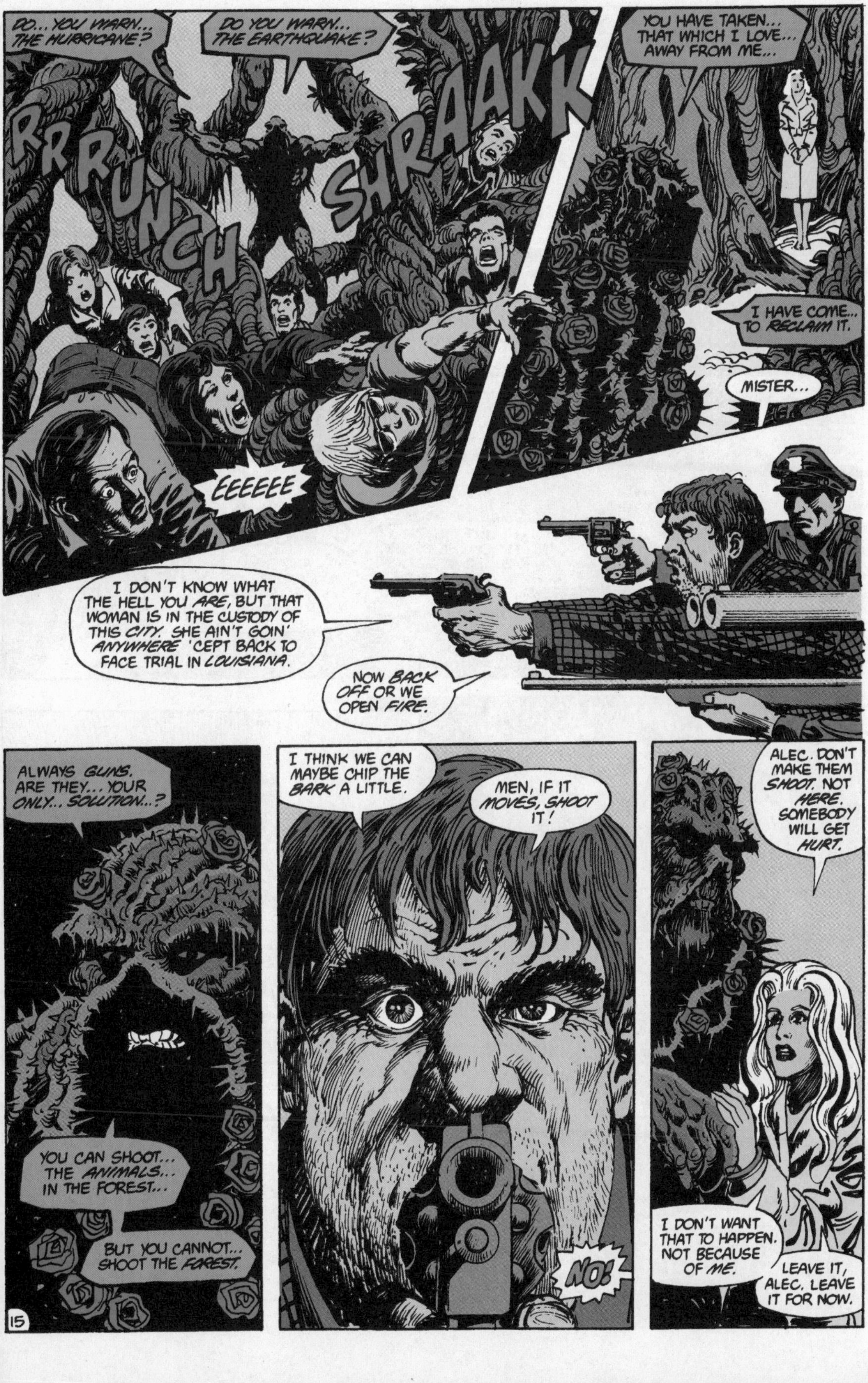
DO... YOU WARN... THE HURRICANE?
DO YOU WARN... THE EARTHQUAKE?
RRRUNCH
SHRAAKK
EEEEEE
YOU HAVE TAKEN... THAT WHICH I LOVE... AWAY FROM ME...
I HAVE COME... TO RECLAIM IT.
MISTER...
I DON'T KNOW WHAT THE HELL YOU ARE, BUT THAT WOMAN IS IN THE CUSTODY OF THIS CITY. SHE AIN'T GOIN' ANYWHERE 'CEPT BACK TO FACE TRIAL IN LOUISIANA.
NOW BACK OFF OR WE OPEN FIRE.
ALWAYS GUNS. ARE THEY... YOUR ONLY... SOLUTION...?
YOU CAN SHOOT... THE ANIMALS... IN THE FOREST...
BUT YOU CANNOT... SHOOT THE FOREST.
15
I THINK WE CAN MAYBE CHIP THE BARK A LITTLE.
MEN, IF IT MOVES, SHOOT IT!
NO!
ALEC. DON'T MAKE THEM SHOOT. NOT HERE. SOMEBODY WILL GET HURT.
I DON'T WANT THAT TO HAPPEN. NOT BECAUSE OF ME.
LEAVE IT, ALEC. LEAVE IT FOR NOW.

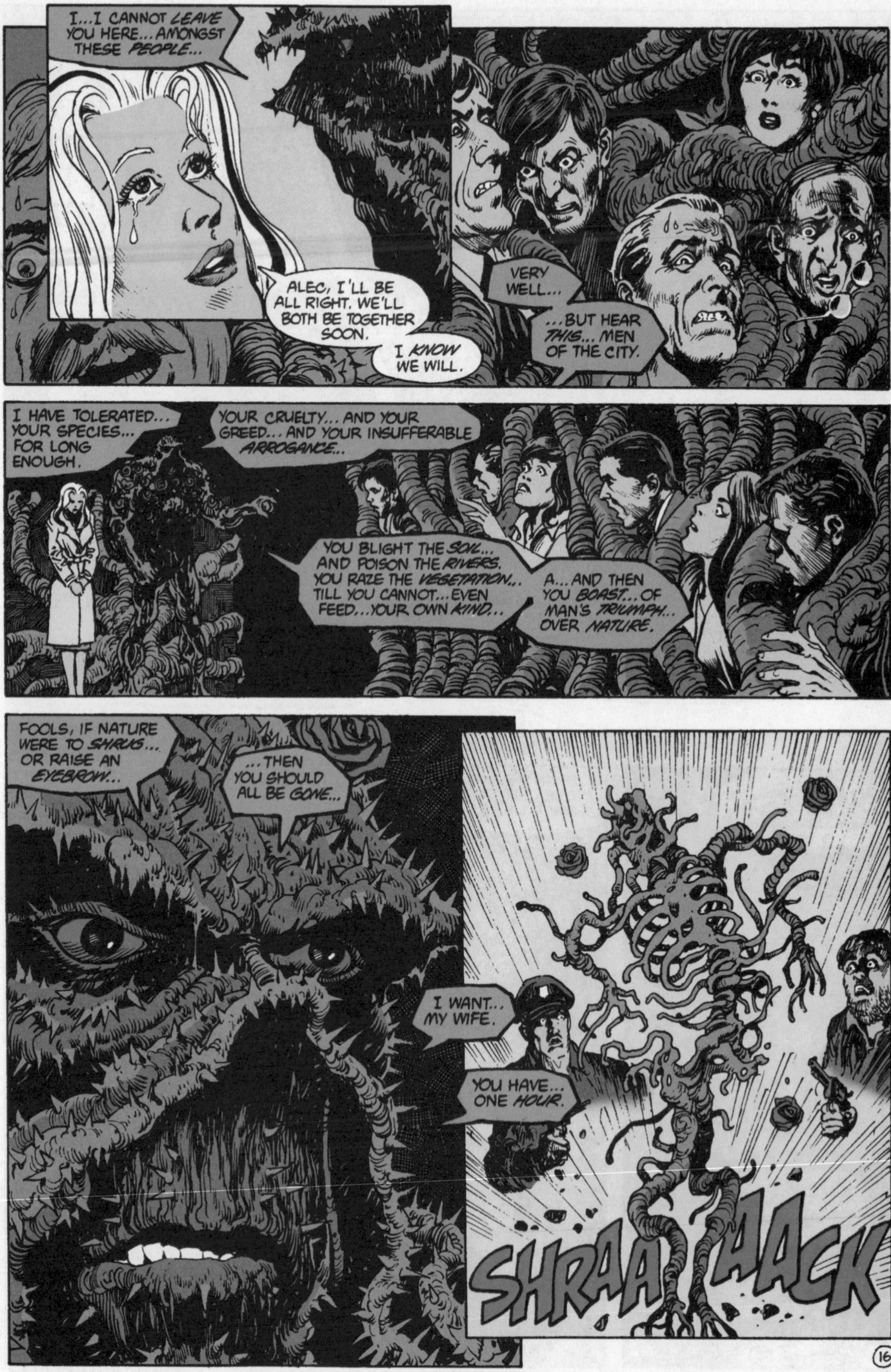
I...I CANNOT LEAVE YOU HERE... AMONGST THESE PEOPLE...
ALEC, I'LL BE ALL RIGHT. WE'LL BOTH BE TOGETHER SOON.
I KNOW WE WILL.
VERY WELL...
...BUT HEAR THIS... MEN OF THE CITY.
I HAVE TOLERATED... YOUR SPECIES... FOR LONG ENOUGH.
YOUR CRUELTY... AND YOUR GREED... AND YOUR INSUFFERABLE ARROGANCE...
YOU BLIGHT THE SOIL... AND POISON THE RIVERS. YOU RAZE THE VEGETATION... TILL YOU CANNOT... EVEN FEED... YOUR OWN KIND...
A... AND THEN YOU BOAST... OF MAN'S TRIUMPH... OVER NATURE.
FOOLS, IF NATURE WERE TO SHRUG... OR RAISE AN EYEBROW...
...THEN YOU SHOULD ALL BE GONE...
I WANT... MY WIFE.
YOU HAVE... ONE HOUR.
SHRAAAACK
16

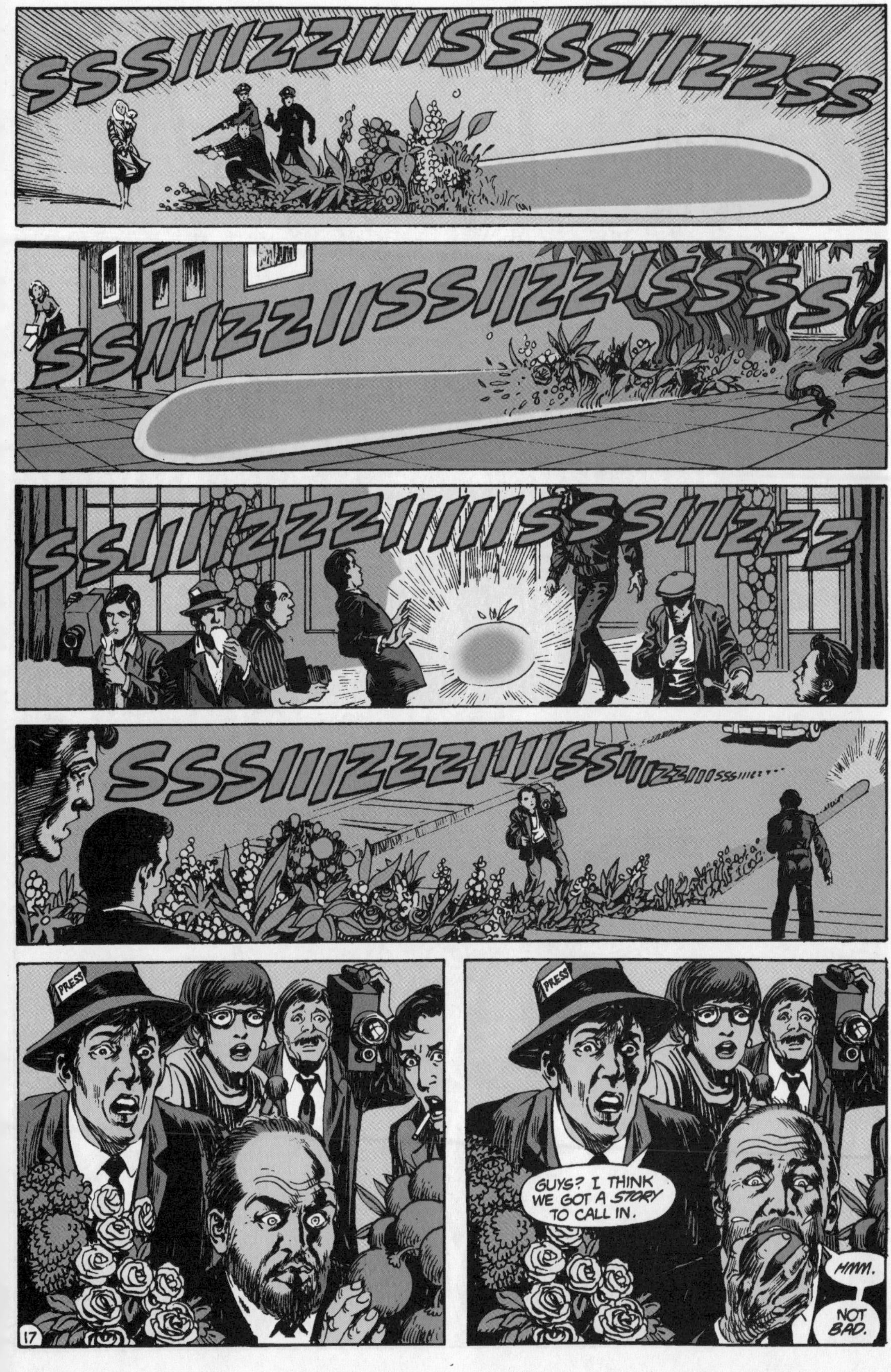

GUYS? I THINK WE GOT A *STORY* TO CALL IN.
HMM.
NOT *BAD*.
17

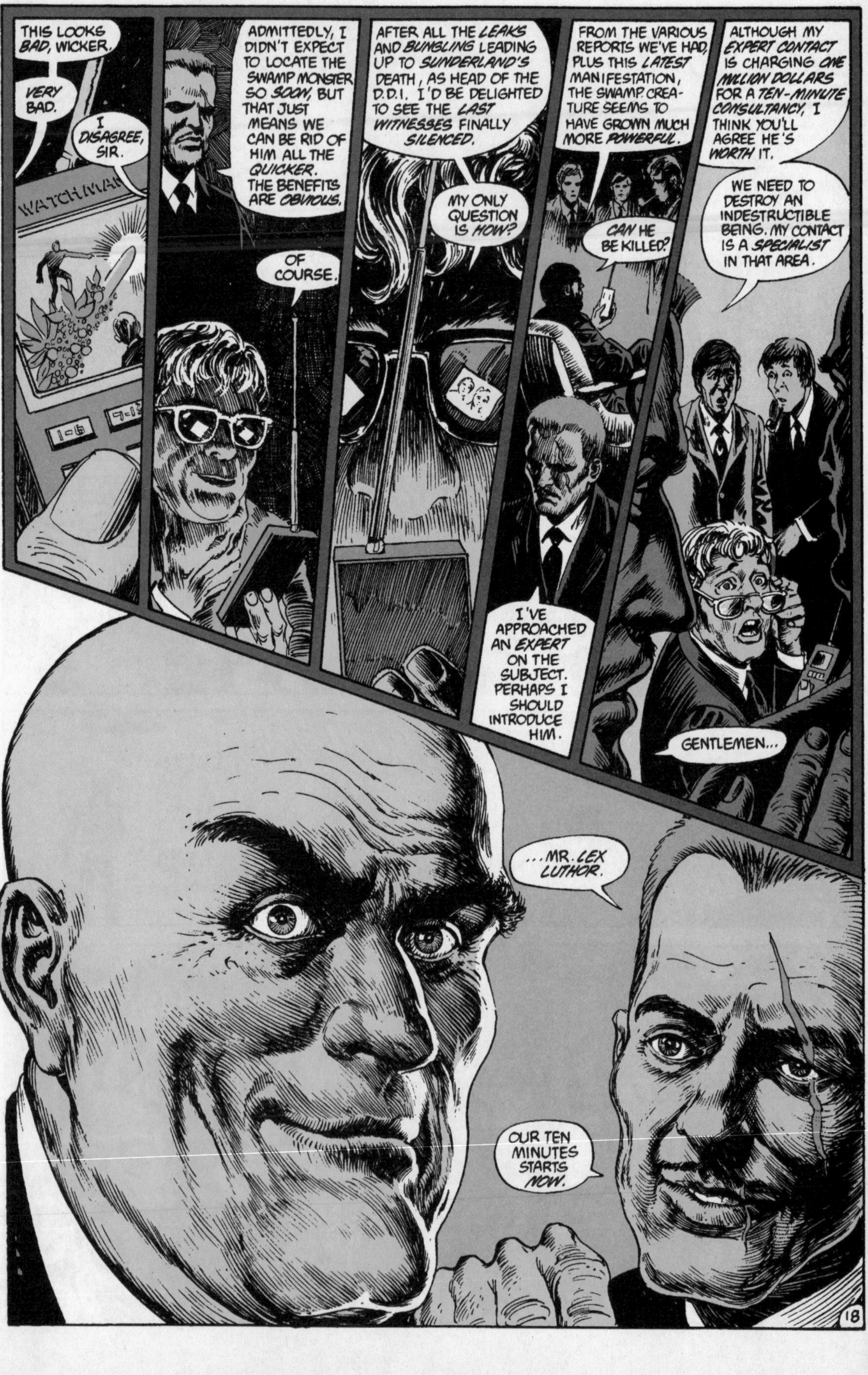
THIS LOOKS BAD, WICKER.
VERY BAD.
I DISAGREE, SIR.
ADMITTEDLY, I DIDN'T EXPECT TO LOCATE THE SWAMP MONSTER SO SOON, BUT THAT JUST MEANS WE CAN BE RID OF HIM ALL THE QUICKER. THE BENEFITS ARE OBVIOUS.
OF COURSE.
AFTER ALL THE LEAKS AND BUNGLING LEADING UP TO SUNDERLAND'S DEATH, AS HEAD OF THE D.D.I. I'D BE DELIGHTED TO SEE THE LAST WITNESSES FINALLY SILENCED.
MY ONLY QUESTION IS HOW?
FROM THE VARIOUS REPORTS WE'VE HAD, PLUS THIS LATEST MANIFESTATION, THE SWAMP CREATURE SEEMS TO HAVE GROWN MUCH MORE POWERFUL.
CAN HE BE KILLED?
I'VE APPROACHED AN EXPERT ON THE SUBJECT. PERHAPS I SHOULD INTRODUCE HIM.
ALTHOUGH MY EXPERT CONTACT IS CHARGING ONE MILLION DOLLARS FOR A TEN-MINUTE CONSULTANCY, I THINK YOU'LL AGREE HE'S WORTH IT.
WE NEED TO DESTROY AN INDESTRUCTIBLE BEING. MY CONTACT IS A SPECIALIST IN THAT AREA.
GENTLEMEN...
...MR. LEX LUTHOR.
OUR TEN MINUTES STARTS NOW.
18

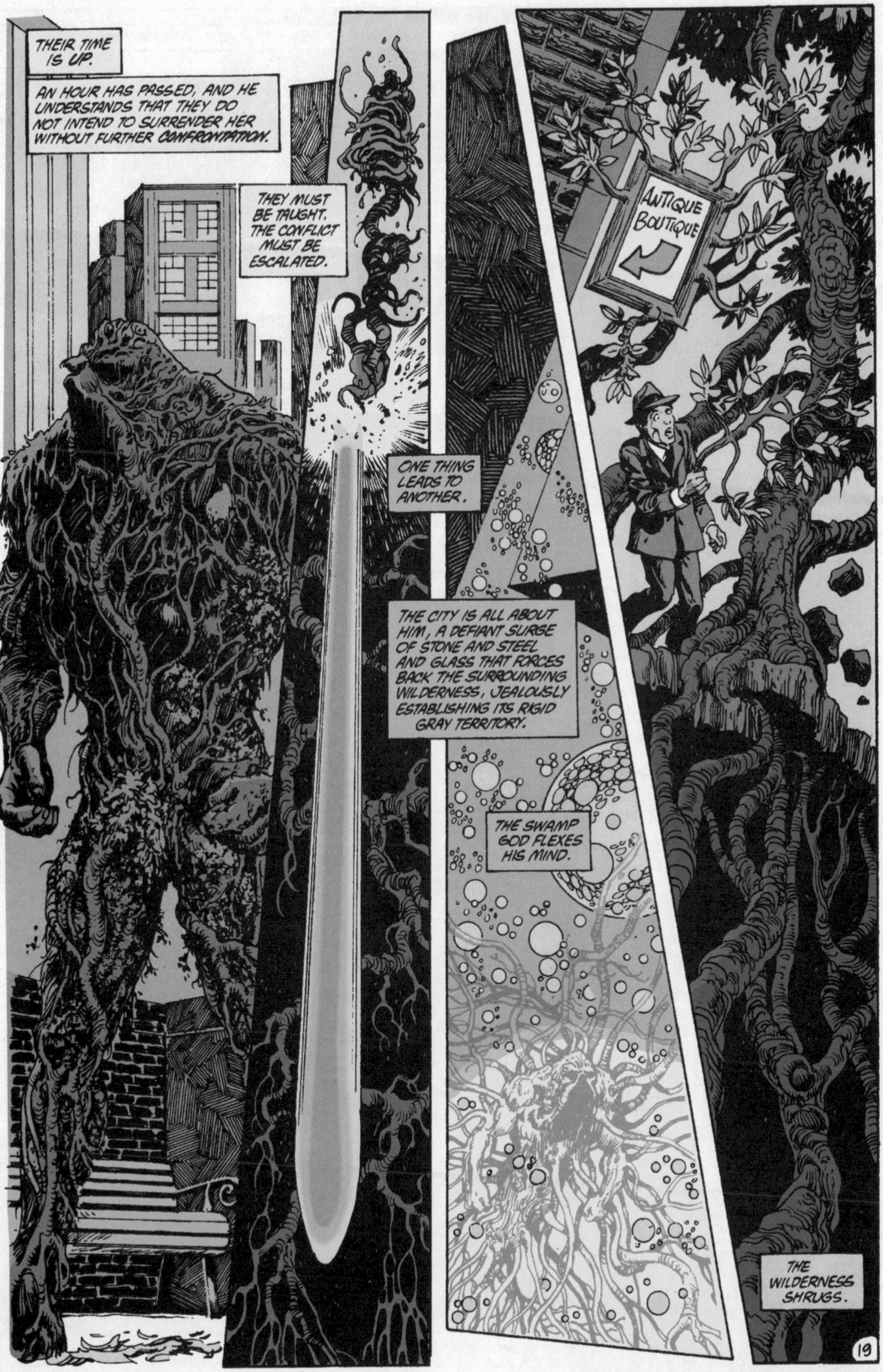
THEIR TIME IS UP.
AN HOUR HAS PASSED, AND HE UNDERSTANDS THAT THEY DO NOT INTEND TO SURRENDER HER WITHOUT FURTHER CONFRONTATION.
THEY MUST BE TAUGHT. THE CONFLICT MUST BE ESCALATED.
ONE THING LEADS TO ANOTHER.
THE CITY IS ALL ABOUT HIM, A DEFIANT SURGE OF STONE AND STEEL AND GLASS THAT FORCES BACK THE SURROUNDING WILDERNESS, JEALOUSLY ESTABLISHING ITS RIGID GRAY TERRITORY.
ANTIQUE BOUTIQUE
THE SWAMP GOD FLEXES HIS MIND.
THE WILDERNESS SHRUGS.
19

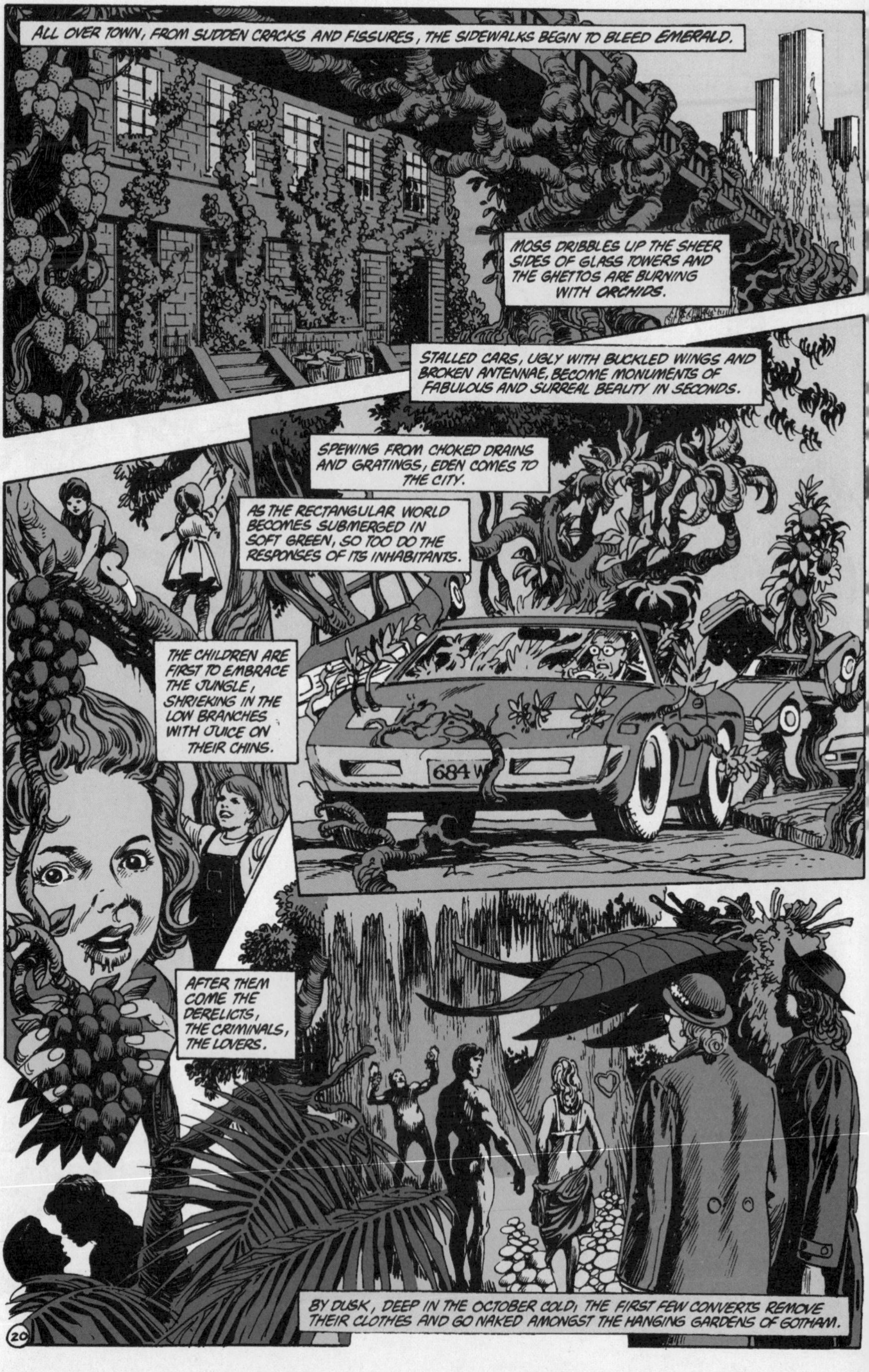
ALL OVER TOWN, FROM SUDDEN CRACKS AND FISSURES, THE SIDEWALKS BEGIN TO BLEED EMERALD.
MOSS DRIBBLES UP THE SHEER SIDES OF GLASS TOWERS AND THE GHETTOS ARE BURNING WITH ORCHIDS.
STALLED CARS, UGLY WITH BUCKLED WINGS AND BROKEN ANTENNAE, BECOME MONUMENTS OF FABULOUS AND SURREAL BEAUTY IN SECONDS.
SPEWING FROM CHOKED DRAINS AND GRATINGS, EDEN COMES TO THE CITY.
AS THE RECTANGULAR WORLD BECOMES SUBMERGED IN SOFT GREEN, SO TOO DO THE RESPONSES OF ITS INHABITANTS.
684 W
THE CHILDREN ARE FIRST TO EMBRACE THE JUNGLE, SHRIEKING IN THE LOW BRANCHES WITH JUICE ON THEIR CHINS.
AFTER THEM COME THE DERELICTS, THE CRIMINALS, THE LOVERS.
BY DUSK, DEEP IN THE OCTOBER COLD, THE FIRST FEW CONVERTS REMOVE THEIR CLOTHES AND GO NAKED AMONGST THE HANGING GARDENS OF GOTHAM.
20

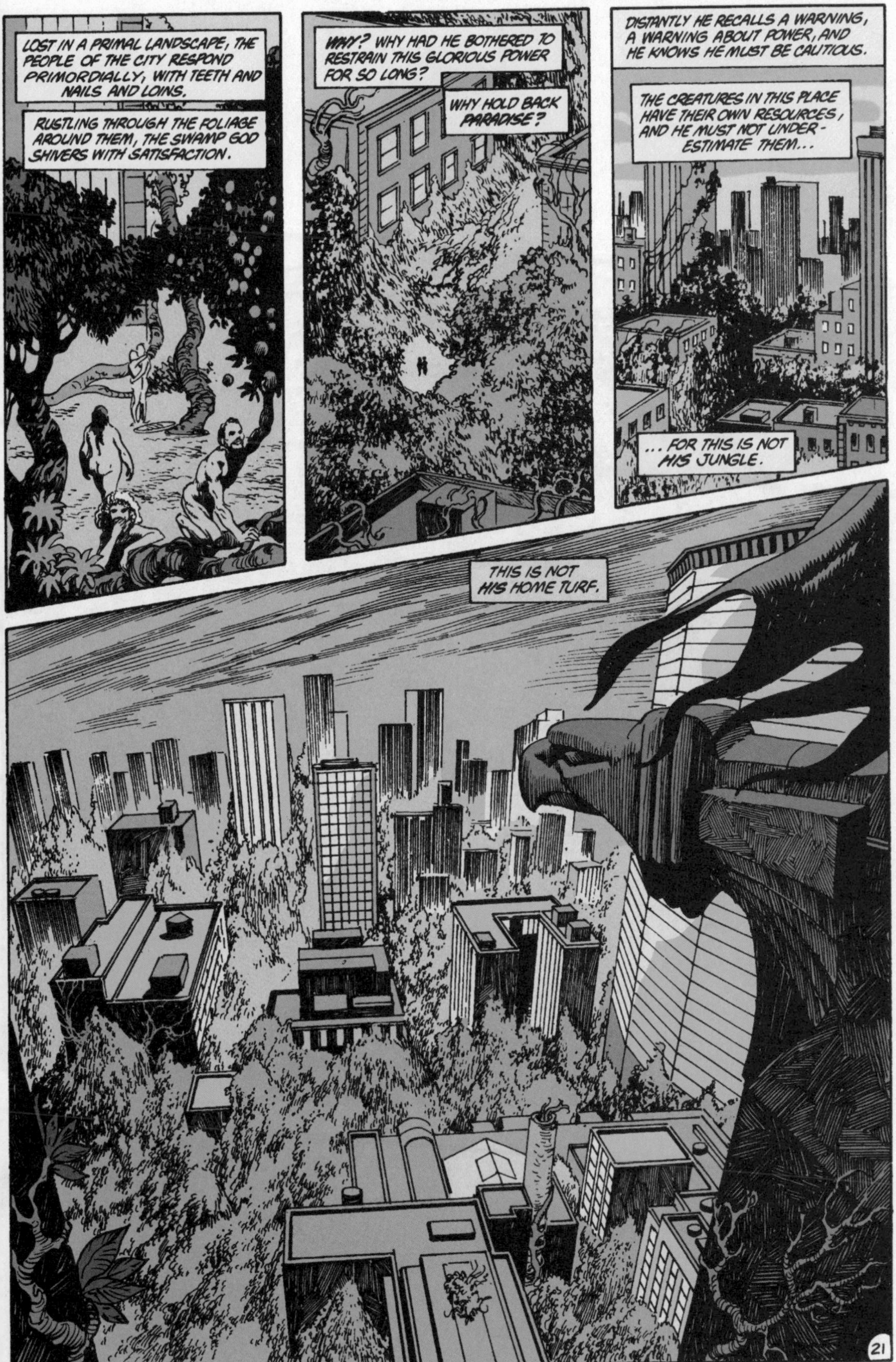
LOST IN A PRIMAL LANDSCAPE, THE PEOPLE OF THE CITY RESPOND PRIMORDIALLY, WITH TEETH AND NAILS AND LOINS.
RUSTLING THROUGH THE FOLIAGE AROUND THEM, THE SWAMP GOD SHIVERS WITH SATISFACTION.
WHY? WHY HAD HE BOTHERED TO RESTRAIN THIS GLORIOUS POWER FOR SO LONG?
WHY HOLD BACK PARADISE?
DISTANTLY HE RECALLS A WARNING, A WARNING ABOUT POWER, AND HE KNOWS HE MUST BE CAUTIOUS.
THE CREATURES IN THIS PLACE HAVE THEIR OWN RESOURCES, AND HE MUST NOT UNDER-ESTIMATE THEM...
... FOR THIS IS NOT HIS JUNGLE.
THIS IS NOT HIS HOME TURF.
21

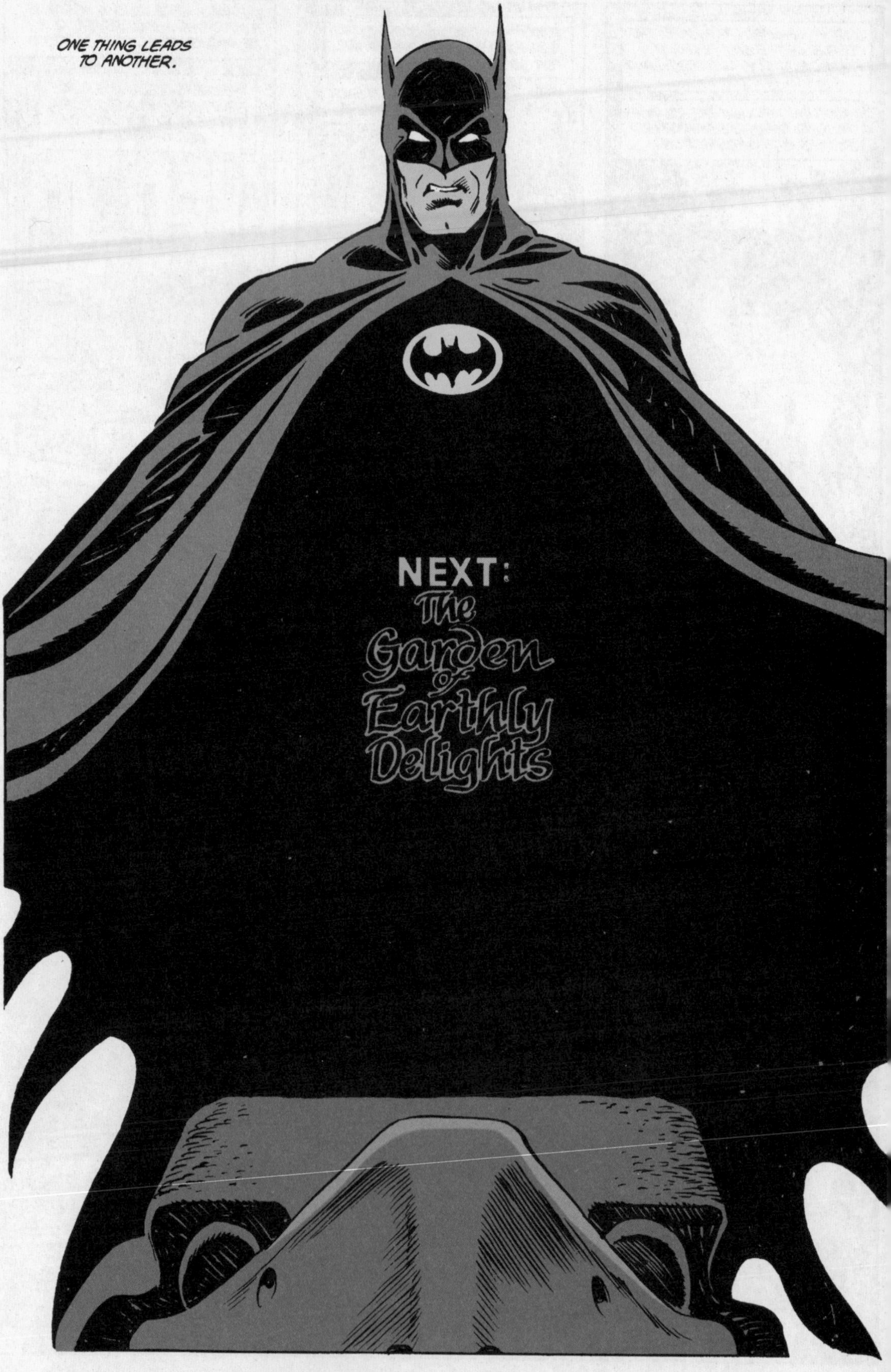
ONE THING LEADS TO ANOTHER.
NEXT:
The Garden of Earthly Delights

CHAPTER 3

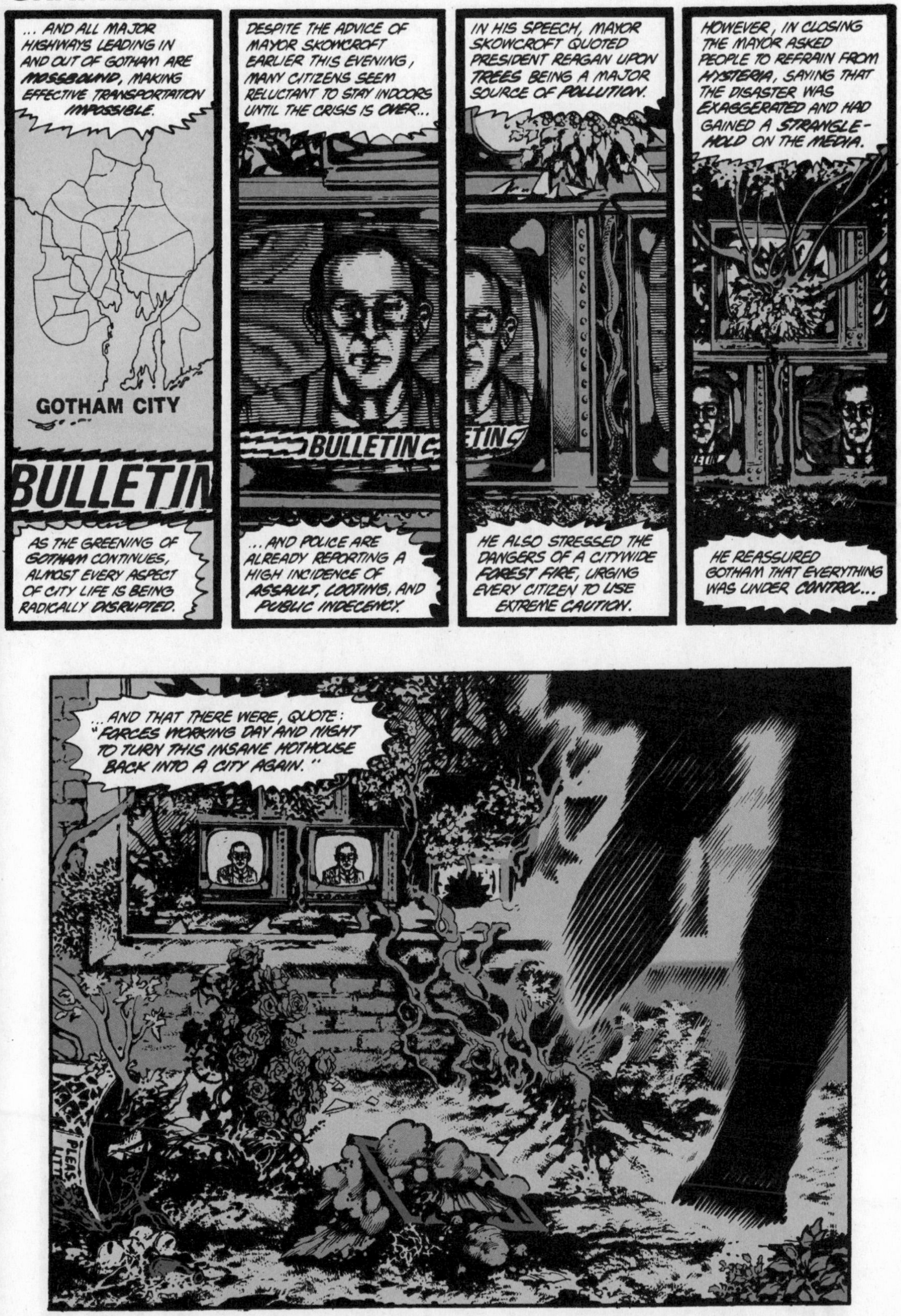
... AND ALL MAJOR HIGHWAYS LEADING IN AND OUT OF GOTHAM ARE MOSSBOUND, MAKING EFFECTIVE TRANSPORTATION IMPOSSIBLE.
GOTHAM CITY
BULLETIN
AS THE GREENING OF GOTHAM CONTINUES, ALMOST EVERY ASPECT OF CITY LIFE IS BEING RADICALLY DISRUPTED.
DESPITE THE ADVICE OF MAYOR SKOWCROFT EARLIER THIS EVENING, MANY CITIZENS SEEM RELUCTANT TO STAY INDOORS UNTIL THE CRISIS IS OVER...
BULLETIN
... AND POLICE ARE ALREADY REPORTING A HIGH INCIDENCE OF ASSAULT, LOOTING, AND PUBLIC INDECENCY.
IN HIS SPEECH, MAYOR SKOWCROFT QUOTED PRESIDENT REAGAN UPON TREES BEING A MAJOR SOURCE OF POLLUTION.
HE ALSO STRESSED THE DANGERS OF A CITYWIDE FOREST FIRE, URGING EVERY CITIZEN TO USE EXTREME CAUTION.
HOWEVER, IN CLOSING THE MAYOR ASKED PEOPLE TO REFRAIN FROM HYSTERIA, SAYING THAT THE DISASTER WAS EXAGGERATED AND HAD GAINED A STRANGLE-HOLD ON THE MEDIA.
HE REASSURED GOTHAM THAT EVERYTHING WAS UNDER CONTROL...
... AND THAT THERE WERE, QUOTE: "FORCES WORKING DAY AND NIGHT TO TURN THIS INSANE HOTHOUSE BACK INTO A CITY AGAIN."

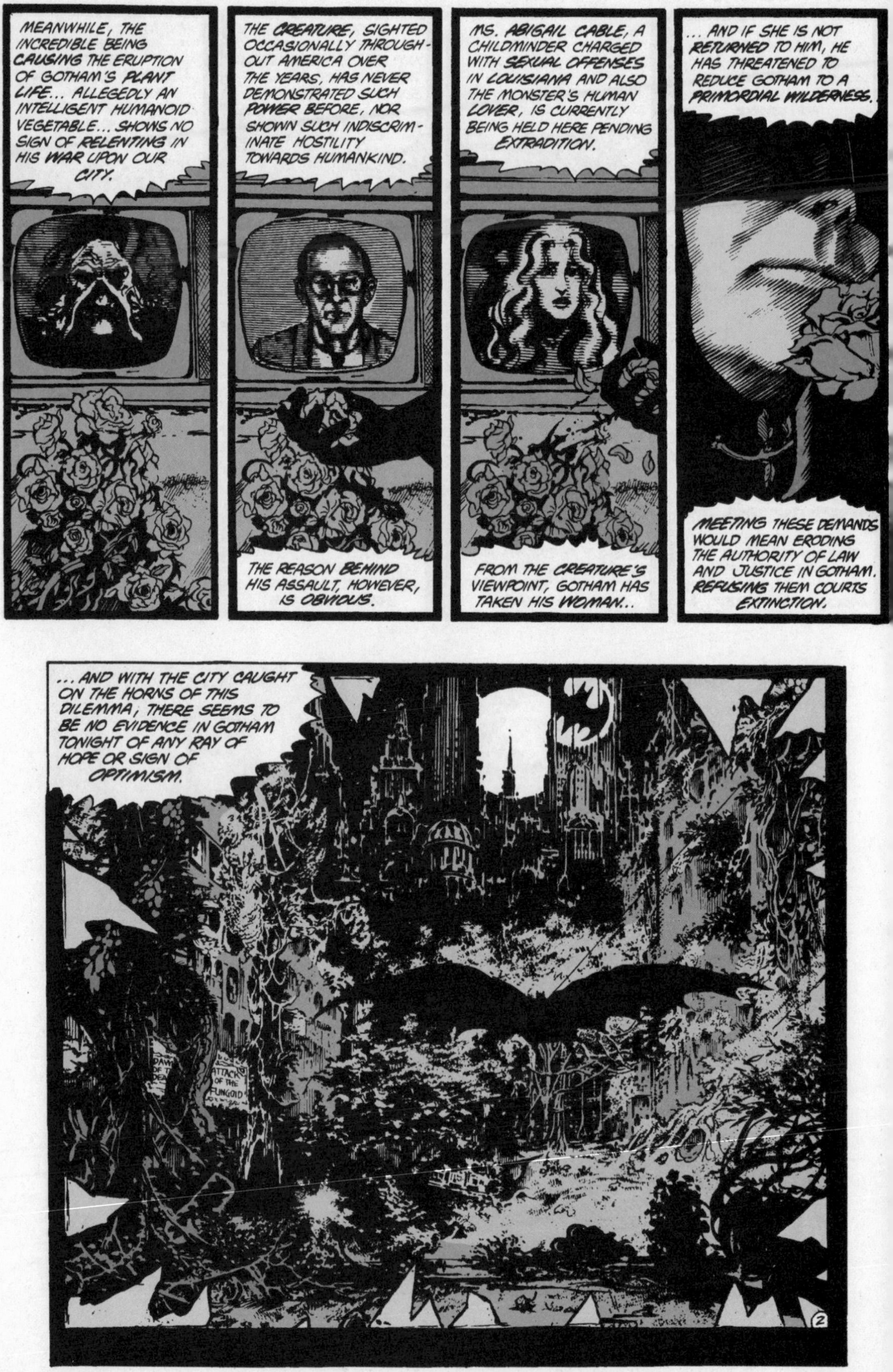
MEANWHILE, THE INCREDIBLE BEING CAUSING THE ERUPTION OF GOTHAM'S PLANT LIFE... ALLEGEDLY AN INTELLIGENT HUMANOID VEGETABLE... SHOWS NO SIGN OF RELENTING IN HIS WAR UPON OUR CITY.
THE CREATURE, SIGHTED OCCASIONALLY THROUGH-OUT AMERICA OVER THE YEARS, HAS NEVER DEMONSTRATED SUCH POWER BEFORE, NOR SHOWN SUCH INDISCRIM-INATE HOSTILITY TOWARDS HUMANKIND.
THE REASON BEHIND HIS ASSAULT, HOWEVER, IS OBVIOUS.
MS. ABIGAIL CABLE, A CHILDMINDER CHARGED WITH SEXUAL OFFENSES IN LOUISIANA AND ALSO THE MONSTER'S HUMAN LOVER, IS CURRENTLY BEING HELD HERE PENDING EXTRADITION.
FROM THE CREATURE'S VIEWPOINT, GOTHAM HAS TAKEN HIS WOMAN...
... AND IF SHE IS NOT RETURNED TO HIM, HE HAS THREATENED TO REDUCE GOTHAM TO A PRIMORDIAL WILDERNESS.
MEETING THESE DEMANDS WOULD MEAN ERODING THE AUTHORITY OF LAW AND JUSTICE IN GOTHAM. REFUSING THEM COURTS EXTINCTION.
... AND WITH THE CITY CAUGHT ON THE HORNS OF THIS DILEMMA, THERE SEEMS TO BE NO EVIDENCE IN GOTHAM TONIGHT OF ANY RAY OF HOPE OR SIGN OF OPTIMISM.
ATTACK OF THE FUNGOID
2

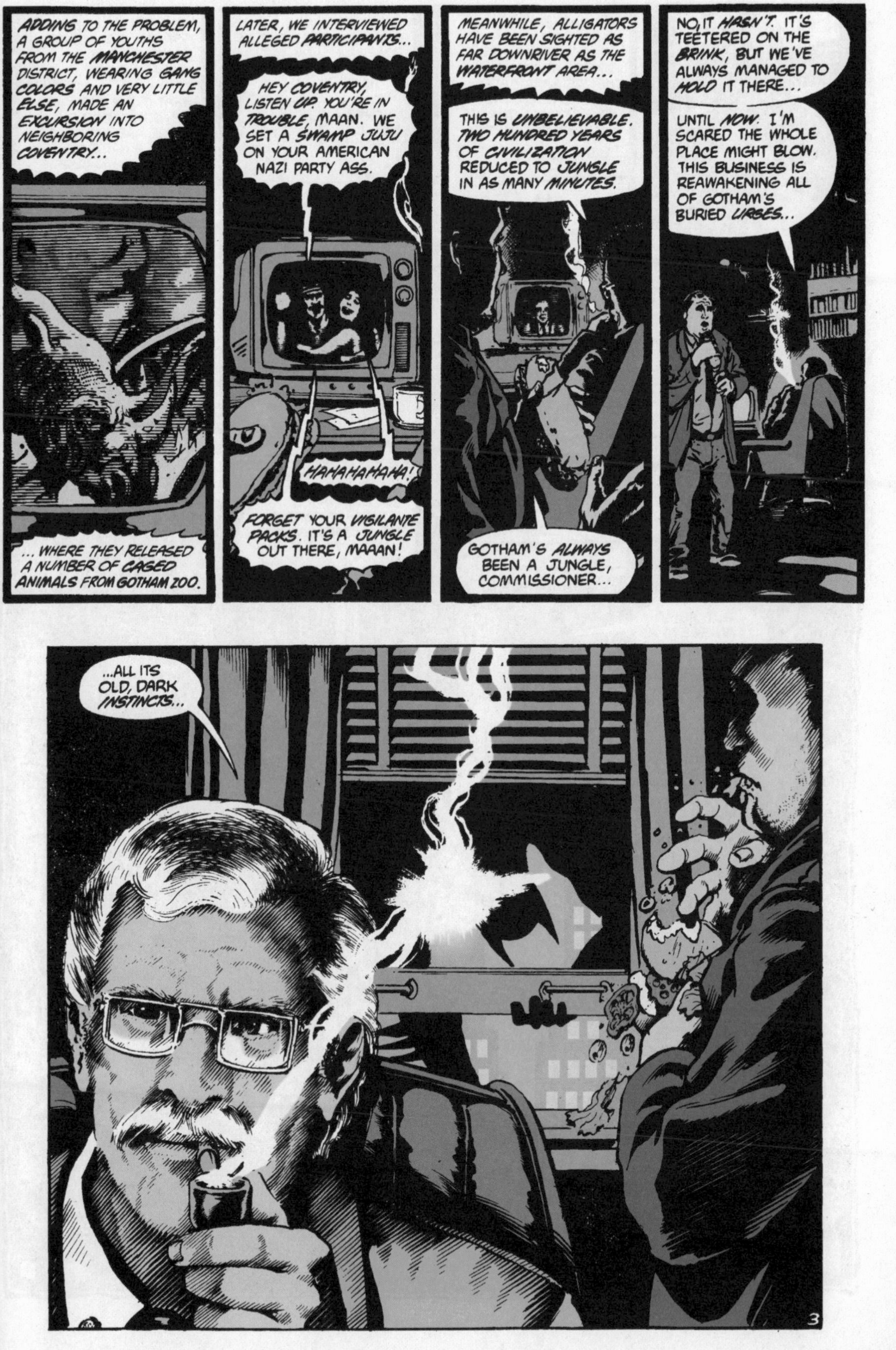
ADDING TO THE PROBLEM, A GROUP OF YOUTHS FROM THE MANCHESTER DISTRICT, WEARING GANG COLORS AND VERY LITTLE ELSE, MADE AN EXCURSION INTO NEIGHBORING COVENTRY...
... WHERE THEY RELEASED A NUMBER OF CAGED ANIMALS FROM GOTHAM ZOO.
LATER, WE INTERVIEWED ALLEGED PARTICIPANTS...
HEY COVENTRY, LISTEN UP. YOU'RE IN TROUBLE, MAAN. WE SET A SWAMP JUJU ON YOUR AMERICAN NAZI PARTY ASS.
HAHAHAHAHA!
FORGET YOUR VIGILANTE PACKS. IT'S A JUNGLE OUT THERE, MAAAN!
MEANWHILE, ALLIGATORS HAVE BEEN SIGHTED AS FAR DOWNRIVER AS THE WATERFRONT AREA...
THIS IS UNBELIEVABLE. TWO HUNDRED YEARS OF CIVILIZATION REDUCED TO JUNGLE IN AS MANY MINUTES.
GOTHAM'S ALWAYS BEEN A JUNGLE, COMMISSIONER...
NO, IT HASN'T. IT'S TEETERED ON THE BRINK, BUT WE'VE ALWAYS MANAGED TO HOLD IT THERE...
UNTIL NOW. I'M SCARED THE WHOLE PLACE MIGHT BLOW. THIS BUSINESS IS REAWAKENING ALL OF GOTHAM'S BURIED URGES...
...ALL ITS OLD, DARK INSTINCTS...
3

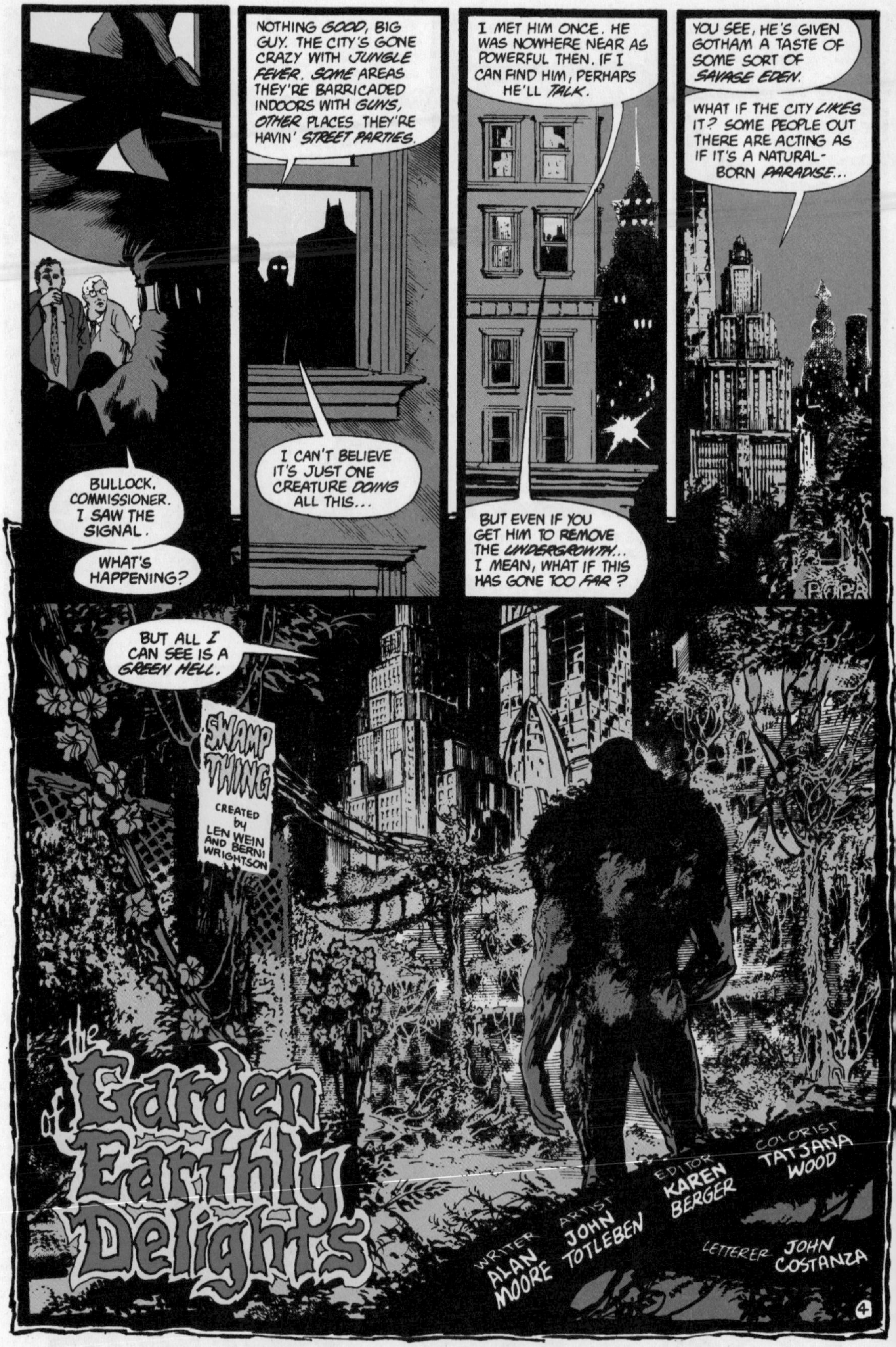
BULLOCK. COMMISSIONER. I SAW THE SIGNAL.
WHAT'S HAPPENING?
NOTHING GOOD, BIG GUY. THE CITY'S GONE CRAZY WITH JUNGLE FEVER. SOME AREAS THEY'RE BARRICADED INDOORS WITH GUNS, OTHER PLACES THEY'RE HAVIN' STREET PARTIES.
I CAN'T BELIEVE IT'S JUST ONE CREATURE DOING ALL THIS...
I MET HIM ONCE. HE WAS NOWHERE NEAR AS POWERFUL THEN. IF I CAN FIND HIM, PERHAPS HE'LL TALK.
BUT EVEN IF YOU GET HIM TO REMOVE THE UNDERGROWTH... I MEAN, WHAT IF THIS HAS GONE TOO FAR?
YOU SEE, HE'S GIVEN GOTHAM A TASTE OF SOME SORT OF SAVAGE EDEN.
WHAT IF THE CITY LIKES IT? SOME PEOPLE OUT THERE ARE ACTING AS IF IT'S A NATURAL-BORN PARADISE...
BUT ALL I CAN SEE IS A GREEN HELL.
SWAMP THING
CREATED by LEN WEIN AND BERNI WRIGHTSON
the Garden of Earthly Delights
WRITER ALAN MOORE
ARTIST JOHN TOTLEBEN
EDITOR KAREN BERGER
COLORIST TATJANA WOOD
LETTERER JOHN COSTANZA
4

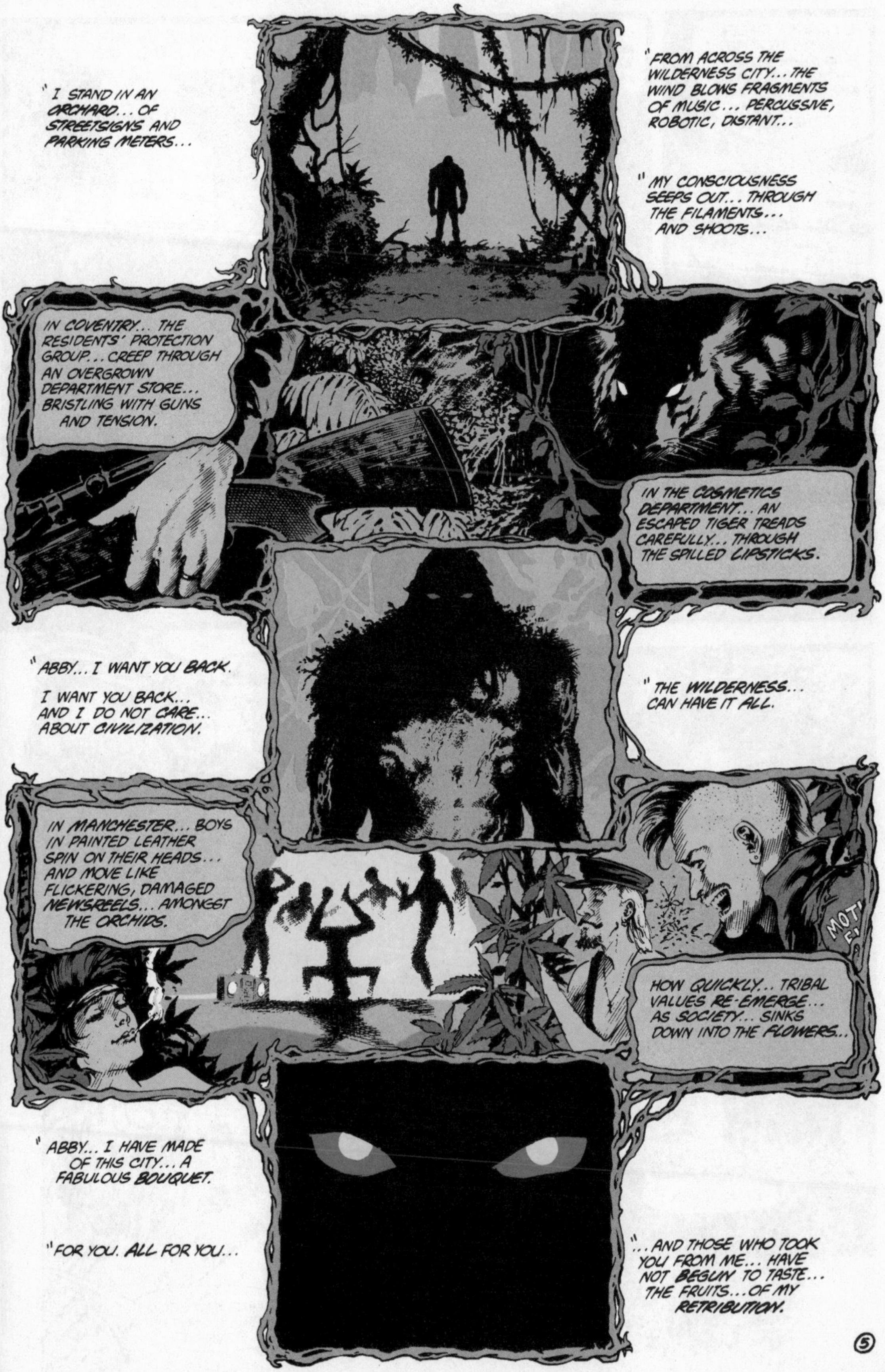
"I STAND IN AN ORCHARD... OF STREETSIGNS AND PARKING METERS...
"FROM ACROSS THE WILDERNESS CITY... THE WIND BLOWS FRAGMENTS OF MUSIC... PERCUSSIVE, ROBOTIC, DISTANT...
"MY CONSCIOUSNESS SEEPS OUT... THROUGH THE FILAMENTS... AND SHOOTS...
IN COVENTRY... THE RESIDENTS' PROTECTION GROUP... CREEP THROUGH AN OVERGROWN DEPARTMENT STORE... BRISTLING WITH GUNS AND TENSION.
IN THE COSMETICS DEPARTMENT... AN ESCAPED TIGER TREADS CAREFULLY... THROUGH THE SPILLED LIPSTICKS.
"ABBY... I WANT YOU BACK.
I WANT YOU BACK... AND I DO NOT CARE... ABOUT CIVILIZATION.
"THE WILDERNESS... CAN HAVE IT ALL.
IN MANCHESTER... BOYS IN PAINTED LEATHER SPIN ON THEIR HEADS... AND MOVE LIKE FLICKERING, DAMAGED NEWSREELS... AMONGST THE ORCHIDS.
HOW QUICKLY... TRIBAL VALUES RE-EMERGE... AS SOCIETY... SINKS DOWN INTO THE FLOWERS...
"ABBY... I HAVE MADE OF THIS CITY... A FABULOUS BOUQUET.
"FOR YOU. ALL FOR YOU...
"... AND THOSE WHO TOOK YOU FROM ME... HAVE NOT BEGUN TO TASTE... THE FRUITS... OF MY RETRIBUTION.
5

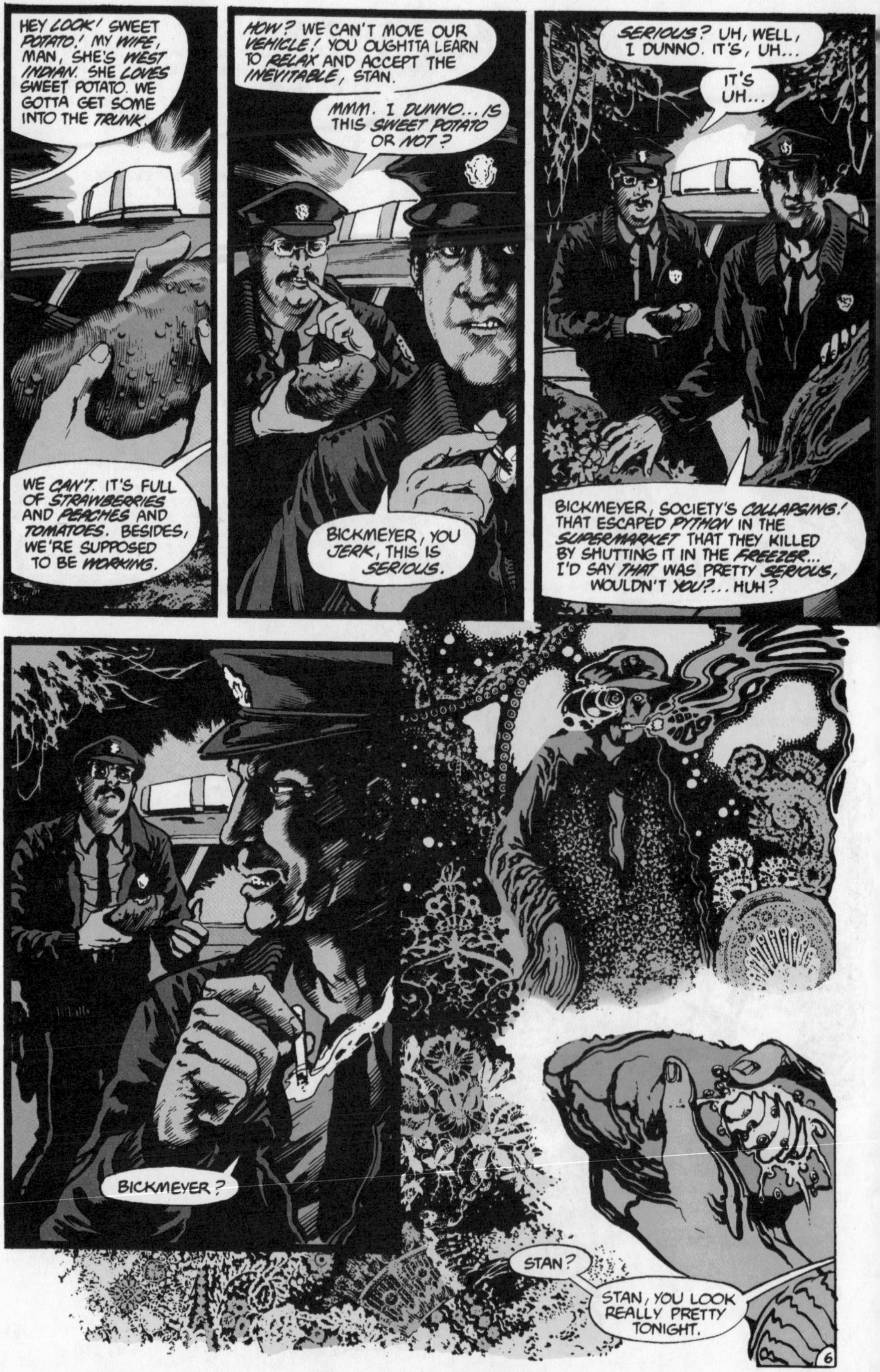
HEY LOOK! SWEET POTATO! MY WIFE, MAN, SHE'S WEST INDIAN. SHE LOVES SWEET POTATO. WE GOTTA GET SOME INTO THE TRUNK.
WE CAN'T. IT'S FULL OF STRAWBERRIES AND PEACHES AND TOMATOES. BESIDES, WE'RE SUPPOSED TO BE WORKING.
HOW? WE CAN'T MOVE OUR VEHICLE! YOU OUGHTTA LEARN TO RELAX AND ACCEPT THE INEVITABLE, STAN.
MMM. I DUNNO... IS THIS SWEET POTATO OR NOT?
BICKMEYER, YOU JERK, THIS IS SERIOUS.
SERIOUS? UH, WELL, I DUNNO. IT'S, UH...
IT'S UH...
BICKMEYER, SOCIETY'S COLLAPSING! THAT ESCAPED PYTHON IN THE SUPERMARKET THAT THEY KILLED BY SHUTTING IT IN THE FREEZER... I'D SAY THAT WAS PRETTY SERIOUS, WOULDN'T YOU?... HUH?
BICKMEYER?
STAN?
STAN, YOU LOOK REALLY PRETTY TONIGHT.
6

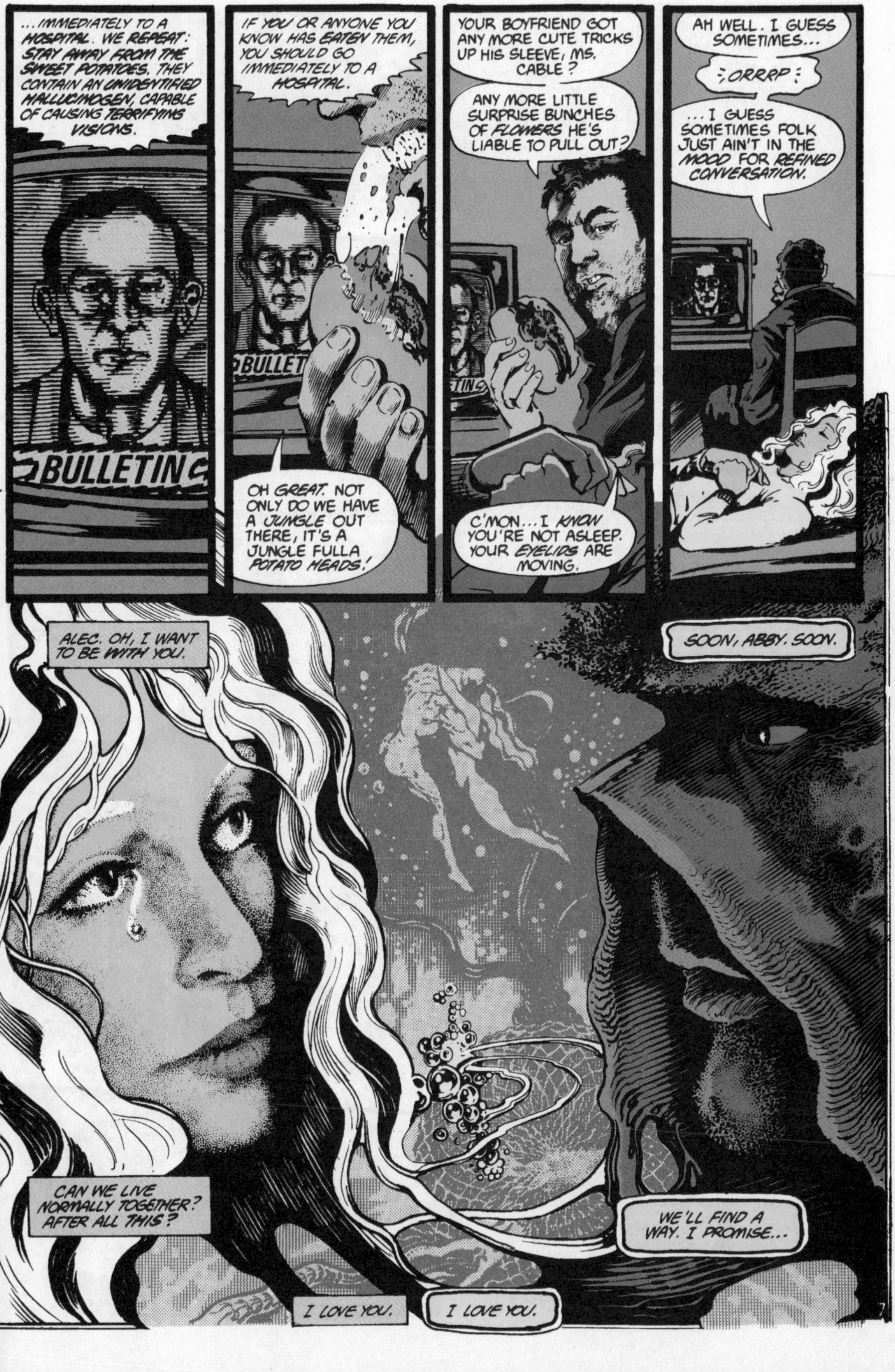
...IMMEDIATELY TO A HOSPITAL. WE REPEAT: STAY AWAY FROM THE SWEET POTATOES. THEY CONTAIN AN UNIDENTIFIED HALLUCINOGEN, CAPABLE OF CAUSING TERRIFYING VISIONS.
BULLETIN
IF YOU OR ANYONE YOU KNOW HAS EATEN THEM, YOU SHOULD GO IMMEDIATELY TO A HOSPITAL.
BULLET
OH GREAT. NOT ONLY DO WE HAVE A JUNGLE OUT THERE, IT'S A JUNGLE FULLA POTATO HEADS!
YOUR BOYFRIEND GOT ANY MORE CUTE TRICKS UP HIS SLEEVE, MS. CABLE?
ANY MORE LITTLE SURPRISE BUNCHES OF FLOWERS HE'S LIABLE TO PULL OUT?
C'MON... I KNOW YOU'RE NOT ASLEEP. YOUR EYELIDS ARE MOVING.
AH WELL. I GUESS SOMETIMES...
ORRRP
...I GUESS SOMETIMES FOLK JUST AIN'T IN THE MOOD FOR REFINED CONVERSATION.
ALEC. OH, I WANT TO BE WITH YOU.
SOON, ABBY. SOON.
CAN WE LIVE NORMALLY TOGETHER? AFTER ALL THIS?
WE'LL FIND A WAY. I PROMISE...
I LOVE YOU.
I LOVE YOU.
7

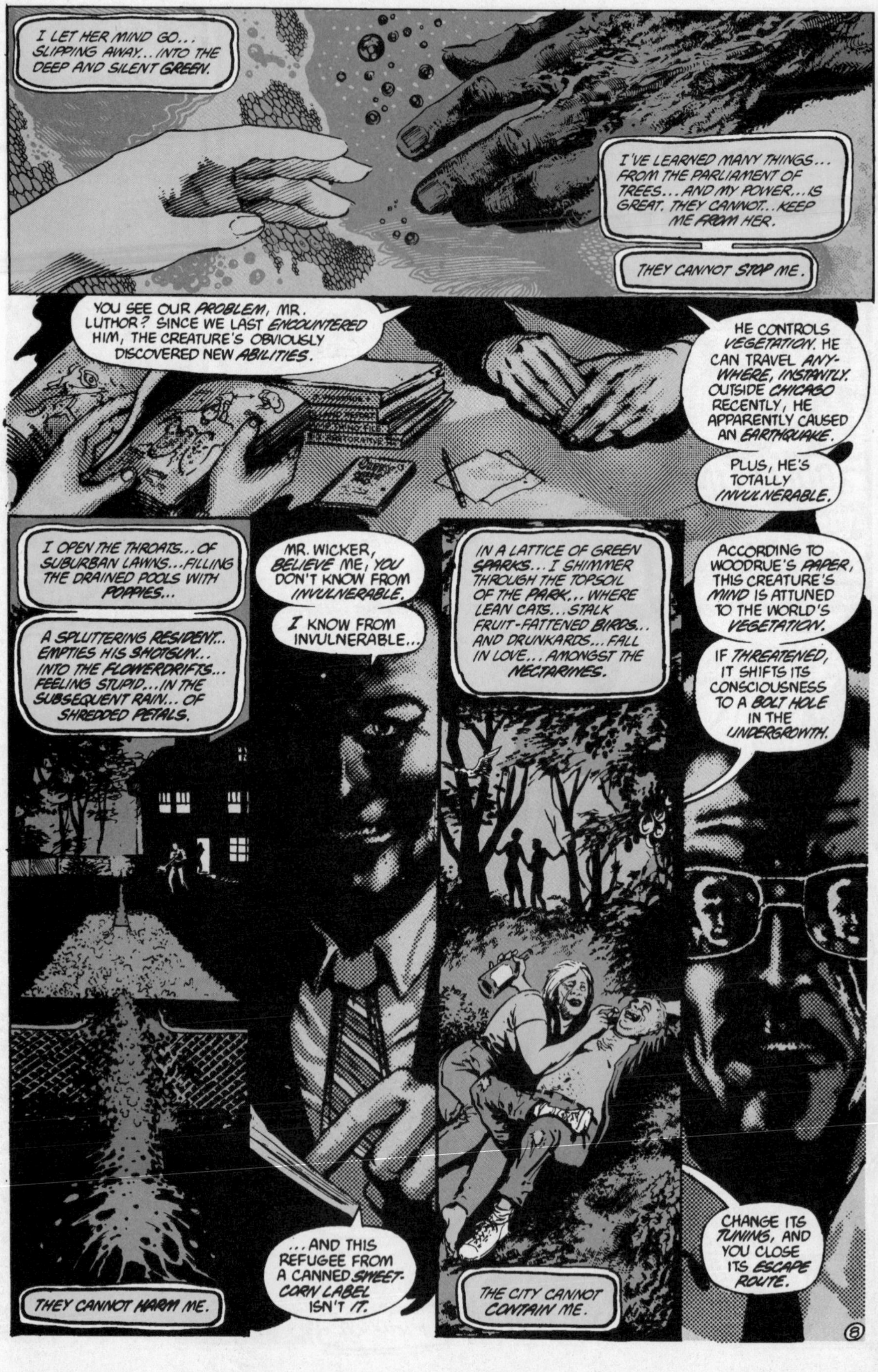
I LET HER MIND GO... SLIPPING AWAY... INTO THE DEEP AND SILENT GREEN.
I'VE LEARNED MANY THINGS... FROM THE PARLIAMENT OF TREES... AND MY POWER... IS GREAT. THEY CANNOT... KEEP ME FROM HER.
THEY CANNOT STOP ME.
YOU SEE OUR PROBLEM, MR. LUTHOR? SINCE WE LAST ENCOUNTERED HIM, THE CREATURE'S OBVIOUSLY DISCOVERED NEW ABILITIES.
HE CONTROLS VEGETATION. HE CAN TRAVEL ANYWHERE, INSTANTLY. OUTSIDE CHICAGO RECENTLY, HE APPARENTLY CAUSED AN EARTHQUAKE.
PLUS, HE'S TOTALLY INVULNERABLE.
I OPEN THE THROATS... OF SUBURBAN LAWNS... FILLING THE DRAINED POOLS WITH POPPIES...
A SPLUTTERING RESIDENT... EMPTIES HIS SHOTGUN... INTO THE FLOWERDRIFTS... FEELING STUPID... IN THE SUBSEQUENT RAIN... OF SHREDDED PETALS.
THEY CANNOT HARM ME.
MR. WICKER, BELIEVE ME, YOU DON'T KNOW FROM INVULNERABLE.
I KNOW FROM INVULNERABLE...
...AND THIS REFUGEE FROM A CANNED SWEET-CORN LABEL ISN'T IT.
IN A LATTICE OF GREEN SPARKS... I SHIMMER THROUGH THE TOPSOIL OF THE PARK... WHERE LEAN CATS... STALK FRUIT-FATTENED BIRDS... AND DRUNKARDS... FALL IN LOVE... AMONGST THE NECTARINES.
THE CITY CANNOT CONTAIN ME.
ACCORDING TO WOODRUE'S PAPER, THIS CREATURE'S MIND IS ATTUNED TO THE WORLD'S VEGETATION.
IF THREATENED, IT SHIFTS ITS CONSCIOUSNESS TO A BOLT HOLE IN THE UNDERGROWTH.
CHANGE ITS TUNING, AND YOU CLOSE ITS ESCAPE ROUTE.
8

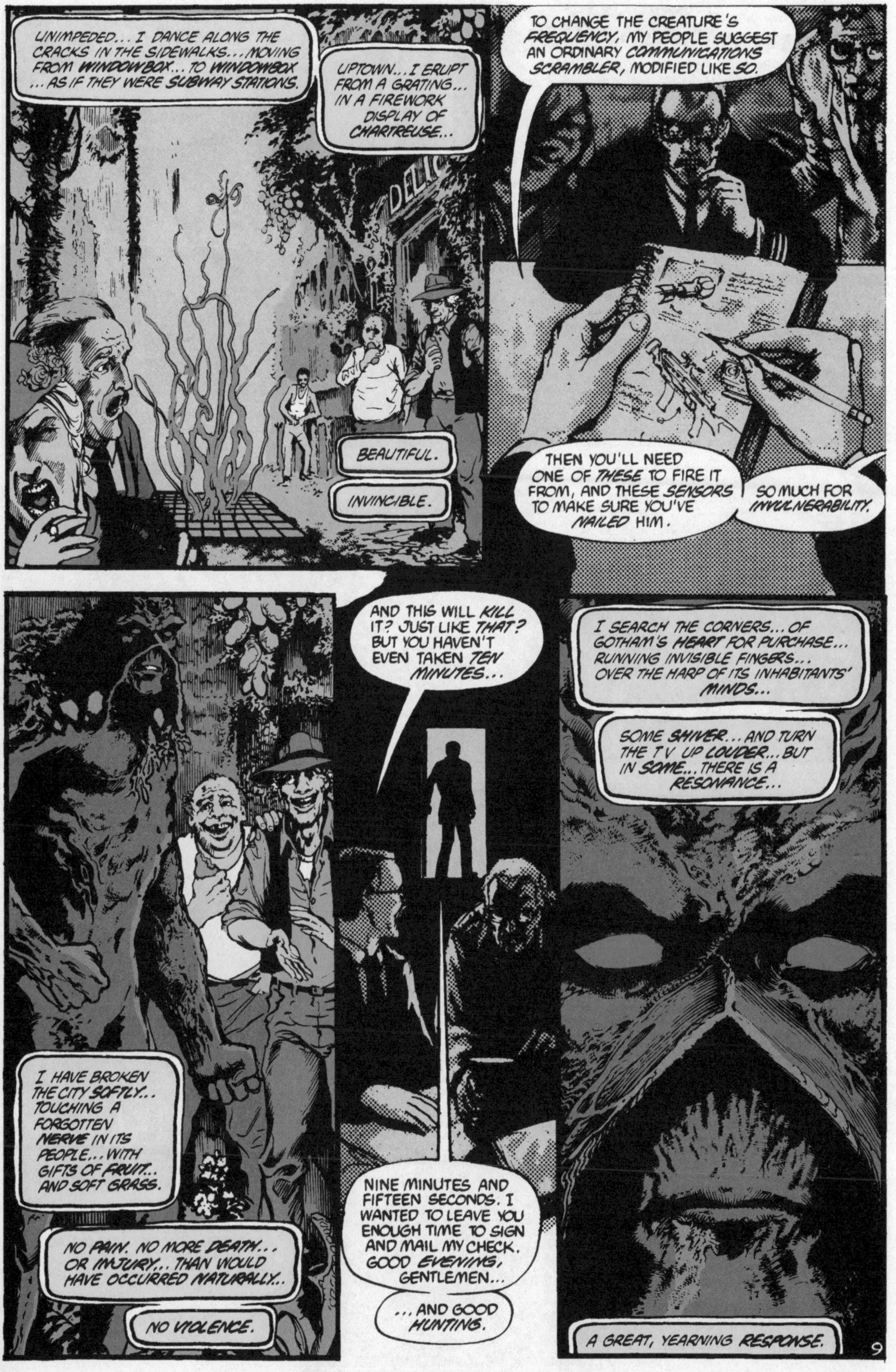
UNIMPEDED... I DANCE ALONG THE CRACKS IN THE SIDEWALKS... MOVING FROM WINDOWBOX... TO WINDOWBOX ... AS IF THEY WERE SUBWAY STATIONS.
UPTOWN... I ERUPT FROM A GRATING... IN A FIREWORK DISPLAY OF CHARTREUSE...
BEAUTIFUL.
INVINCIBLE.
TO CHANGE THE CREATURE'S FREQUENCY, MY PEOPLE SUGGEST AN ORDINARY COMMUNICATIONS SCRAMBLER, MODIFIED LIKE SO.
THEN YOU'LL NEED ONE OF THESE TO FIRE IT FROM, AND THESE SENSORS TO MAKE SURE YOU'VE NAILED HIM.
SO MUCH FOR INVULNERABILITY.
I HAVE BROKEN THE CITY SOFTLY... TOUCHING A FORGOTTEN NERVE IN ITS PEOPLE... WITH GIFTS OF FRUIT... AND SOFT GRASS.
NO PAIN. NO MORE DEATH... OR INJURY... THAN WOULD HAVE OCCURRED NATURALLY...
NO VIOLENCE.
AND THIS WILL KILL IT? JUST LIKE THAT? BUT YOU HAVEN'T EVEN TAKEN TEN MINUTES...
NINE MINUTES AND FIFTEEN SECONDS. I WANTED TO LEAVE YOU ENOUGH TIME TO SIGN AND MAIL MY CHECK. GOOD EVENING, GENTLEMEN...
...AND GOOD HUNTING.
I SEARCH THE CORNERS... OF GOTHAM'S HEART FOR PURCHASE... RUNNING INVISIBLE FINGERS... OVER THE HARP OF ITS INHABITANTS' MINDS...
SOME SHIVER... AND TURN THE TV UP LOUDER... BUT IN SOME... THERE IS A RESONANCE...
A GREAT, YEARNING RESPONSE.
9

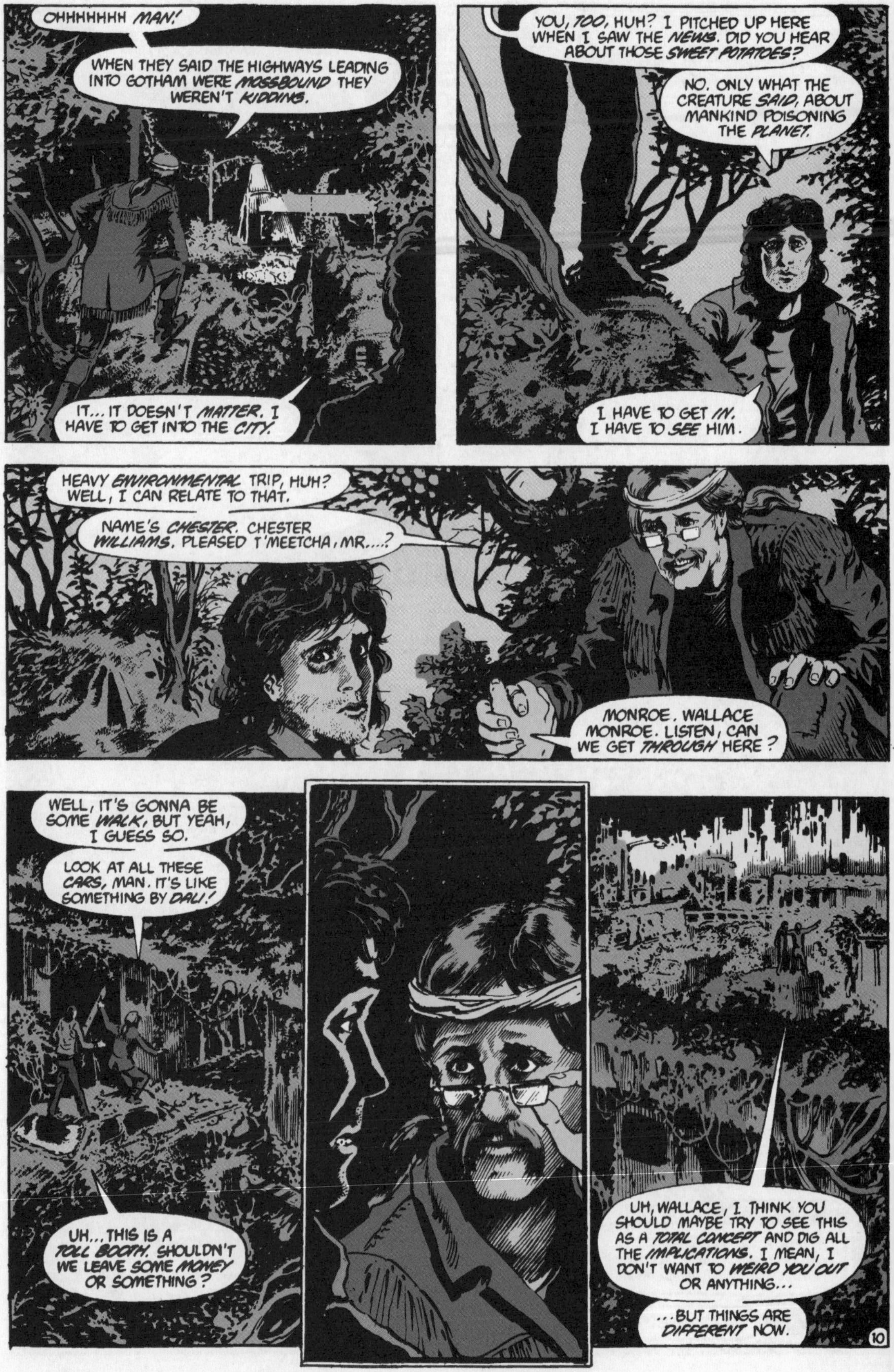
OHHHHHHH MAN!
WHEN THEY SAID THE HIGHWAYS LEADING INTO GOTHAM WERE MOSSBOUND THEY WEREN'T KIDDING.
IT... IT DOESN'T MATTER. I HAVE TO GET INTO THE CITY.
YOU, TOO, HUH? I PITCHED UP HERE WHEN I SAW THE NEWS. DID YOU HEAR ABOUT THOSE SWEET POTATOES?
NO. ONLY WHAT THE CREATURE SAID, ABOUT MANKIND POISONING THE PLANET.
I HAVE TO GET IN. I HAVE TO SEE HIM.
HEAVY ENVIRONMENTAL TRIP, HUH? WELL, I CAN RELATE TO THAT.
NAME'S CHESTER. CHESTER WILLIAMS. PLEASED T'MEETCHA, MR....?
MONROE. WALLACE MONROE. LISTEN, CAN WE GET THROUGH HERE?
WELL, IT'S GONNA BE SOME WALK, BUT YEAH, I GUESS SO.
LOOK AT ALL THESE CARS, MAN. IT'S LIKE SOMETHING BY DALI!
UH... THIS IS A TOLL BOOTH. SHOULDN'T WE LEAVE SOME MONEY OR SOMETHING?
UH, WALLACE, I THINK YOU SHOULD MAYBE TRY TO SEE THIS AS A TOTAL CONCEPT AND DIG ALL THE IMPLICATIONS. I MEAN, I DON'T WANT TO WEIRD YOU OUT OR ANYTHING...
...BUT THINGS ARE DIFFERENT NOW.
10

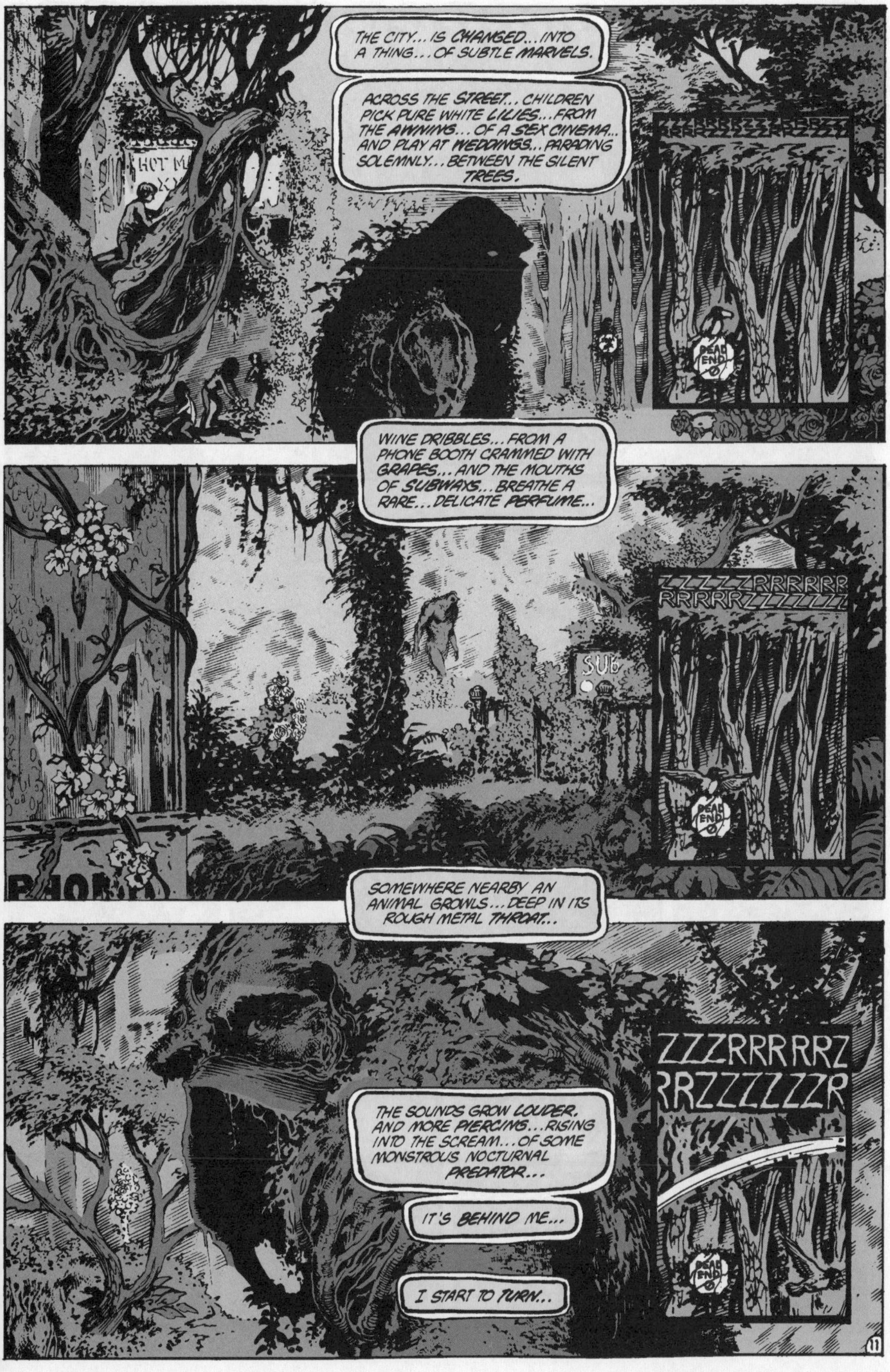
THE CITY... IS CHANGED... INTO A THING... OF SUBTLE MARVELS.
ACROSS THE STREET... CHILDREN PICK PURE WHITE LILIES... FROM THE AWNINGS... OF A SEX CINEMA... AND PLAY AT WEDDINGS... PARADING SOLEMNLY... BETWEEN THE SILENT TREES.
HOT M
DEAD END
WINE DRIBBLES... FROM A PHONE BOOTH CRAMMED WITH GRAPES... AND THE MOUTHS OF SUBWAYS... BREATHE A RARE... DELICATE PERFUME...
ZZZZZRRRRRR
RRRRRZZZZZZ
SUB
DEAD END
SOMEWHERE NEARBY AN ANIMAL GROWLS... DEEP IN ITS ROUGH METAL THROAT...
ZZZRRRRRZ
RRZZZZZZR
THE SOUNDS GROW LOUDER, AND MORE PIERCING... RISING INTO THE SCREAM... OF SOME MONSTROUS NOCTURNAL PREDATOR...
IT'S BEHIND ME...
DEAD END
I START TO TURN...
11

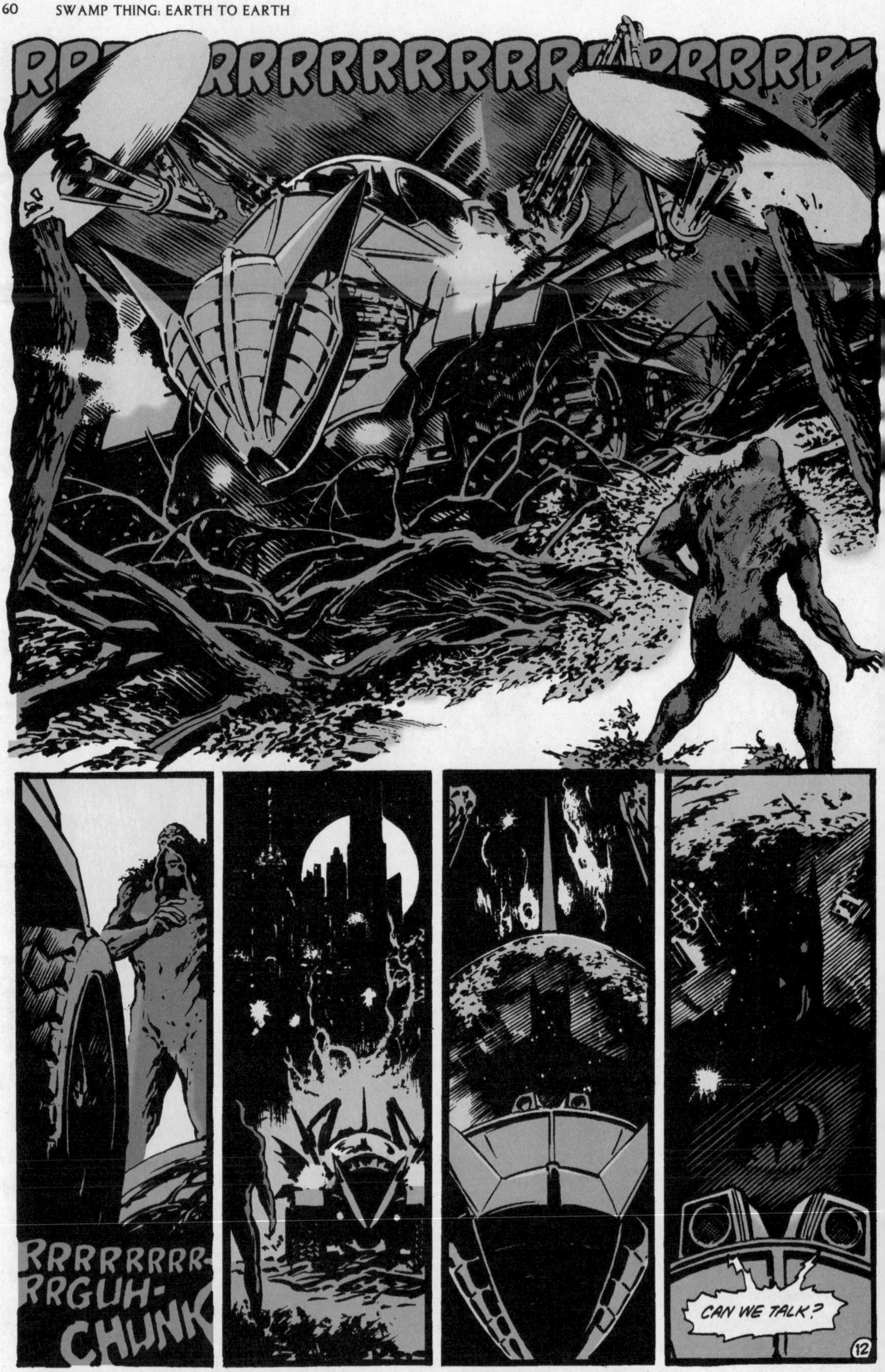
RRRRRRRRRRRRRRRRRRRRRRR
RRRRRRRRR-
RRGUH-
CHUNK
CAN WE TALK?
12

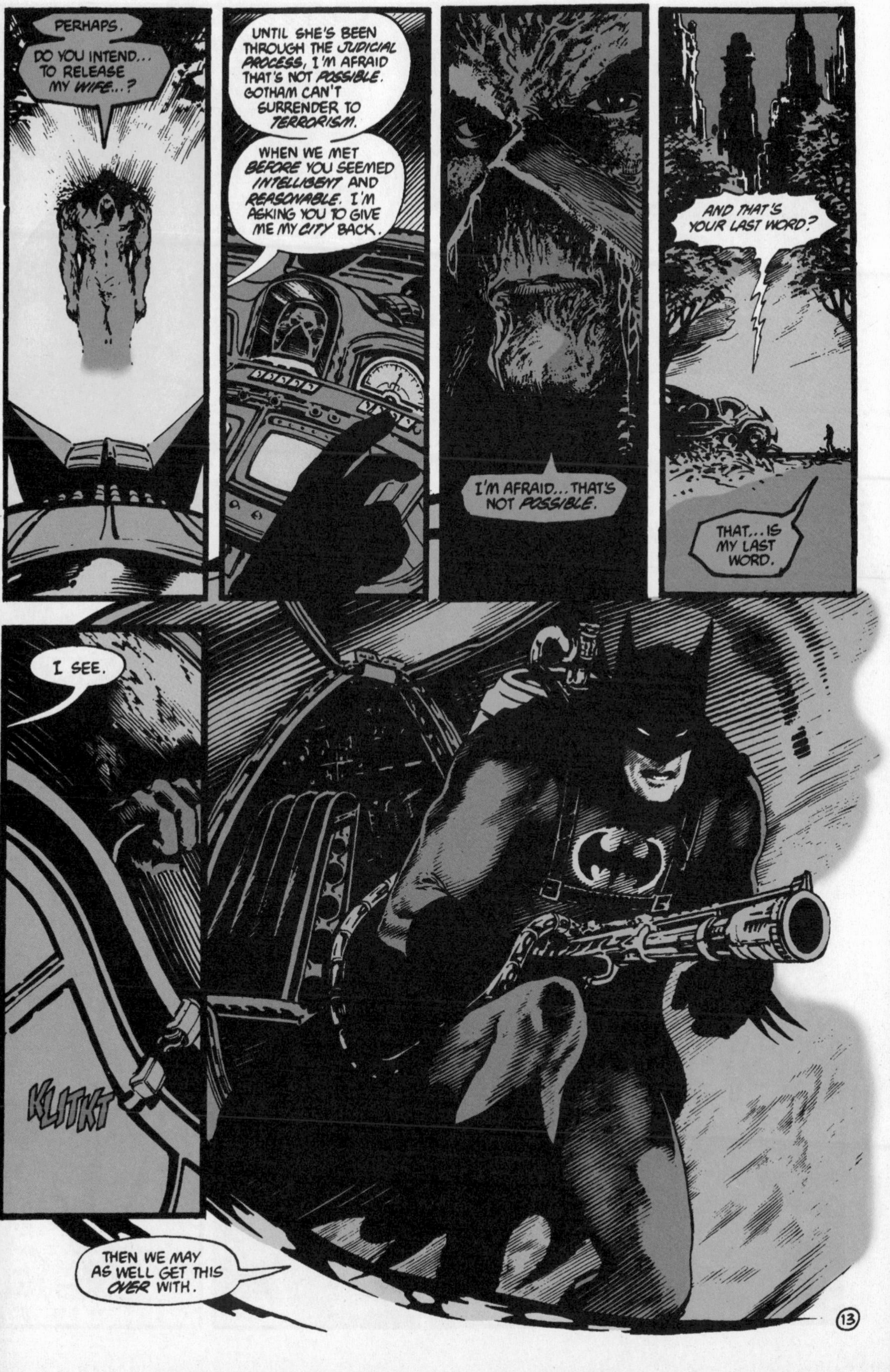
PERHAPS.
DO YOU INTEND... TO RELEASE MY WIFE...?
UNTIL SHE'S BEEN THROUGH THE JUDICIAL PROCESS, I'M AFRAID THAT'S NOT POSSIBLE. GOTHAM CAN'T SURRENDER TO TERRORISM.
WHEN WE MET BEFORE YOU SEEMED INTELLIGENT AND REASONABLE. I'M ASKING YOU TO GIVE ME MY CITY BACK.
I'M AFRAID... THAT'S NOT POSSIBLE.
AND THAT'S YOUR LAST WORD?
THAT... IS MY LAST WORD.
I SEE.
KLITKT
THEN WE MAY AS WELL GET THIS OVER WITH.
13

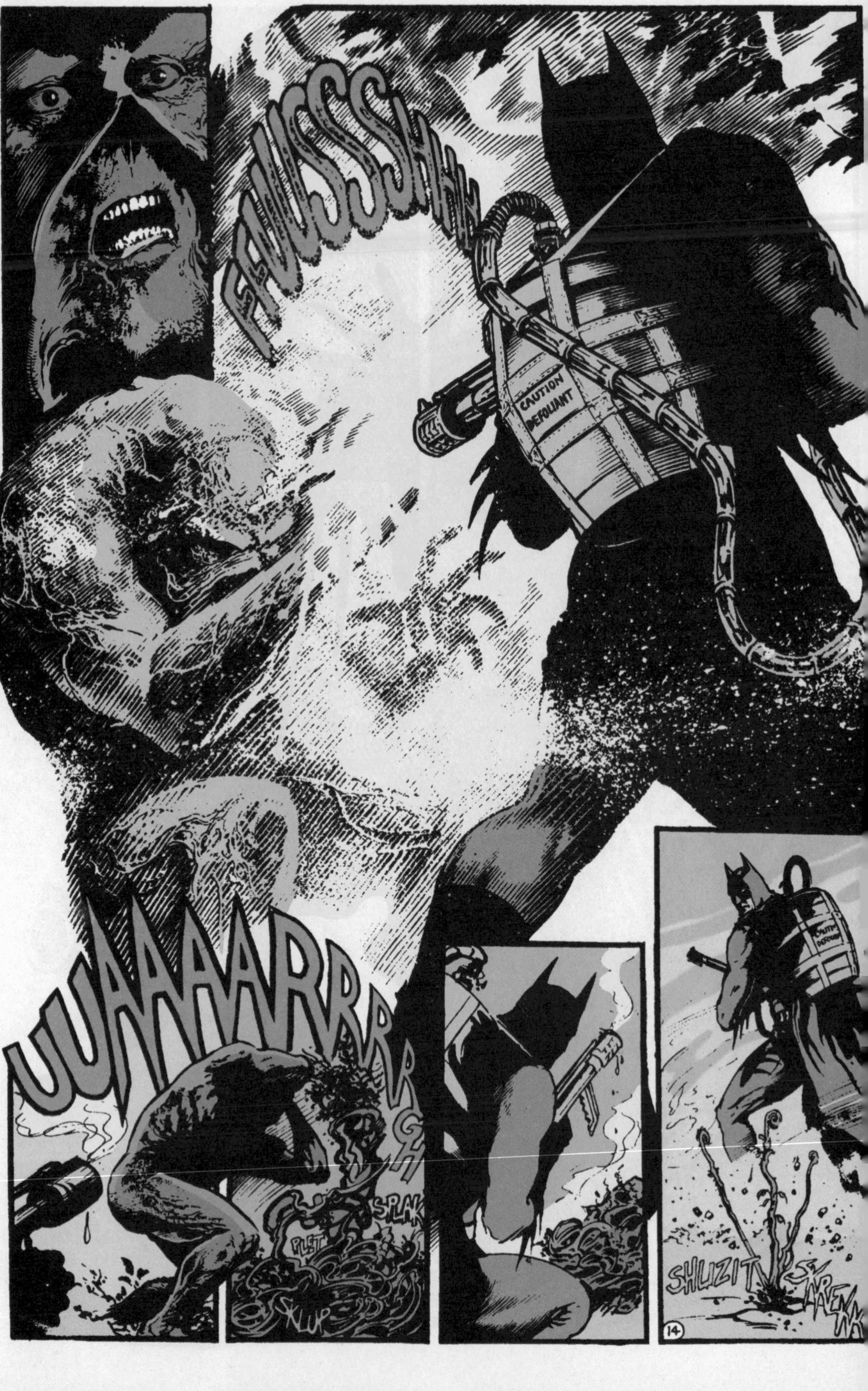
FWUSSSHHH
CAUTION DEFOLIANT
UUAAAARRRRGH
SPLAK
PLUT
SHUZIT
SKREKK
14

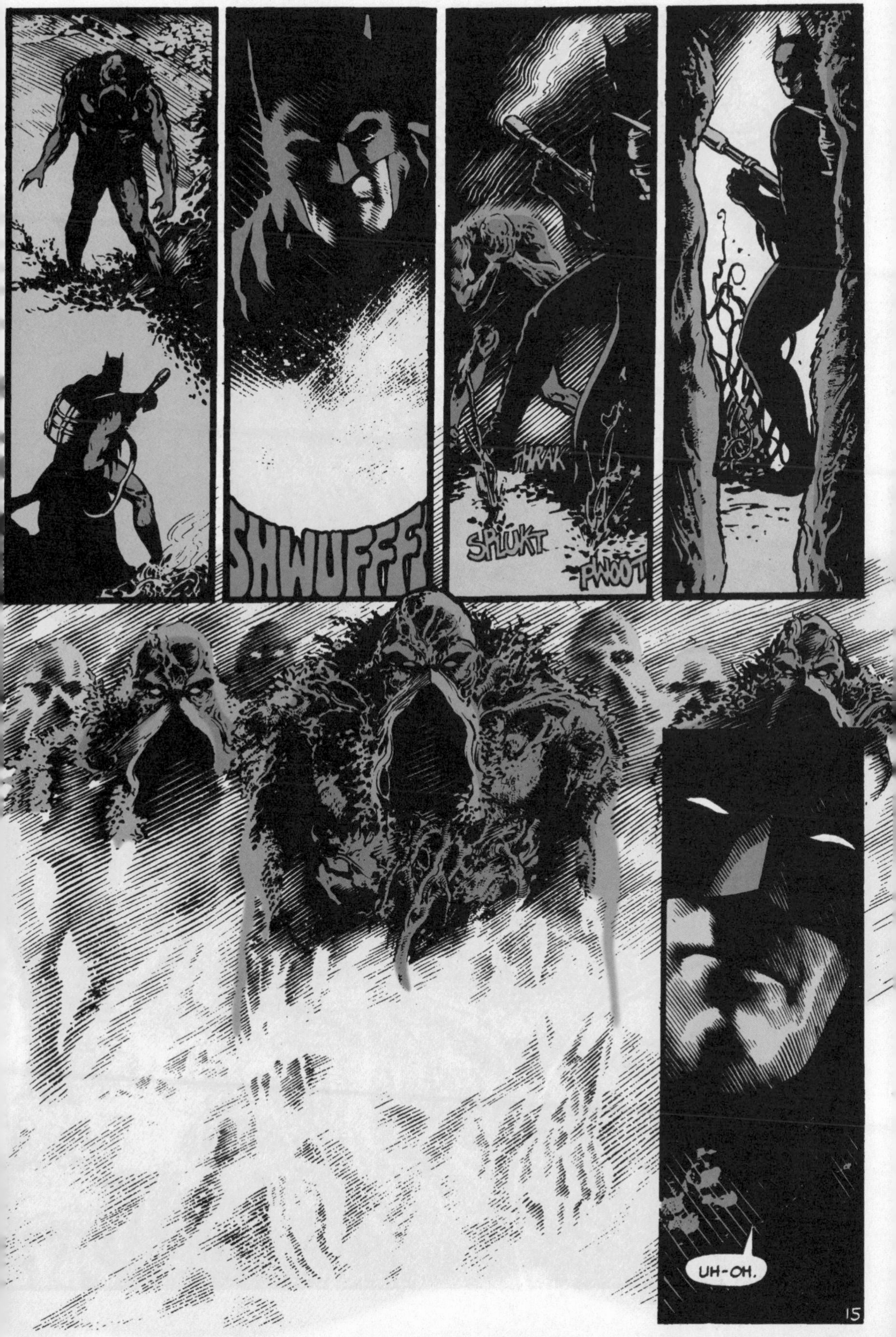
SHWUFFF
THRAK
SPLUKT
PWOOT
UH-OH.
15

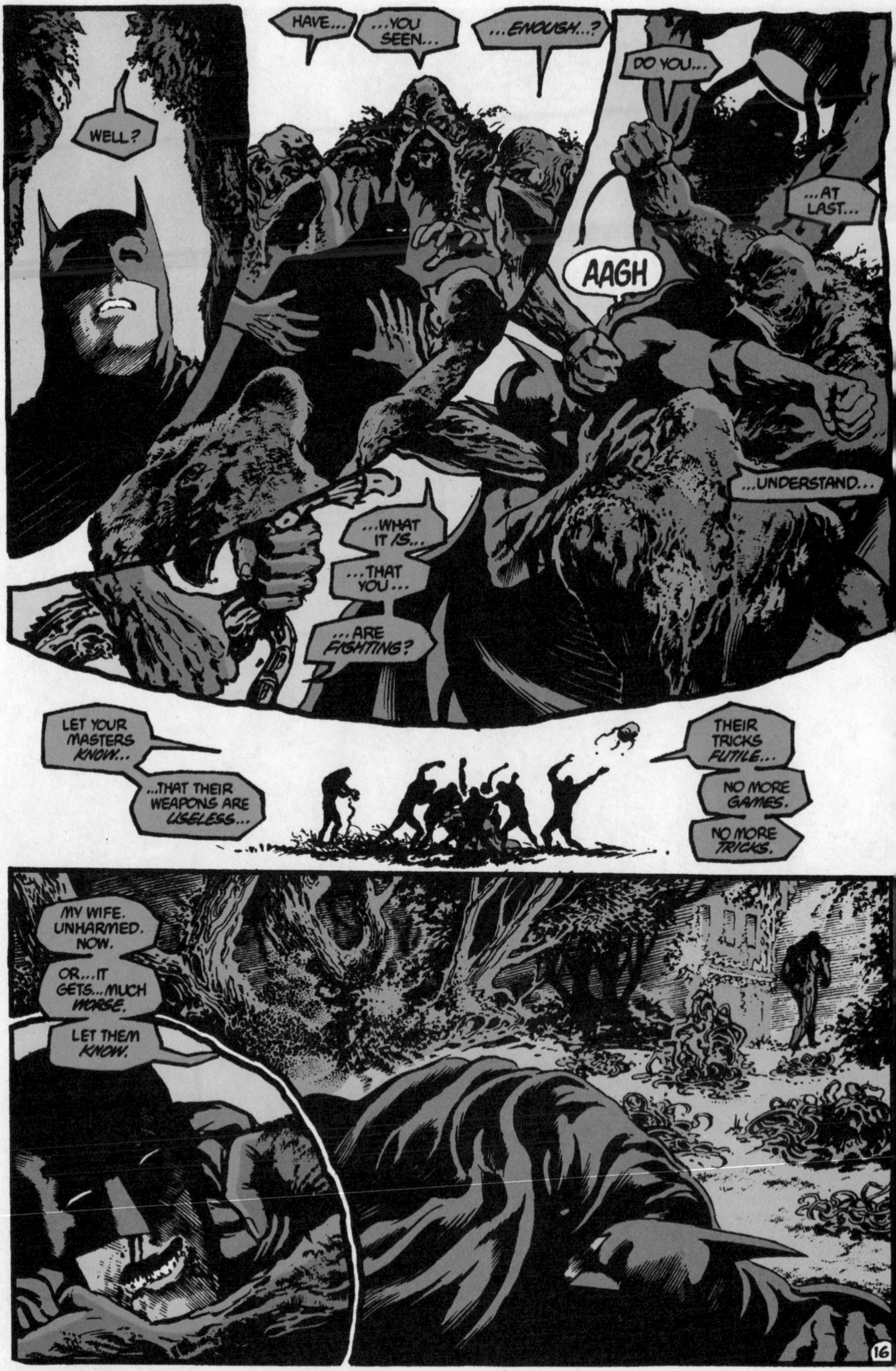
WELL?
HAVE...
...YOU SEEN...
...ENOUGH...?
DO YOU...
...AT LAST...
AAGH
...UNDERSTAND...
...WHAT IT IS...
...THAT YOU...
...ARE FIGHTING?
LET YOUR MASTERS KNOW...
...THAT THEIR WEAPONS ARE USELESS...
THEIR TRICKS FUTILE...
NO MORE GAMES.
NO MORE TRICKS.
MY WIFE. UNHARMED. NOW.
OR...IT GETS...MUCH WORSE.
LET THEM KNOW.
16

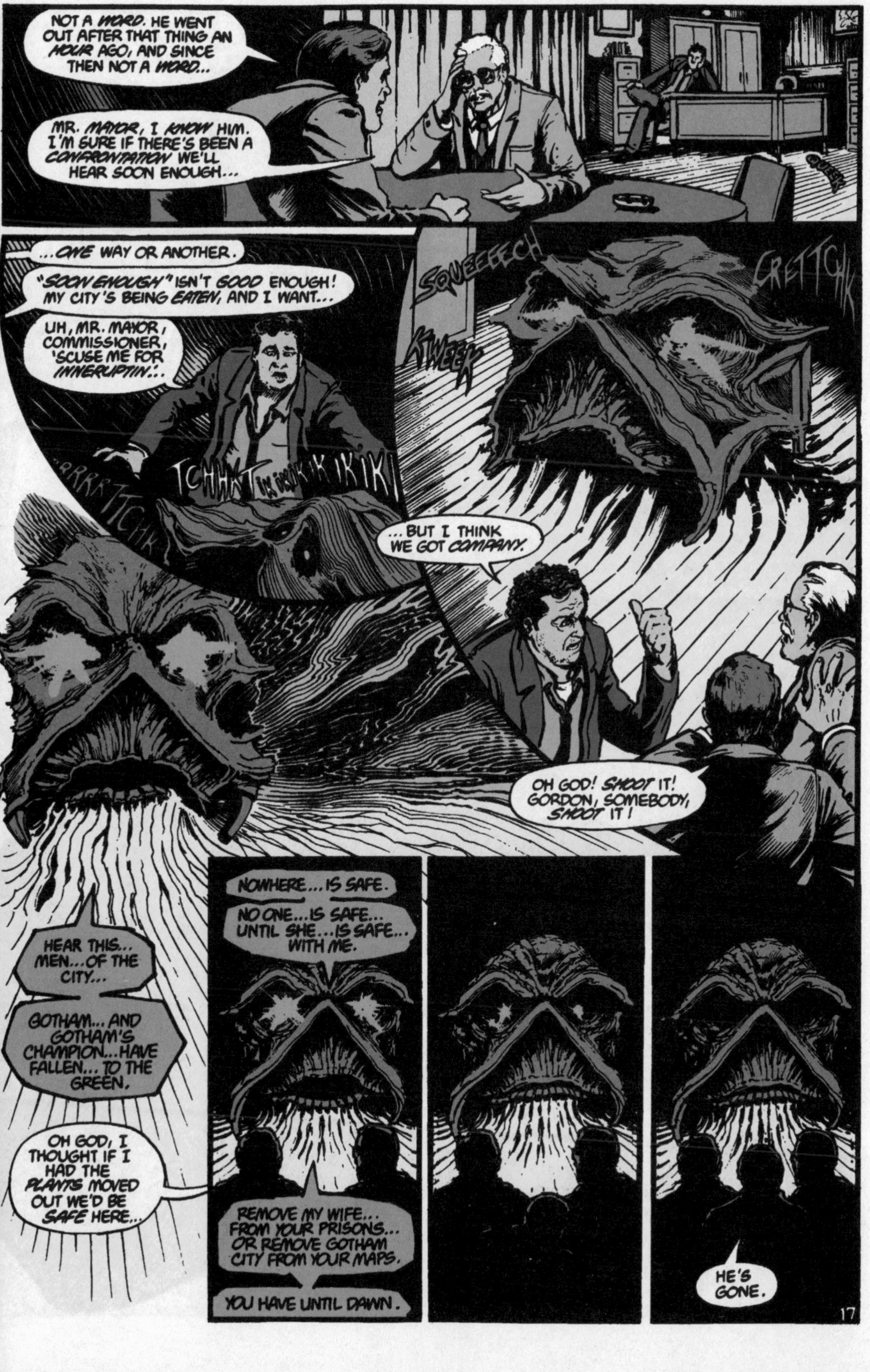
NOT A WORD. HE WENT OUT AFTER THAT THING AN HOUR AGO, AND SINCE THEN NOT A WORD...
MR. MAYOR, I KNOW HIM. I'M SURE IF THERE'S BEEN A CONFRONTATION WE'LL HEAR SOON ENOUGH...
...ONE WAY OR ANOTHER.
"SOON ENOUGH" ISN'T GOOD ENOUGH! MY CITY'S BEING EATEN, AND I WANT...
UH, MR. MAYOR, COMMISSIONER, 'SCUSE ME FOR INNERUPTIN'...
...BUT I THINK WE GOT COMPANY.
SQUEEEECH
CRETTCHK
OH GOD! SHOOT IT! GORDON, SOMEBODY, SHOOT IT!
HEAR THIS... MEN...OF THE CITY...
GOTHAM... AND GOTHAM'S CHAMPION...HAVE FALLEN... TO THE GREEN.
NOWHERE... IS SAFE.
NO ONE...IS SAFE... UNTIL SHE...IS SAFE... WITH ME.
OH GOD, I THOUGHT IF I HAD THE PLANTS MOVED OUT WE'D BE SAFE HERE...
REMOVE MY WIFE... FROM YOUR PRISONS... OR REMOVE GOTHAM CITY FROM YOUR MAPS.
YOU HAVE UNTIL DAWN.
HE'S GONE.
17

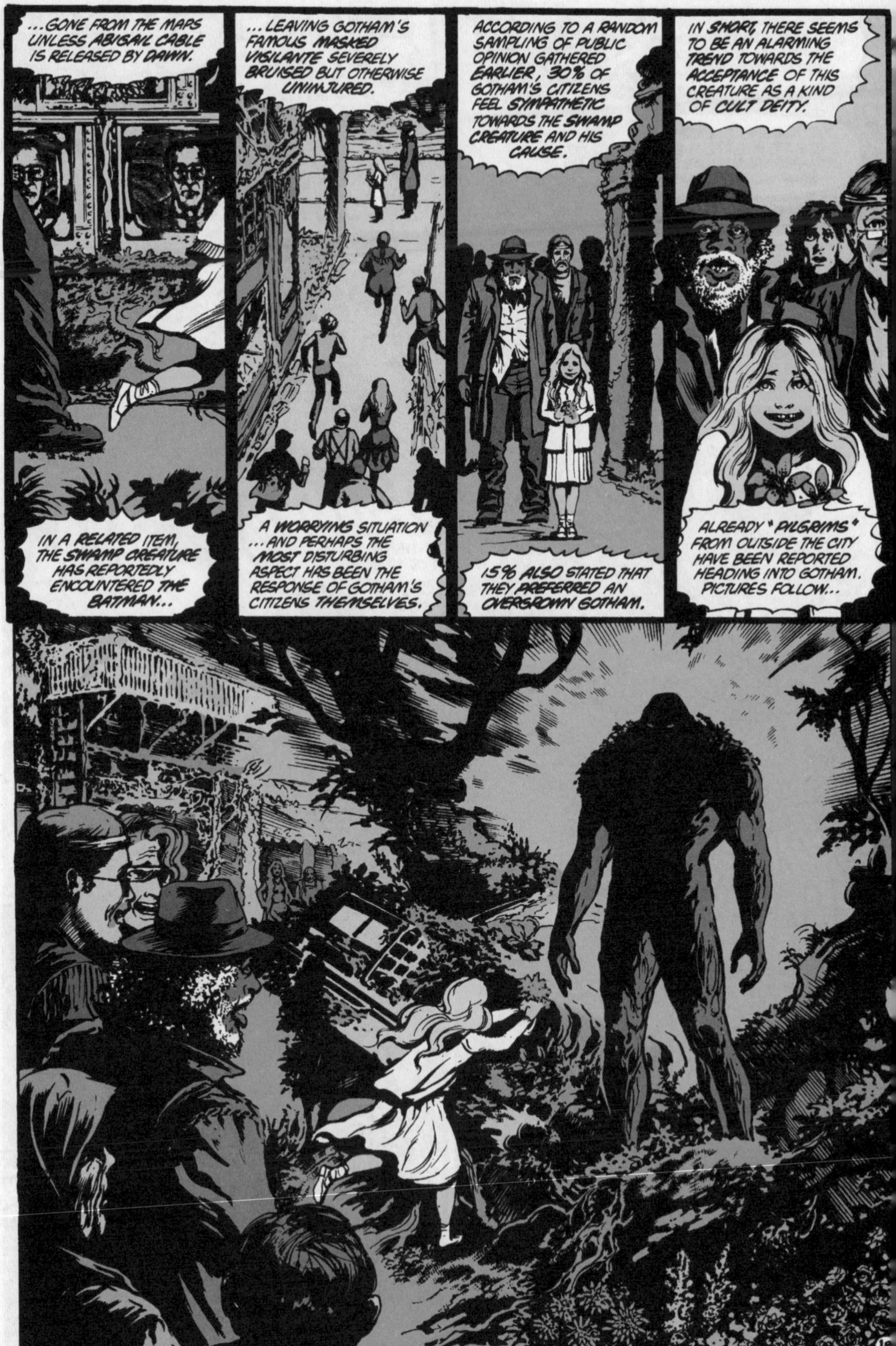
...GONE FROM THE MAPS UNLESS ABIGAIL CABLE IS RELEASED BY DAWN.
IN A RELATED ITEM, THE SWAMP CREATURE HAS REPORTEDLY ENCOUNTERED THE BATMAN...
...LEAVING GOTHAM'S FAMOUS MASKED VIGILANTE SEVERELY BRUISED BUT OTHERWISE UNINJURED.
A WORRYING SITUATION ...AND PERHAPS THE MOST DISTURBING ASPECT HAS BEEN THE RESPONSE OF GOTHAM'S CITIZENS THEMSELVES.
ACCORDING TO A RANDOM SAMPLING OF PUBLIC OPINION GATHERED EARLIER, 30% OF GOTHAM'S CITIZENS FEEL SYMPATHETIC TOWARDS THE SWAMP CREATURE AND HIS CAUSE.
15% ALSO STATED THAT THEY PREFERRED AN OVERGROWN GOTHAM.
IN SHORT, THERE SEEMS TO BE AN ALARMING TREND TOWARDS THE ACCEPTANCE OF THIS CREATURE AS A KIND OF CULT DEITY.
ALREADY "PILGRIMS" FROM OUTSIDE THE CITY HAVE BEEN REPORTED HEADING INTO GOTHAM. PICTURES FOLLOW...
18

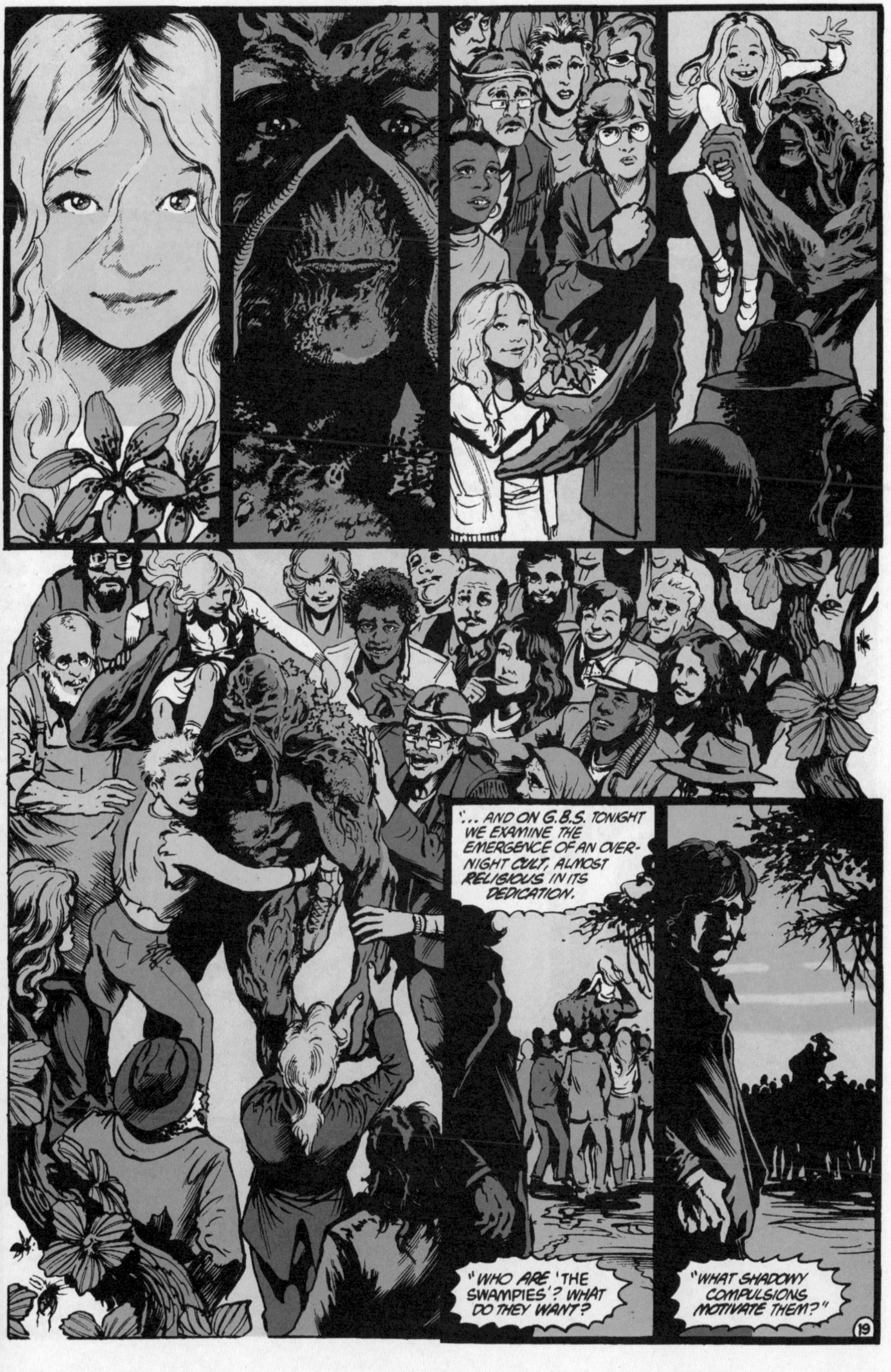
"... AND ON G.B.S. TONIGHT WE EXAMINE THE EMERGENCE OF AN OVER-NIGHT CULT, ALMOST RELIGIOUS IN ITS DEDICATION.
"WHO ARE 'THE SWAMPIES'? WHAT DO THEY WANT?
"WHAT SHADOWY COMPULSIONS MOTIVATE THEM?"
19

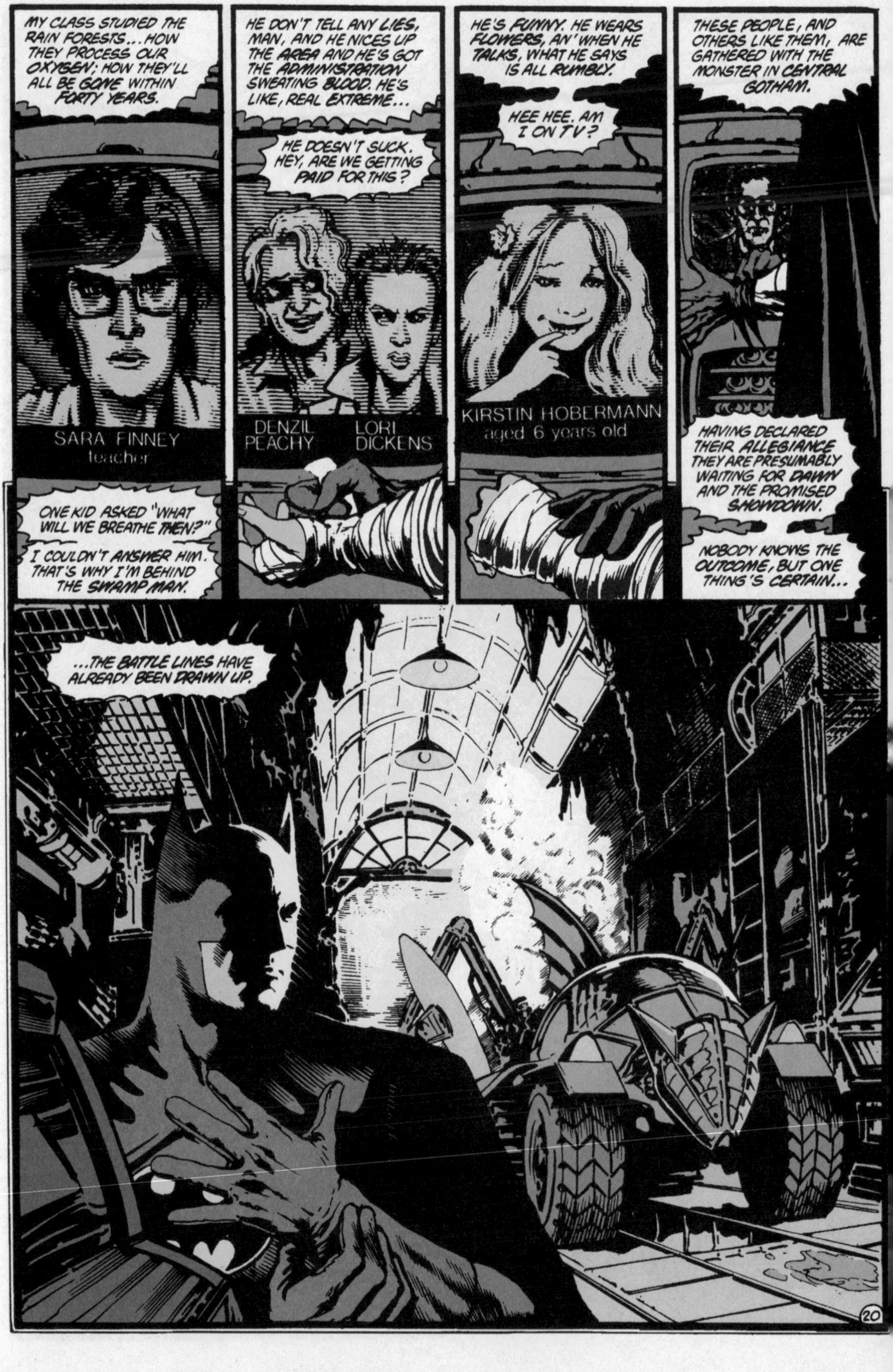
MY CLASS STUDIED THE RAIN FORESTS... HOW THEY PROCESS OUR OXYGEN; HOW THEY'LL ALL BE GONE WITHIN FORTY YEARS.
SARA FINNEY
teacher
ONE KID ASKED "WHAT WILL WE BREATHE THEN?"
I COULDN'T ANSWER HIM. THAT'S WHY I'M BEHIND THE SWAMP MAN.
HE DON'T TELL ANY LIES, MAN, AND HE NICES UP THE AREA AND HE'S GOT THE ADMINISTRATION SWEATING BLOOD. HE'S LIKE, REAL EXTREME...
HE DOESN'T SUCK. HEY, ARE WE GETTING PAID FOR THIS?
DENZIL PEACHY
LORI DICKENS
HE'S FUNNY. HE WEARS FLOWERS, AN' WHEN HE TALKS, WHAT HE SAYS IS ALL RUMBLY.
HEE HEE. AM I ON TV?
KIRSTIN HOBERMANN
aged 6 years old
THESE PEOPLE, AND OTHERS LIKE THEM, ARE GATHERED WITH THE MONSTER IN CENTRAL GOTHAM.
HAVING DECLARED THEIR ALLEGIANCE THEY ARE PRESUMABLY WAITING FOR DAWN AND THE PROMISED SHOWDOWN.
NOBODY KNOWS THE OUTCOME, BUT ONE THING'S CERTAIN...
...THE BATTLE LINES HAVE ALREADY BEEN DRAWN UP.
20

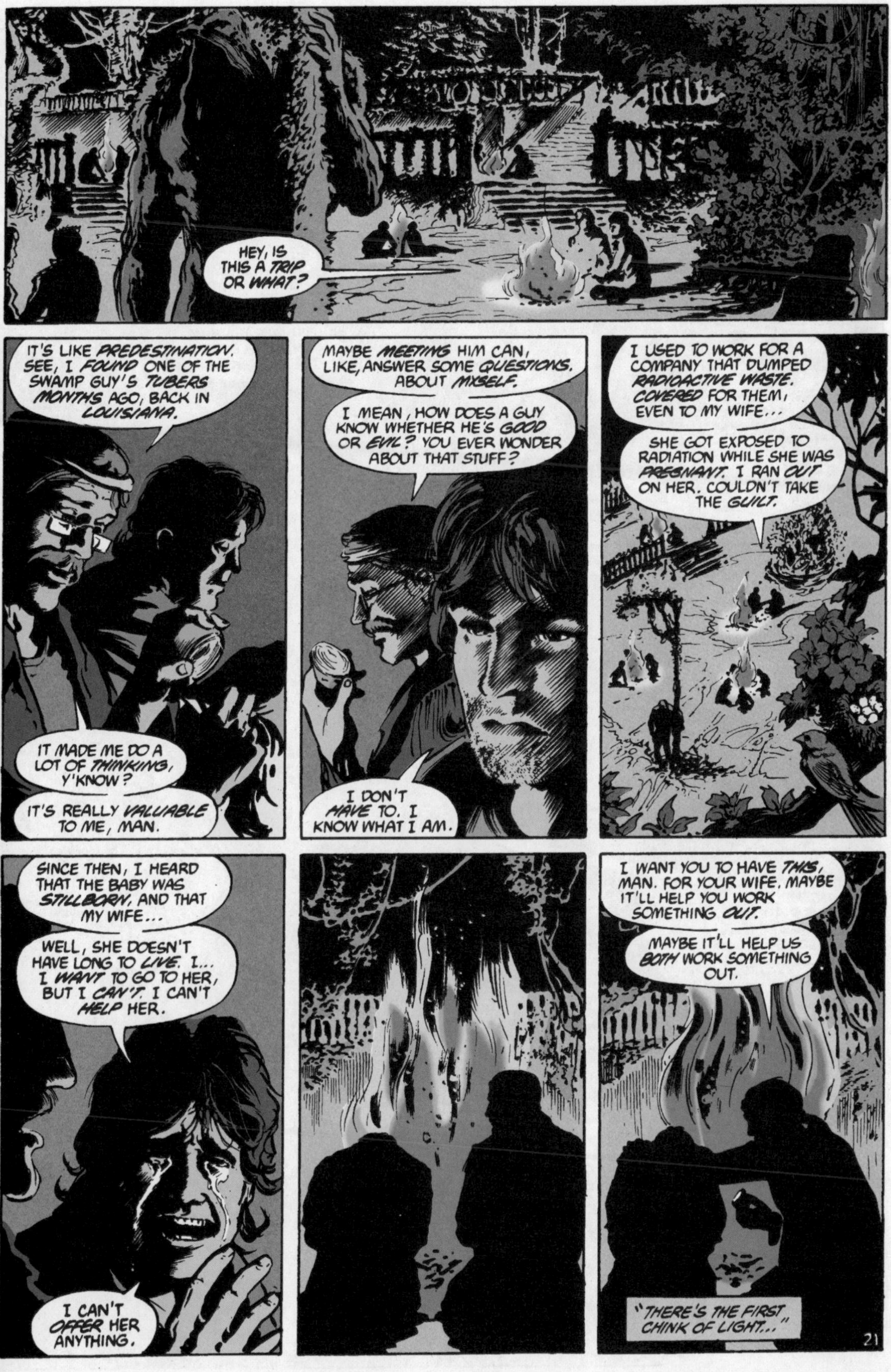
HEY, IS THIS A TRIP OR WHAT?
IT'S LIKE PREDESTINATION. SEE, I FOUND ONE OF THE SWAMP GUY'S TUBERS MONTHS AGO, BACK IN LOUISIANA.
IT MADE ME DO A LOT OF THINKING, Y'KNOW?
IT'S REALLY VALUABLE TO ME, MAN.
MAYBE MEETING HIM CAN, LIKE, ANSWER SOME QUESTIONS. ABOUT MYSELF.
I MEAN, HOW DOES A GUY KNOW WHETHER HE'S GOOD OR EVIL? YOU EVER WONDER ABOUT THAT STUFF?
I DON'T HAVE TO. I KNOW WHAT I AM.
I USED TO WORK FOR A COMPANY THAT DUMPED RADIOACTIVE WASTE. COVERED FOR THEM, EVEN TO MY WIFE...
SHE GOT EXPOSED TO RADIATION WHILE SHE WAS PREGNANT. I RAN OUT ON HER. COULDN'T TAKE THE GUILT.
SINCE THEN, I HEARD THAT THE BABY WAS STILLBORN, AND THAT MY WIFE...
WELL, SHE DOESN'T HAVE LONG TO LIVE. I... I WANT TO GO TO HER, BUT I CAN'T. I CAN'T HELP HER.
I CAN'T OFFER HER ANYTHING.
I WANT YOU TO HAVE THIS, MAN. FOR YOUR WIFE. MAYBE IT'LL HELP YOU WORK SOMETHING OUT.
MAYBE IT'LL HELP US BOTH WORK SOMETHING OUT.
"THERE'S THE FIRST CHINK OF LIGHT..."
21

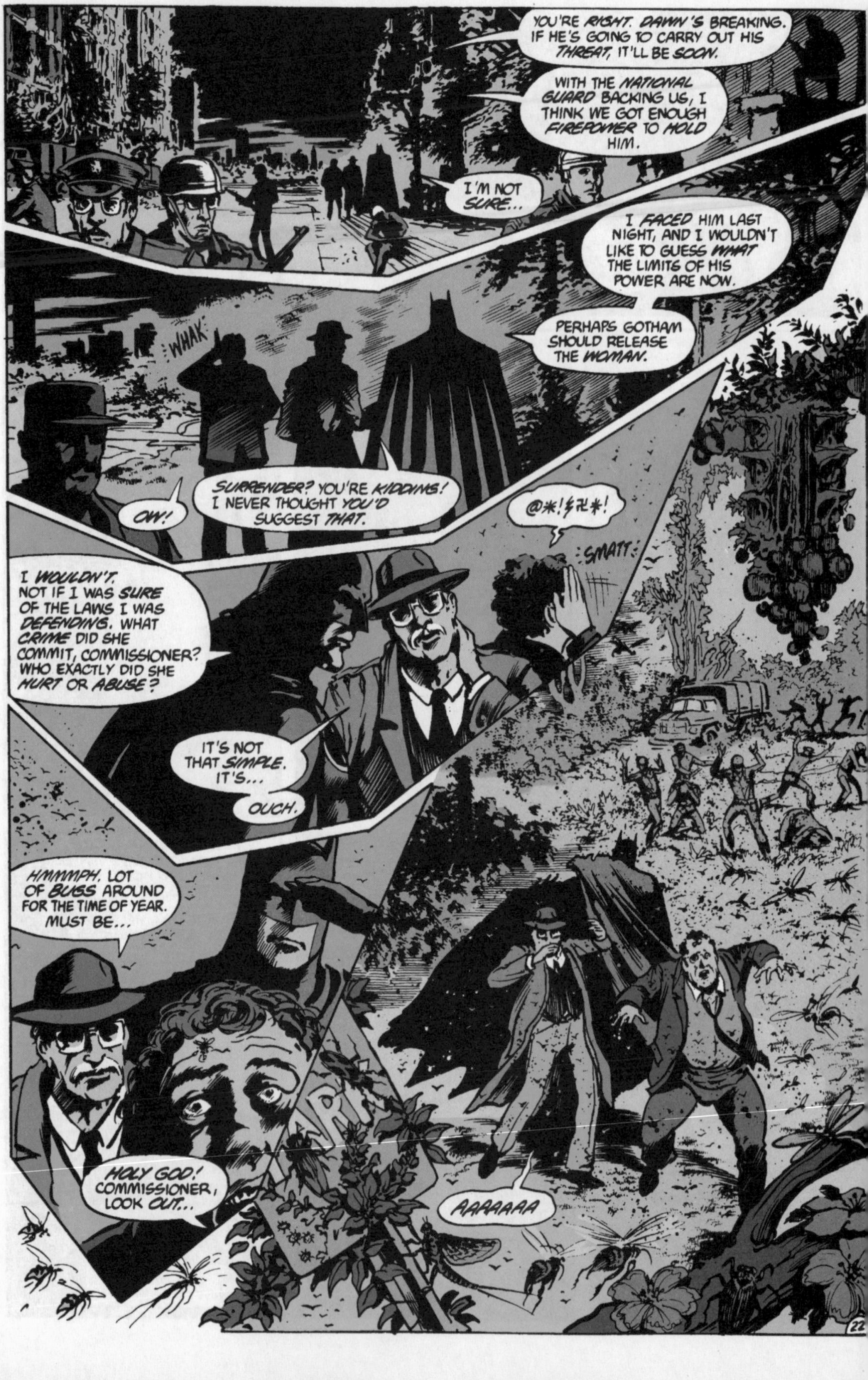
YOU'RE RIGHT. DAWN'S BREAKING. IF HE'S GOING TO CARRY OUT HIS THREAT, IT'LL BE SOON.
WITH THE NATIONAL GUARD BACKING US, I THINK WE GOT ENOUGH FIREPOWER TO HOLD HIM.
I'M NOT SURE...
I FACED HIM LAST NIGHT, AND I WOULDN'T LIKE TO GUESS WHAT THE LIMITS OF HIS POWER ARE NOW.
PERHAPS GOTHAM SHOULD RELEASE THE WOMAN.
WHAK
OW!
SURRENDER? YOU'RE KIDDING! I NEVER THOUGHT YOU'D SUGGEST THAT.
@*!ϟ卍*!
SMATT
I WOULDN'T. NOT IF I WAS SURE OF THE LAWS I WAS DEFENDING. WHAT CRIME DID SHE COMMIT, COMMISSIONER? WHO EXACTLY DID SHE HURT OR ABUSE?
IT'S NOT THAT SIMPLE. IT'S...
OUCH.
HMMMPH. LOT OF BUGS AROUND FOR THE TIME OF YEAR. MUST BE...
HOLY GOD! COMMISSIONER, LOOK OUT...
AAAAAAA
22

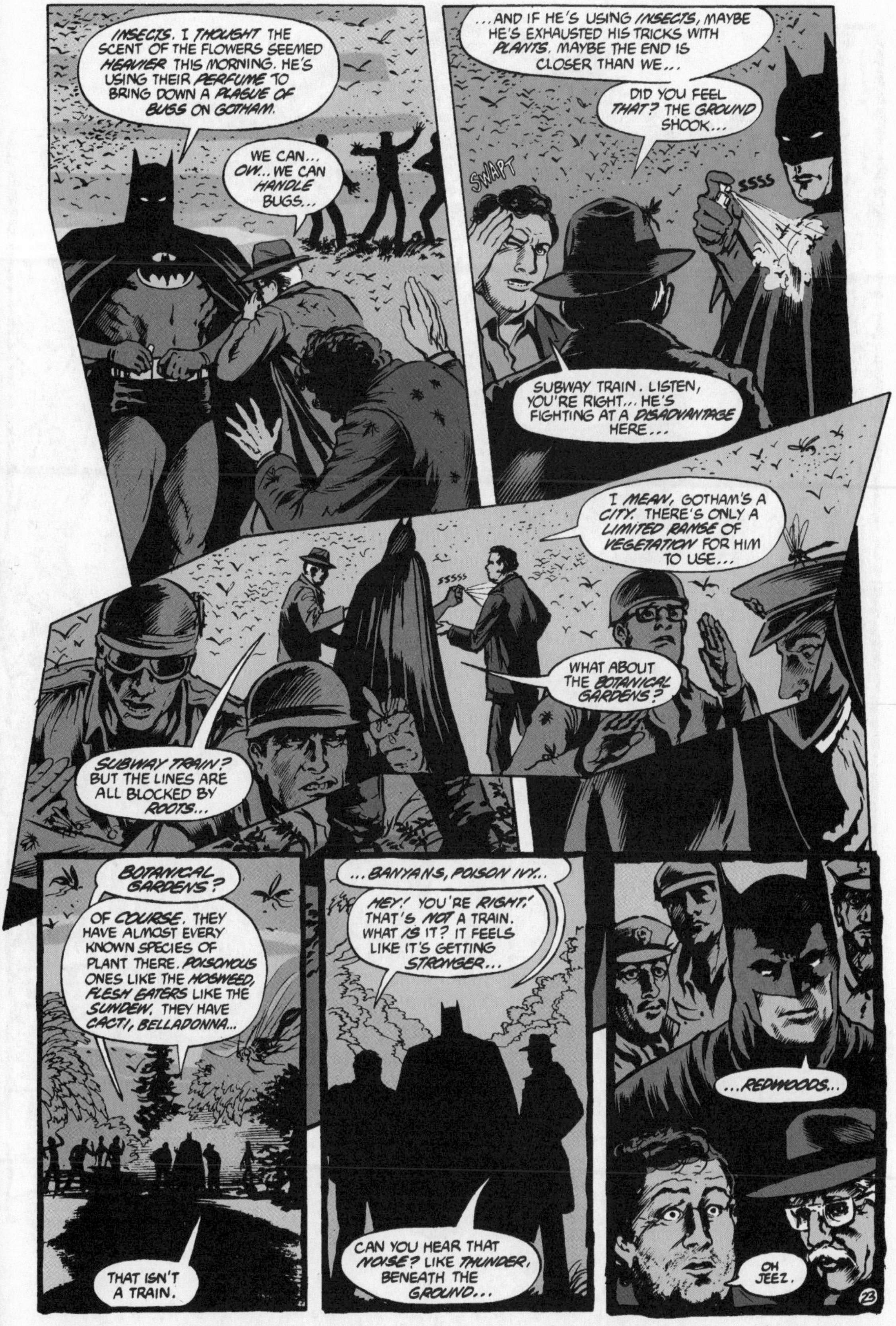

INSECTS. I THOUGHT THE SCENT OF THE FLOWERS SEEMED HEAVIER THIS MORNING. HE'S USING THEIR PERFUME TO BRING DOWN A PLAGUE OF BUGS ON GOTHAM.
WE CAN... OW... WE CAN HANDLE BUGS...
...AND IF HE'S USING INSECTS, MAYBE HE'S EXHAUSTED HIS TRICKS WITH PLANTS. MAYBE THE END IS CLOSER THAN WE...
DID YOU FEEL THAT? THE GROUND SHOOK...
SWAPT
SSSS
SUBWAY TRAIN. LISTEN, YOU'RE RIGHT... HE'S FIGHTING AT A DISADVANTAGE HERE...
I MEAN, GOTHAM'S A CITY. THERE'S ONLY A LIMITED RANGE OF VEGETATION FOR HIM TO USE...
SSSSS
WHAT ABOUT THE BOTANICAL GARDENS?
SUBWAY TRAIN? BUT THE LINES ARE ALL BLOCKED BY ROOTS...
BOTANICAL GARDENS?
OF COURSE. THEY HAVE ALMOST EVERY KNOWN SPECIES OF PLANT THERE. POISONOUS ONES LIKE THE HOGWEED, FLESH EATERS LIKE THE SUNDEW. THEY HAVE CACTI, BELLADONNA...
THAT ISN'T A TRAIN.
...BANYANS, POISON IVY...
HEY! YOU'RE RIGHT! THAT'S NOT A TRAIN. WHAT IS IT? IT FEELS LIKE IT'S GETTING STRONGER...
CAN YOU HEAR THAT NOISE? LIKE THUNDER, BENEATH THE GROUND...
...REDWOODS...
OH JEEZ.
23

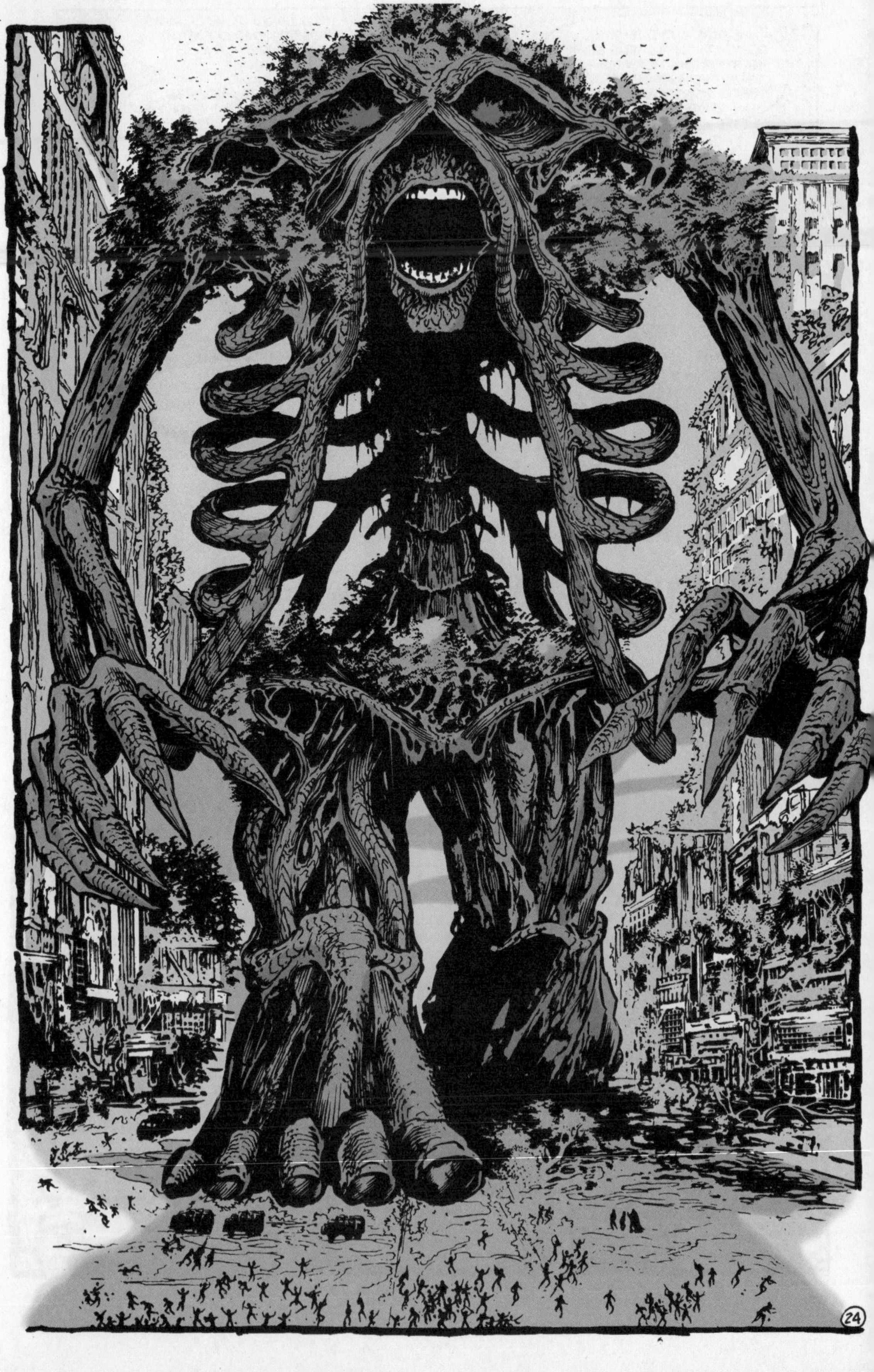
24

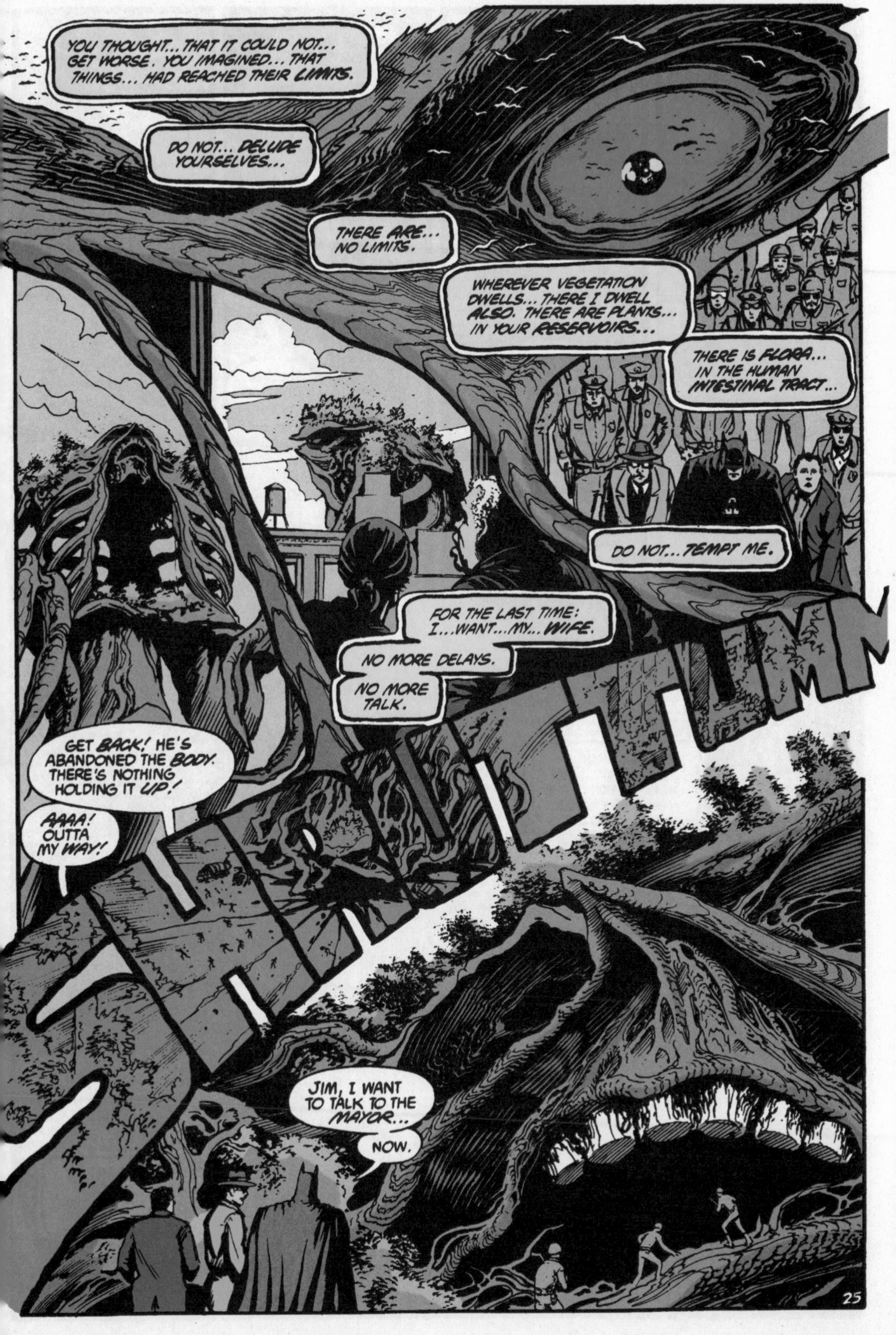
YOU THOUGHT... THAT IT COULD NOT... GET WORSE. YOU IMAGINED... THAT THINGS... HAD REACHED THEIR LIMITS.
DO NOT... DELUDE YOURSELVES...
THERE ARE... NO LIMITS.
WHEREVER VEGETATION DWELLS... THERE I DWELL ALSO. THERE ARE PLANTS... IN YOUR RESERVOIRS...
THERE IS FLORA... IN THE HUMAN INTESTINAL TRACT...
DO NOT... TEMPT ME.
FOR THE LAST TIME: I... WANT... MY... WIFE.
NO MORE DELAYS.
NO MORE TALK.
GET BACK! HE'S ABANDONED THE BODY. THERE'S NOTHING HOLDING IT UP!
AAAA! OUTTA MY WAY!
JIM, I WANT TO TALK TO THE MAYOR...
NOW.
25

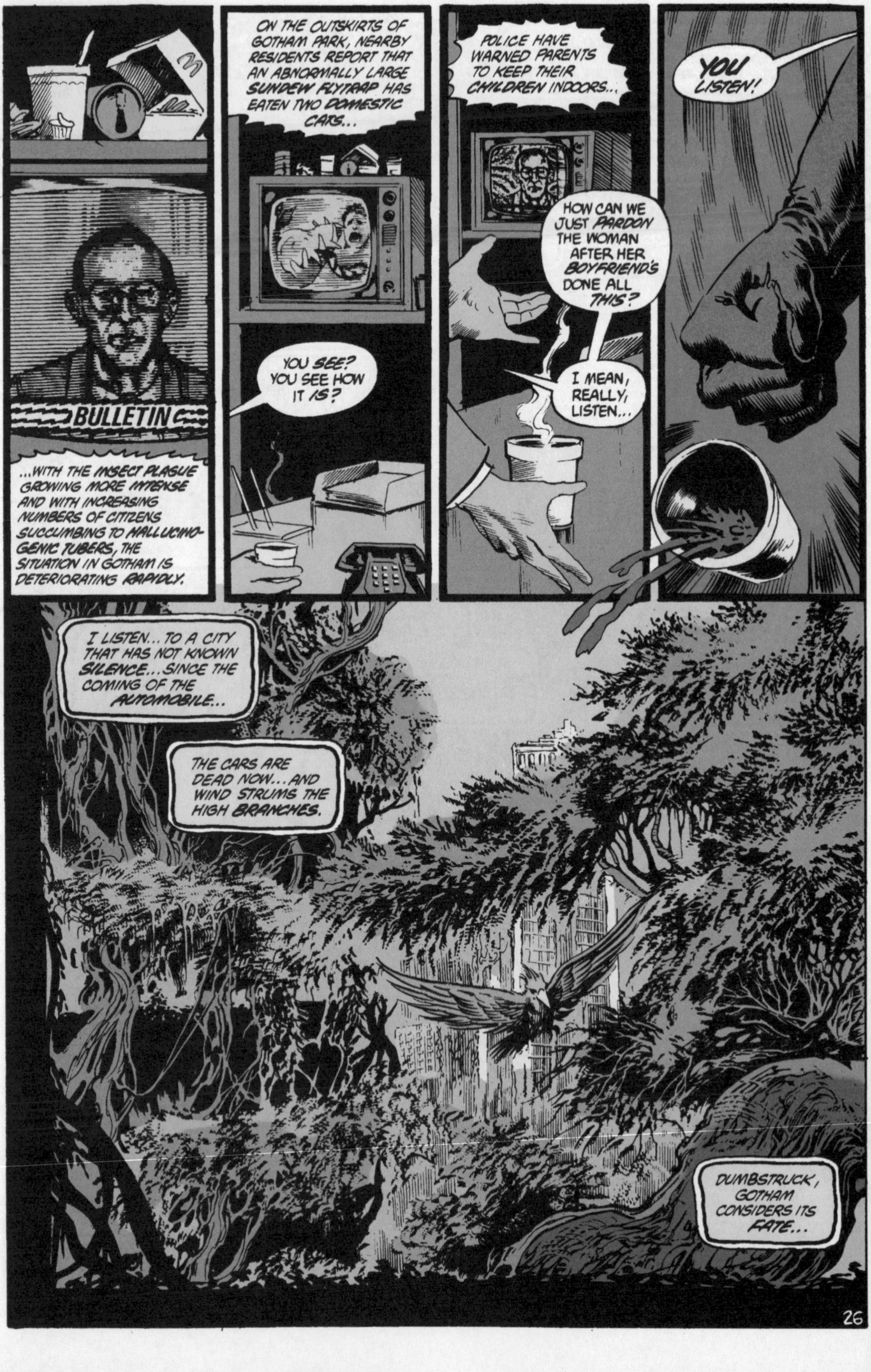
BULLETIN
...WITH THE INSECT PLAGUE GROWING MORE INTENSE AND WITH INCREASING NUMBERS OF CITIZENS SUCCUMBING TO HALLUCINOGENIC TUBERS, THE SITUATION IN GOTHAM IS DETERIORATING RAPIDLY.
ON THE OUTSKIRTS OF GOTHAM PARK, NEARBY RESIDENTS REPORT THAT AN ABNORMALLY LARGE SUNDEW FLYTRAP HAS EATEN TWO DOMESTIC CATS...
YOU SEE? YOU SEE HOW IT IS?
POLICE HAVE WARNED PARENTS TO KEEP THEIR CHILDREN INDOORS...
HOW CAN WE JUST PARDON THE WOMAN AFTER HER BOYFRIEND'S DONE ALL THIS?
I MEAN, REALLY, LISTEN...
YOU LISTEN!
I LISTEN... TO A CITY THAT HAS NOT KNOWN SILENCE... SINCE THE COMING OF THE AUTOMOBILE...
THE CARS ARE DEAD NOW... AND WIND STRUMS THE HIGH BRANCHES.
DUMBSTRUCK, GOTHAM CONSIDERS ITS FATE...
26

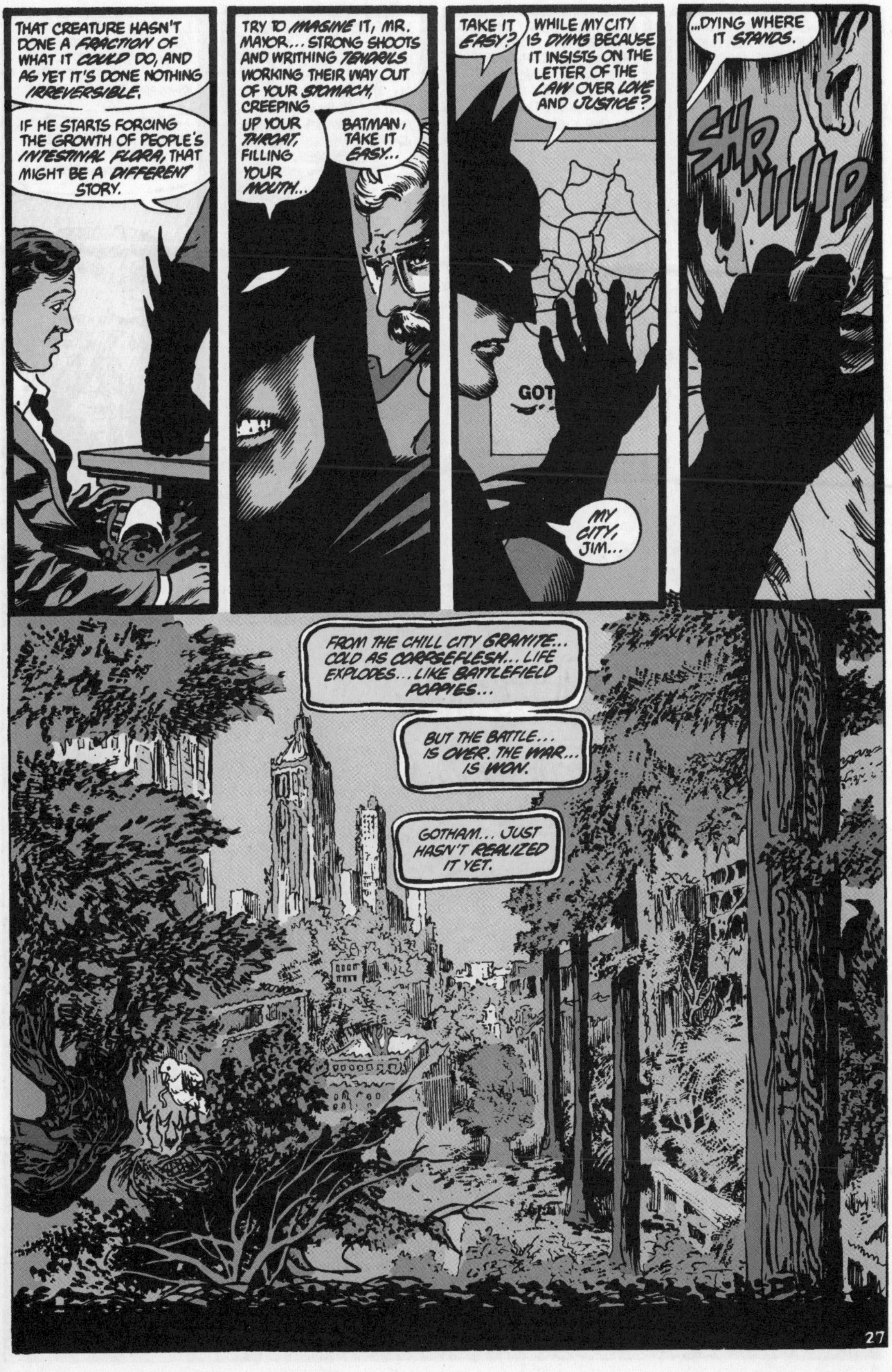
THAT CREATURE HASN'T DONE A FRACTION OF WHAT IT COULD DO, AND AS YET IT'S DONE NOTHING IRREVERSIBLE.
IF HE STARTS FORCING THE GROWTH OF PEOPLE'S INTESTINAL FLORA, THAT MIGHT BE A DIFFERENT STORY.
TRY TO IMAGINE IT, MR. MAYOR... STRONG SHOOTS AND WRITHING TENDRILS WORKING THEIR WAY OUT OF YOUR STOMACH, CREEPING UP YOUR THROAT, FILLING YOUR MOUTH...
BATMAN, TAKE IT EASY...
TAKE IT EASY?
WHILE MY CITY IS DYING BECAUSE IT INSISTS ON THE LETTER OF THE LAW OVER LOVE AND JUSTICE?
GOT
MY CITY, JIM...
...DYING WHERE IT STANDS.
SHRIIIIP
FROM THE CHILL CITY GRANITE... COLD AS CORPSEFLESH... LIFE EXPLODES... LIKE BATTLEFIELD POPPIES...
BUT THE BATTLE... IS OVER. THE WAR... IS WON.
GOTHAM... JUST HASN'T REALIZED IT YET.
27

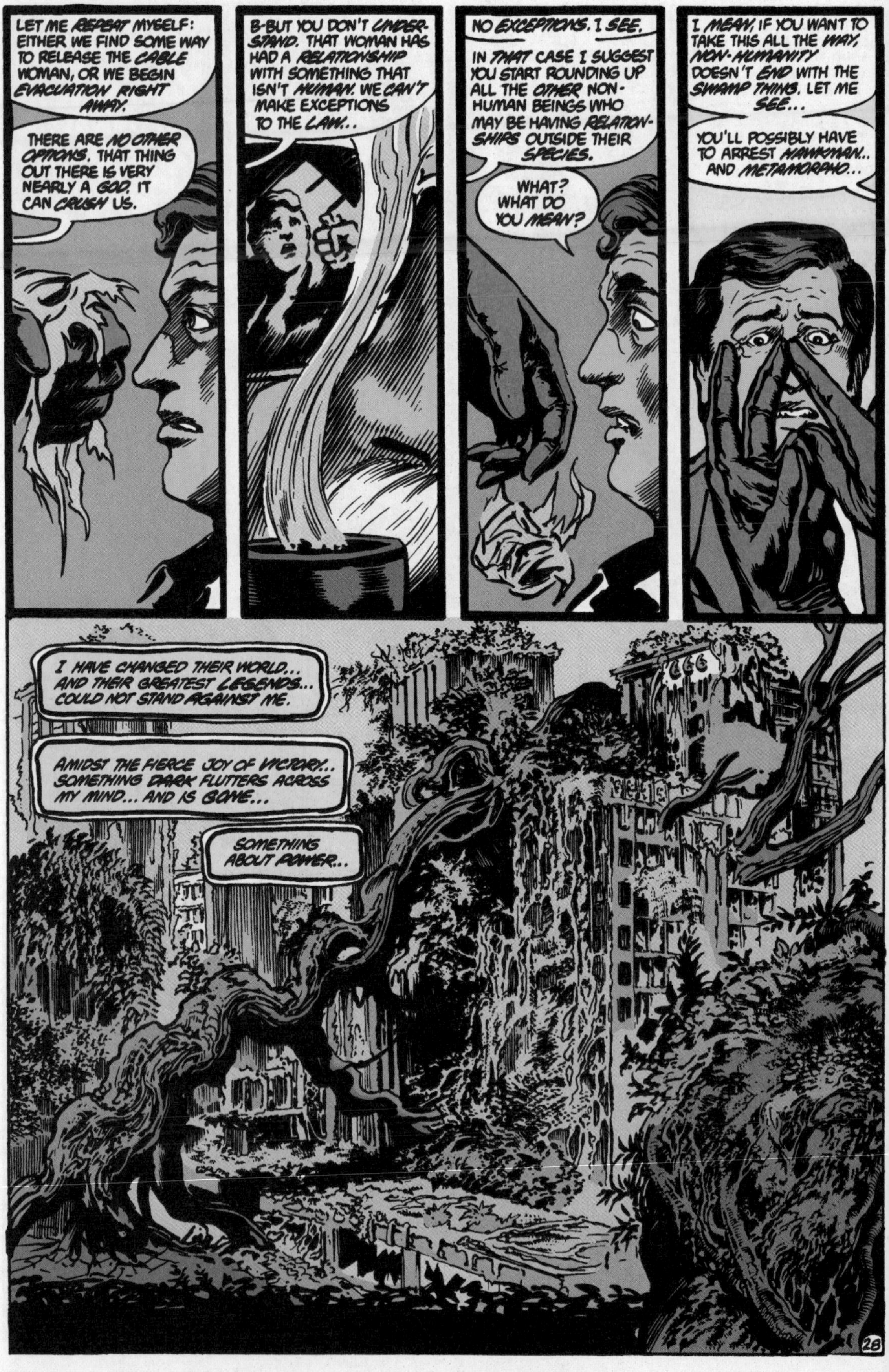
LET ME REPEAT MYSELF: EITHER WE FIND SOME WAY TO RELEASE THE CABLE WOMAN, OR WE BEGIN EVACUATION RIGHT AWAY.
THERE ARE NO OTHER OPTIONS. THAT THING OUT THERE IS VERY NEARLY A GOD. IT CAN CRUSH US.
B-BUT YOU DON'T UNDERSTAND. THAT WOMAN HAS HAD A RELATIONSHIP WITH SOMETHING THAT ISN'T HUMAN. WE CAN'T MAKE EXCEPTIONS TO THE LAW...
NO EXCEPTIONS. I SEE.
IN THAT CASE I SUGGEST YOU START ROUNDING UP ALL THE OTHER NON-HUMAN BEINGS WHO MAY BE HAVING RELATIONSHIPS OUTSIDE THEIR SPECIES.
WHAT? WHAT DO YOU MEAN?
I MEAN, IF YOU WANT TO TAKE THIS ALL THE WAY, NON-HUMANITY DOESN'T END WITH THE SWAMP THING. LET ME SEE...
YOU'LL POSSIBLY HAVE TO ARREST HAWKMAN... AND METAMORPHO...
I HAVE CHANGED THEIR WORLD... AND THEIR GREATEST LEGENDS... COULD NOT STAND AGAINST ME.
AMIDST THE FIERCE JOY OF VICTORY... SOMETHING DARK FLUTTERS ACROSS MY MIND... AND IS GONE...
SOMETHING ABOUT POWER...
28

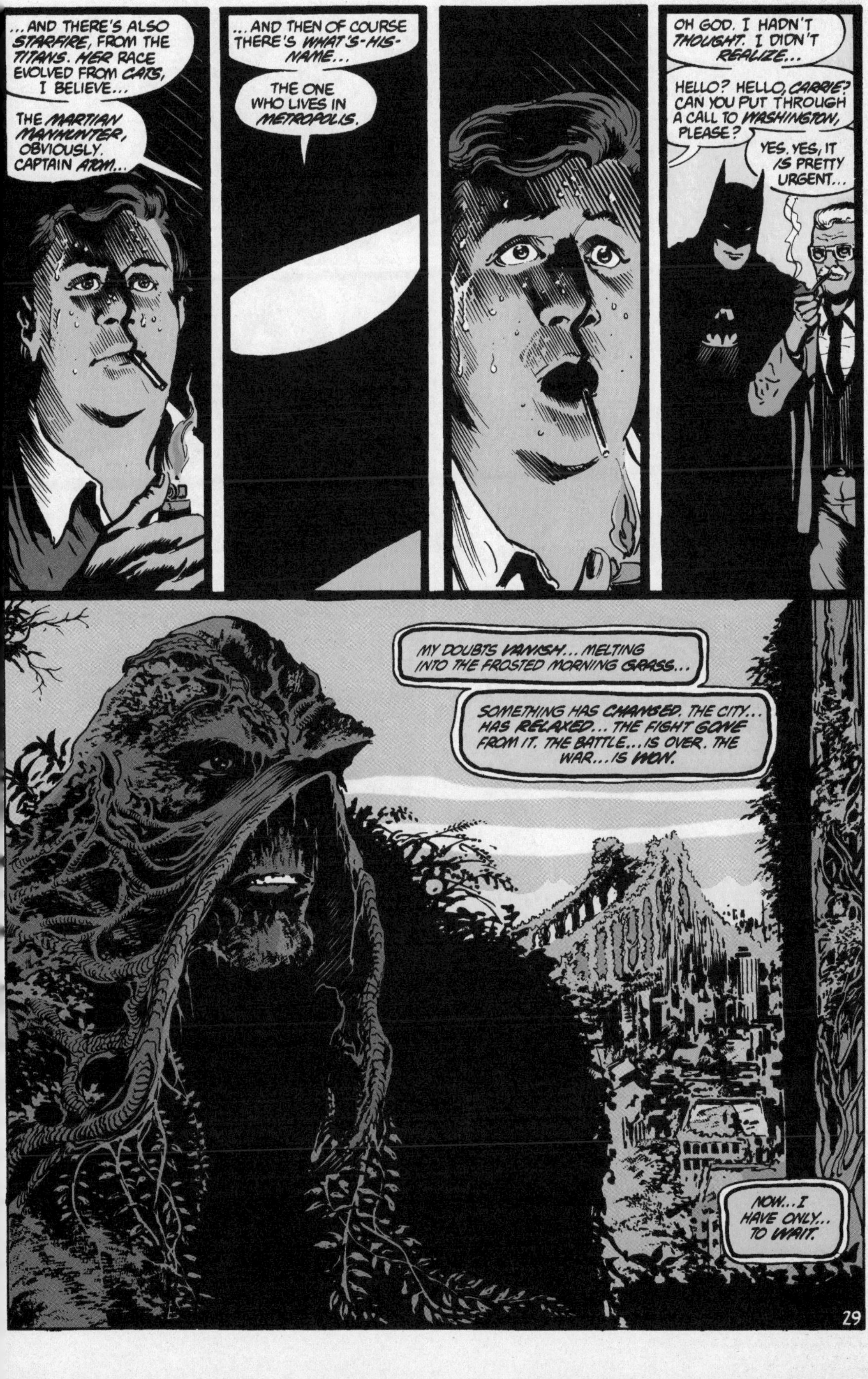
...AND THERE'S ALSO STARFIRE, FROM THE TITANS. HER RACE EVOLVED FROM CATS, I BELIEVE...
THE MARTIAN MANHUNTER, OBVIOUSLY. CAPTAIN ATOM...
...AND THEN OF COURSE THERE'S WHAT'S-HIS-NAME...
THE ONE WHO LIVES IN METROPOLIS.
OH GOD. I HADN'T THOUGHT. I DIDN'T REALIZE...
HELLO? HELLO, CARRIE? CAN YOU PUT THROUGH A CALL TO WASHINGTON, PLEASE?
YES. YES, IT IS PRETTY URGENT...
MY DOUBTS VANISH... MELTING INTO THE FROSTED MORNING GRASS...
SOMETHING HAS CHANGED. THE CITY... HAS RELAXED... THE FIGHT GONE FROM IT. THE BATTLE... IS OVER. THE WAR... IS WON.
NOW... I HAVE ONLY... TO WAIT.
29

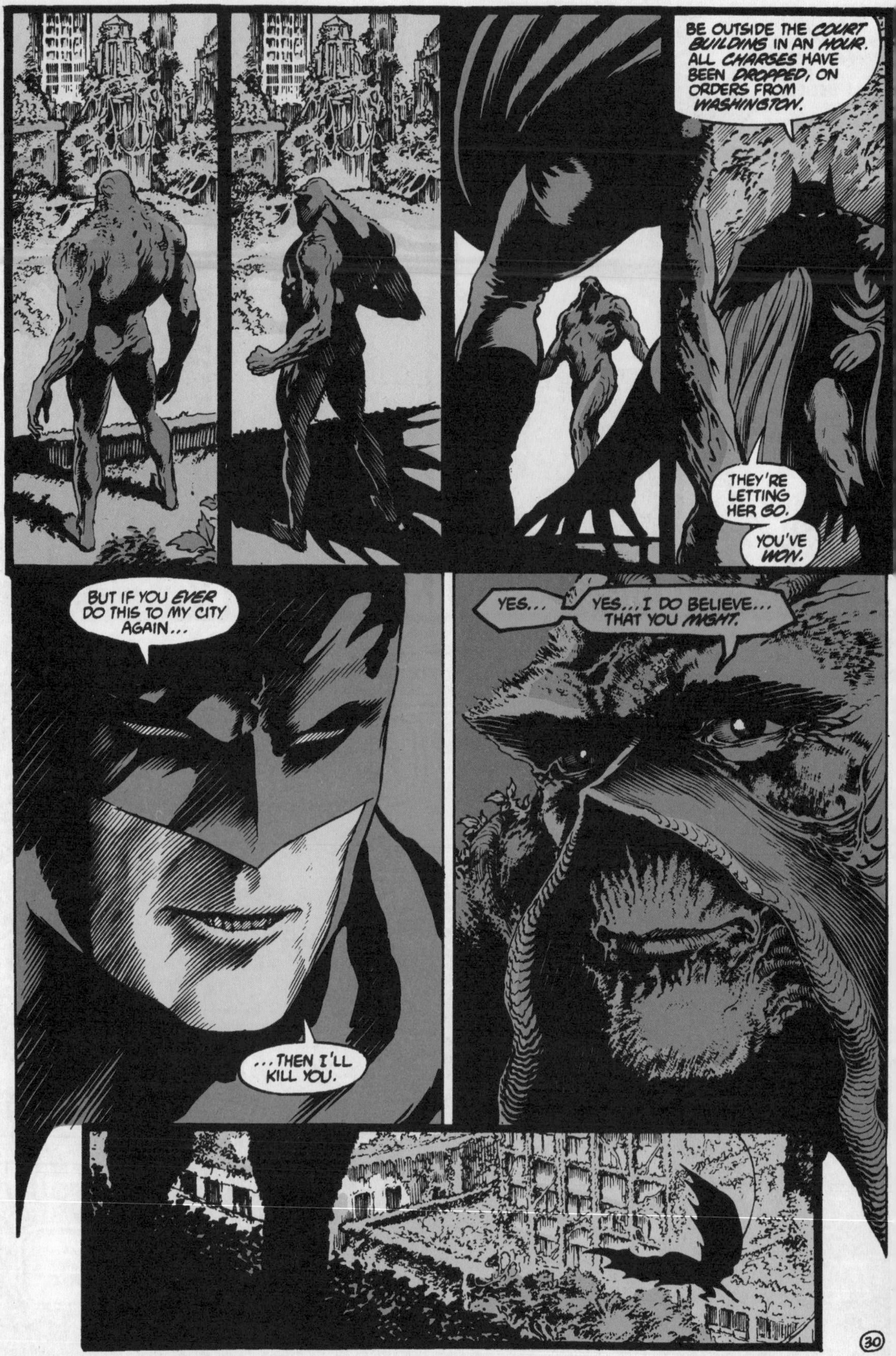
BE OUTSIDE THE COURT BUILDINGS IN AN HOUR. ALL CHARGES HAVE BEEN DROPPED, ON ORDERS FROM WASHINGTON.
THEY'RE LETTING HER GO.
YOU'VE WON.
BUT IF YOU EVER DO THIS TO MY CITY AGAIN...
...THEN I'LL KILL YOU.
YES...
YES... I DO BELIEVE... THAT YOU MIGHT.
30

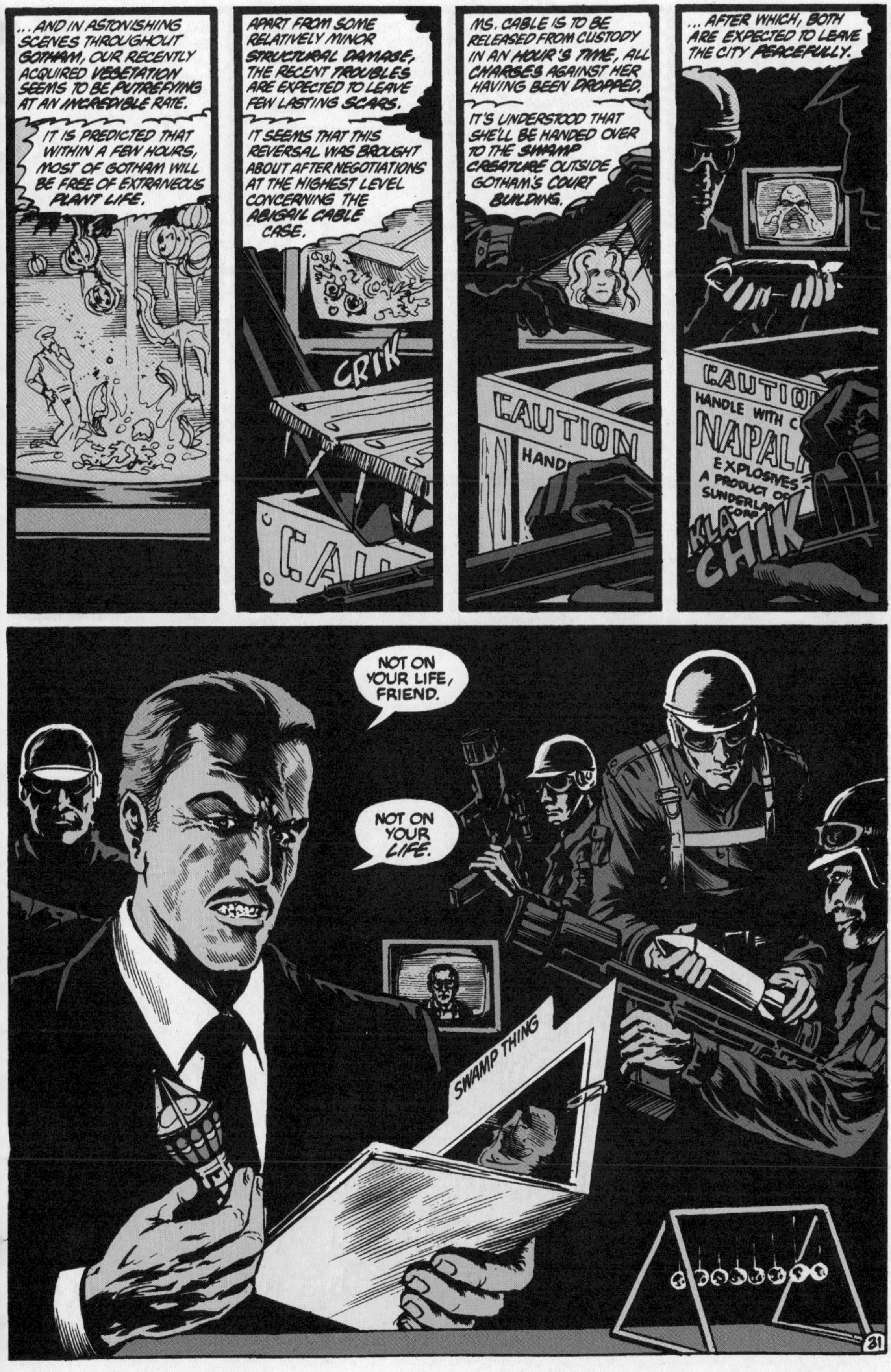
...AND IN ASTONISHING SCENES THROUGHOUT GOTHAM, OUR RECENTLY ACQUIRED VEGETATION SEEMS TO BE PUTREFYING AT AN INCREDIBLE RATE.
IT IS PREDICTED THAT WITHIN A FEW HOURS, MOST OF GOTHAM WILL BE FREE OF EXTRANEOUS PLANT LIFE.
APART FROM SOME RELATIVELY MINOR STRUCTURAL DAMAGE, THE RECENT TROUBLES ARE EXPECTED TO LEAVE FEW LASTING SCARS.
IT SEEMS THAT THIS REVERSAL WAS BROUGHT ABOUT AFTER NEGOTIATIONS AT THE HIGHEST LEVEL CONCERNING THE ABIGAIL CABLE CASE.
CRIK
MS. CABLE IS TO BE RELEASED FROM CUSTODY IN AN HOUR'S TIME, ALL CHARGES AGAINST HER HAVING BEEN DROPPED.
IT'S UNDERSTOOD THAT SHE'LL BE HANDED OVER TO THE SWAMP CREATURE OUTSIDE GOTHAM'S COURT BUILDING.
CAUTION
HAND
...AFTER WHICH, BOTH ARE EXPECTED TO LEAVE THE CITY PEACEFULLY.
CAUTIO
HANDLE WITH C
NAPAL
EXPLOSIVES
A PRODUCT OF
SUNDERLA
CORP
KLA CHIK
NOT ON YOUR LIFE, FRIEND.
NOT ON YOUR LIFE.
SWAMP THING
31

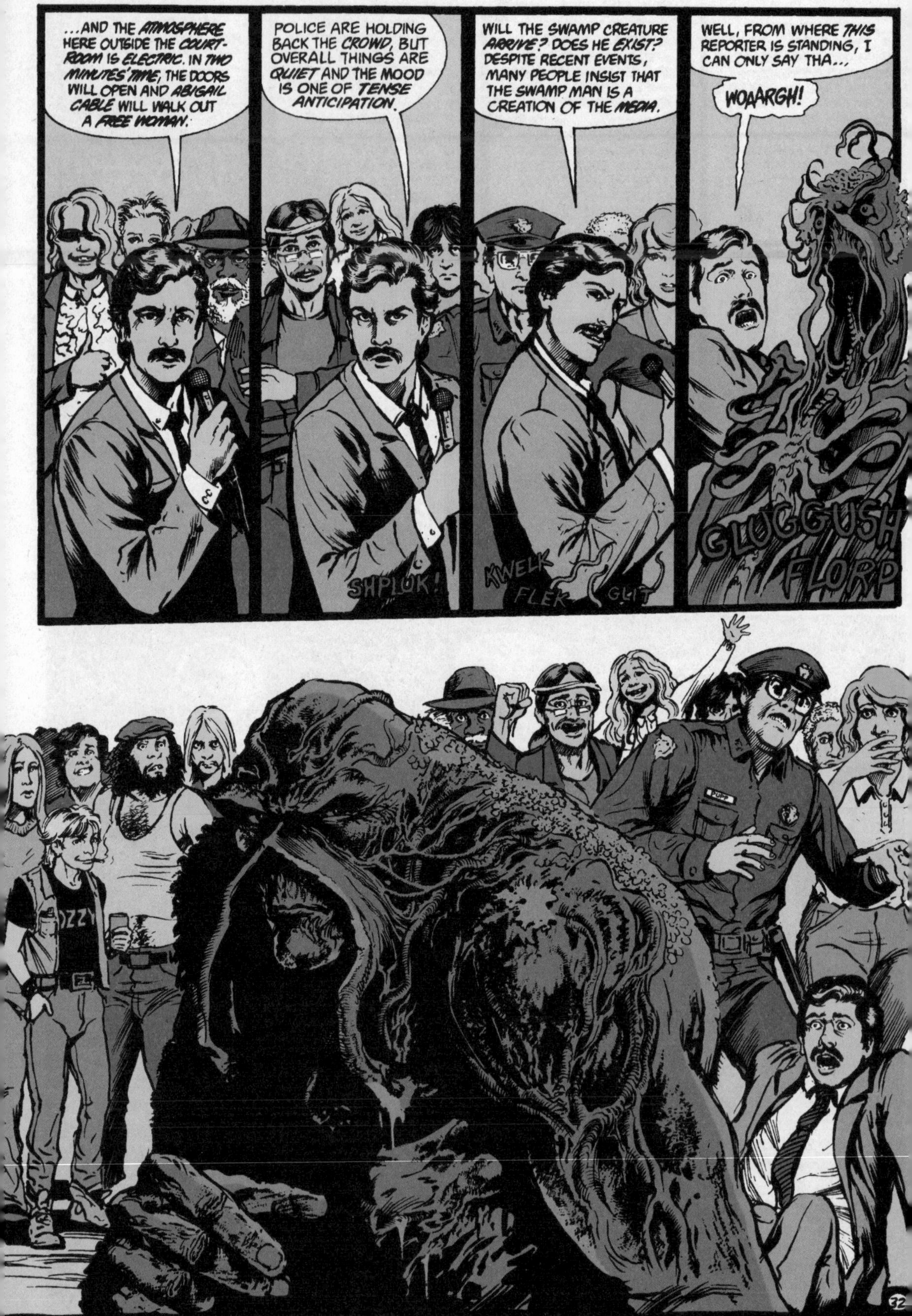
...AND THE ATMOSPHERE HERE OUTSIDE THE COURT-ROOM IS ELECTRIC. IN TWO MINUTES' TIME, THE DOORS WILL OPEN AND ABIGAIL CABLE WILL WALK OUT A FREE WOMAN.
POLICE ARE HOLDING BACK THE CROWD, BUT OVERALL THINGS ARE QUIET AND THE MOOD IS ONE OF TENSE ANTICIPATION.
SHPLUK!
WILL THE SWAMP CREATURE ARRIVE? DOES HE EXIST? DESPITE RECENT EVENTS, MANY PEOPLE INSIST THAT THE SWAMP MAN IS A CREATION OF THE MEDIA.
KWELK
FLEK
GLIT
WELL, FROM WHERE THIS REPORTER IS STANDING, I CAN ONLY SAY THA...
WOAARGH!
GLUGGUSH
FLORP
OZZY
PUPP
32

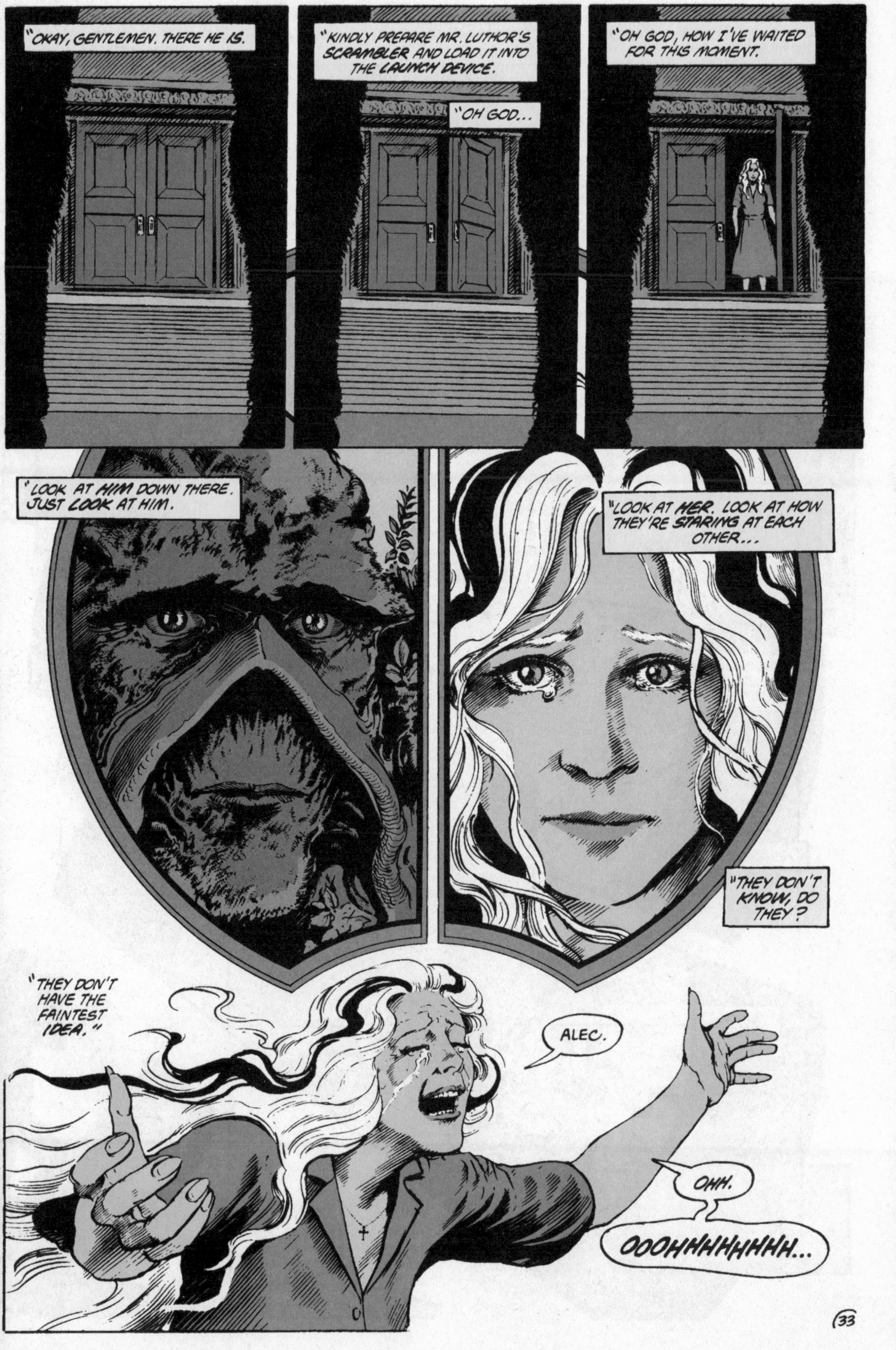
"OKAY, GENTLEMEN. THERE HE IS.
"KINDLY PREPARE MR. LUTHOR'S SCRAMBLER AND LOAD IT INTO THE LAUNCH DEVICE.
"OH GOD...
"OH GOD, HOW I'VE WAITED FOR THIS MOMENT.
"LOOK AT HIM DOWN THERE. JUST LOOK AT HIM.
"LOOK AT HER. LOOK AT HOW THEY'RE STARING AT EACH OTHER...
"THEY DON'T KNOW, DO THEY?
"THEY DON'T HAVE THE FAINTEST IDEA."
ALEC.
OHH.
OOOHHHHHHHH...
33

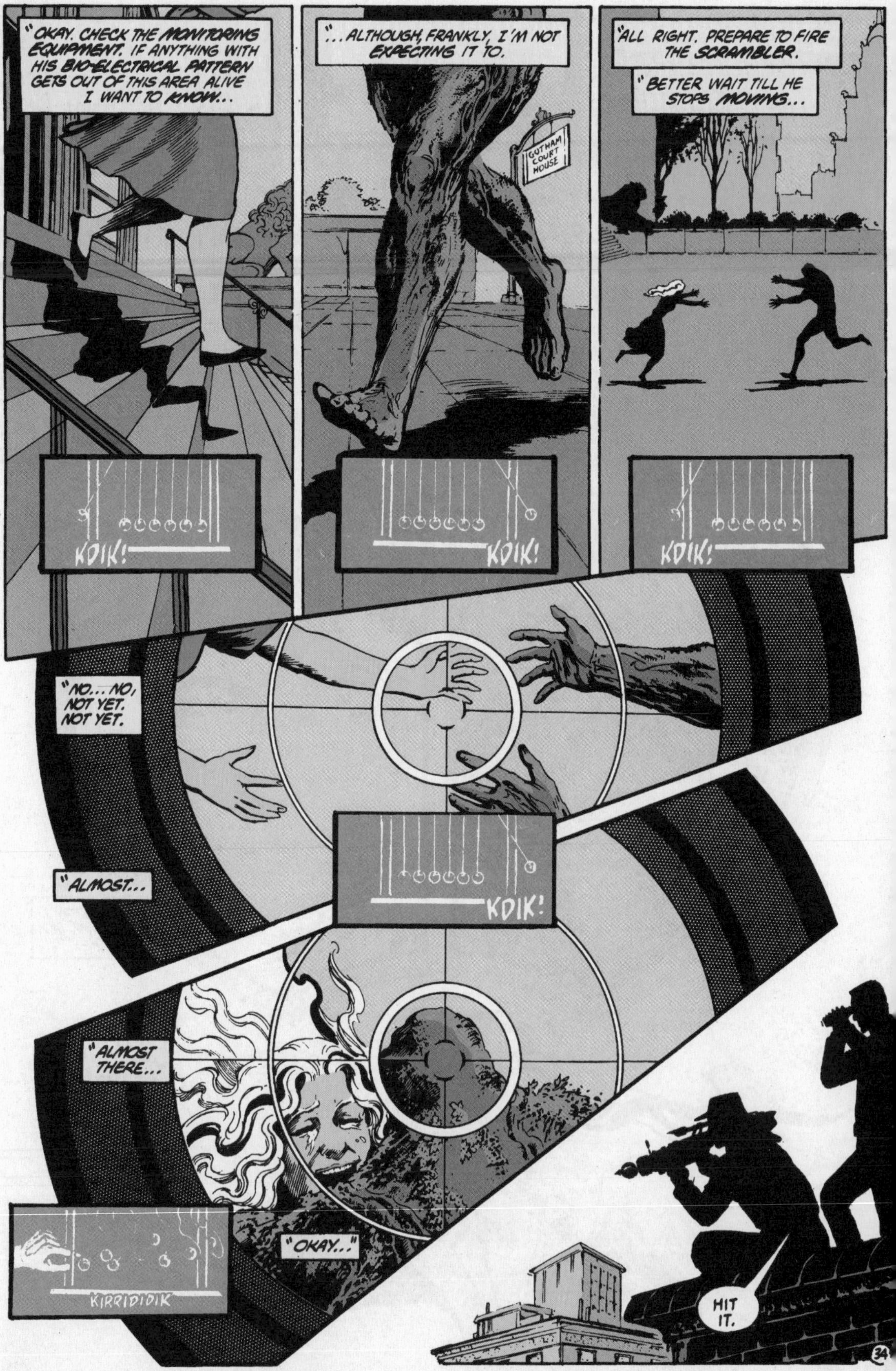
"OKAY. CHECK THE MONITORING EQUIPMENT. IF ANYTHING WITH HIS BIO-ELECTRICAL PATTERN GETS OUT OF THIS AREA ALIVE I WANT TO KNOW...
KDIK!
"...ALTHOUGH, FRANKLY, I'M NOT EXPECTING IT TO.
GOTHAM COURT HOUSE
KDIK!
"ALL RIGHT. PREPARE TO FIRE THE SCRAMBLER.
"BETTER WAIT TILL HE STOPS MOVING...
KDIK!
"NO... NO, NOT YET. NOT YET.
"ALMOST...
KDIK!
"ALMOST THERE...
KIRRIDIDIK
"OKAY..."
HIT IT.
34

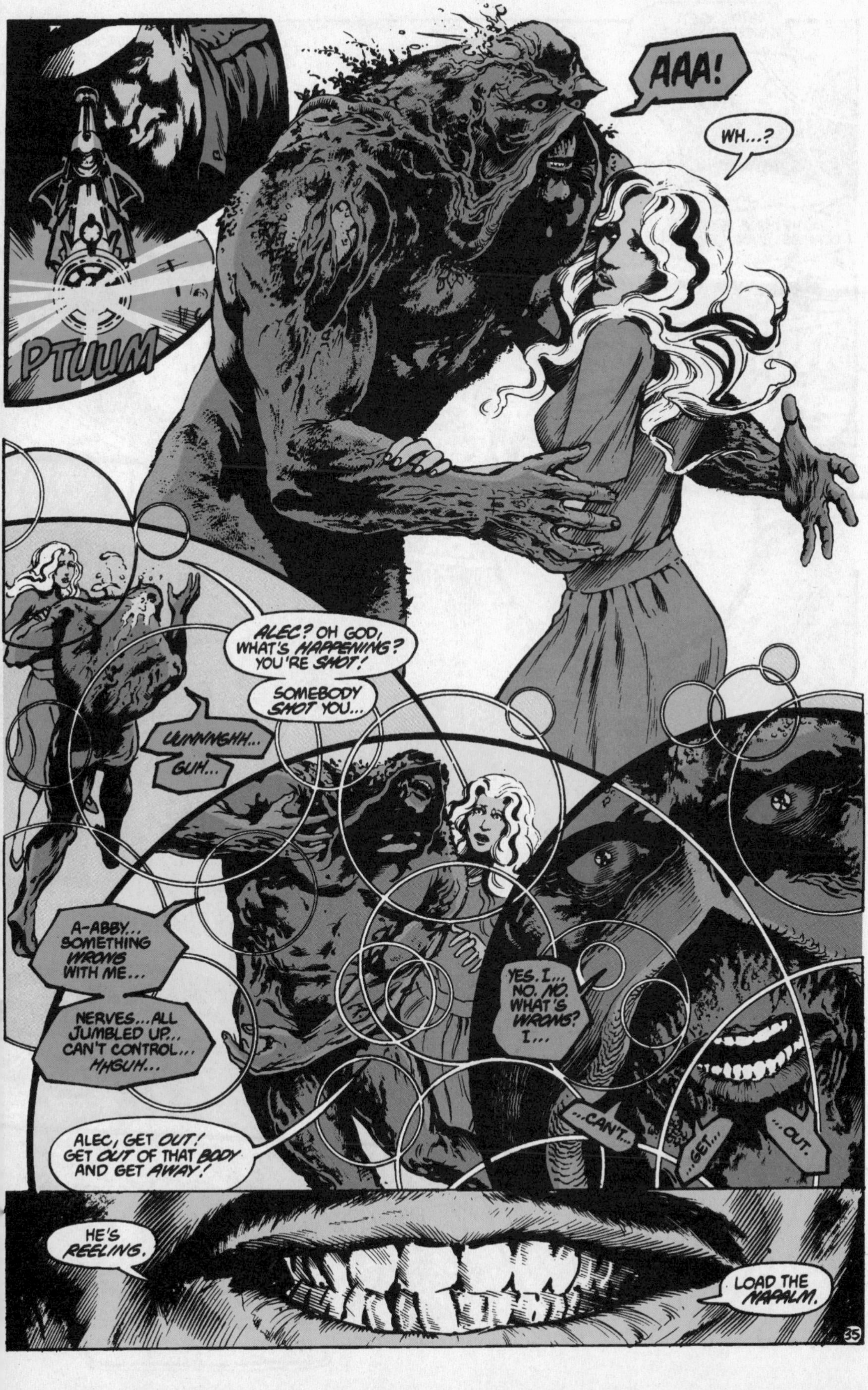
PTUUM
AAA!
WH...?
ALEC? OH GOD, WHAT'S HAPPENING? YOU'RE SHOT!
SOMEBODY SHOT YOU...
UUNNNGHH... GUH...
A-ABBY... SOMETHING WRONG WITH ME...
NERVES... ALL JUMBLED UP... CAN'T CONTROL... HHGUH...
YES. I... NO. NO. WHAT'S WRONG? I...
ALEC, GET OUT! GET OUT OF THAT BODY AND GET AWAY!
...CAN'T...
...GET...
...OUT.
HE'S REELING.
LOAD THE NAPALM.
35

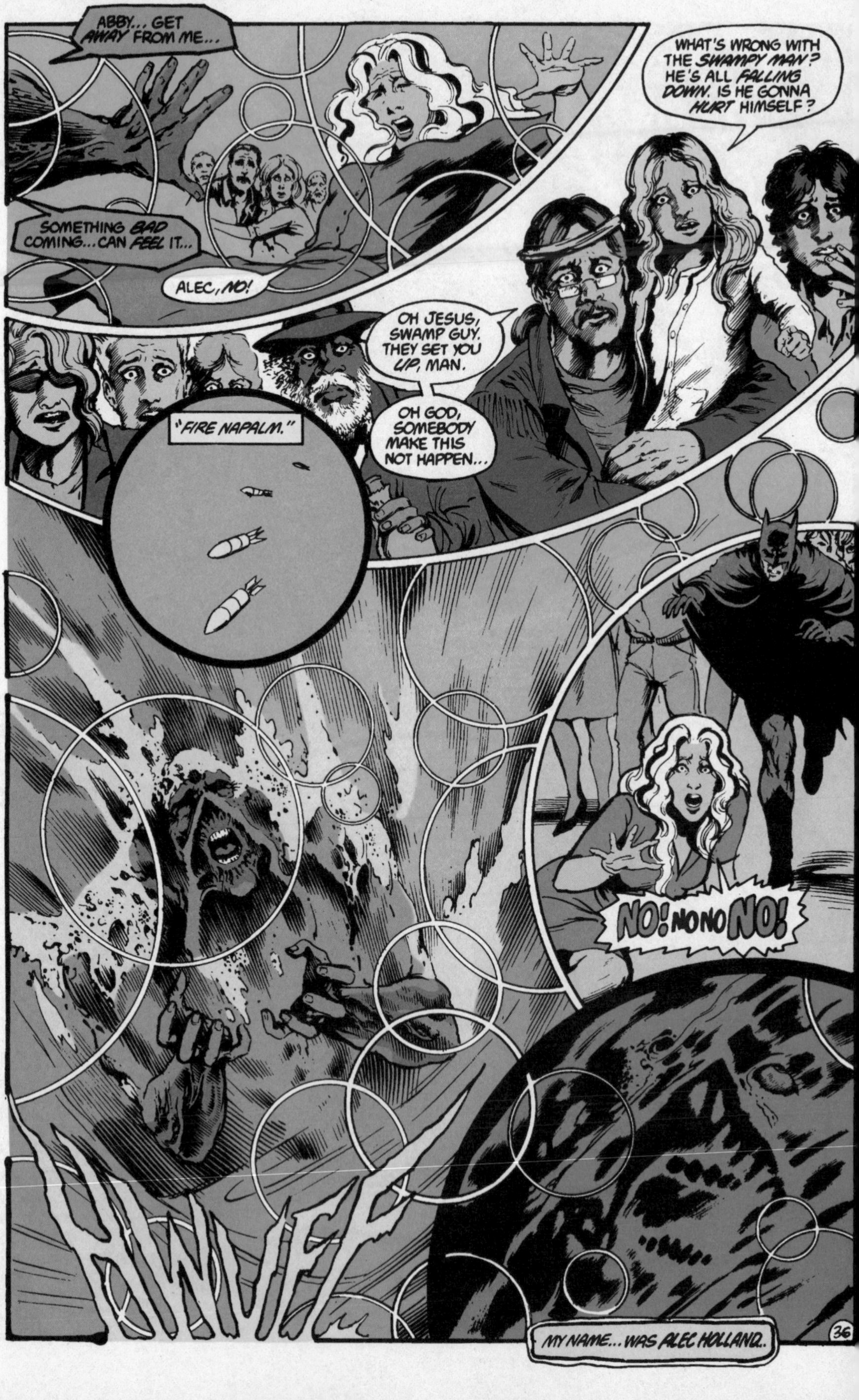
ABBY... GET AWAY FROM ME...
SOMETHING BAD COMING... CAN FEEL IT...
ALEC, NO!
WHAT'S WRONG WITH THE SWAMPY MAN? HE'S ALL FALLING DOWN. IS HE GONNA HURT HIMSELF?
OH JESUS, SWAMP GUY. THEY SET YOU UP, MAN.
OH GOD, SOMEBODY MAKE THIS NOT HAPPEN...
"FIRE NAPALM."
NO! NO NO NO!
HWUFF
MY NAME... WAS ALEC HOLLAND...
36

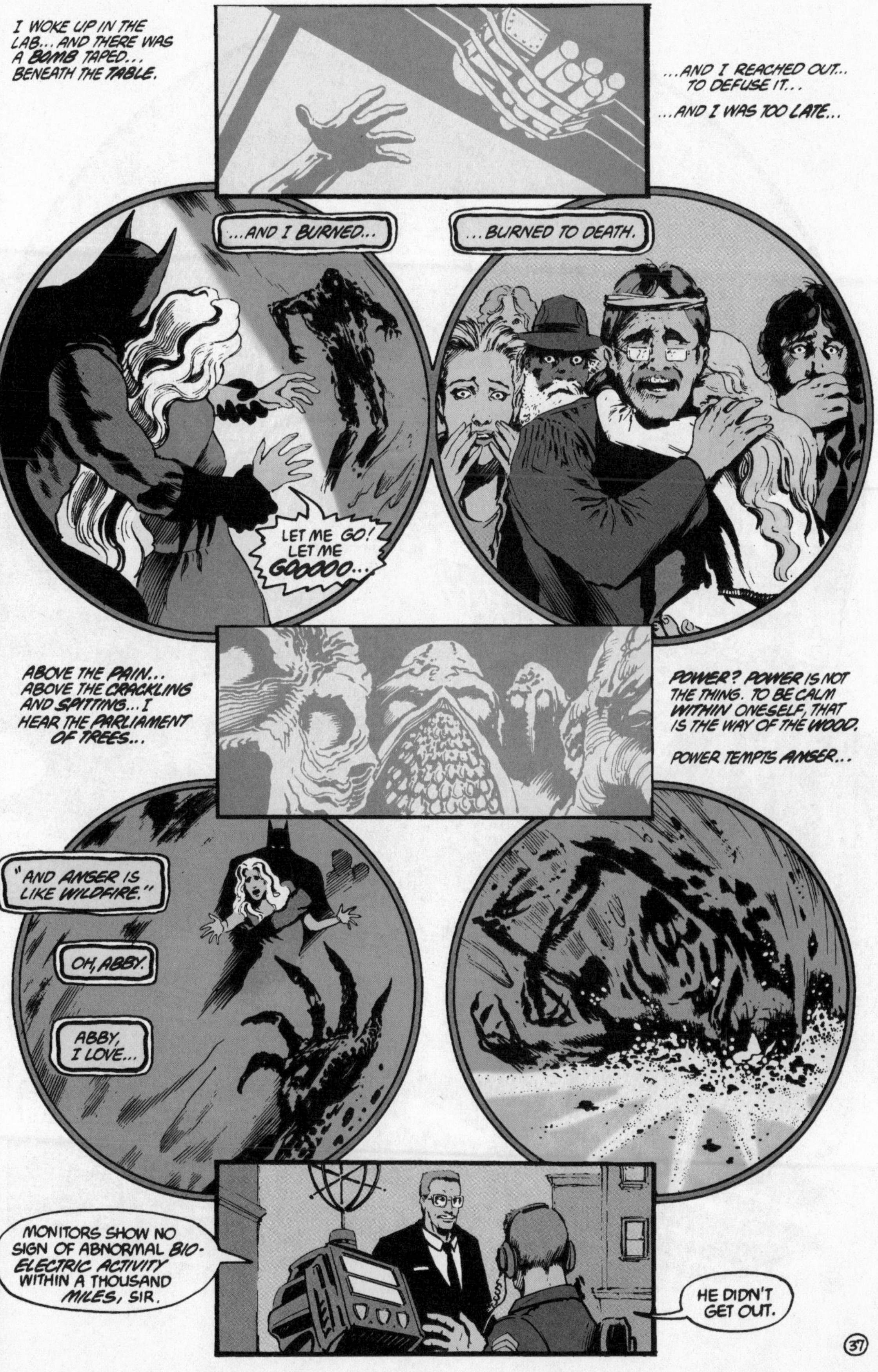
I WOKE UP IN THE LAB... AND THERE WAS A BOMB TAPED... BENEATH THE TABLE.
...AND I REACHED OUT... TO DEFUSE IT...
...AND I WAS TOO LATE...
...AND I BURNED...
...BURNED TO DEATH.
LET ME GO! LET ME GOOOOO...
ABOVE THE PAIN... ABOVE THE CRACKLING AND SPITTING... I HEAR THE PARLIAMENT OF TREES...
POWER? POWER IS NOT THE THING. TO BE CALM WITHIN ONESELF, THAT IS THE WAY OF THE WOOD.
POWER TEMPTS ANGER...
"AND ANGER IS LIKE WILDFIRE."
OH, ABBY.
ABBY, I LOVE...
MONITORS SHOW NO SIGN OF ABNORMAL BIO-ELECTRIC ACTIVITY WITHIN A THOUSAND MILES, SIR.
HE DIDN'T GET OUT.
37

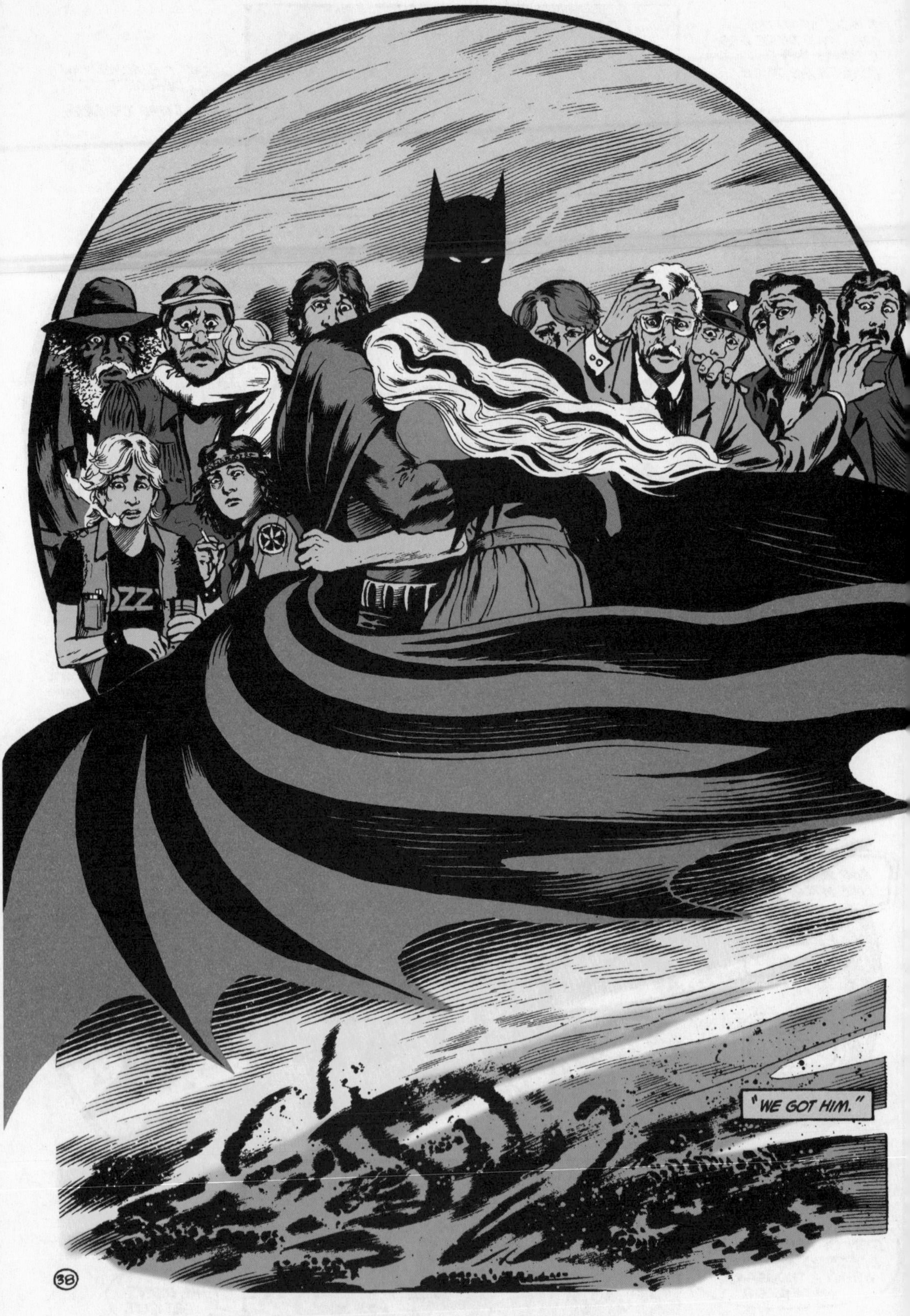
"WE GOT HIM."
38

Chapter 4

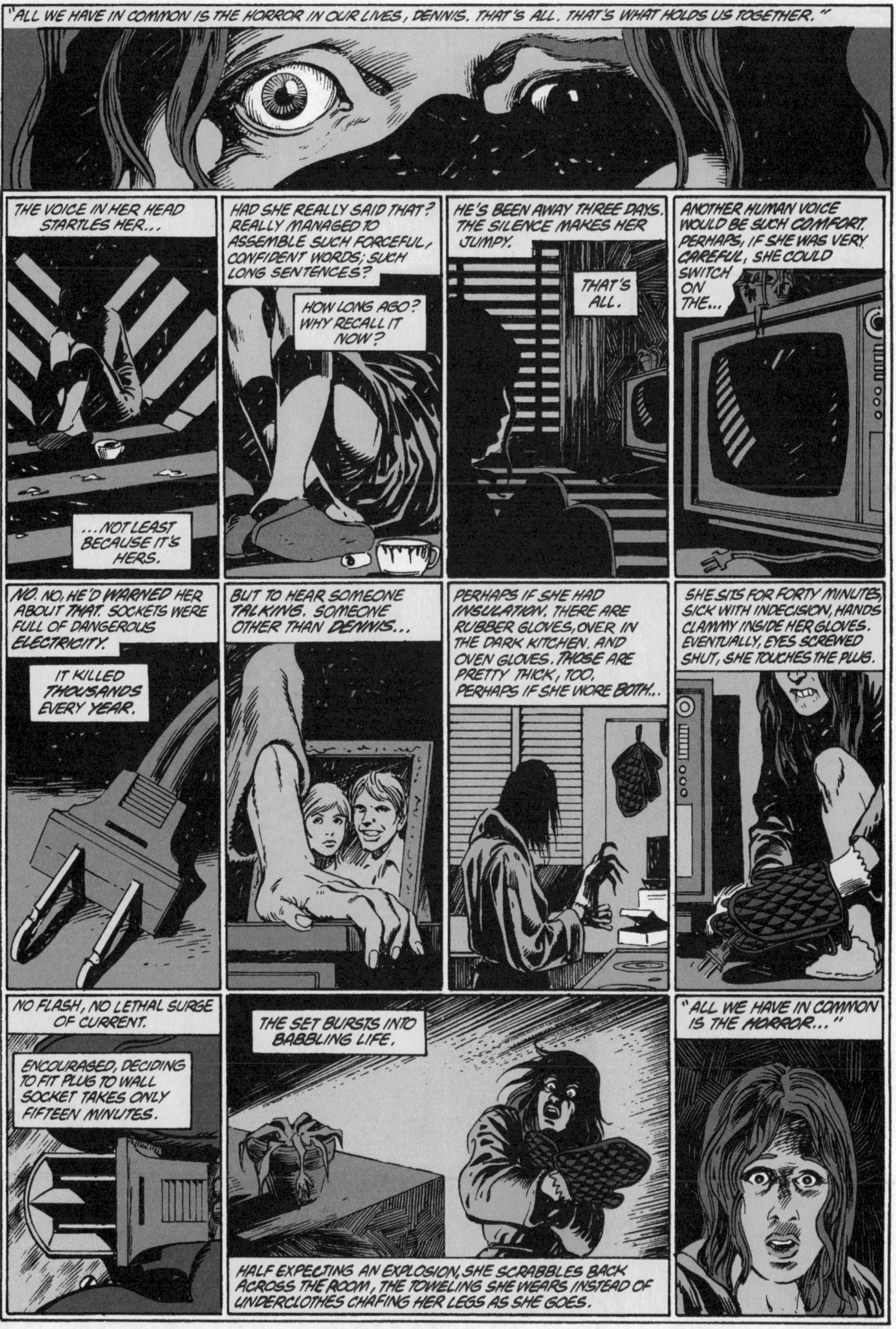
"ALL WE HAVE IN COMMON IS THE HORROR IN OUR LIVES, DENNIS. THAT'S ALL. THAT'S WHAT HOLDS US TOGETHER."
THE VOICE IN HER HEAD STARTLES HER...
...NOT LEAST BECAUSE IT'S HERS.
HAD SHE REALLY SAID THAT? REALLY MANAGED TO ASSEMBLE SUCH FORCEFUL, CONFIDENT WORDS; SUCH LONG SENTENCES?
HOW LONG AGO? WHY RECALL IT NOW?
HE'S BEEN AWAY THREE DAYS. THE SILENCE MAKES HER JUMPY.
THAT'S ALL.
ANOTHER HUMAN VOICE WOULD BE SUCH COMFORT. PERHAPS, IF SHE WAS VERY CAREFUL, SHE COULD SWITCH ON THE...
NO. NO, HE'D WARNED HER ABOUT THAT. SOCKETS WERE FULL OF DANGEROUS ELECTRICITY.
IT KILLED THOUSANDS EVERY YEAR.
BUT TO HEAR SOMEONE TALKING. SOMEONE OTHER THAN DENNIS...
PERHAPS IF SHE HAD INSULATION. THERE ARE RUBBER GLOVES, OVER IN THE DARK KITCHEN. AND OVEN GLOVES. THOSE ARE PRETTY THICK, TOO. PERHAPS IF SHE WORE BOTH...
SHE SITS FOR FORTY MINUTES, SICK WITH INDECISION, HANDS CLAMMY INSIDE HER GLOVES. EVENTUALLY, EYES SCREWED SHUT, SHE TOUCHES THE PLUG.
NO FLASH, NO LETHAL SURGE OF CURRENT.
ENCOURAGED, DECIDING TO FIT PLUG TO WALL SOCKET TAKES ONLY FIFTEEN MINUTES.
THE SET BURSTS INTO BABBLING LIFE.
HALF EXPECTING AN EXPLOSION, SHE SCRABBLES BACK ACROSS THE ROOM, THE TOWELING SHE WEARS INSTEAD OF UNDERCLOTHES CHAFING HER LEGS AS SHE GOES.
"ALL WE HAVE IN COMMON IS THE HORROR..."

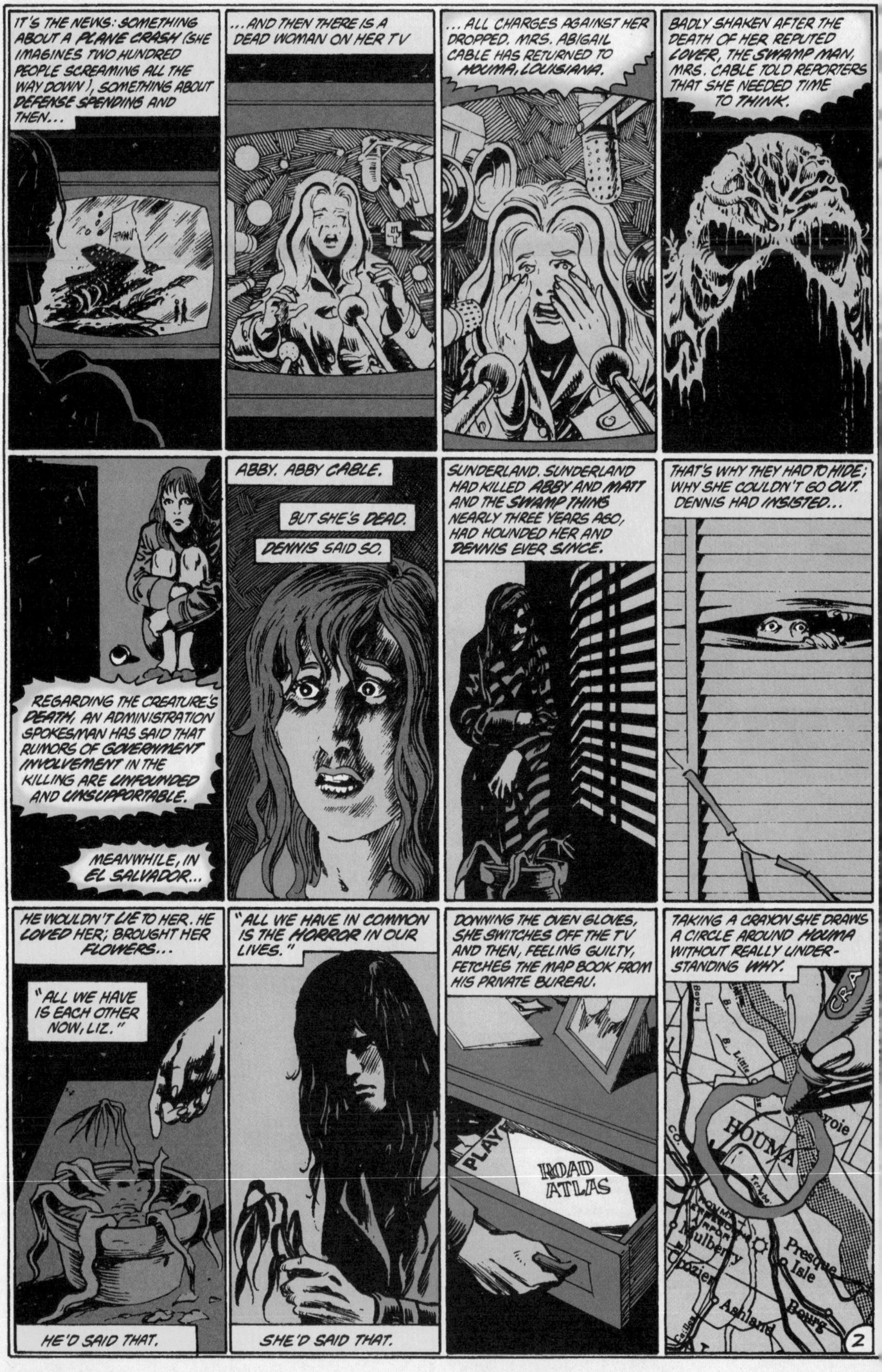
IT'S THE NEWS: SOMETHING ABOUT A PLANE CRASH (SHE IMAGINES TWO HUNDRED PEOPLE SCREAMING ALL THE WAY DOWN), SOMETHING ABOUT DEFENSE SPENDING AND THEN...
...AND THEN THERE IS A DEAD WOMAN ON HER TV
...ALL CHARGES AGAINST HER DROPPED. MRS. ABIGAIL CABLE HAS RETURNED TO HOUMA, LOUISIANA.
BADLY SHAKEN AFTER THE DEATH OF HER REPUTED LOVER, THE SWAMP MAN, MRS. CABLE TOLD REPORTERS THAT SHE NEEDED TIME TO THINK.
REGARDING THE CREATURE'S DEATH, AN ADMINISTRATION SPOKESMAN HAS SAID THAT RUMORS OF GOVERNMENT INVOLVEMENT IN THE KILLING ARE UNFOUNDED AND UNSUPPORTABLE.
MEANWHILE, IN EL SALVADOR...
ABBY. ABBY CABLE.
BUT SHE'S DEAD.
DENNIS SAID SO.
SUNDERLAND. SUNDERLAND HAD KILLED ABBY AND MATT AND THE SWAMP THING NEARLY THREE YEARS AGO, HAD HOUNDED HER AND DENNIS EVER SINCE.
THAT'S WHY THEY HAD TO HIDE; WHY SHE COULDN'T GO OUT. DENNIS HAD INSISTED...
HE WOULDN'T LIE TO HER. HE LOVED HER; BROUGHT HER FLOWERS...
"ALL WE HAVE IS EACH OTHER NOW, LIZ."
HE'D SAID THAT.
"ALL WE HAVE IN COMMON IS THE HORROR IN OUR LIVES."
SHE'D SAID THAT.
DONNING THE OVEN GLOVES, SHE SWITCHES OFF THE TV AND THEN, FEELING GUILTY, FETCHES THE MAP BOOK FROM HIS PRIVATE BUREAU.
PLAY
ROAD ATLAS
TAKING A CRAYON SHE DRAWS A CIRCLE AROUND HOUMA WITHOUT REALLY UNDERSTANDING WHY.
CRA
HOUMA
Presque Isle
Mulberry
Ashland
Bourg
2

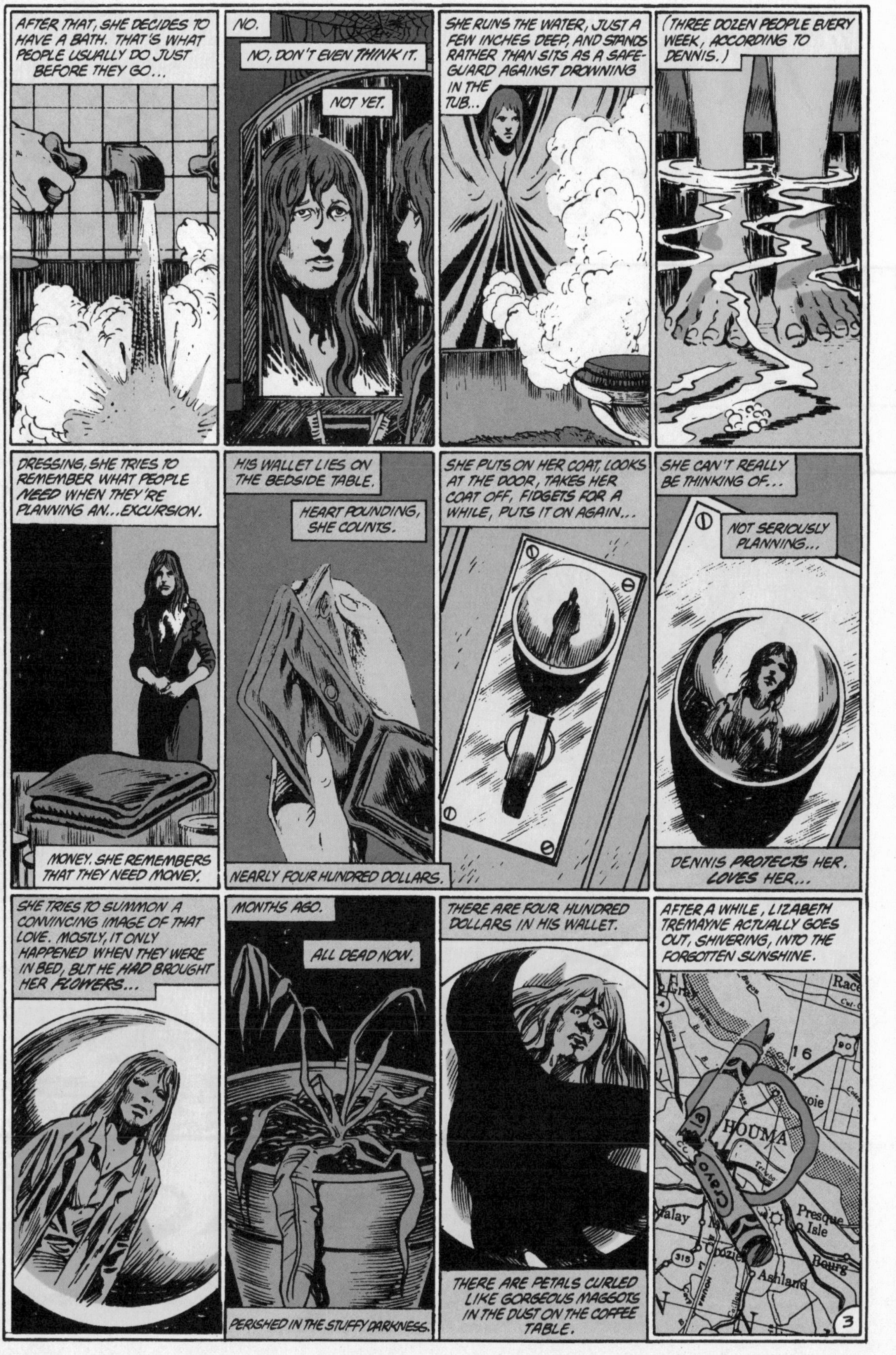
AFTER THAT, SHE DECIDES TO HAVE A BATH. THAT'S WHAT PEOPLE USUALLY DO JUST BEFORE THEY GO...
NO.
NO, DON'T EVEN THINK IT.
NOT YET.
SHE RUNS THE WATER, JUST A FEW INCHES DEEP, AND STANDS RATHER THAN SITS AS A SAFE-GUARD AGAINST DROWNING IN THE TUB...
(THREE DOZEN PEOPLE EVERY WEEK, ACCORDING TO DENNIS.)
DRESSING, SHE TRIES TO REMEMBER WHAT PEOPLE NEED WHEN THEY'RE PLANNING AN...EXCURSION.
MONEY. SHE REMEMBERS THAT THEY NEED MONEY.
HIS WALLET LIES ON THE BEDSIDE TABLE.
HEART POUNDING, SHE COUNTS.
NEARLY FOUR HUNDRED DOLLARS.
SHE PUTS ON HER COAT, LOOKS AT THE DOOR, TAKES HER COAT OFF, FIDGETS FOR A WHILE, PUTS IT ON AGAIN...
SHE CAN'T REALLY BE THINKING OF...
NOT SERIOUSLY PLANNING...
DENNIS PROTECTS HER. LOVES HER...
SHE TRIES TO SUMMON A CONVINCING IMAGE OF THAT LOVE. MOSTLY, IT ONLY HAPPENED WHEN THEY WERE IN BED, BUT HE HAD BROUGHT HER FLOWERS...
MONTHS AGO.
ALL DEAD NOW.
PERISHED IN THE STUFFY DARKNESS.
THERE ARE FOUR HUNDRED DOLLARS IN HIS WALLET.
THERE ARE PETALS CURLED LIKE GORGEOUS MAGGOTS IN THE DUST ON THE COFFEE TABLE.
AFTER A WHILE, LIZABETH TREMAYNE ACTUALLY GOES OUT, SHIVERING, INTO THE FORGOTTEN SUNSHINE.
HOUMA
Presque Isle
Ashland
Bourg
3

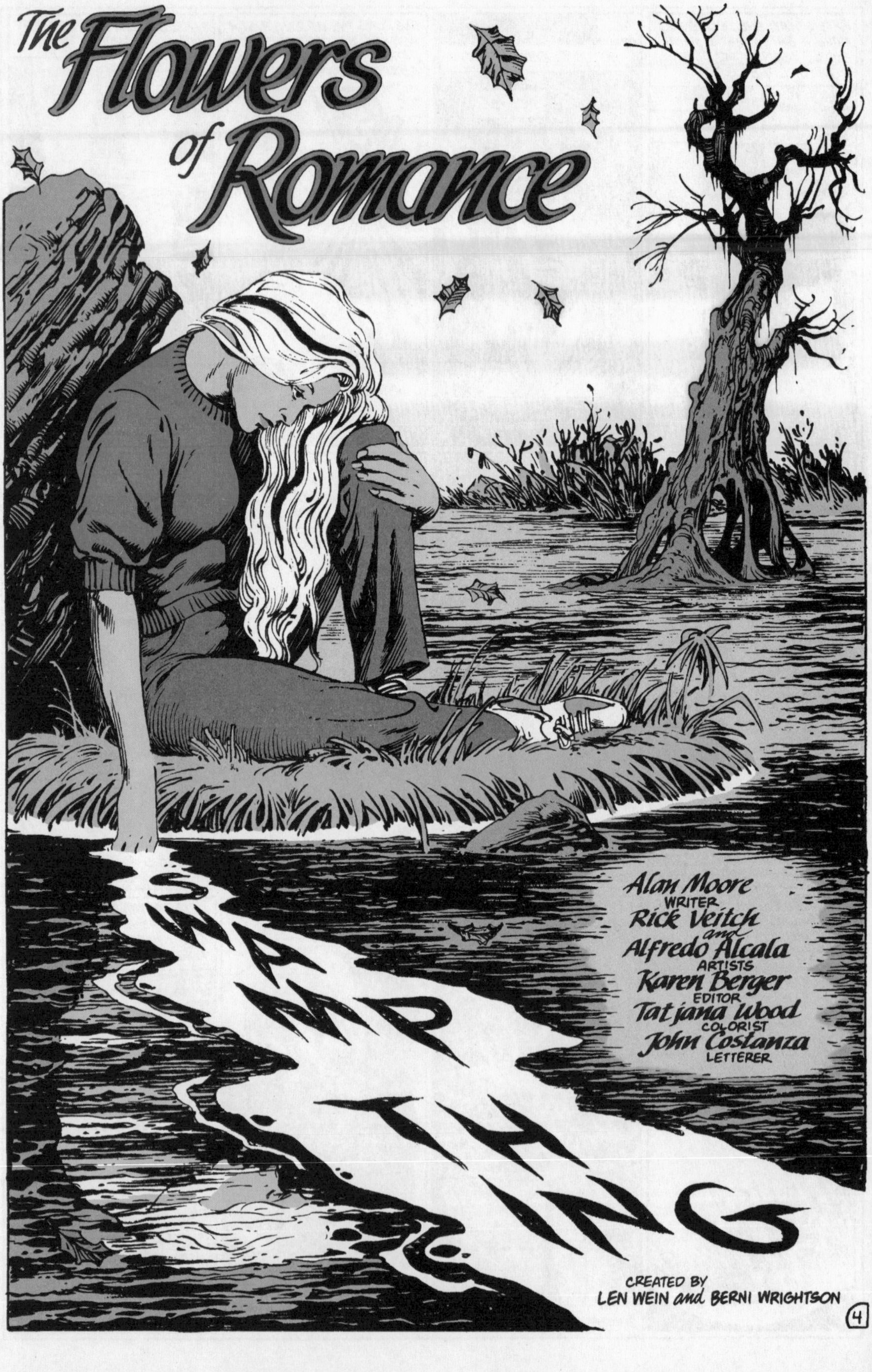
The Flowers of Romance
SWAMP THING
Alan Moore
WRITER
Rick Veitch
and
Alfredo Alcala
ARTISTS
Karen Berger
EDITOR
Tatjana Wood
COLORIST
John Costanza
LETTERER
CREATED BY
LEN WEIN and BERNI WRIGHTSON
4

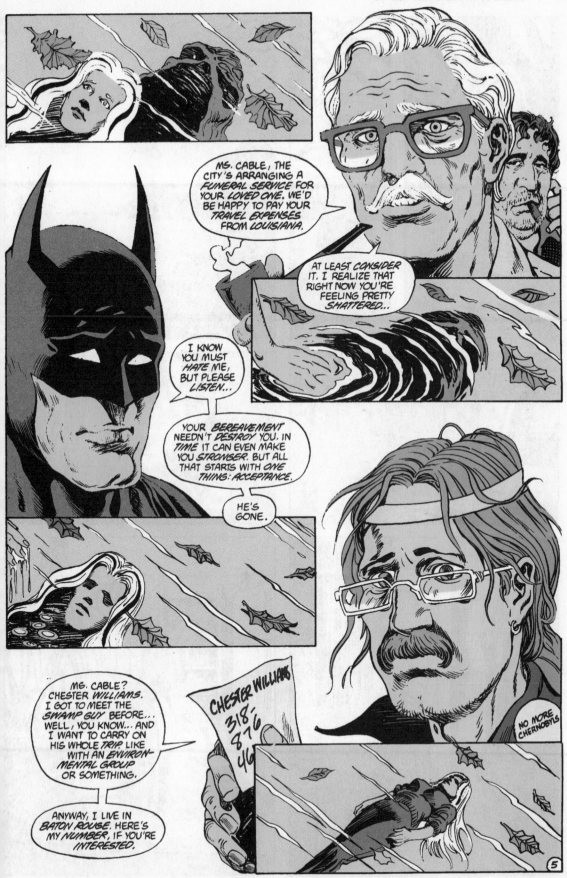

MS. CABLE, THE CITY'S ARRANGING A *FUNERAL SERVICE* FOR YOUR *LOVED ONE*. WE'D BE HAPPY TO PAY YOUR *TRAVEL EXPENSES* FROM *LOUISIANA*.

AT LEAST *CONSIDER* IT. I REALIZE THAT RIGHT NOW YOU'RE FEELING PRETTY *SHATTERED*...

I KNOW YOU MUST *HATE* ME, BUT PLEASE *LISTEN*...

YOUR *BEREAVEMENT* NEEDN'T *DESTROY* YOU. IN *TIME* IT CAN EVEN MAKE YOU *STRONGER*. BUT ALL THAT STARTS WITH *ONE THING: ACCEPTANCE*.

HE'S GONE.

MS. CABLE? CHESTER *WILLIAMS*. I GOT TO MEET THE *SWAMP GUY* BEFORE... WELL, YOU KNOW... AND I WANT TO CARRY ON HIS WHOLE *TRIP*, LIKE WITH AN *ENVIRON-MENTAL GROUP* OR SOMETHING.

ANYWAY, I LIVE IN *BATON ROUGE*, HERE'S MY *NUMBER*, IF YOU'RE *INTERESTED*.

CHESTER WILLIAMS
318-
876-
46

NO MORE CHERNOBYLS

5

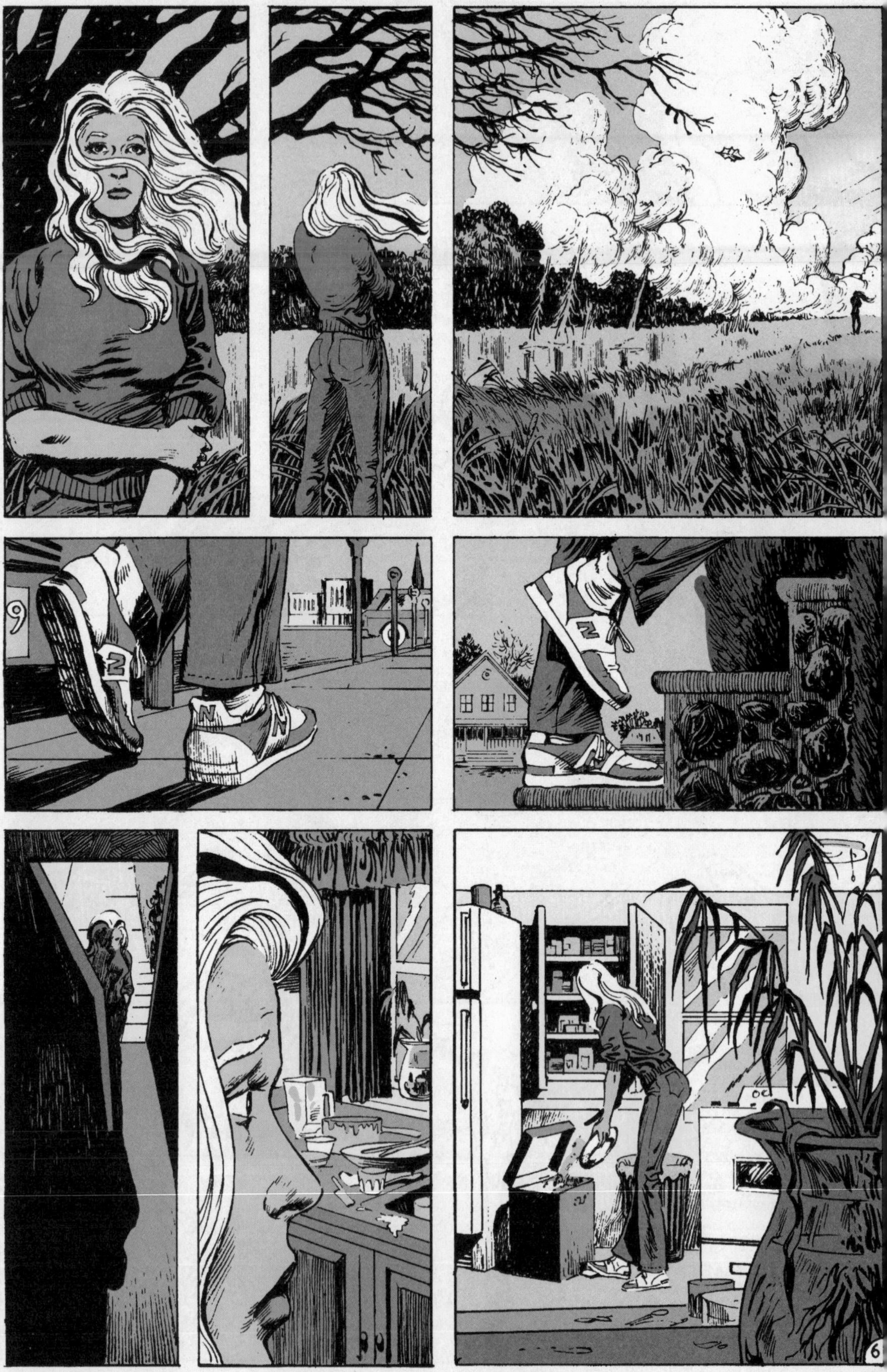

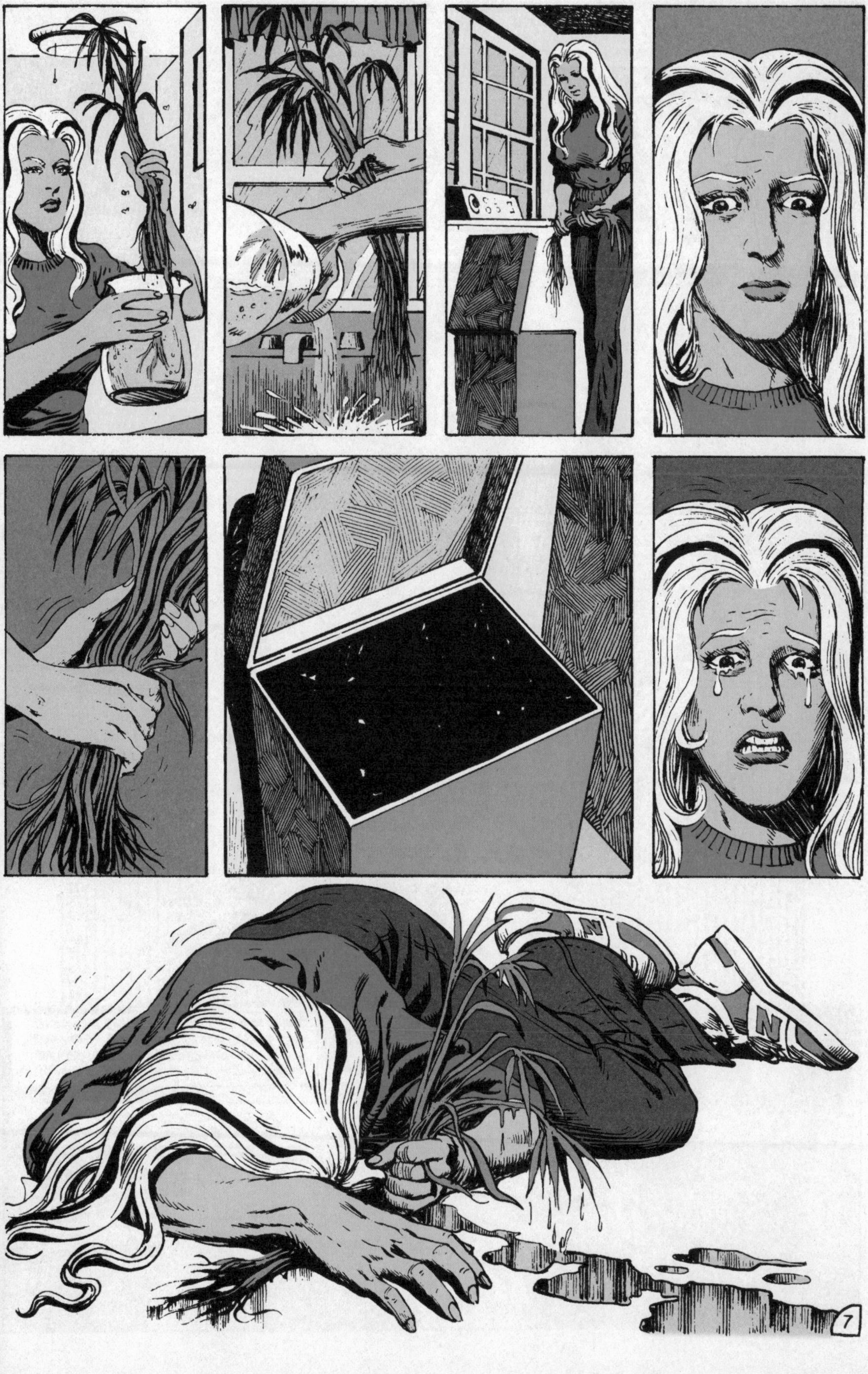
7

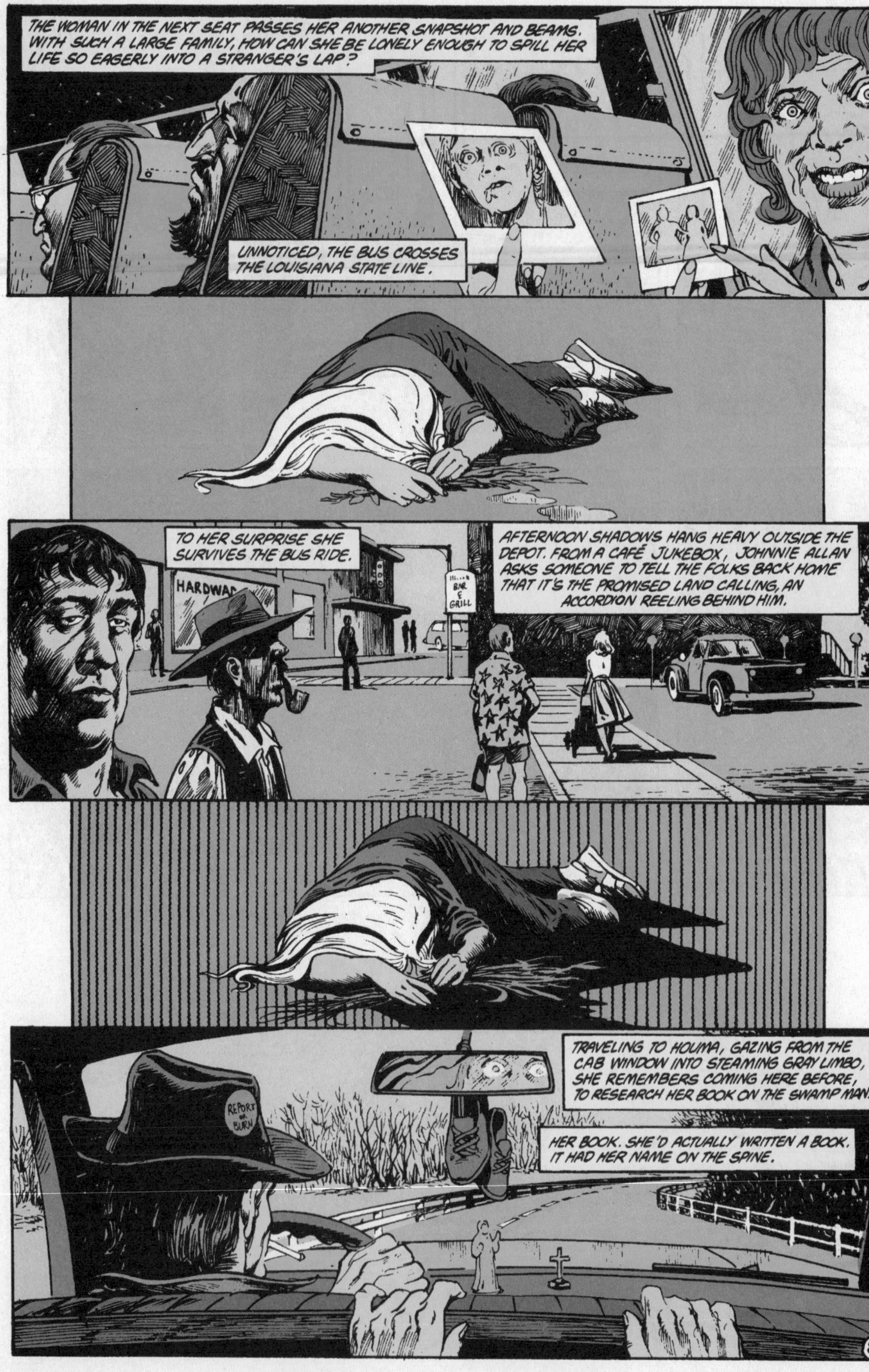
THE WOMAN IN THE NEXT SEAT PASSES HER ANOTHER SNAPSHOT AND BEAMS. WITH SUCH A LARGE FAMILY, HOW CAN SHE BE LONELY ENOUGH TO SPILL HER LIFE SO EAGERLY INTO A STRANGER'S LAP?
UNNOTICED, THE BUS CROSSES THE LOUISIANA STATE LINE.
TO HER SURPRISE SHE SURVIVES THE BUS RIDE.
AFTERNOON SHADOWS HANG HEAVY OUTSIDE THE DEPOT. FROM A CAFÉ JUKEBOX, JOHNNIE ALLAN ASKS SOMEONE TO TELL THE FOLKS BACK HOME THAT IT'S THE PROMISED LAND CALLING, AN ACCORDION REELING BEHIND HIM.
TRAVELING TO HOUMA, GAZING FROM THE CAB WINDOW INTO STEAMING GRAY LIMBO, SHE REMEMBERS COMING HERE BEFORE, TO RESEARCH HER BOOK ON THE SWAMP MAN.
HER BOOK. SHE'D ACTUALLY WRITTEN A BOOK. IT HAD HER NAME ON THE SPINE.
8

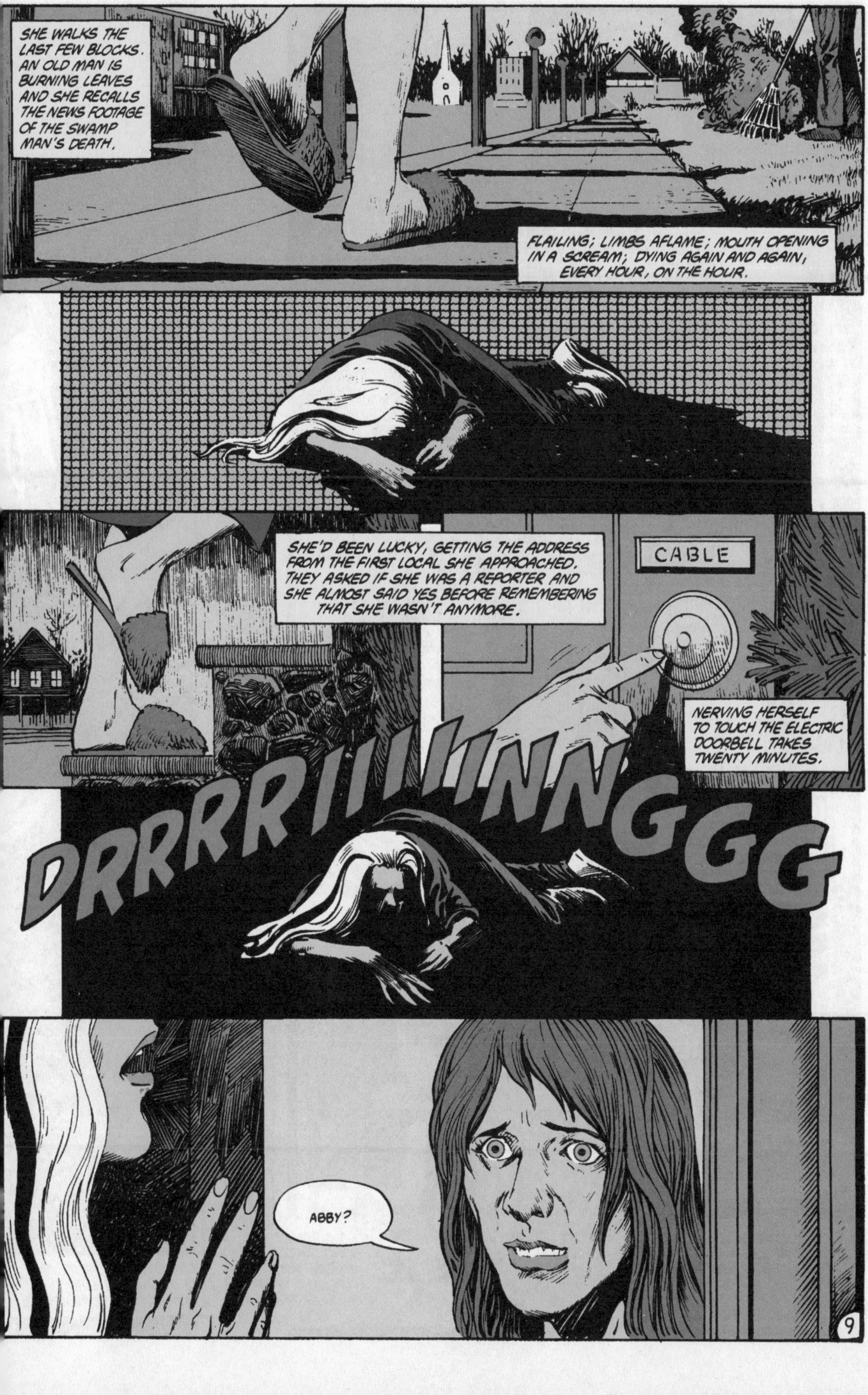
SHE WALKS THE LAST FEW BLOCKS. AN OLD MAN IS BURNING LEAVES AND SHE RECALLS THE NEWS FOOTAGE OF THE SWAMP MAN'S DEATH.
FLAILING; LIMBS AFLAME; MOUTH OPENING IN A SCREAM; DYING AGAIN AND AGAIN, EVERY HOUR, ON THE HOUR.
SHE'D BEEN LUCKY, GETTING THE ADDRESS FROM THE FIRST LOCAL SHE APPROACHED. THEY ASKED IF SHE WAS A REPORTER AND SHE ALMOST SAID YES BEFORE REMEMBERING THAT SHE WASN'T ANYMORE.
CABLE
NERVING HERSELF TO TOUCH THE ELECTRIC DOORBELL TAKES TWENTY MINUTES.
DRRRRIIIIINNGGG
ABBY?
9

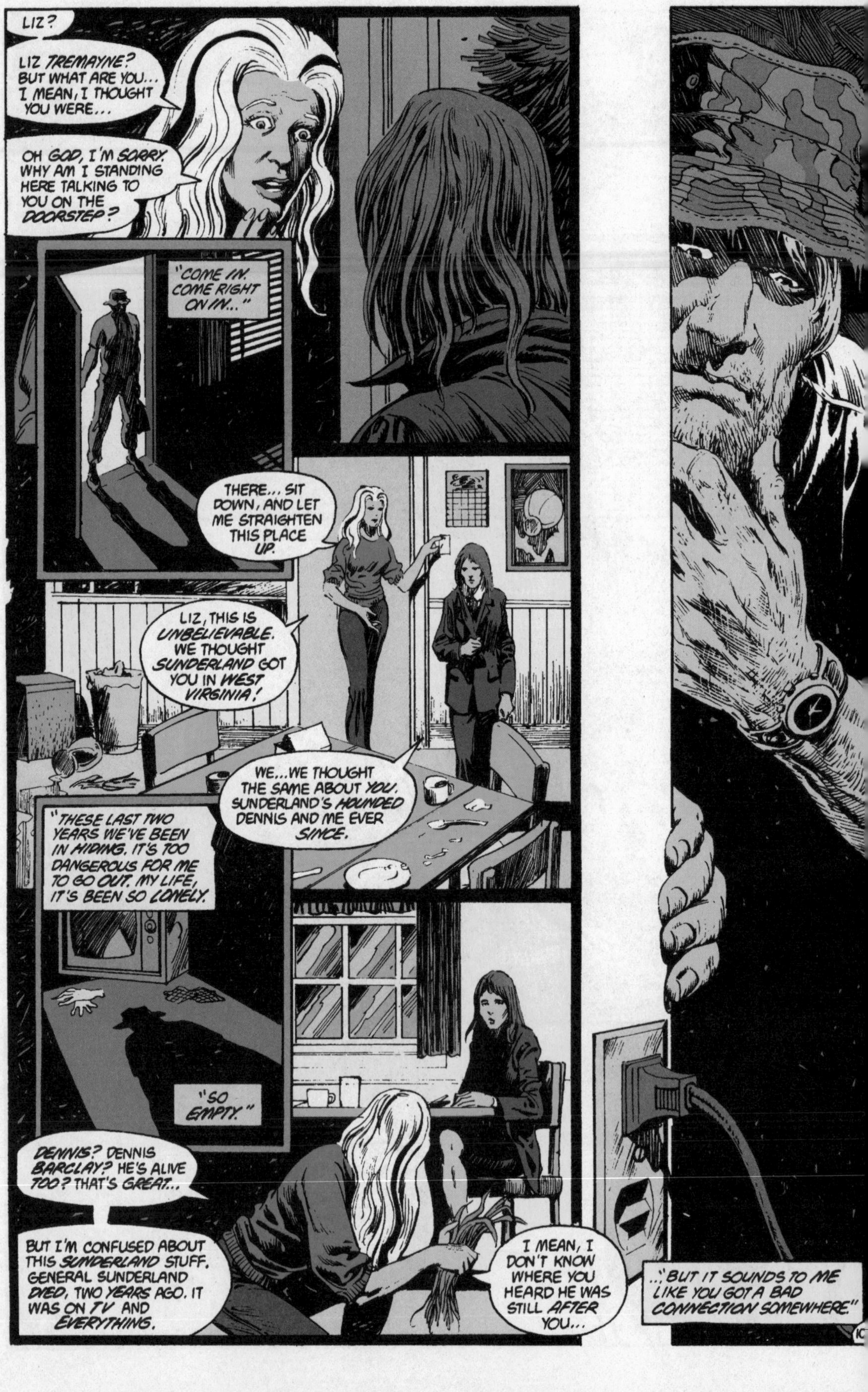
LIZ?
LIZ TREMAYNE? BUT WHAT ARE YOU... I MEAN, I THOUGHT YOU WERE...
OH GOD, I'M SORRY. WHY AM I STANDING HERE TALKING TO YOU ON THE DOORSTEP?
"COME IN. COME RIGHT ON IN..."
THERE... SIT DOWN, AND LET ME STRAIGHTEN THIS PLACE UP.
LIZ, THIS IS UNBELIEVABLE. WE THOUGHT SUNDERLAND GOT YOU IN WEST VIRGINIA!
WE...WE THOUGHT THE SAME ABOUT YOU. SUNDERLAND'S HOUNDED DENNIS AND ME EVER SINCE.
"THESE LAST TWO YEARS WE'VE BEEN IN HIDING. IT'S TOO DANGEROUS FOR ME TO GO OUT. MY LIFE, IT'S BEEN SO LONELY.
"SO EMPTY."
DENNIS? DENNIS BARCLAY? HE'S ALIVE TOO? THAT'S GREAT...
BUT I'M CONFUSED ABOUT THIS SUNDERLAND STUFF. GENERAL SUNDERLAND DIED, TWO YEARS AGO. IT WAS ON TV AND EVERYTHING.
I MEAN, I DON'T KNOW WHERE YOU HEARD HE WAS STILL AFTER YOU...
..."BUT IT SOUNDS TO ME LIKE YOU GOT A BAD CONNECTION SOMEWHERE."

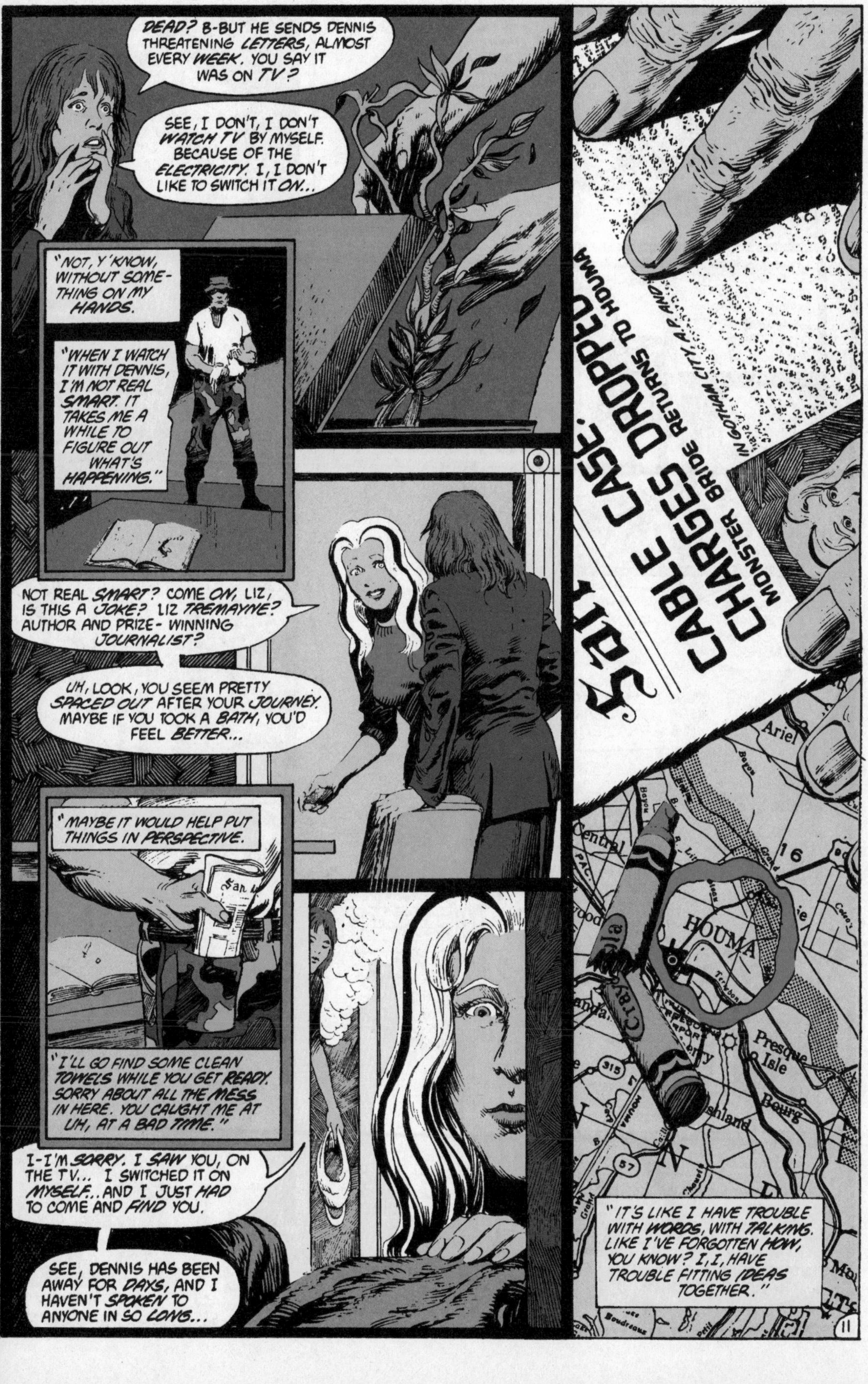
DEAD? B-BUT HE SENDS DENNIS THREATENING LETTERS, ALMOST EVERY WEEK. YOU SAY IT WAS ON TV?
SEE, I DON'T, I DON'T WATCH TV BY MYSELF. BECAUSE OF THE ELECTRICITY. I, I DON'T LIKE TO SWITCH IT ON...
"NOT, Y'KNOW, WITHOUT SOMETHING ON MY HANDS.
"WHEN I WATCH IT WITH DENNIS, I'M NOT REAL SMART. IT TAKES ME A WHILE TO FIGURE OUT WHAT'S HAPPENING."
NOT REAL SMART? COME ON, LIZ, IS THIS A JOKE? LIZ TREMAYNE? AUTHOR AND PRIZE-WINNING JOURNALIST?
UH, LOOK, YOU SEEM PRETTY SPACED OUT AFTER YOUR JOURNEY. MAYBE IF YOU TOOK A BATH, YOU'D FEEL BETTER...
"MAYBE IT WOULD HELP PUT THINGS IN PERSPECTIVE.
"I'LL GO FIND SOME CLEAN TOWELS WHILE YOU GET READY. SORRY ABOUT ALL THE MESS IN HERE. YOU CAUGHT ME AT UH, AT A BAD TIME."
I-I'M SORRY. I SAW YOU, ON THE TV... I SWITCHED IT ON MYSELF... AND I JUST HAD TO COME AND FIND YOU.
SEE, DENNIS HAS BEEN AWAY FOR DAYS, AND I HAVEN'T SPOKEN TO ANYONE IN SO LONG...
San
CABLE CASE: CHARGES DROPPED
MONSTER BRIDE RETURNS TO HOUMA
IN GOTHAM CITY, A.P. AND
Ariel
Central
HOUMA
Presque Isle
Bourg
16
315
57
"IT'S LIKE I HAVE TROUBLE WITH WORDS, WITH TALKING. LIKE I'VE FORGOTTEN HOW, YOU KNOW? I, I, HAVE TROUBLE FITTING IDEAS TOGETHER."
11

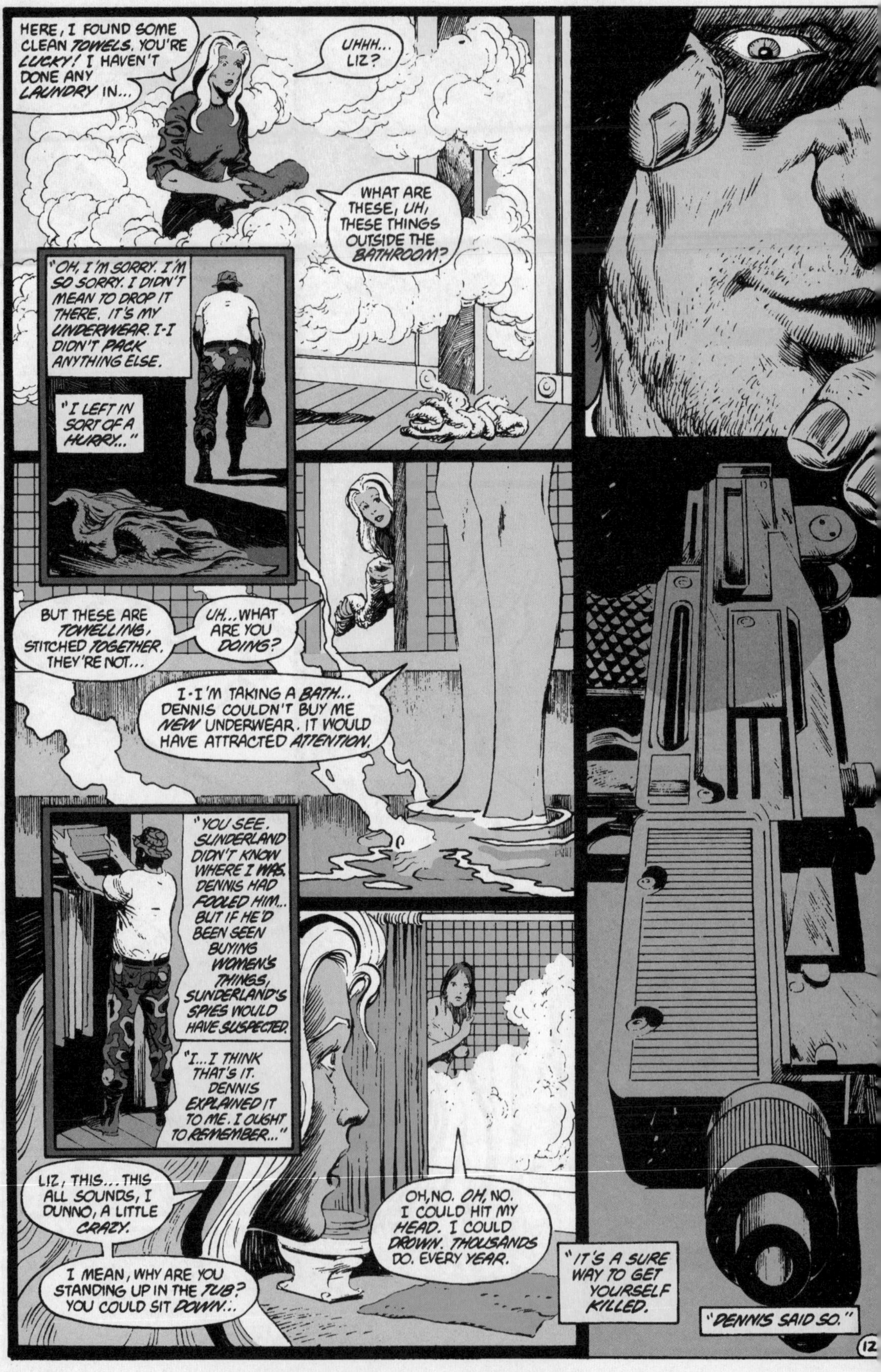
HERE, I FOUND SOME CLEAN TOWELS. YOU'RE LUCKY! I HAVEN'T DONE ANY LAUNDRY IN...
UHHH... LIZ?
WHAT ARE THESE, UH, THESE THINGS OUTSIDE THE BATHROOM?
"OH, I'M SORRY. I'M SO SORRY. I DIDN'T MEAN TO DROP IT THERE. IT'S MY UNDERWEAR. I-I DIDN'T PACK ANYTHING ELSE.
"I LEFT IN SORT OF A HURRY..."
BUT THESE ARE TOWELLING, STITCHED TOGETHER. THEY'RE NOT...
UH... WHAT ARE YOU DOING?
I-I'M TAKING A BATH... DENNIS COULDN'T BUY ME NEW UNDERWEAR. IT WOULD HAVE ATTRACTED ATTENTION.
"YOU SEE. SUNDERLAND DIDN'T KNOW WHERE I WAS. DENNIS HAD FOOLED HIM... BUT IF HE'D BEEN SEEN BUYING WOMEN'S THINGS, SUNDERLAND'S SPIES WOULD HAVE SUSPECTED.
"I... I THINK THAT'S IT. DENNIS EXPLAINED IT TO ME. I OUGHT TO REMEMBER..."
LIZ, THIS... THIS ALL SOUNDS, I DUNNO, A LITTLE CRAZY.
I MEAN, WHY ARE YOU STANDING UP IN THE TUB? YOU COULD SIT DOWN...
OH, NO. OH, NO. I COULD HIT MY HEAD. I COULD DROWN. THOUSANDS DO. EVERY YEAR.
"IT'S A SURE WAY TO GET YOURSELF KILLED.
"DENNIS SAID SO."
12

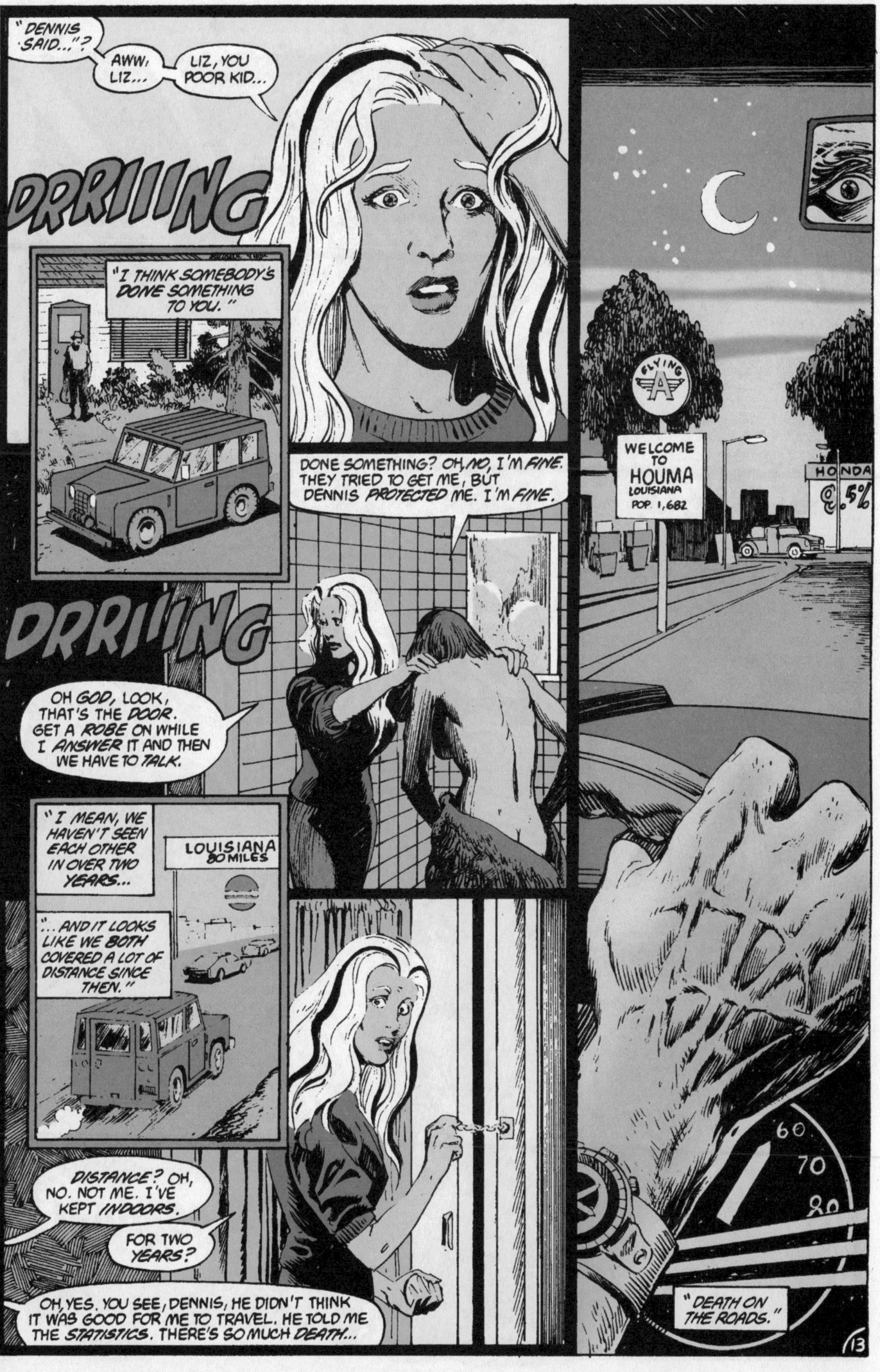
"DENNIS SAID..."?
AWW, LIZ...
LIZ, YOU POOR KID...
DRRIIING
"I THINK SOMEBODY'S DONE SOMETHING TO YOU."
DONE SOMETHING? OH, NO, I'M FINE. THEY TRIED TO GET ME, BUT DENNIS PROTECTED ME. I'M FINE.
DRRIIING
OH GOD, LOOK, THAT'S THE DOOR. GET A ROBE ON WHILE I ANSWER IT AND THEN WE HAVE TO TALK.
"I MEAN, WE HAVEN'T SEEN EACH OTHER IN OVER TWO YEARS...
LOUISIANA 80 MILES
"...AND IT LOOKS LIKE WE BOTH COVERED A LOT OF DISTANCE SINCE THEN."
DISTANCE? OH, NO. NOT ME. I'VE KEPT INDOORS.
FOR TWO YEARS?
OH, YES. YOU SEE, DENNIS, HE DIDN'T THINK IT WAS GOOD FOR ME TO TRAVEL. HE TOLD ME THE STATISTICS. THERE'S SO MUCH DEATH...
FLYING A
WELCOME TO HOUMA LOUISIANA POP. 1,682
HONDA
60
70
80
"DEATH ON THE ROADS."
13

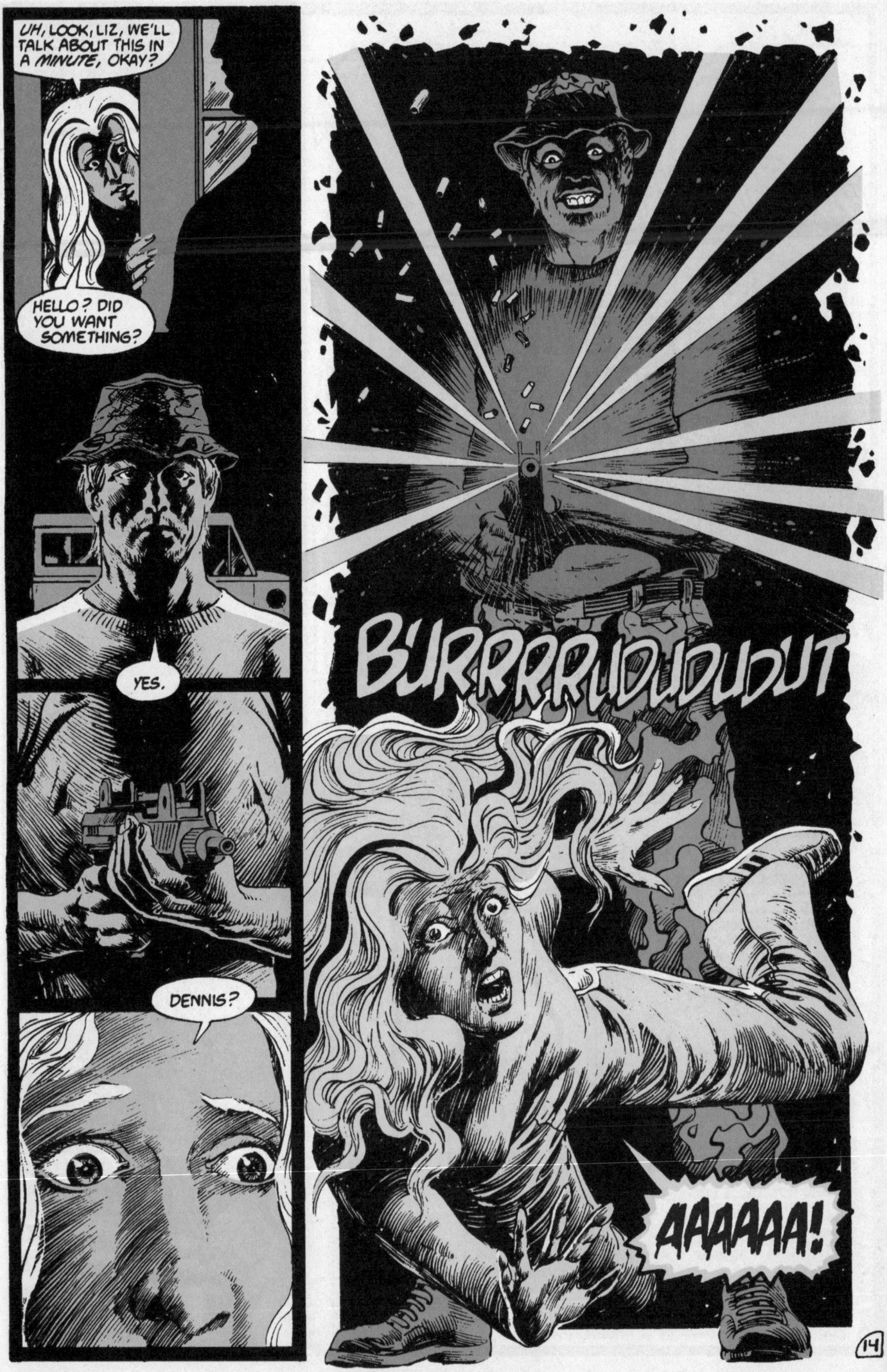
UH, LOOK, LIZ, WE'LL TALK ABOUT THIS IN A *MINUTE*, OKAY?
HELLO? DID YOU WANT SOMETHING?
YES.
DENNIS?
BURRRRRUDUDUDUT
AAAAAA!
14

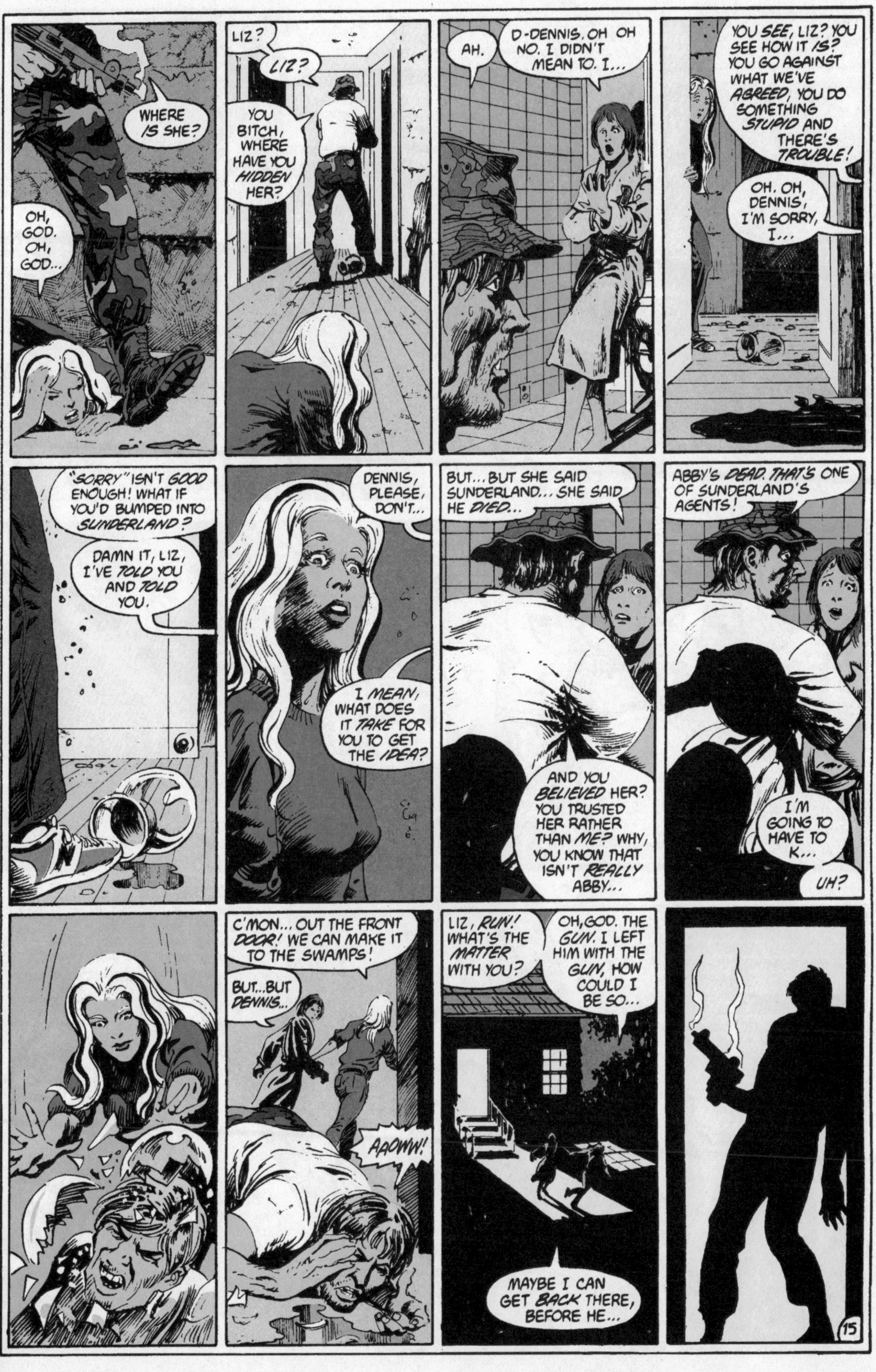
WHERE IS SHE?
OH, GOD. OH, GOD...
LIZ?
LIZ?
YOU BITCH, WHERE HAVE YOU HIDDEN HER?
AH.
D-DENNIS. OH OH NO. I DIDN'T MEAN TO. I...
YOU SEE, LIZ? YOU SEE HOW IT IS? YOU GO AGAINST WHAT WE'VE AGREED, YOU DO SOMETHING STUPID AND THERE'S TROUBLE!
OH. OH, DENNIS, I'M SORRY, I...
"SORRY" ISN'T GOOD ENOUGH! WHAT IF YOU'D BUMPED INTO SUNDERLAND?
DAMN IT, LIZ, I'VE TOLD YOU AND TOLD YOU.
DENNIS, PLEASE, DON'T...
I MEAN, WHAT DOES IT TAKE FOR YOU TO GET THE IDEA?
BUT... BUT SHE SAID SUNDERLAND... SHE SAID HE DIED...
AND YOU BELIEVED HER? YOU TRUSTED HER RATHER THAN ME? WHY, YOU KNOW THAT ISN'T REALLY ABBY...
ABBY'S DEAD. THAT'S ONE OF SUNDERLAND'S AGENTS!
I'M GOING TO HAVE TO K...
UH?
C'MON... OUT THE FRONT DOOR! WE CAN MAKE IT TO THE SWAMPS!
BUT...BUT DENNIS...
AAOWW!
LIZ, RUN! WHAT'S THE MATTER WITH YOU?
OH, GOD. THE GUN. I LEFT HIM WITH THE GUN, HOW COULD I BE SO...
MAYBE I CAN GET BACK THERE, BEFORE HE...
15

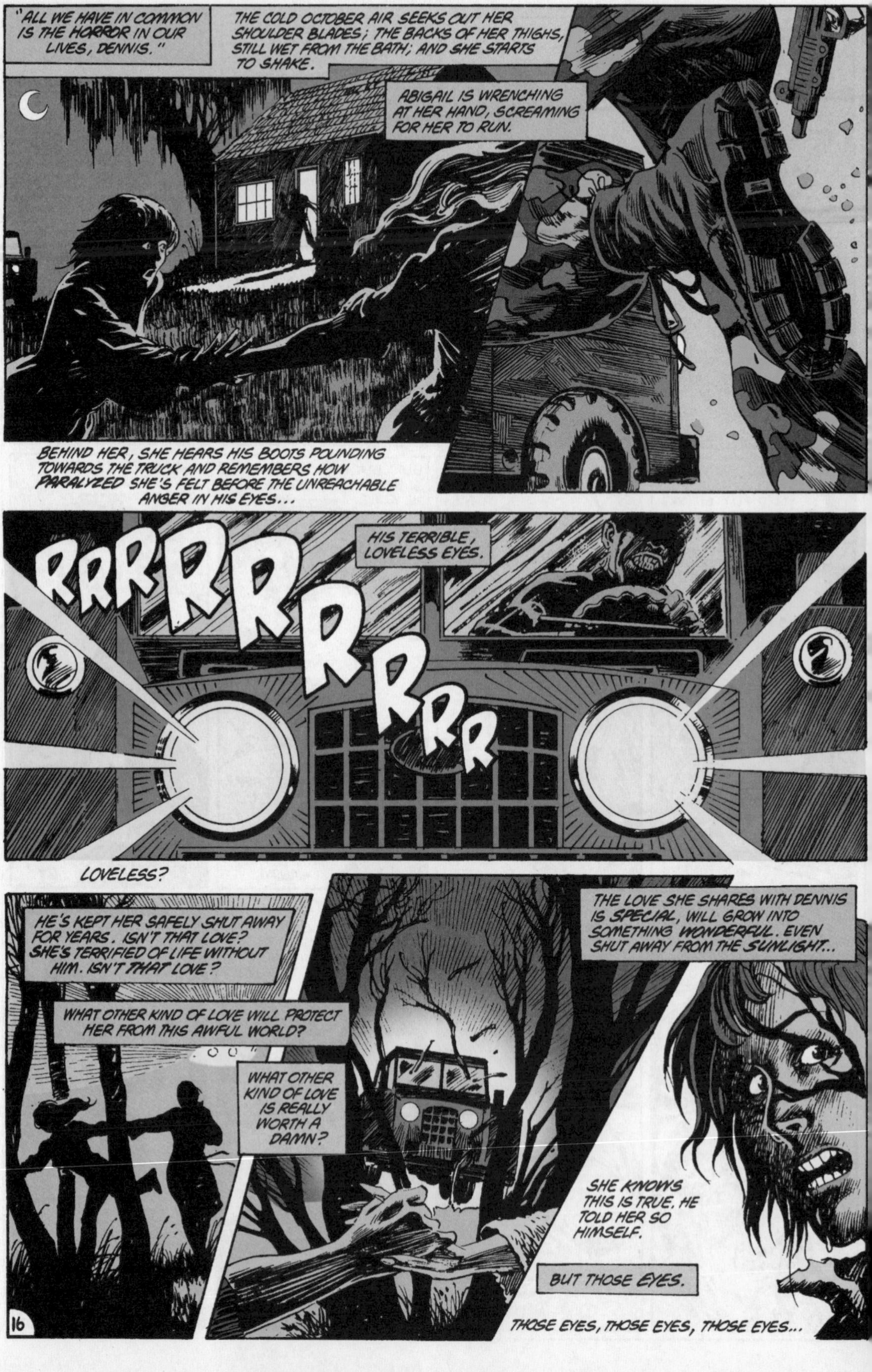
"ALL WE HAVE IN COMMON IS THE HORROR IN OUR LIVES, DENNIS."
THE COLD OCTOBER AIR SEEKS OUT HER SHOULDER BLADES; THE BACKS OF HER THIGHS, STILL WET FROM THE BATH; AND SHE STARTS TO SHAKE.
ABIGAIL IS WRENCHING AT HER HAND, SCREAMING FOR HER TO RUN.
BEHIND HER, SHE HEARS HIS BOOTS POUNDING TOWARDS THE TRUCK AND REMEMBERS HOW PARALYZED SHE'S FELT BEFORE THE UNREACHABLE ANGER IN HIS EYES...
HIS TERRIBLE, LOVELESS EYES.
RRRRRRRRRR
LOVELESS?
HE'S KEPT HER SAFELY SHUT AWAY FOR YEARS. ISN'T THAT LOVE? SHE'S TERRIFIED OF LIFE WITHOUT HIM. ISN'T THAT LOVE?
WHAT OTHER KIND OF LOVE WILL PROTECT HER FROM THIS AWFUL WORLD?
WHAT OTHER KIND OF LOVE IS REALLY WORTH A DAMN?
THE LOVE SHE SHARES WITH DENNIS IS SPECIAL, WILL GROW INTO SOMETHING WONDERFUL. EVEN SHUT AWAY FROM THE SUNLIGHT...
SHE KNOWS THIS IS TRUE. HE TOLD HER SO HIMSELF.
BUT THOSE EYES.
THOSE EYES, THOSE EYES, THOSE EYES...
16

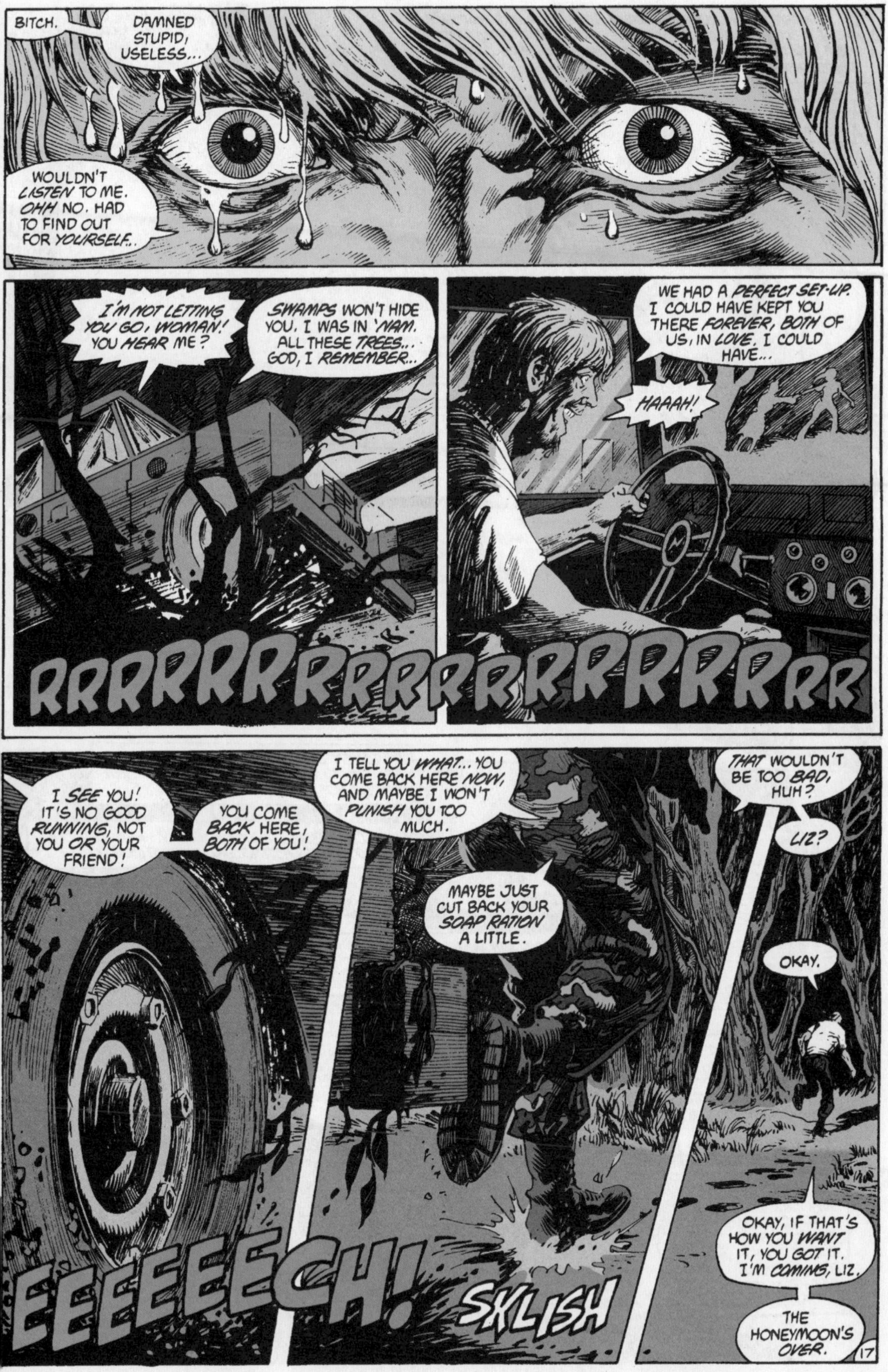
BITCH.
DAMNED STUPID, USELESS...
WOULDN'T LISTEN TO ME. OHH NO. HAD TO FIND OUT FOR YOURSELF...
I'M NOT LETTING YOU GO, WOMAN! YOU HEAR ME?
SWAMPS WON'T HIDE YOU. I WAS IN 'NAM. ALL THESE TREES... GOD, I REMEMBER...
WE HAD A PERFECT SET-UP. I COULD HAVE KEPT YOU THERE FOREVER, BOTH OF US, IN LOVE. I COULD HAVE...
HAAAH!
RRRRRRRRRRRRRRRRRRRRRR
I SEE YOU! IT'S NO GOOD RUNNING, NOT YOU OR YOUR FRIEND!
YOU COME BACK HERE, BOTH OF YOU!
I TELL YOU WHAT... YOU COME BACK HERE NOW, AND MAYBE I WON'T PUNISH YOU TOO MUCH.
MAYBE JUST CUT BACK YOUR SOAP RATION A LITTLE.
THAT WOULDN'T BE TOO BAD, HUH?
LIZ?
OKAY.
OKAY, IF THAT'S HOW YOU WANT IT, YOU GOT IT. I'M COMING, LIZ.
THE HONEYMOON'S OVER.
EEEEEECH!
SKLISH
17

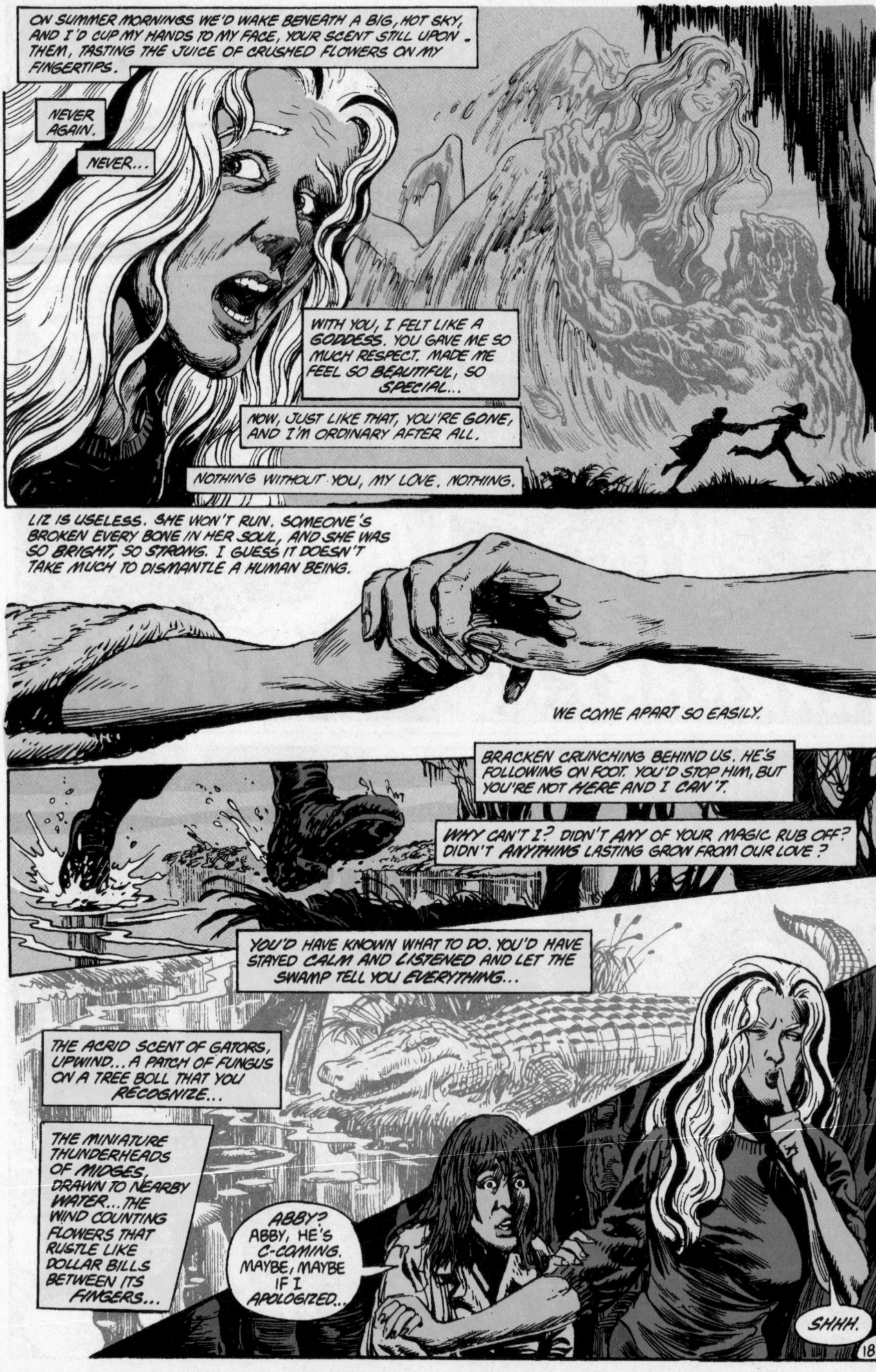
ON SUMMER MORNINGS WE'D WAKE BENEATH A BIG, HOT SKY, AND I'D CUP MY HANDS TO MY FACE, YOUR SCENT STILL UPON THEM, TASTING THE JUICE OF CRUSHED FLOWERS ON MY FINGERTIPS.
NEVER AGAIN.
NEVER...
WITH YOU, I FELT LIKE A GODDESS. YOU GAVE ME SO MUCH RESPECT. MADE ME FEEL SO BEAUTIFUL, SO SPECIAL...
NOW, JUST LIKE THAT, YOU'RE GONE, AND I'M ORDINARY AFTER ALL.
NOTHING WITHOUT YOU, MY LOVE. NOTHING.
LIZ IS USELESS. SHE WON'T RUN. SOMEONE'S BROKEN EVERY BONE IN HER SOUL, AND SHE WAS SO BRIGHT, SO STRONG. I GUESS IT DOESN'T TAKE MUCH TO DISMANTLE A HUMAN BEING.
WE COME APART SO EASILY.
BRACKEN CRUNCHING BEHIND US. HE'S FOLLOWING ON FOOT. YOU'D STOP HIM, BUT YOU'RE NOT HERE AND I CAN'T.
WHY CAN'T I? DIDN'T ANY OF YOUR MAGIC RUB OFF? DIDN'T ANYTHING LASTING GROW FROM OUR LOVE?
YOU'D HAVE KNOWN WHAT TO DO. YOU'D HAVE STAYED CALM AND LISTENED AND LET THE SWAMP TELL YOU EVERYTHING...
THE ACRID SCENT OF GATORS, UPWIND... A PATCH OF FUNGUS ON A TREE BOLL THAT YOU RECOGNIZE...
THE MINIATURE THUNDERHEADS OF MIDGES, DRAWN TO NEARBY WATER... THE WIND COUNTING FLOWERS THAT RUSTLE LIKE DOLLAR BILLS BETWEEN ITS FINGERS...
ABBY? ABBY, HE'S C-COMING. MAYBE, MAYBE IF I APOLOGIZED...
SHHH.
18

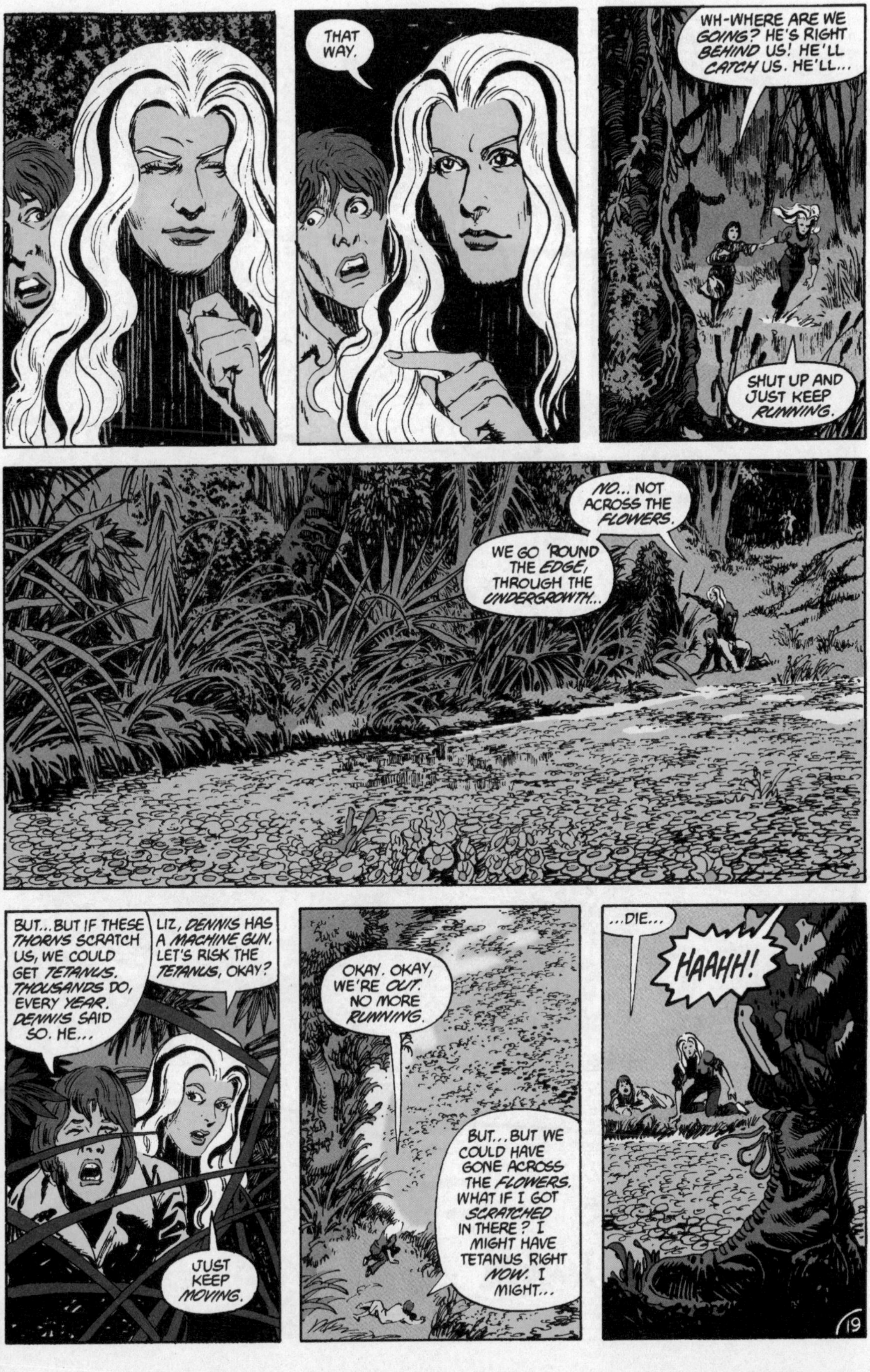
THAT WAY.
WH-WHERE ARE WE GOING? HE'S RIGHT BEHIND US! HE'LL CATCH US. HE'LL...
SHUT UP AND JUST KEEP RUNNING.
NO... NOT ACROSS THE FLOWERS.
WE GO 'ROUND THE EDGE, THROUGH THE UNDERGROWTH...
BUT... BUT IF THESE THORNS SCRATCH US, WE COULD GET TETANUS. THOUSANDS DO, EVERY YEAR. DENNIS SAID SO. HE...
LIZ, DENNIS HAS A MACHINE GUN. LET'S RISK THE TETANUS, OKAY?
JUST KEEP MOVING.
OKAY. OKAY, WE'RE OUT. NO MORE RUNNING.
BUT... BUT WE COULD HAVE GONE ACROSS THE FLOWERS. WHAT IF I GOT SCRATCHED IN THERE? I MIGHT HAVE TETANUS RIGHT NOW. I MIGHT...
...DIE...
HAAHH!
19

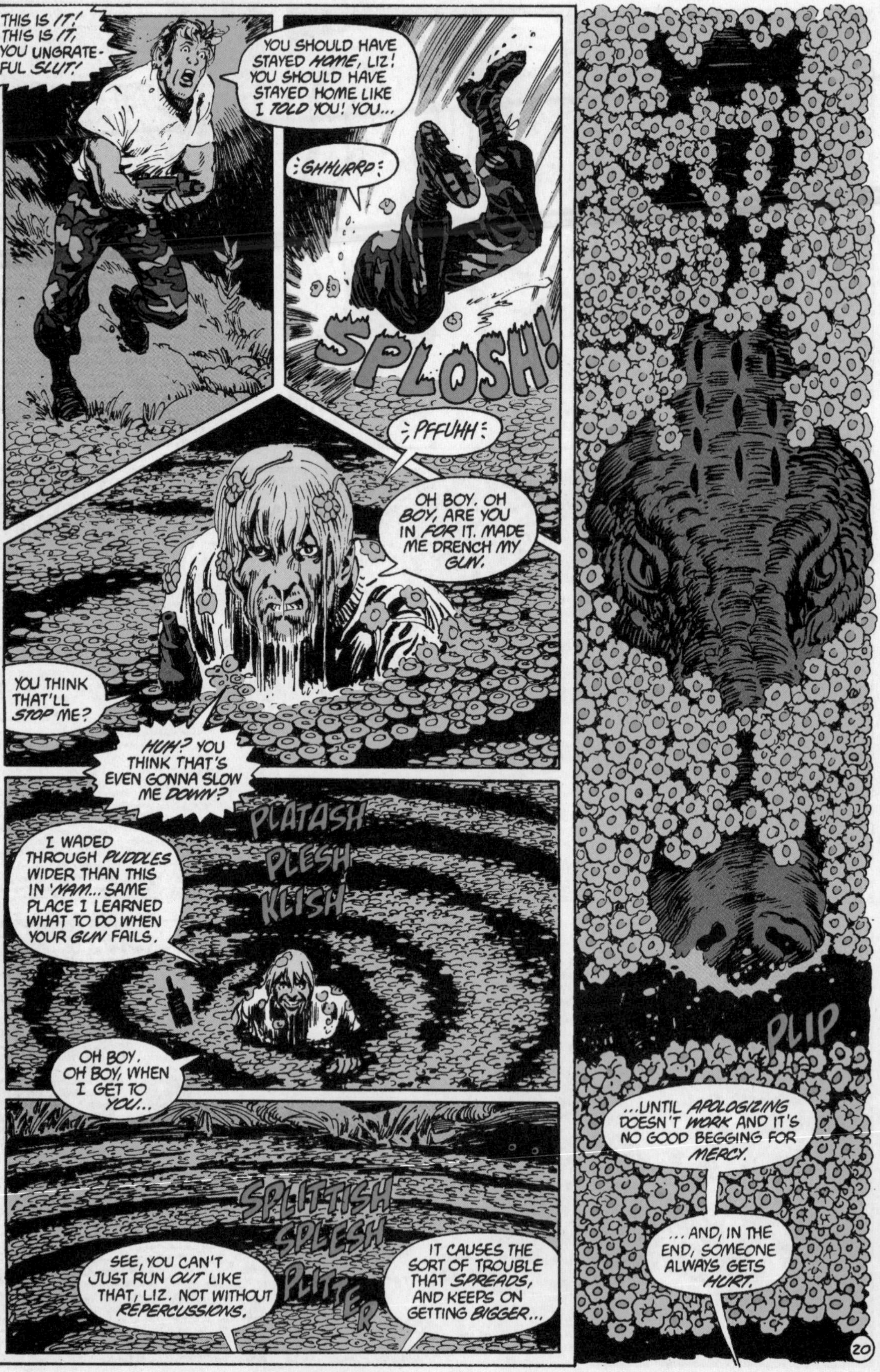
THIS IS IT! THIS IS IT, YOU UNGRATEFUL SLUT!
YOU SHOULD HAVE STAYED HOME, LIZ! YOU SHOULD HAVE STAYED HOME LIKE I TOLD YOU! YOU...
GHHURRP
SPLOSH!
PFFUHH
OH BOY. OH BOY, ARE YOU IN FOR IT. MADE ME DRENCH MY GUN.
YOU THINK THAT'LL STOP ME?
HUH? YOU THINK THAT'S EVEN GONNA SLOW ME DOWN?
PLATASH
PLESH
KLISH
I WADED THROUGH PUDDLES WIDER THAN THIS IN 'NAM... SAME PLACE I LEARNED WHAT TO DO WHEN YOUR GUN FAILS.
OH BOY. OH BOY, WHEN I GET TO YOU...
SPLITTISH
SPLESH
PLITTER
SEE, YOU CAN'T JUST RUN OUT LIKE THAT, LIZ. NOT WITHOUT REPERCUSSIONS.
IT CAUSES THE SORT OF TROUBLE THAT SPREADS, AND KEEPS ON GETTING BIGGER...
PLIP
...UNTIL APOLOGIZING DOESN'T WORK AND IT'S NO GOOD BEGGING FOR MERCY.
... AND, IN THE END, SOMEONE ALWAYS GETS HURT.
20

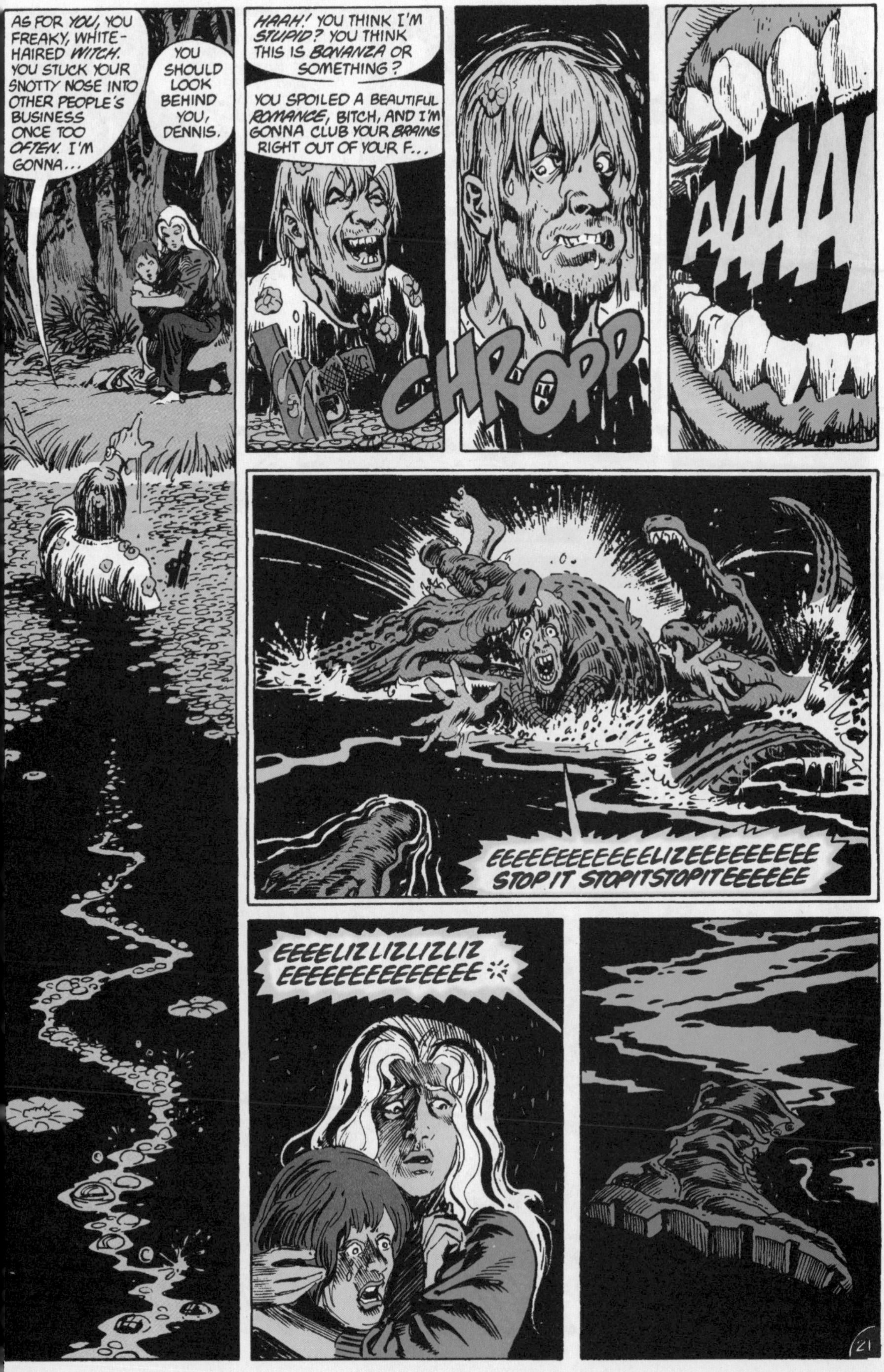
AS FOR YOU, YOU FREAKY, WHITE-HAIRED WITCH. YOU STUCK YOUR SNOTTY NOSE INTO OTHER PEOPLE'S BUSINESS ONCE TOO OFTEN. I'M GONNA...
YOU SHOULD LOOK BEHIND YOU, DENNIS.
HAAH! YOU THINK I'M STUPID? YOU THINK THIS IS BONANZA OR SOMETHING?
YOU SPOILED A BEAUTIFUL ROMANCE, BITCH, AND I'M GONNA CLUB YOUR BRAINS RIGHT OUT OF YOUR F...
CHROPP
AAAA
EEEEEEEEEEEELIZEEEEEEEEEE STOP IT STOPITSTOPITEEEEEE
EEEELIZLIZLIZLIZ EEEEEEEEEEEEEE
21

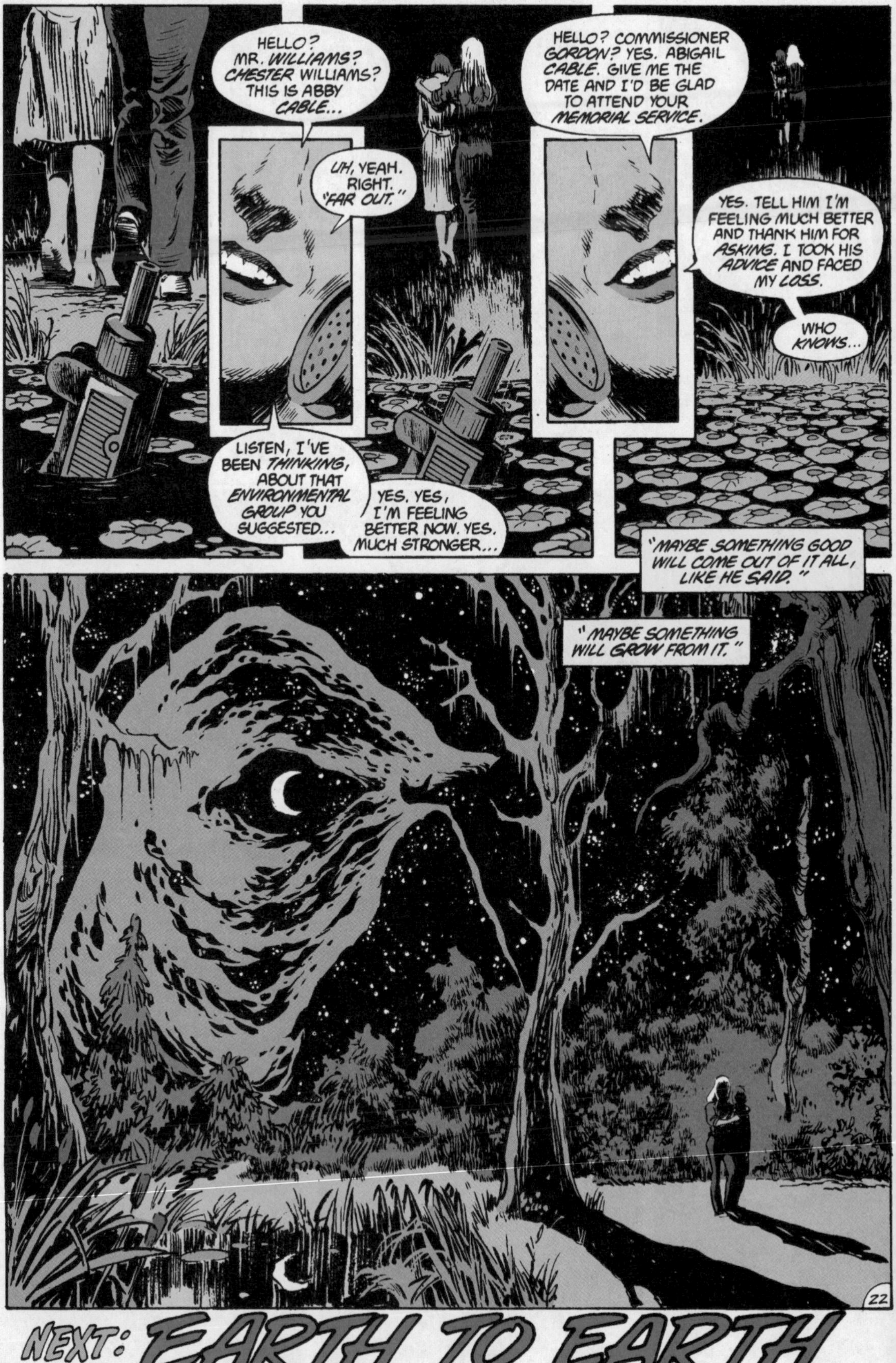
HELLO? MR. WILLIAMS? CHESTER WILLIAMS? THIS IS ABBY CABLE...
UH, YEAH. RIGHT. "FAR OUT."
LISTEN, I'VE BEEN THINKING, ABOUT THAT ENVIRONMENTAL GROUP YOU SUGGESTED...
YES. YES, I'M FEELING BETTER NOW. YES. MUCH STRONGER...
HELLO? COMMISSIONER GORDON? YES. ABIGAIL CABLE. GIVE ME THE DATE AND I'D BE GLAD TO ATTEND YOUR MEMORIAL SERVICE.
YES. TELL HIM I'M FEELING MUCH BETTER AND THANK HIM FOR ASKING. I TOOK HIS ADVICE AND FACED MY LOSS.
WHO KNOWS...
"MAYBE SOMETHING GOOD WILL COME OUT OF IT ALL, LIKE HE SAID."
"MAYBE SOMETHING WILL GROW FROM IT."
22
NEXT: EARTH TO EARTH

Chapter 5

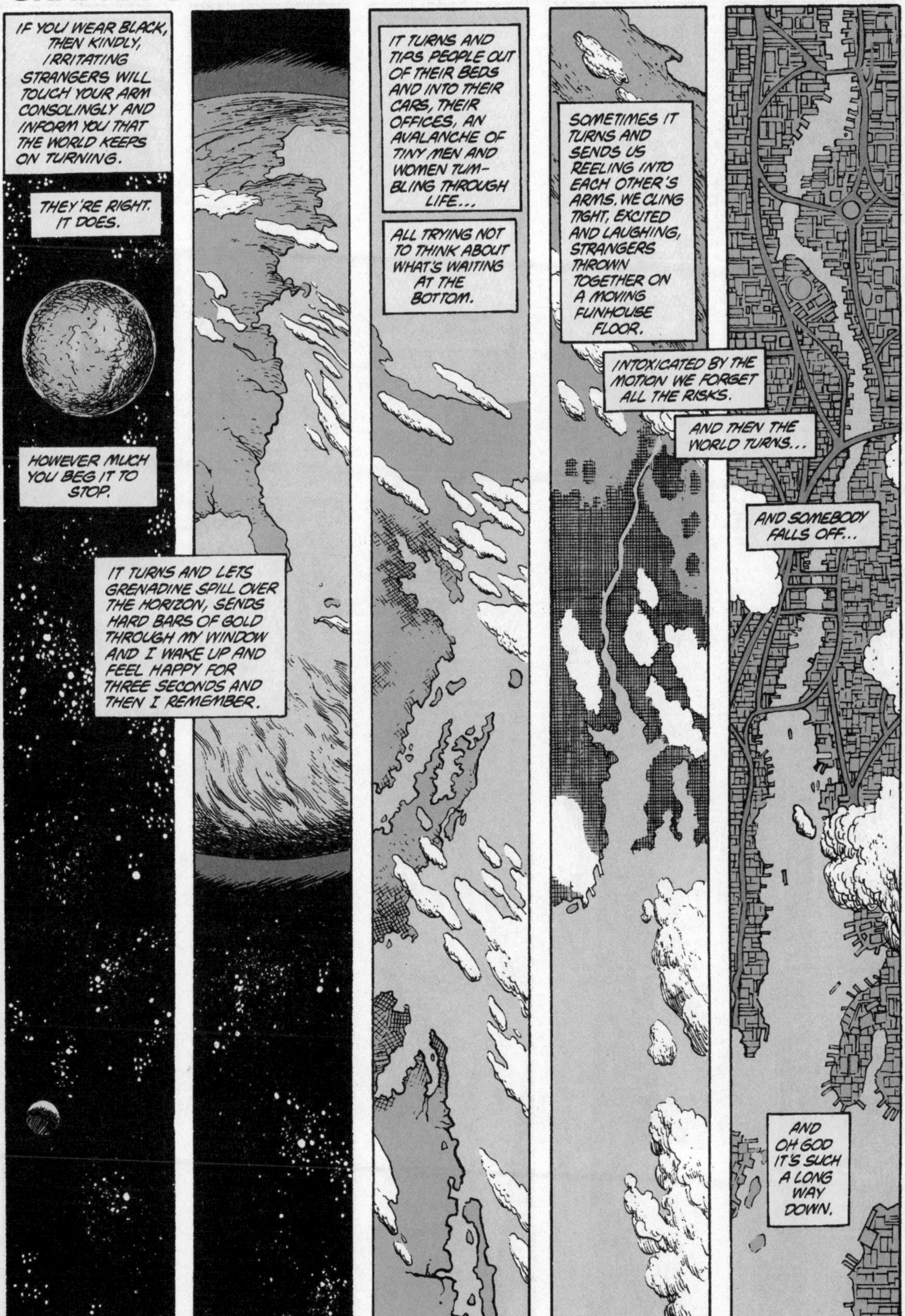
IF YOU WEAR BLACK, THEN KINDLY, IRRITATING STRANGERS WILL TOUCH YOUR ARM CONSOLINGLY AND INFORM YOU THAT THE WORLD KEEPS ON TURNING.
THEY'RE RIGHT. IT DOES.
HOWEVER MUCH YOU BEG IT TO STOP.
IT TURNS AND LETS GRENADINE SPILL OVER THE HORIZON, SENDS HARD BARS OF GOLD THROUGH MY WINDOW AND I WAKE UP AND FEEL HAPPY FOR THREE SECONDS AND THEN I REMEMBER.
IT TURNS AND TIPS PEOPLE OUT OF THEIR BEDS AND INTO THEIR CARS, THEIR OFFICES, AN AVALANCHE OF TINY MEN AND WOMEN TUMBLING THROUGH LIFE...
ALL TRYING NOT TO THINK ABOUT WHAT'S WAITING AT THE BOTTOM.
SOMETIMES IT TURNS AND SENDS US REELING INTO EACH OTHER'S ARMS. WE CLING TIGHT, EXCITED AND LAUGHING, STRANGERS THROWN TOGETHER ON A MOVING FUNHOUSE FLOOR.
INTOXICATED BY THE MOTION WE FORGET ALL THE RISKS.
AND THEN THE WORLD TURNS...
AND SOMEBODY FALLS OFF...
AND OH GOD IT'S SUCH A LONG WAY DOWN.

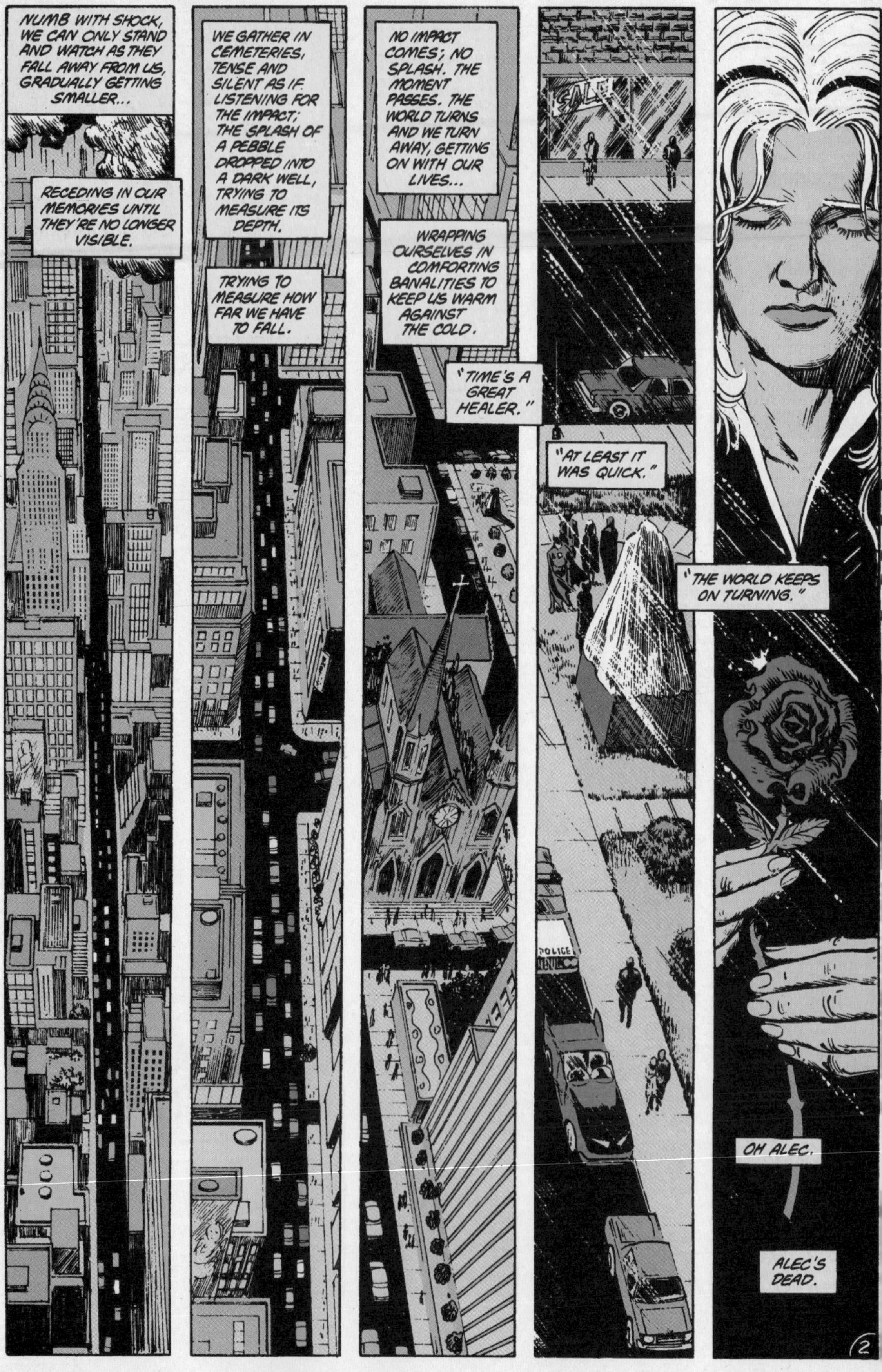
NUMB WITH SHOCK, WE CAN ONLY STAND AND WATCH AS THEY FALL AWAY FROM US, GRADUALLY GETTING SMALLER...
RECEDING IN OUR MEMORIES UNTIL THEY'RE NO LONGER VISIBLE.
WE GATHER IN CEMETERIES, TENSE AND SILENT AS IF LISTENING FOR THE IMPACT; THE SPLASH OF A PEBBLE DROPPED INTO A DARK WELL, TRYING TO MEASURE ITS DEPTH.
TRYING TO MEASURE HOW FAR WE HAVE TO FALL.
NO IMPACT COMES; NO SPLASH. THE MOMENT PASSES. THE WORLD TURNS AND WE TURN AWAY, GETTING ON WITH OUR LIVES...
WRAPPING OURSELVES IN COMFORTING BANALITIES TO KEEP US WARM AGAINST THE COLD.
"TIME'S A GREAT HEALER."
"AT LEAST IT WAS QUICK."
POLICE
"THE WORLD KEEPS ON TURNING."
OH ALEC.
ALEC'S DEAD.
2

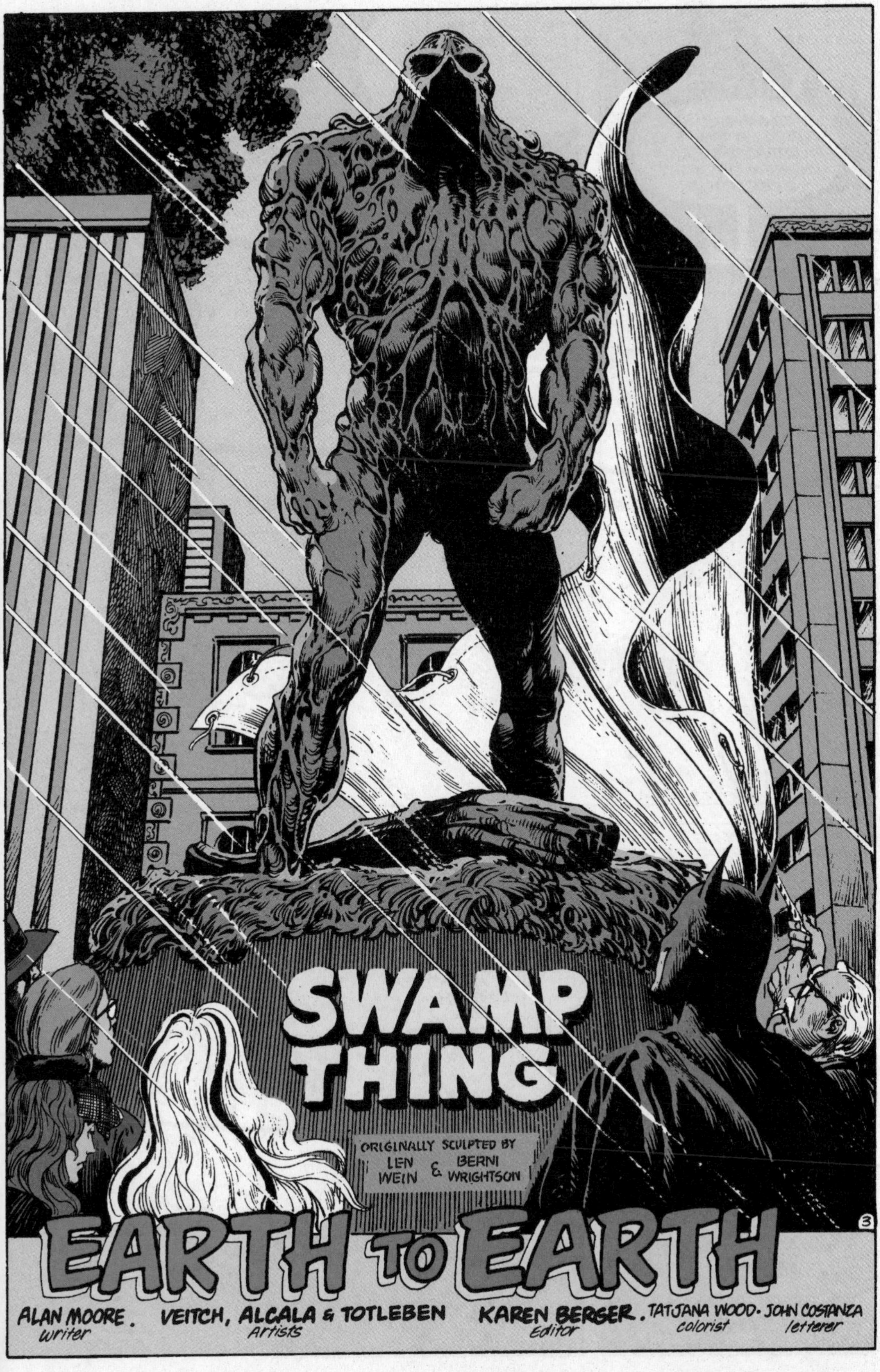
SWAMP THING
ORIGINALLY SCULPTED BY LEN WEIN & BERNI WRIGHTSON
3
EARTH TO EARTH
ALAN MOORE. writer
VEITCH, ALCALA & TOTLEBEN Artists
KAREN BERGER. Editor
TATJANA WOOD. colorist
JOHN COSTANZA letterer

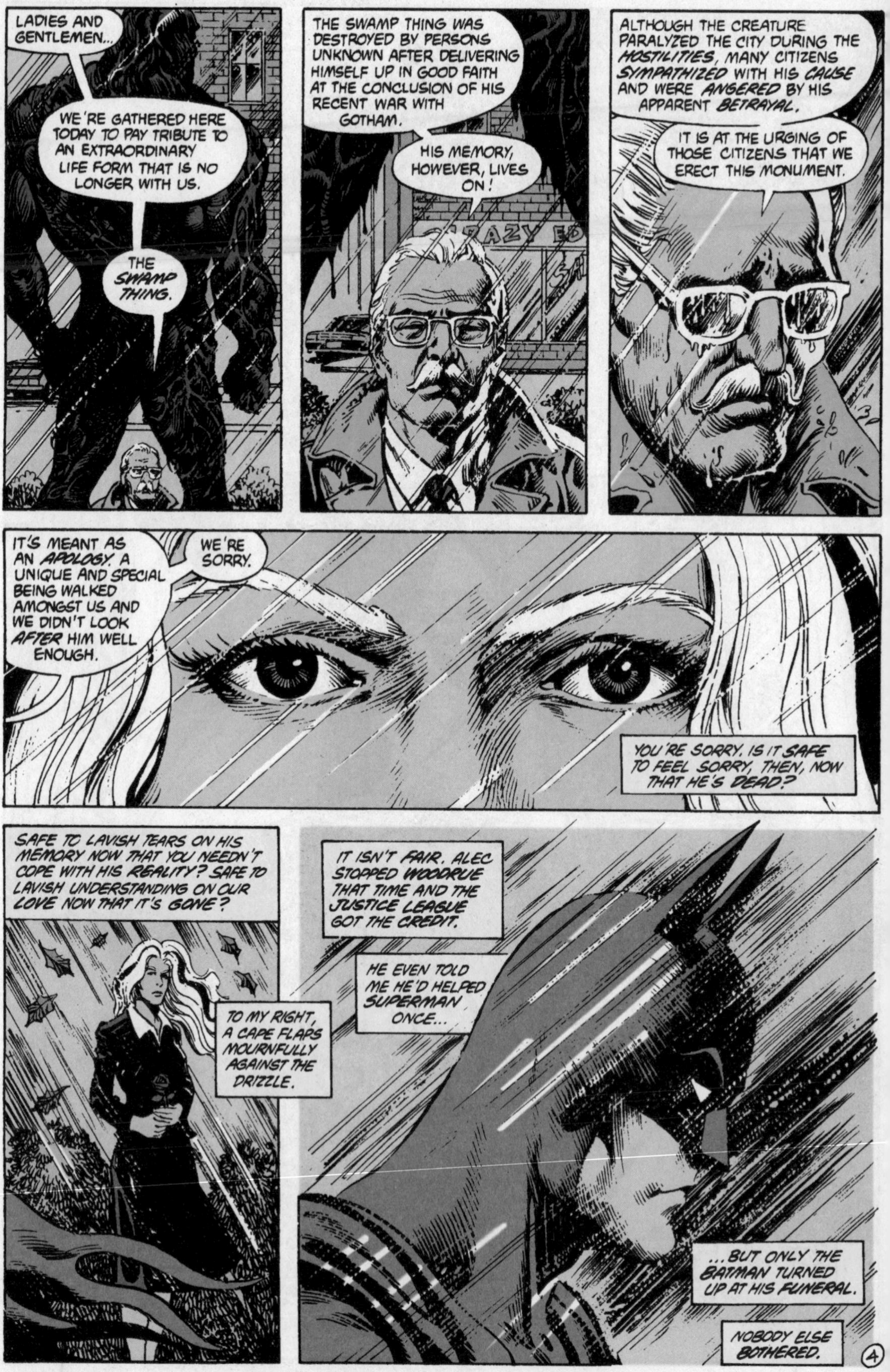
LADIES AND GENTLEMEN...
WE'RE GATHERED HERE TODAY TO PAY TRIBUTE TO AN EXTRAORDINARY LIFE FORM THAT IS NO LONGER WITH US.
THE SWAMP THING.
THE SWAMP THING WAS DESTROYED BY PERSONS UNKNOWN AFTER DELIVERING HIMSELF UP IN GOOD FAITH AT THE CONCLUSION OF HIS RECENT WAR WITH GOTHAM.
HIS MEMORY, HOWEVER, LIVES ON!
ALTHOUGH THE CREATURE PARALYZED THE CITY DURING THE HOSTILITIES, MANY CITIZENS SYMPATHIZED WITH HIS CAUSE AND WERE ANGERED BY HIS APPARENT BETRAYAL.
IT IS AT THE URGING OF THOSE CITIZENS THAT WE ERECT THIS MONUMENT.
IT'S MEANT AS AN APOLOGY. A UNIQUE AND SPECIAL BEING WALKED AMONGST US AND WE DIDN'T LOOK AFTER HIM WELL ENOUGH.
WE'RE SORRY.
YOU'RE SORRY. IS IT SAFE TO FEEL SORRY, THEN, NOW THAT HE'S DEAD?
SAFE TO LAVISH TEARS ON HIS MEMORY NOW THAT YOU NEEDN'T COPE WITH HIS REALITY? SAFE TO LAVISH UNDERSTANDING ON OUR LOVE NOW THAT IT'S GONE?
TO MY RIGHT, A CAPE FLAPS MOURNFULLY AGAINST THE DRIZZLE.
IT ISN'T FAIR. ALEC STOPPED WOODRUE THAT TIME AND THE JUSTICE LEAGUE GOT THE CREDIT.
HE EVEN TOLD ME HE'D HELPED SUPERMAN ONCE...
...BUT ONLY THE BATMAN TURNED UP AT HIS FUNERAL.
NOBODY ELSE BOTHERED.
4

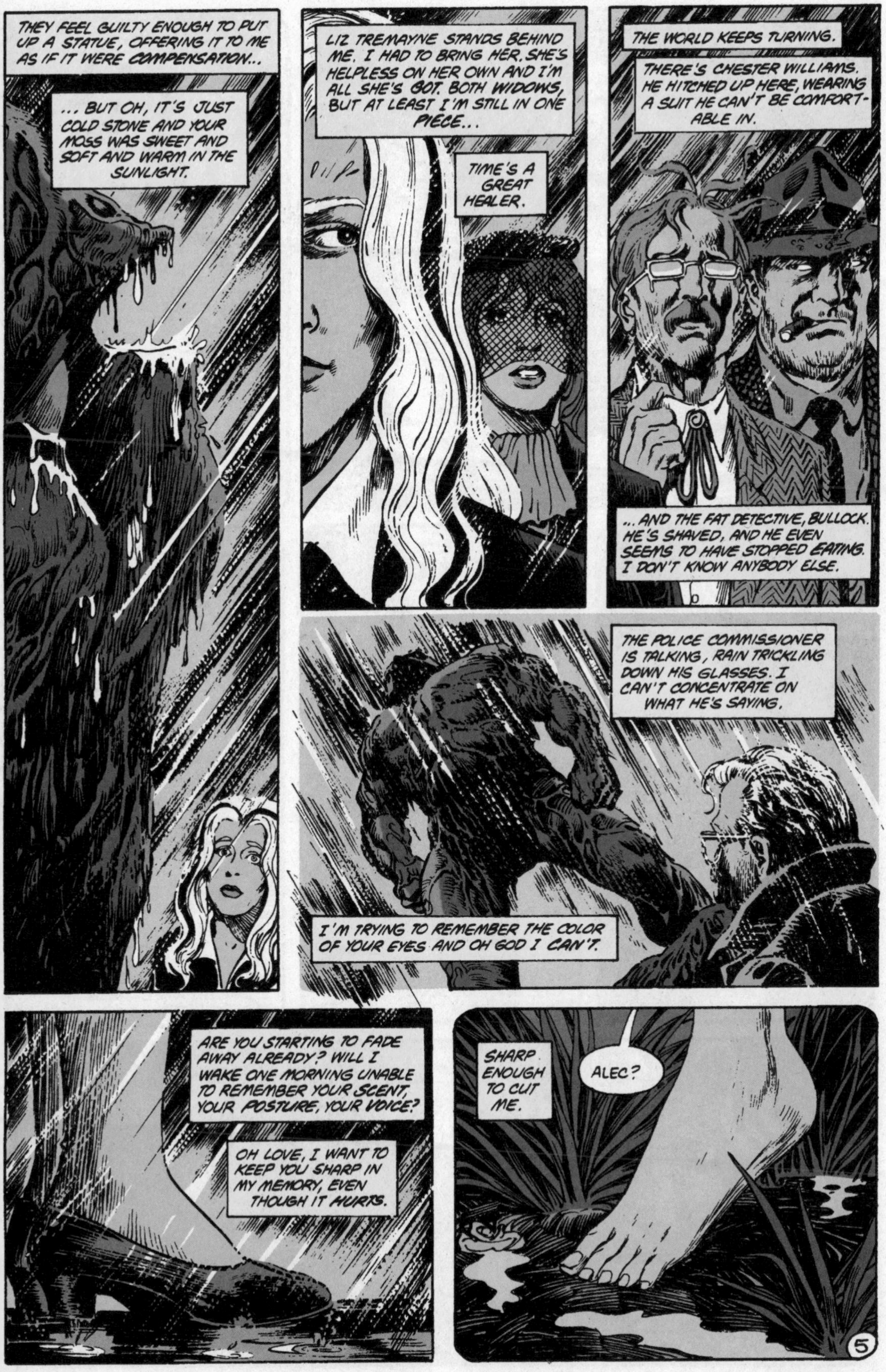
THEY FEEL GUILTY ENOUGH TO PUT UP A STATUE, OFFERING IT TO ME AS IF IT WERE COMPENSATION...
... BUT OH, IT'S JUST COLD STONE AND YOUR MOSS WAS SWEET AND SOFT AND WARM IN THE SUNLIGHT.
LIZ TREMAYNE STANDS BEHIND ME. I HAD TO BRING HER. SHE'S HELPLESS ON HER OWN AND I'M ALL SHE'S GOT. BOTH WIDOWS, BUT AT LEAST I'M STILL IN ONE PIECE...
TIME'S A GREAT HEALER.
THE WORLD KEEPS TURNING.
THERE'S CHESTER WILLIAMS. HE HITCHED UP HERE, WEARING A SUIT HE CAN'T BE COMFORTABLE IN.
... AND THE FAT DETECTIVE, BULLOCK. HE'S SHAVED, AND HE EVEN SEEMS TO HAVE STOPPED EATING. I DON'T KNOW ANYBODY ELSE.
THE POLICE COMMISSIONER IS TALKING, RAIN TRICKLING DOWN HIS GLASSES. I CAN'T CONCENTRATE ON WHAT HE'S SAYING.
I'M TRYING TO REMEMBER THE COLOR OF YOUR EYES AND OH GOD I CAN'T.
ARE YOU STARTING TO FADE AWAY ALREADY? WILL I WAKE ONE MORNING UNABLE TO REMEMBER YOUR SCENT, YOUR POSTURE, YOUR VOICE?
OH LOVE, I WANT TO KEEP YOU SHARP IN MY MEMORY, EVEN THOUGH IT HURTS.
SHARP. ENOUGH TO CUT ME.
ALEC?
5

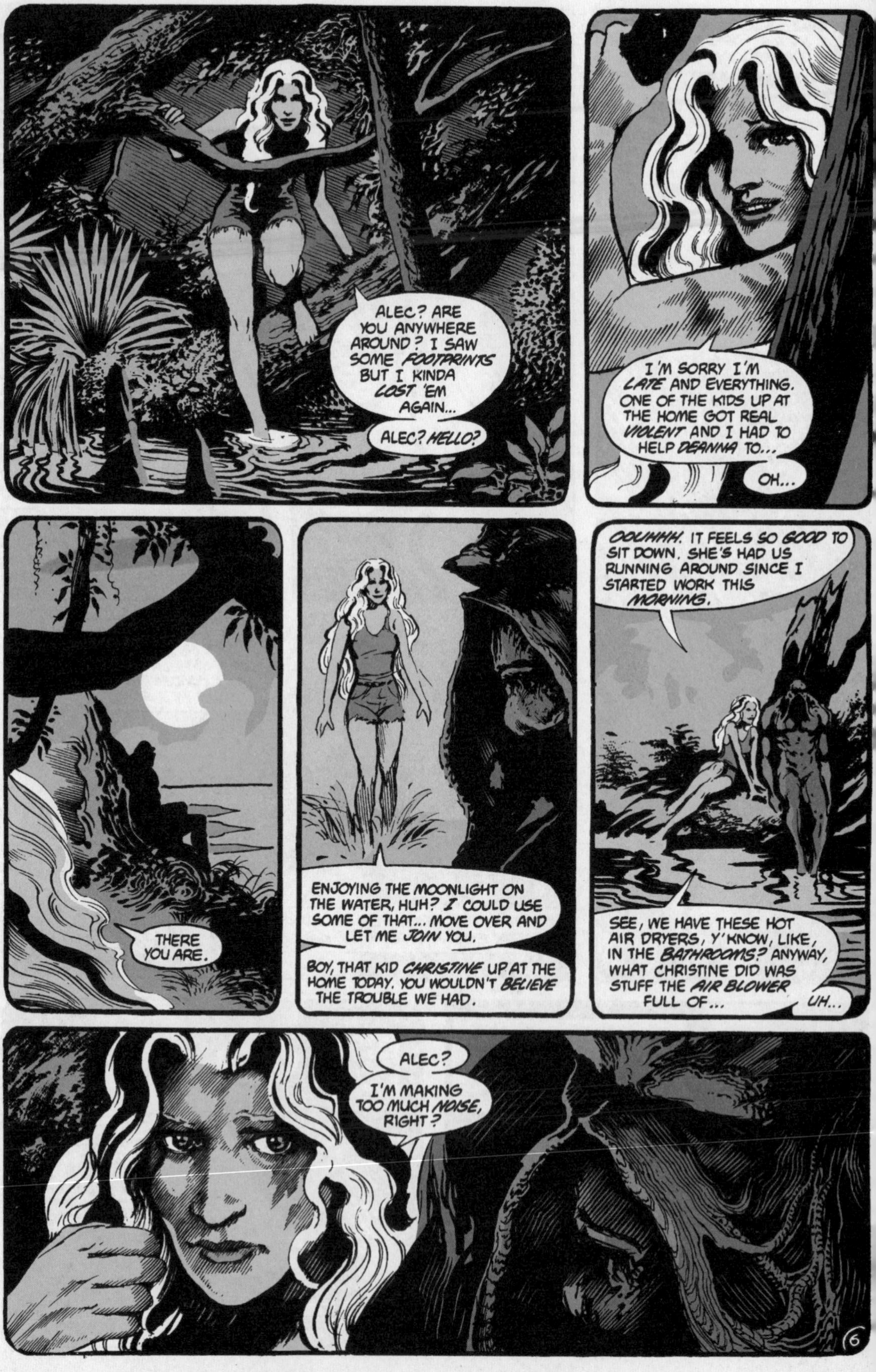
ALEC? ARE YOU ANYWHERE AROUND? I SAW SOME FOOTPRINTS BUT I KINDA LOST 'EM AGAIN...
ALEC? HELLO?
I'M SORRY I'M LATE AND EVERYTHING. ONE OF THE KIDS UP AT THE HOME GOT REAL VIOLENT AND I HAD TO HELP DEANNA TO...
OH...
THERE YOU ARE.
ENJOYING THE MOONLIGHT ON THE WATER, HUH? I COULD USE SOME OF THAT... MOVE OVER AND LET ME JOIN YOU.
BOY, THAT KID CHRISTINE UP AT THE HOME TODAY. YOU WOULDN'T BELIEVE THE TROUBLE WE HAD.
OOUHHH. IT FEELS SO GOOD TO SIT DOWN. SHE'S HAD US RUNNING AROUND SINCE I STARTED WORK THIS MORNING.
SEE, WE HAVE THESE HOT AIR DRYERS, Y'KNOW, LIKE, IN THE BATHROOMS? ANYWAY, WHAT CHRISTINE DID WAS STUFF THE AIR BLOWER FULL OF...
UH...
ALEC?
I'M MAKING TOO MUCH NOISE, RIGHT?
6

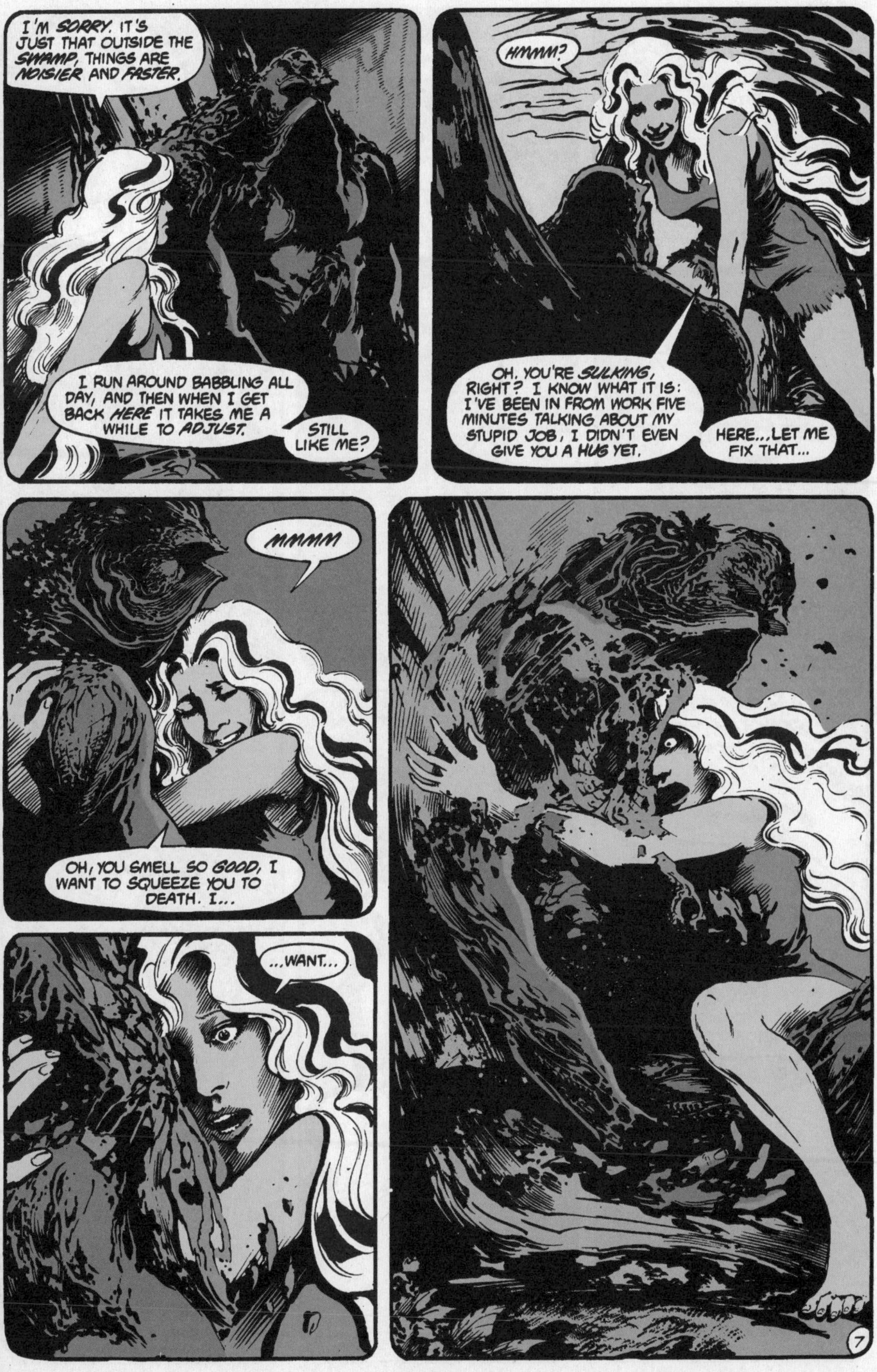
I'M SORRY. IT'S JUST THAT OUTSIDE THE SWAMP, THINGS ARE NOISIER AND FASTER.
I RUN AROUND BABBLING ALL DAY, AND THEN WHEN I GET BACK HERE IT TAKES ME A WHILE TO ADJUST.
STILL LIKE ME?
HMMM?
OH, YOU'RE SULKING, RIGHT? I KNOW WHAT IT IS: I'VE BEEN IN FROM WORK FIVE MINUTES TALKING ABOUT MY STUPID JOB, I DIDN'T EVEN GIVE YOU A HUG YET.
HERE... LET ME FIX THAT...
MMMM
OH, YOU SMELL SO GOOD, I WANT TO SQUEEZE YOU TO DEATH. I...
...WANT...
7

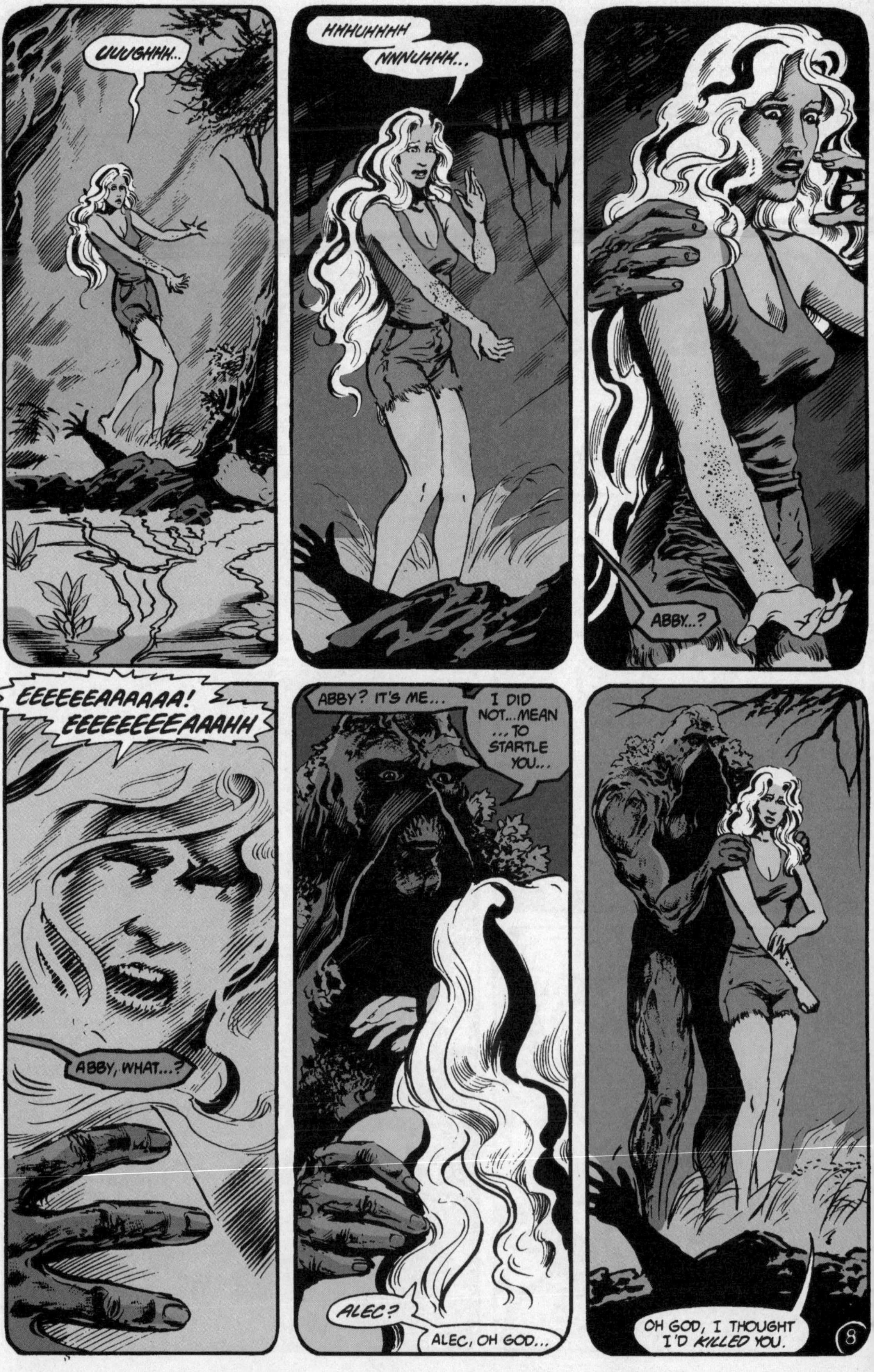
UUUGHHH...
HHHUHHHH
NNNUHHH...
ABBY...?
EEEEEEAAAAAA!
EEEEEEEEAAAHH
ABBY, WHAT...?
ABBY? IT'S ME...
I DID NOT...MEAN ...TO STARTLE YOU...
ALEC?
ALEC, OH GOD...
OH GOD, I THOUGHT I'D KILLED YOU.
8

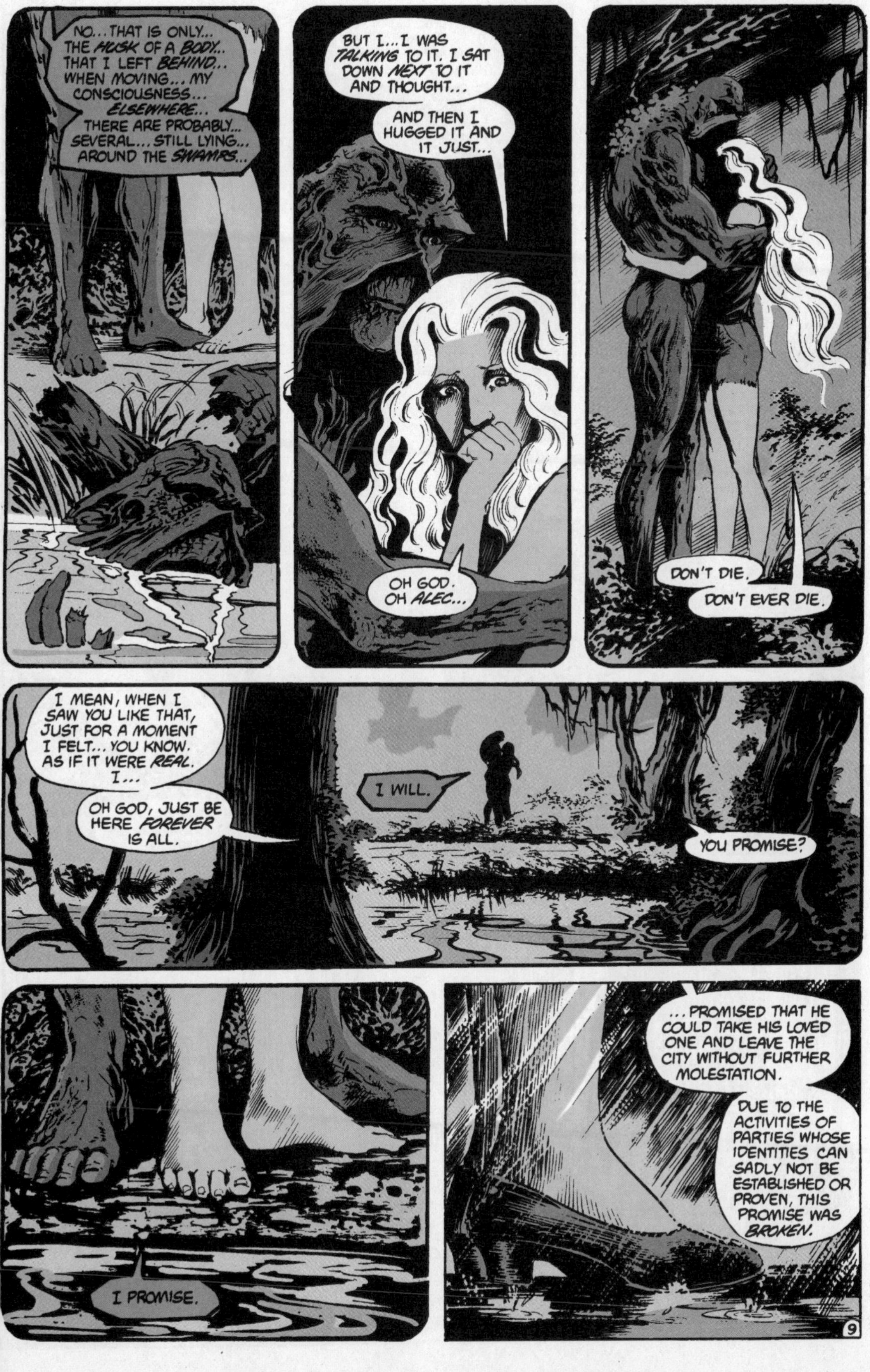
NO... THAT IS ONLY... THE HUSK OF A BODY.. THAT I LEFT BEHIND... WHEN MOVING... MY CONSCIOUSNESS... ELSEWHERE... THERE ARE PROBABLY... SEVERAL... STILL LYING... AROUND THE SWAMPS...
BUT I... I WAS TALKING TO IT. I SAT DOWN NEXT TO IT AND THOUGHT...
AND THEN I HUGGED IT AND IT JUST...
OH GOD. OH ALEC...
DON'T DIE.
DON'T EVER DIE.
I MEAN, WHEN I SAW YOU LIKE THAT, JUST FOR A MOMENT I FELT... YOU KNOW. AS IF IT WERE REAL. I...
OH GOD, JUST BE HERE FOREVER IS ALL.
I WILL.
YOU PROMISE?
I PROMISE.
...PROMISED THAT HE COULD TAKE HIS LOVED ONE AND LEAVE THE CITY WITHOUT FURTHER MOLESTATION.
DUE TO THE ACTIVITIES OF PARTIES WHOSE IDENTITIES CAN SADLY NOT BE ESTABLISHED OR PROVEN, THIS PROMISE WAS BROKEN.
9

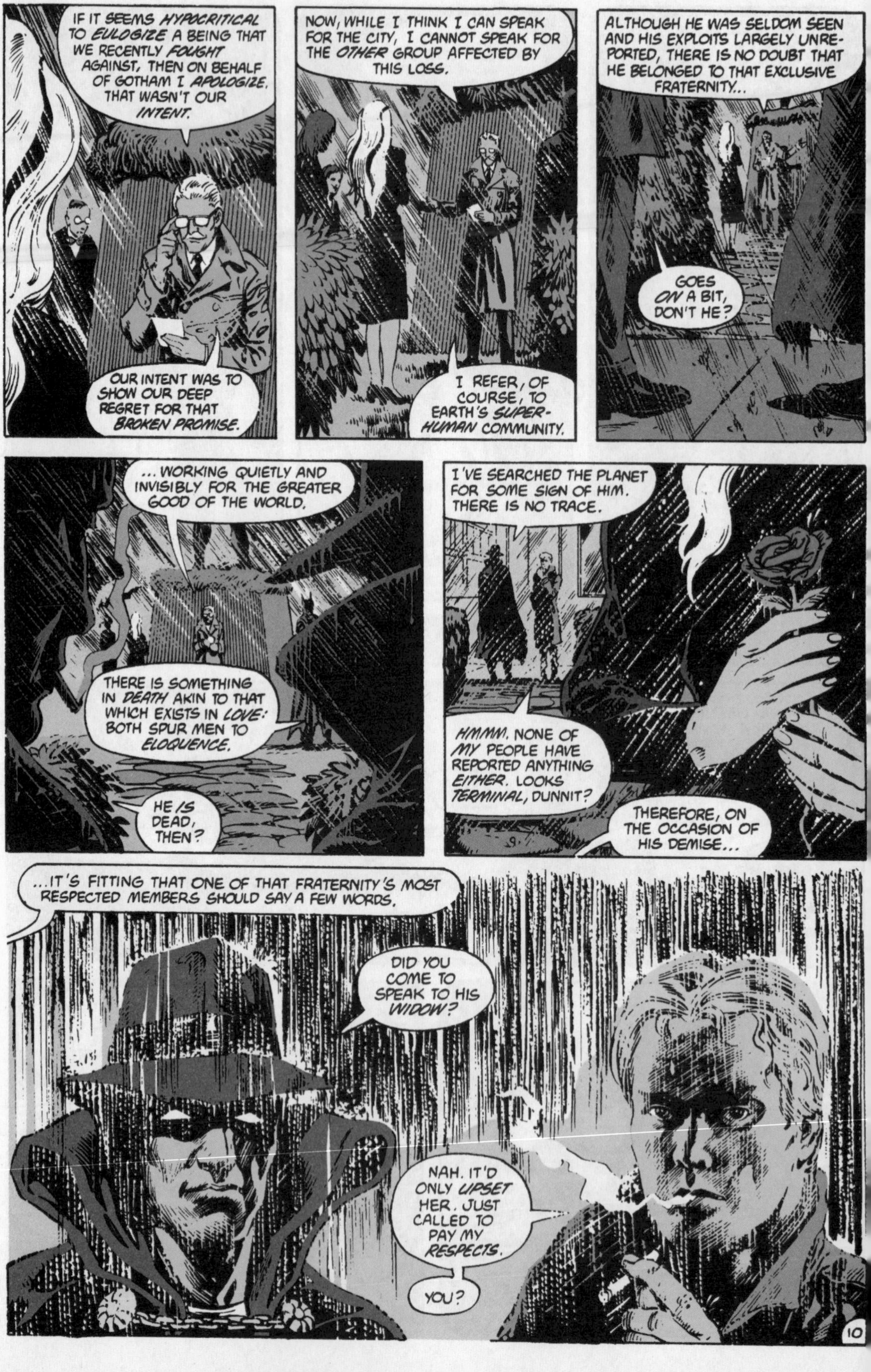
IF IT SEEMS HYPOCRITICAL TO EULOGIZE A BEING THAT WE RECENTLY FOUGHT AGAINST, THEN ON BEHALF OF GOTHAM I APOLOGIZE. THAT WASN'T OUR INTENT.
OUR INTENT WAS TO SHOW OUR DEEP REGRET FOR THAT BROKEN PROMISE.
NOW, WHILE I THINK I CAN SPEAK FOR THE CITY, I CANNOT SPEAK FOR THE OTHER GROUP AFFECTED BY THIS LOSS.
I REFER, OF COURSE, TO EARTH'S SUPER-HUMAN COMMUNITY.
ALTHOUGH HE WAS SELDOM SEEN AND HIS EXPLOITS LARGELY UNRE-PORTED, THERE IS NO DOUBT THAT HE BELONGED TO THAT EXCLUSIVE FRATERNITY...
GOES ON A BIT, DON'T HE?
...WORKING QUIETLY AND INVISIBLY FOR THE GREATER GOOD OF THE WORLD.
THERE IS SOMETHING IN DEATH AKIN TO THAT WHICH EXISTS IN LOVE: BOTH SPUR MEN TO ELOQUENCE.
HE IS DEAD, THEN?
I'VE SEARCHED THE PLANET FOR SOME SIGN OF HIM. THERE IS NO TRACE.
HMMM. NONE OF MY PEOPLE HAVE REPORTED ANYTHING EITHER. LOOKS TERMINAL, DUNNIT?
THEREFORE, ON THE OCCASION OF HIS DEMISE...
...IT'S FITTING THAT ONE OF THAT FRATERNITY'S MOST RESPECTED MEMBERS SHOULD SAY A FEW WORDS.
DID YOU COME TO SPEAK TO HIS WIDOW?
NAH. IT'D ONLY UPSET HER. JUST CALLED TO PAY MY RESPECTS.
YOU?
10

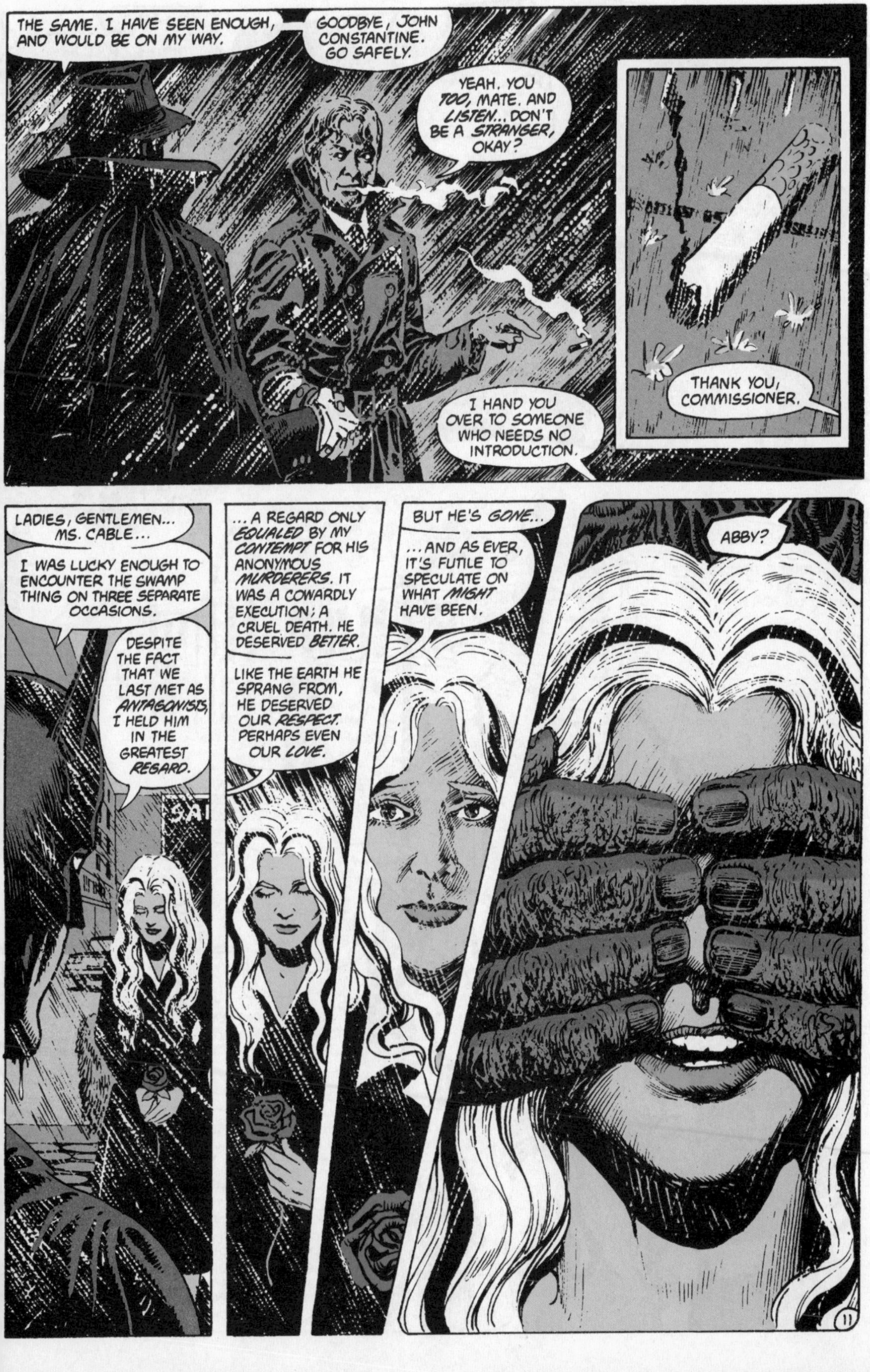
THE SAME. I HAVE SEEN ENOUGH, AND WOULD BE ON MY WAY.
GOODBYE, JOHN CONSTANTINE. GO SAFELY.
YEAH. YOU TOO, MATE. AND LISTEN... DON'T BE A STRANGER, OKAY?
I HAND YOU OVER TO SOMEONE WHO NEEDS NO INTRODUCTION.
THANK YOU, COMMISSIONER.
LADIES, GENTLEMEN... MS. CABLE...
I WAS LUCKY ENOUGH TO ENCOUNTER THE SWAMP THING ON THREE SEPARATE OCCASIONS.
DESPITE THE FACT THAT WE LAST MET AS ANTAGONISTS, I HELD HIM IN THE GREATEST REGARD.
... A REGARD ONLY EQUALED BY MY CONTEMPT FOR HIS ANONYMOUS MURDERERS. IT WAS A COWARDLY EXECUTION; A CRUEL DEATH. HE DESERVED BETTER.
LIKE THE EARTH HE SPRANG FROM, HE DESERVED OUR RESPECT. PERHAPS EVEN OUR LOVE.
BUT HE'S GONE...
... AND AS EVER, IT'S FUTILE TO SPECULATE ON WHAT MIGHT HAVE BEEN.
ABBY?
11

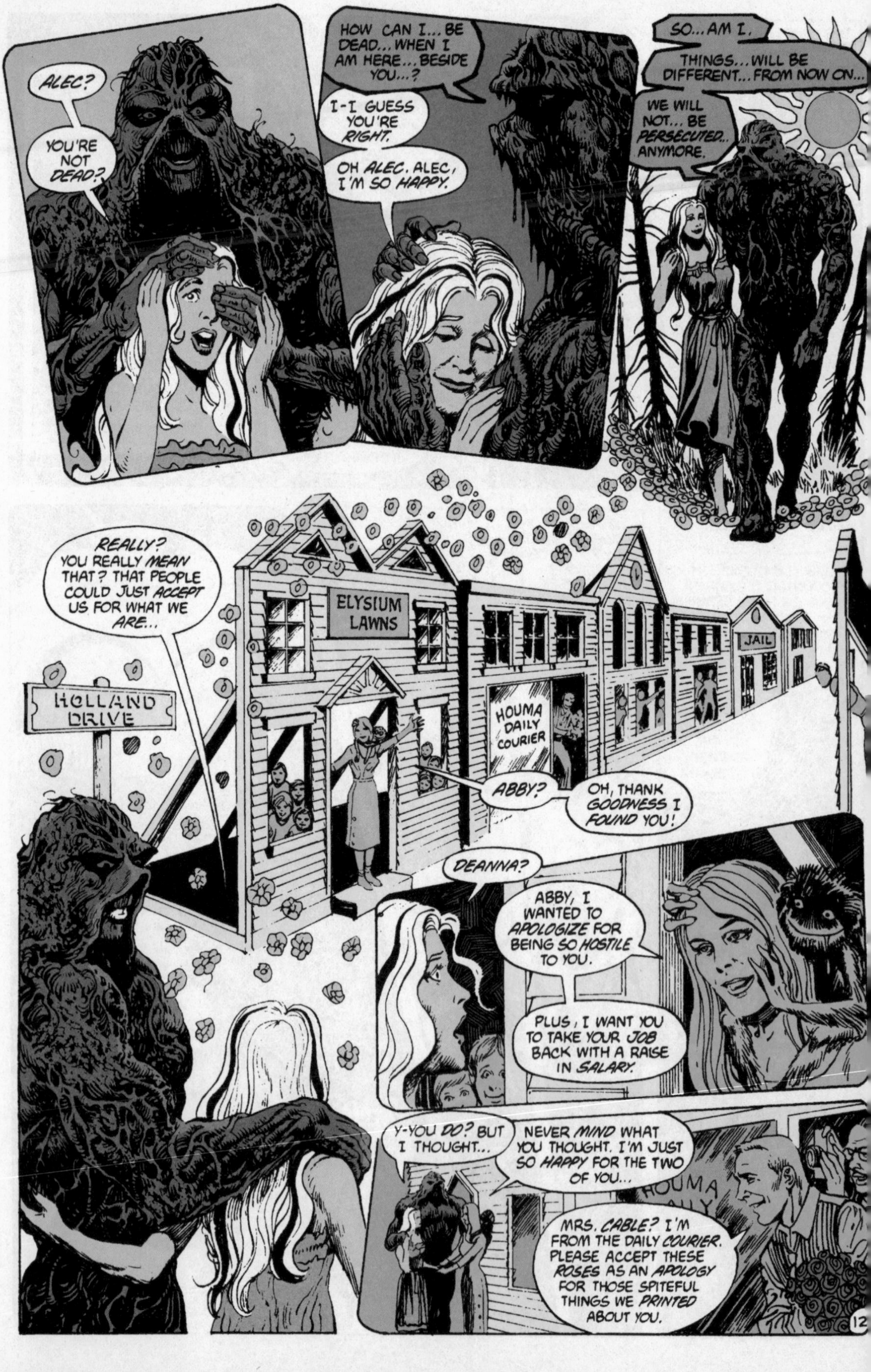
ALEC?
YOU'RE NOT DEAD?
HOW CAN I... BE DEAD... WHEN I AM HERE... BESIDE YOU...?
I-I GUESS YOU'RE RIGHT.
OH ALEC. ALEC, I'M SO HAPPY.
SO... AM I.
THINGS... WILL BE DIFFERENT... FROM NOW ON...
WE WILL NOT... BE PERSECUTED... ANYMORE.
REALLY? YOU REALLY MEAN THAT? THAT PEOPLE COULD JUST ACCEPT US FOR WHAT WE ARE...
ELYSIUM LAWNS
HOLLAND DRIVE
HOUMA DAILY COURIER
JAIL
ABBY?
OH, THANK GOODNESS I FOUND YOU!
DEANNA?
ABBY, I WANTED TO APOLOGIZE FOR BEING SO HOSTILE TO YOU.
PLUS, I WANT YOU TO TAKE YOUR JOB BACK WITH A RAISE IN SALARY.
Y-YOU DO? BUT I THOUGHT...
NEVER MIND WHAT YOU THOUGHT. I'M JUST SO HAPPY FOR THE TWO OF YOU...
MRS. CABLE? I'M FROM THE DAILY COURIER. PLEASE ACCEPT THESE ROSES AS AN APOLOGY FOR THOSE SPITEFUL THINGS WE PRINTED ABOUT YOU.
12

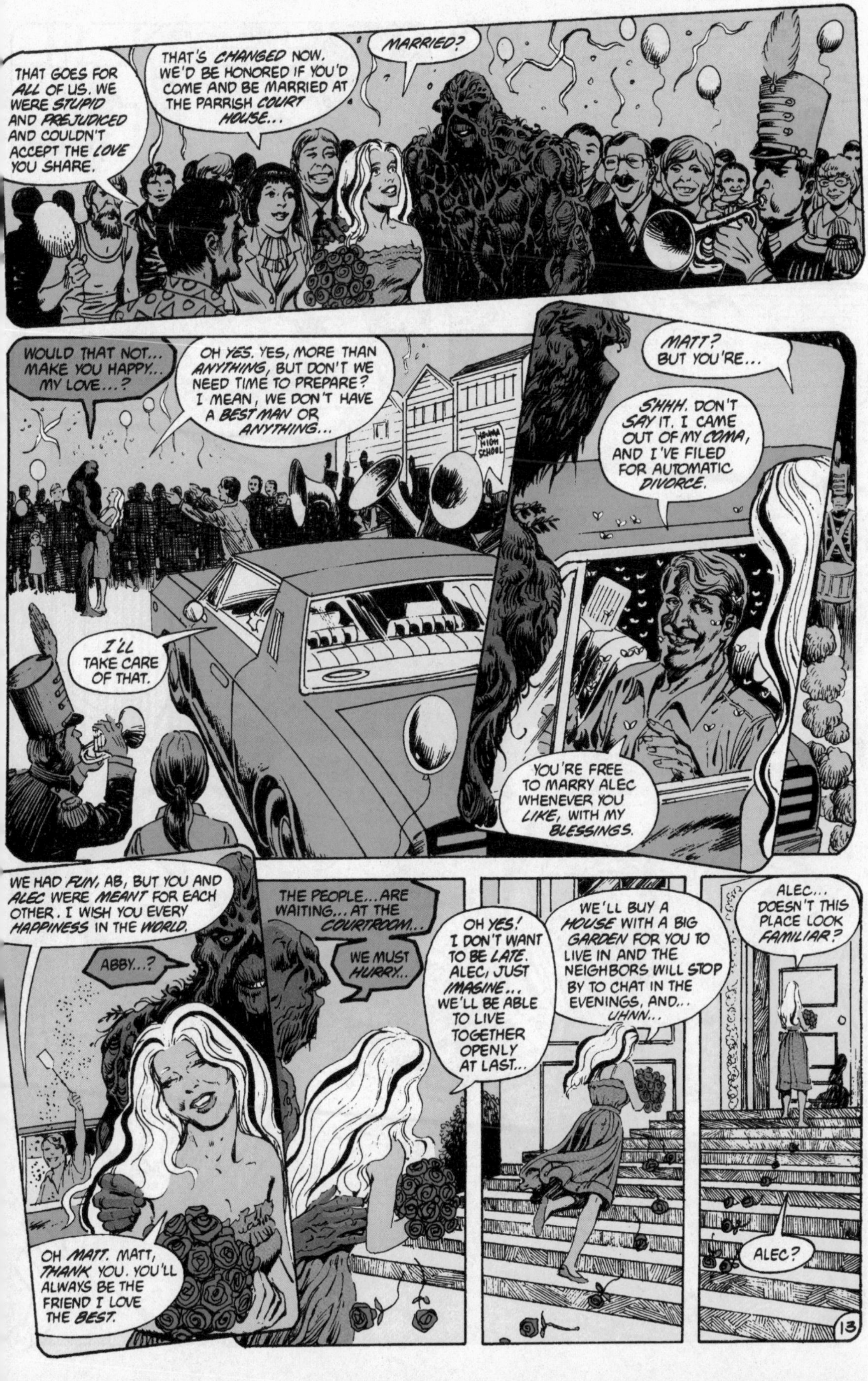
THAT GOES FOR ALL OF US. WE WERE STUPID AND PREJUDICED AND COULDN'T ACCEPT THE LOVE YOU SHARE.
THAT'S CHANGED NOW. WE'D BE HONORED IF YOU'D COME AND BE MARRIED AT THE PARRISH COURT HOUSE...
MARRIED?
WOULD THAT NOT... MAKE YOU HAPPY... MY LOVE...?
OH YES. YES, MORE THAN ANYTHING, BUT DON'T WE NEED TIME TO PREPARE? I MEAN, WE DON'T HAVE A BEST MAN OR ANYTHING...
I'LL TAKE CARE OF THAT.
MATT? BUT YOU'RE...
SHHH. DON'T SAY IT. I CAME OUT OF MY COMA, AND I'VE FILED FOR AUTOMATIC DIVORCE.
YOU'RE FREE TO MARRY ALEC WHENEVER YOU LIKE, WITH MY BLESSINGS.
WE HAD FUN, AB, BUT YOU AND ALEC WERE MEANT FOR EACH OTHER. I WISH YOU EVERY HAPPINESS IN THE WORLD.
ABBY...?
OH MATT. MATT, THANK YOU. YOU'LL ALWAYS BE THE FRIEND I LOVE THE BEST.
THE PEOPLE...ARE WAITING... AT THE COURTROOM...
WE MUST HURRY...
OH YES! I DON'T WANT TO BE LATE. ALEC, JUST IMAGINE... WE'LL BE ABLE TO LIVE TOGETHER OPENLY AT LAST...
WE'LL BUY A HOUSE WITH A BIG GARDEN FOR YOU TO LIVE IN AND THE NEIGHBORS WILL STOP BY TO CHAT IN THE EVENINGS, AND... UHNN...
ALEC... DOESN'T THIS PLACE LOOK FAMILIAR?
ALEC?
13

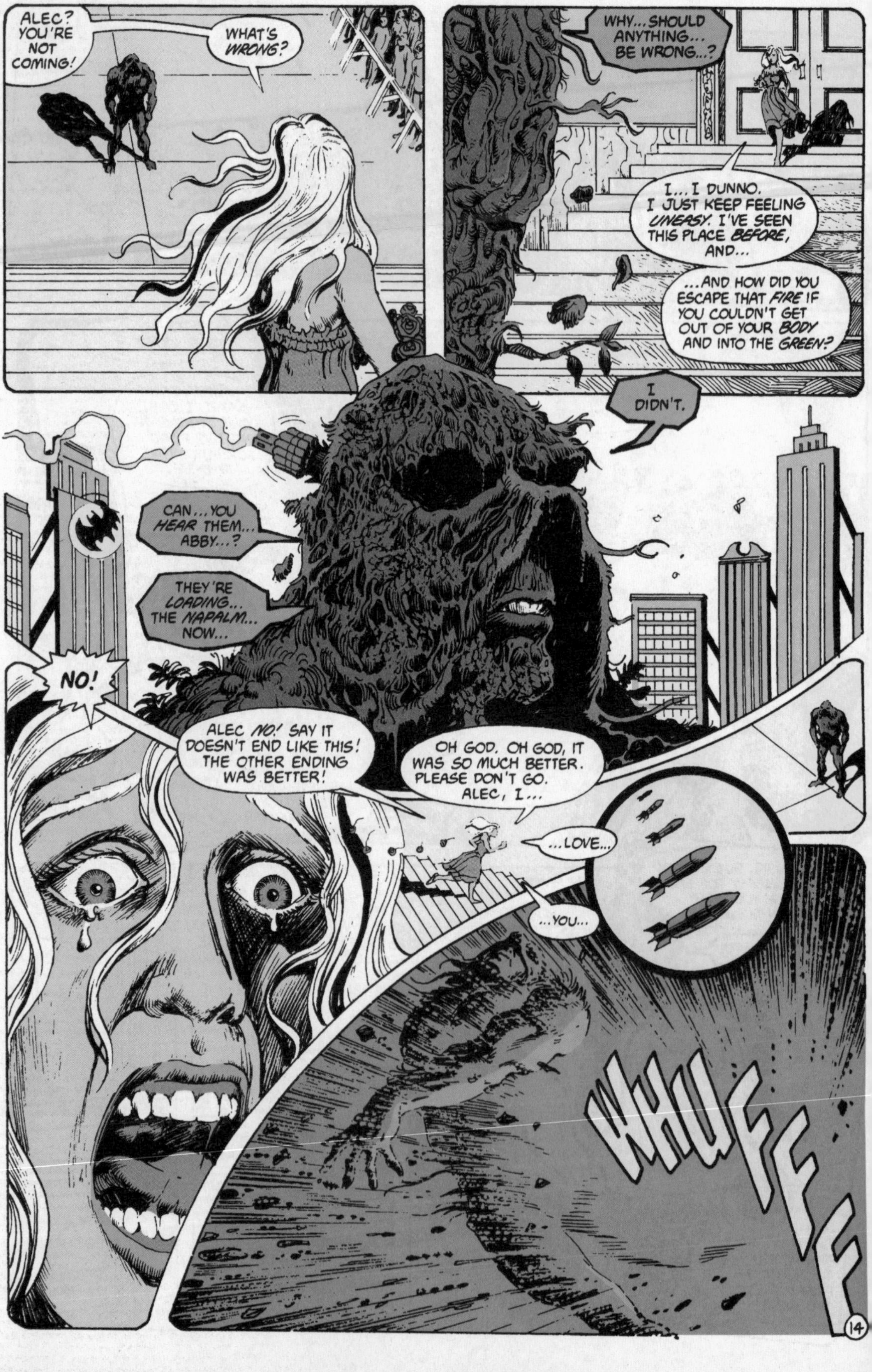
ALEC? YOU'RE NOT COMING!
WHAT'S WRONG?
WHY... SHOULD ANYTHING... BE WRONG...?
I... I DUNNO. I JUST KEEP FEELING UNEASY. I'VE SEEN THIS PLACE BEFORE, AND...
...AND HOW DID YOU ESCAPE THAT FIRE IF YOU COULDN'T GET OUT OF YOUR BODY AND INTO THE GREEN?
I DIDN'T.
CAN... YOU HEAR THEM... ABBY...?
THEY'RE LOADING... THE NAPALM... NOW...
NO!
ALEC NO! SAY IT DOESN'T END LIKE THIS! THE OTHER ENDING WAS BETTER!
OH GOD. OH GOD, IT WAS SO MUCH BETTER. PLEASE DON'T GO. ALEC, I...
...LOVE...
...YOU...
WHUFFF
14

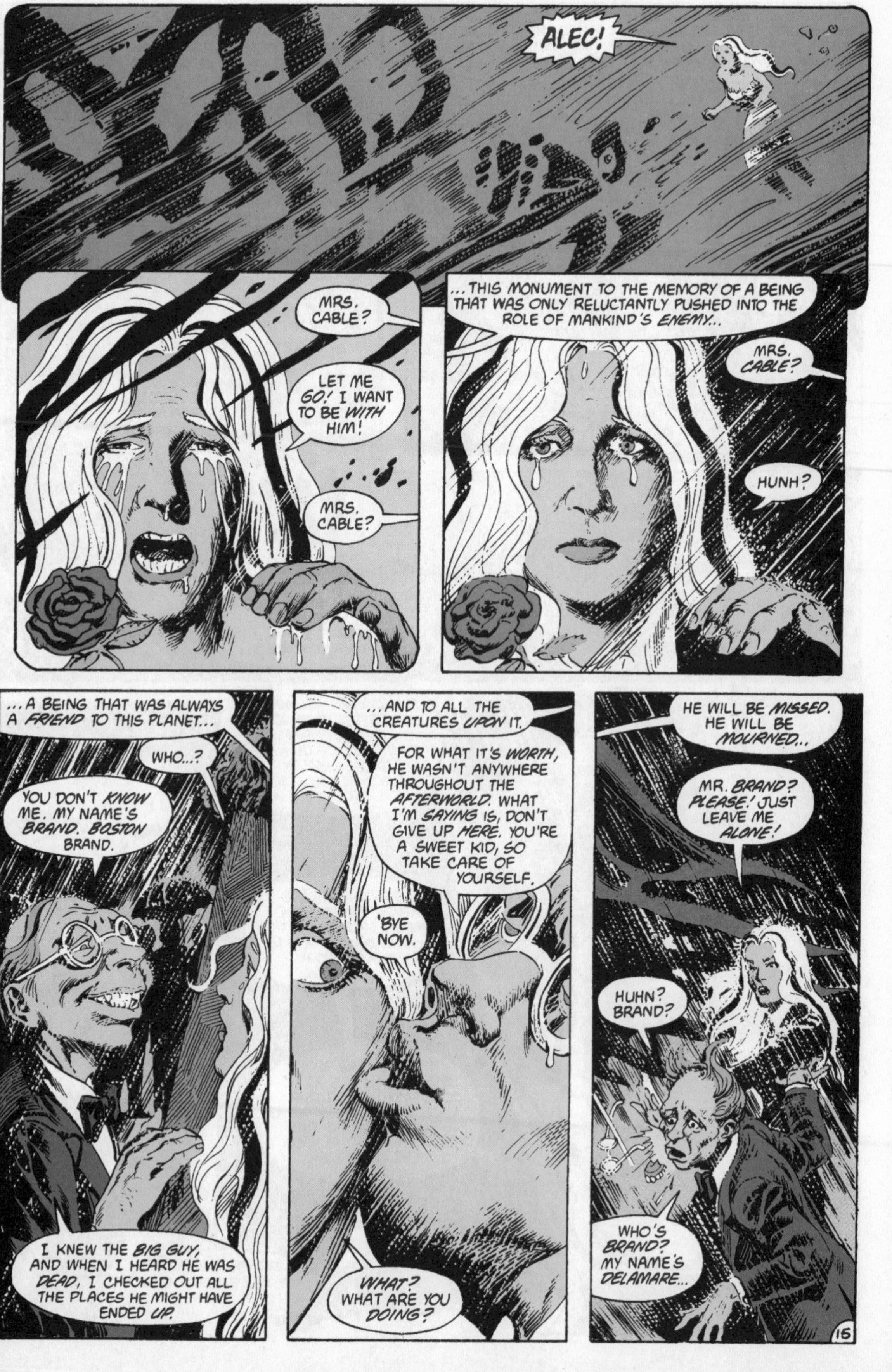
ALEC!
MRS. CABLE?
LET ME GO! I WANT TO BE WITH HIM!
MRS. CABLE?
...THIS MONUMENT TO THE MEMORY OF A BEING THAT WAS ONLY RELUCTANTLY PUSHED INTO THE ROLE OF MANKIND'S ENEMY...
MRS. CABLE?
HUNH?
...A BEING THAT WAS ALWAYS A FRIEND TO THIS PLANET...
WHO...?
YOU DON'T KNOW ME. MY NAME'S BRAND. BOSTON BRAND.
I KNEW THE BIG GUY, AND WHEN I HEARD HE WAS DEAD, I CHECKED OUT ALL THE PLACES HE MIGHT HAVE ENDED UP.
...AND TO ALL THE CREATURES UPON IT.
FOR WHAT IT'S WORTH, HE WASN'T ANYWHERE THROUGHOUT THE AFTERWORLD. WHAT I'M SAYING IS, DON'T GIVE UP HERE. YOU'RE A SWEET KID, SO TAKE CARE OF YOURSELF.
'BYE NOW.
WHAT? WHAT ARE YOU DOING?
HE WILL BE MISSED. HE WILL BE MOURNED...
MR. BRAND? PLEASE! JUST LEAVE ME ALONE!
HUHN? BRAND?
WHO'S BRAND? MY NAME'S DELAMARE...
15

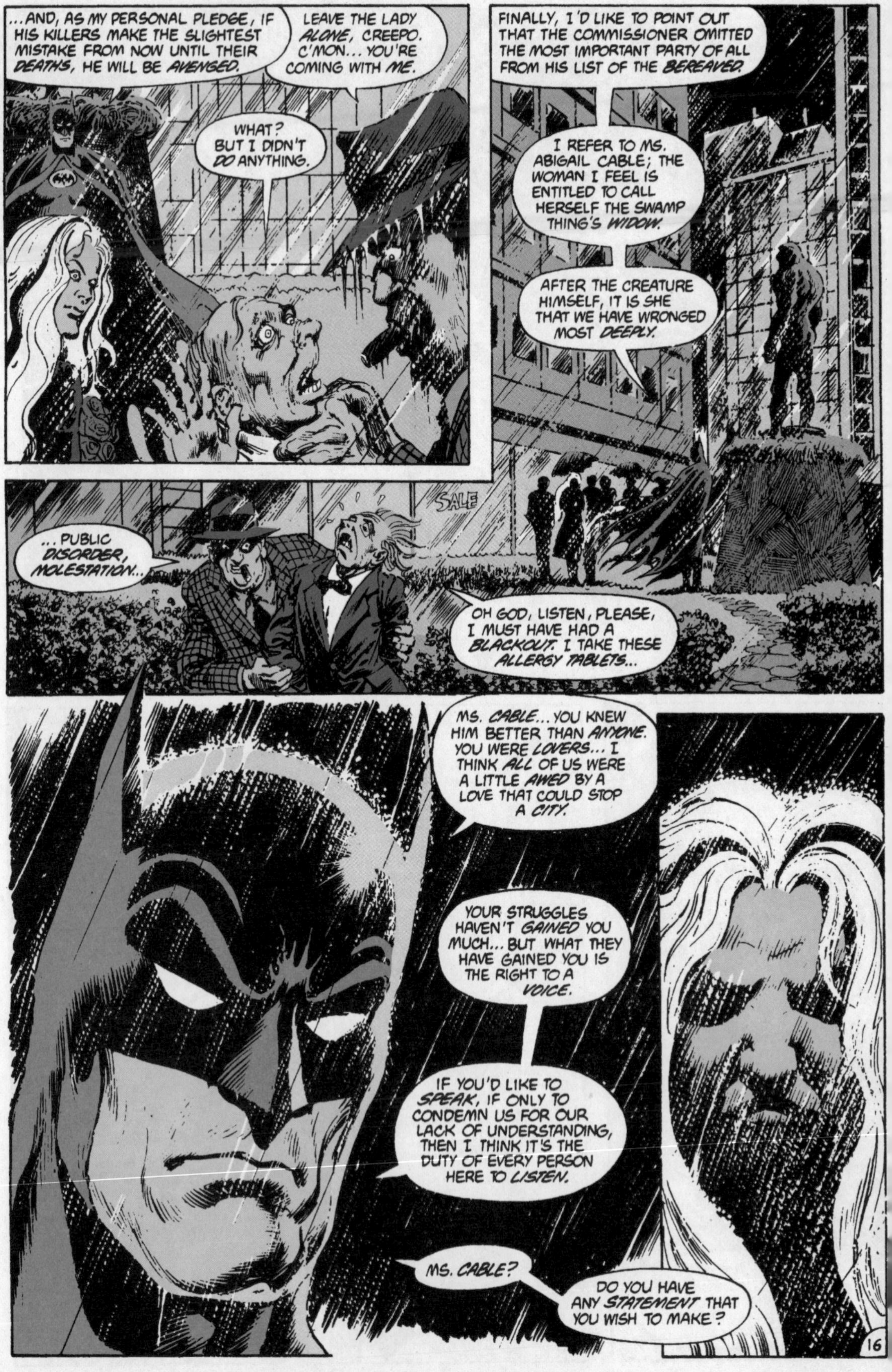
...AND, AS MY PERSONAL PLEDGE, IF HIS KILLERS MAKE THE SLIGHTEST MISTAKE FROM NOW UNTIL THEIR DEATHS, HE WILL BE AVENGED.
LEAVE THE LADY ALONE, CREEPO. C'MON... YOU'RE COMING WITH ME.
WHAT? BUT I DIDN'T DO ANYTHING.
FINALLY, I'D LIKE TO POINT OUT THAT THE COMMISSIONER OMITTED THE MOST IMPORTANT PARTY OF ALL FROM HIS LIST OF THE BEREAVED.
I REFER TO MS. ABIGAIL CABLE; THE WOMAN I FEEL IS ENTITLED TO CALL HERSELF THE SWAMP THING'S WIDOW.
AFTER THE CREATURE HIMSELF, IT IS SHE THAT WE HAVE WRONGED MOST DEEPLY.
SALE
...PUBLIC DISORDER, MOLESTATION...
OH GOD, LISTEN, PLEASE, I MUST HAVE HAD A BLACKOUT. I TAKE THESE ALLERGY TABLETS...
MS. CABLE... YOU KNEW HIM BETTER THAN ANYONE. YOU WERE LOVERS... I THINK ALL OF US WERE A LITTLE AWED BY A LOVE THAT COULD STOP A CITY.
YOUR STRUGGLES HAVEN'T GAINED YOU MUCH... BUT WHAT THEY HAVE GAINED YOU IS THE RIGHT TO A VOICE.
IF YOU'D LIKE TO SPEAK, IF ONLY TO CONDEMN US FOR OUR LACK OF UNDERSTANDING, THEN I THINK IT'S THE DUTY OF EVERY PERSON HERE TO LISTEN.
MS. CABLE?
DO YOU HAVE ANY STATEMENT THAT YOU WISH TO MAKE?
16

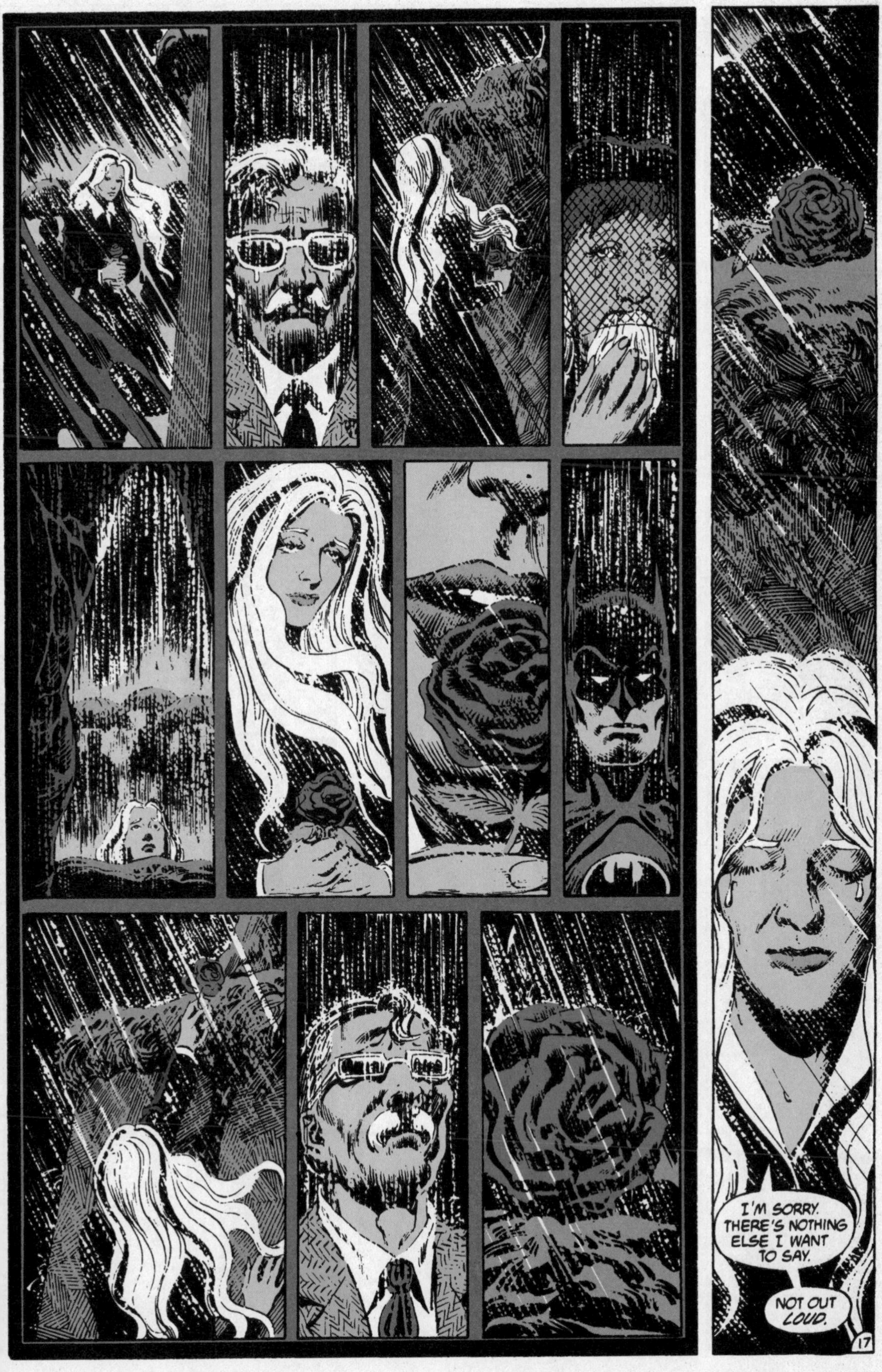
I'M SORRY. THERE'S NOTHING ELSE I WANT TO SAY.
NOT OUT LOUD.
17

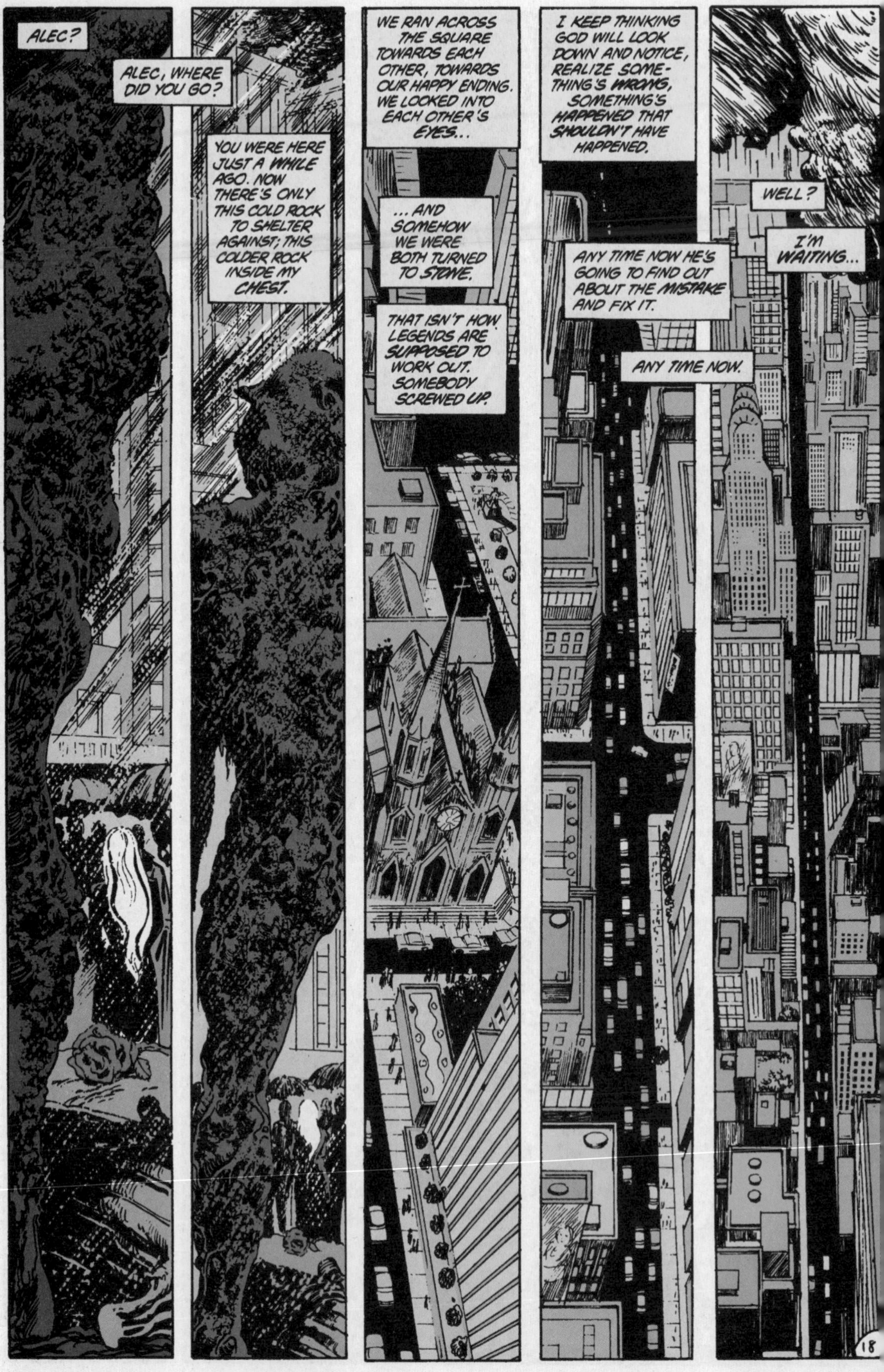
ALEC?
ALEC, WHERE DID YOU GO?
YOU WERE HERE JUST A WHILE AGO. NOW THERE'S ONLY THIS COLD ROCK TO SHELTER AGAINST; THIS COLDER ROCK INSIDE MY CHEST.
WE RAN ACROSS THE SQUARE TOWARDS EACH OTHER, TOWARDS OUR HAPPY ENDING. WE LOOKED INTO EACH OTHER'S EYES...
...AND SOMEHOW WE WERE BOTH TURNED TO STONE.
THAT ISN'T HOW LEGENDS ARE SUPPOSED TO WORK OUT. SOMEBODY SCREWED UP.
I KEEP THINKING GOD WILL LOOK DOWN AND NOTICE, REALIZE SOMETHING'S WRONG, SOMETHING'S HAPPENED THAT SHOULDN'T HAVE HAPPENED.
ANY TIME NOW HE'S GOING TO FIND OUT ABOUT THE MISTAKE AND FIX IT.
ANY TIME NOW.
WELL?
I'M WAITING...
18

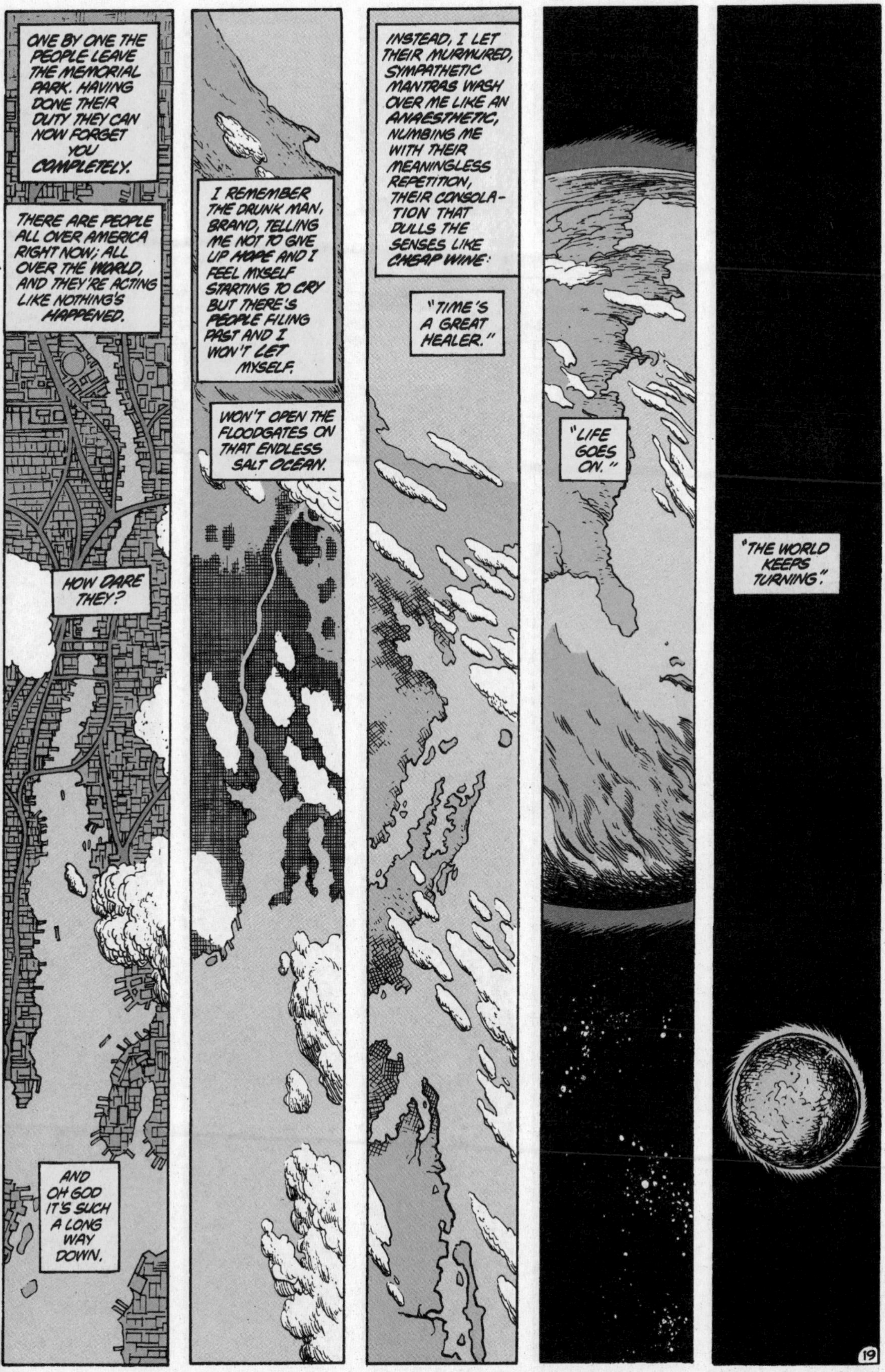
ONE BY ONE THE PEOPLE LEAVE THE MEMORIAL PARK. HAVING DONE THEIR DUTY THEY CAN NOW FORGET YOU COMPLETELY.
THERE ARE PEOPLE ALL OVER AMERICA RIGHT NOW; ALL OVER THE WORLD, AND THEY'RE ACTING LIKE NOTHING'S HAPPENED.
HOW DARE THEY?
AND OH GOD IT'S SUCH A LONG WAY DOWN.
I REMEMBER THE DRUNK MAN, BRAND, TELLING ME NOT TO GIVE UP HOPE AND I FEEL MYSELF STARTING TO CRY BUT THERE'S PEOPLE FILING PAST AND I WON'T LET MYSELF.
WON'T OPEN THE FLOODGATES ON THAT ENDLESS SALT OCEAN.
INSTEAD, I LET THEIR MURMURED, SYMPATHETIC MANTRAS WASH OVER ME LIKE AN ANAESTHETIC, NUMBING ME WITH THEIR MEANINGLESS REPETITION, THEIR CONSOLA-TION THAT DULLS THE SENSES LIKE CHEAP WINE:
"TIME'S A GREAT HEALER."
"LIFE GOES ON."
"THE WORLD KEEPS TURNING."
19

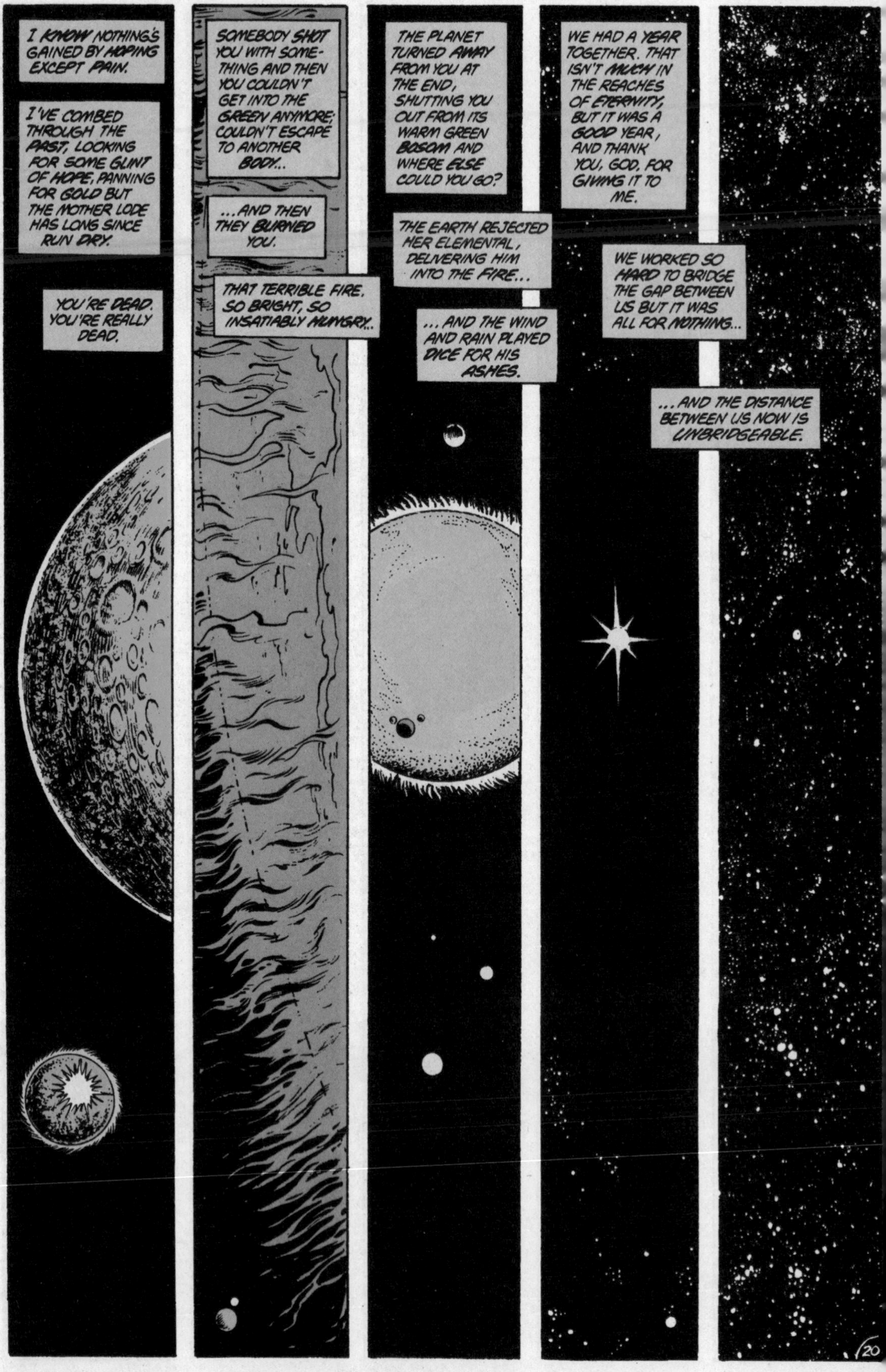
I KNOW NOTHING'S GAINED BY HOPING EXCEPT PAIN.
I'VE COMBED THROUGH THE PAST, LOOKING FOR SOME GLINT OF HOPE, PANNING FOR GOLD BUT THE MOTHER LODE HAS LONG SINCE RUN DRY.
YOU'RE DEAD. YOU'RE REALLY DEAD.
SOMEBODY SHOT YOU WITH SOMETHING AND THEN YOU COULDN'T GET INTO THE GREEN ANYMORE; COULDN'T ESCAPE TO ANOTHER BODY...
...AND THEN THEY BURNED YOU.
THAT TERRIBLE FIRE. SO BRIGHT, SO INSATIABLY HUNGRY...
THE PLANET TURNED AWAY FROM YOU AT THE END, SHUTTING YOU OUT FROM ITS WARM GREEN BOSOM AND WHERE ELSE COULD YOU GO?
THE EARTH REJECTED HER ELEMENTAL, DELIVERING HIM INTO THE FIRE...
...AND THE WIND AND RAIN PLAYED DICE FOR HIS ASHES.
WE HAD A YEAR TOGETHER. THAT ISN'T MUCH IN THE REACHES OF ETERNITY, BUT IT WAS A GOOD YEAR, AND THANK YOU, GOD, FOR GIVING IT TO ME.
WE WORKED SO HARD TO BRIDGE THE GAP BETWEEN US BUT IT WAS ALL FOR NOTHING...
...AND THE DISTANCE BETWEEN US NOW IS UNBRIDGEABLE.
20

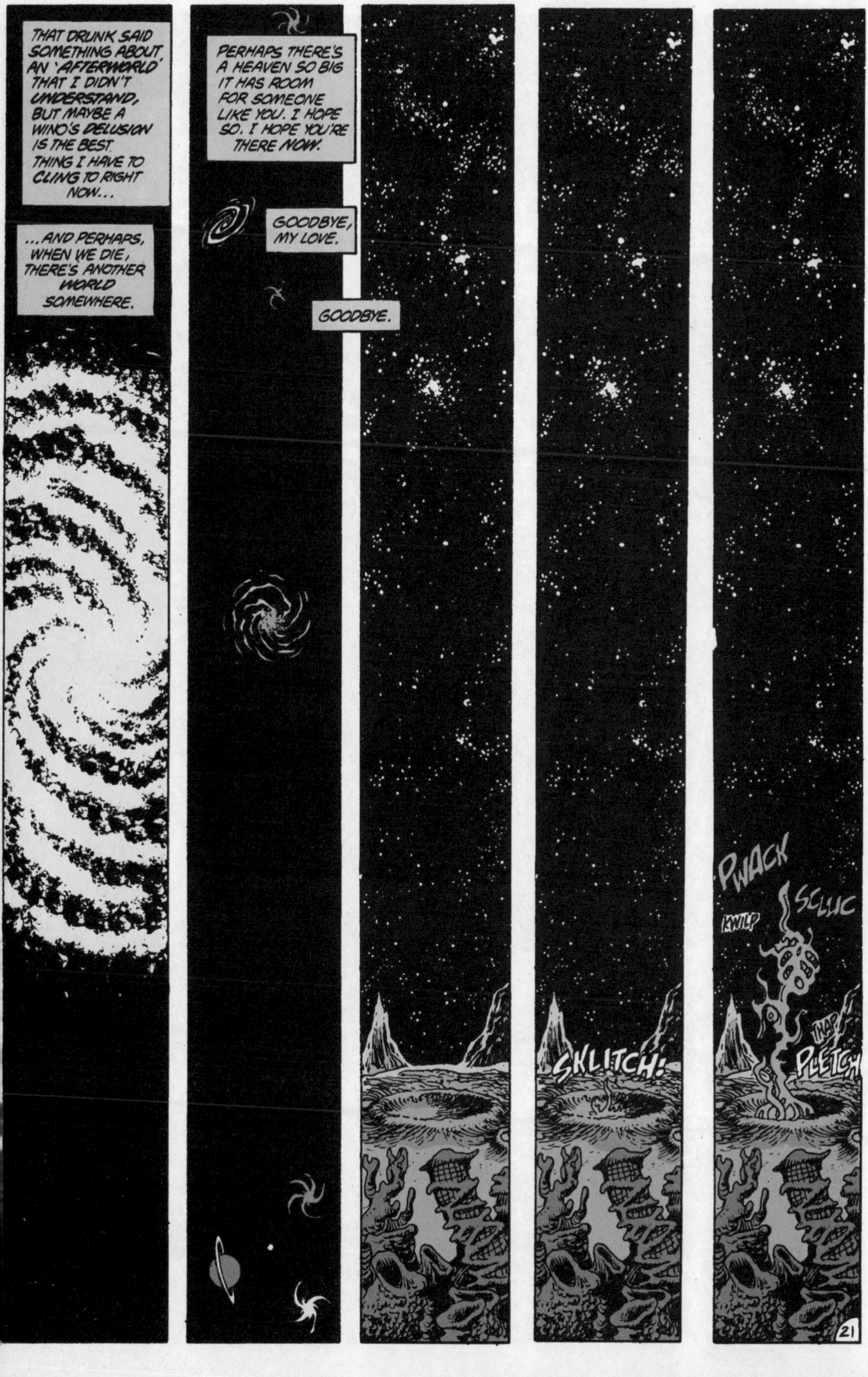
THAT DRUNK SAID SOMETHING ABOUT AN 'AFTERWORLD' THAT I DIDN'T UNDERSTAND, BUT MAYBE A WINO'S DELUSION IS THE BEST THING I HAVE TO CLING TO RIGHT NOW...
...AND PERHAPS, WHEN WE DIE, THERE'S ANOTHER WORLD SOMEWHERE.
PERHAPS THERE'S A HEAVEN SO BIG IT HAS ROOM FOR SOMEONE LIKE YOU. I HOPE SO. I HOPE YOU'RE THERE NOW.
GOODBYE, MY LOVE.
GOODBYE.
SKLITCH!
PWACK
SCLUC
KWILP
THAP
PLETCH
21

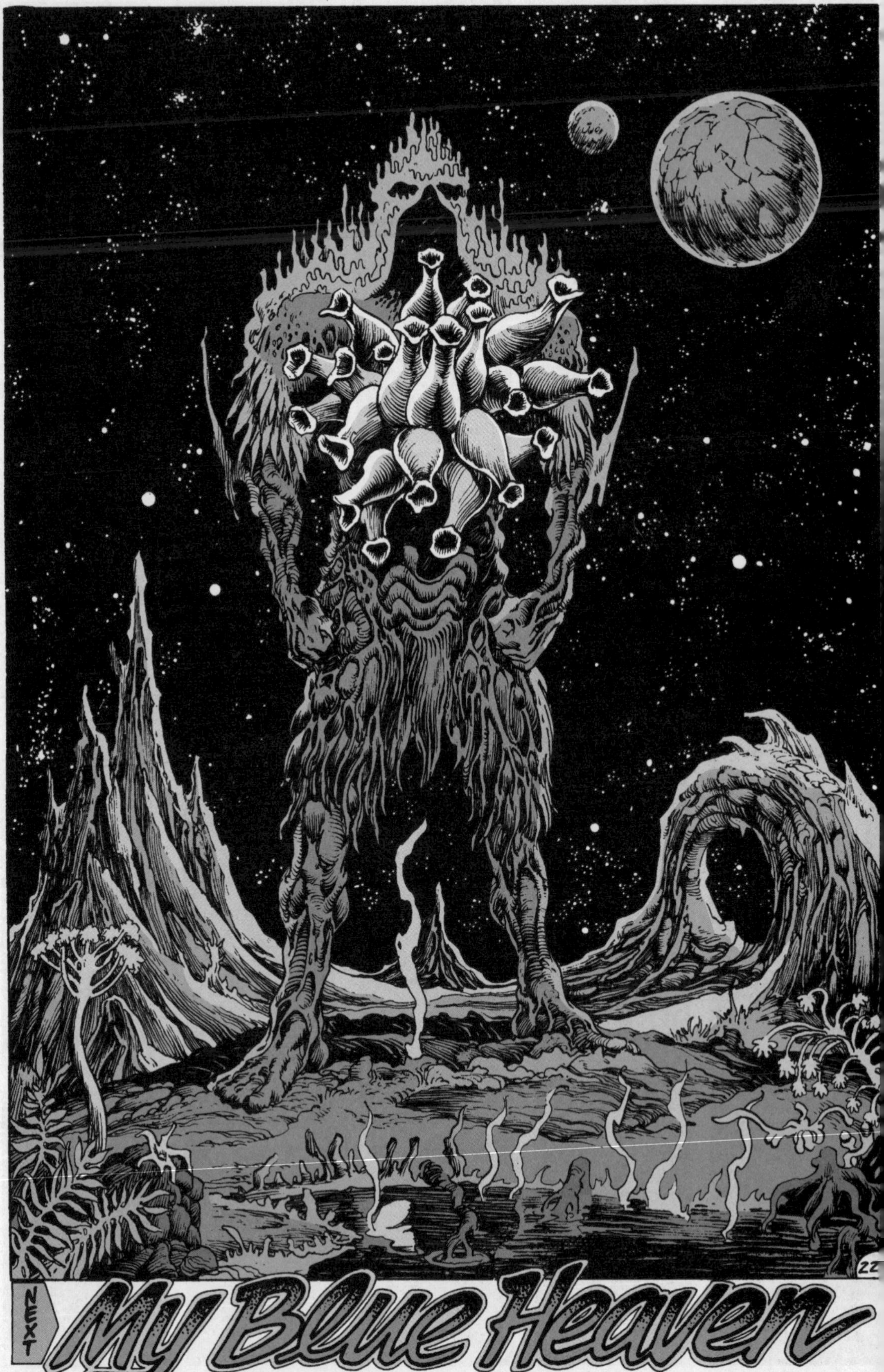
22
NEXT
My Blue Heaven

CHAPTER 6

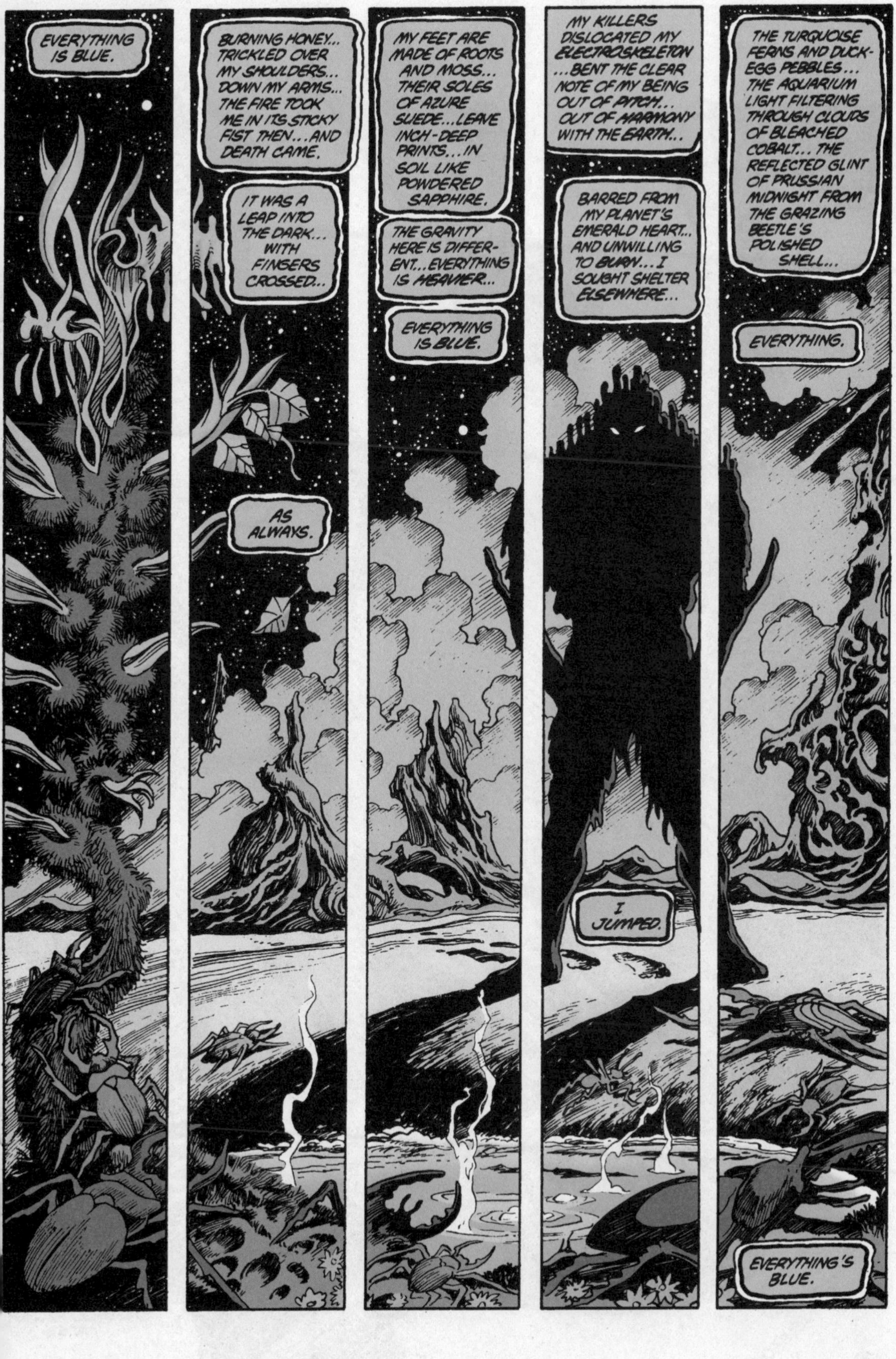
EVERYTHING IS BLUE.
BURNING HONEY... TRICKLED OVER MY SHOULDERS... DOWN MY ARMS... THE FIRE TOOK ME IN ITS STICKY FIST THEN... AND DEATH CAME.
IT WAS A LEAP INTO THE DARK... WITH FINGERS CROSSED...
AS ALWAYS.
MY FEET ARE MADE OF ROOTS AND MOSS... THEIR SOLES OF AZURE SUEDE... LEAVE INCH-DEEP PRINTS... IN SOIL LIKE POWDERED SAPPHIRE.
THE GRAVITY HERE IS DIFFERENT... EVERYTHING IS HEAVIER...
EVERYTHING IS BLUE.
MY KILLERS DISLOCATED MY ELECTROSKELETON ...BENT THE CLEAR NOTE OF MY BEING OUT OF PITCH... OUT OF HARMONY WITH THE EARTH...
BARRED FROM MY PLANET'S EMERALD HEART... AND UNWILLING TO BURN... I SOUGHT SHELTER ELSEWHERE...
I JUMPED.
THE TURQUOISE FERNS AND DUCK-EGG PEBBLES... THE AQUARIUM LIGHT FILTERING THROUGH CLOUDS OF BLEACHED COBALT... THE REFLECTED GLINT OF PRUSSIAN MIDNIGHT FROM THE GRAZING BEETLE'S POLISHED SHELL...
EVERYTHING.
EVERYTHING'S BLUE.

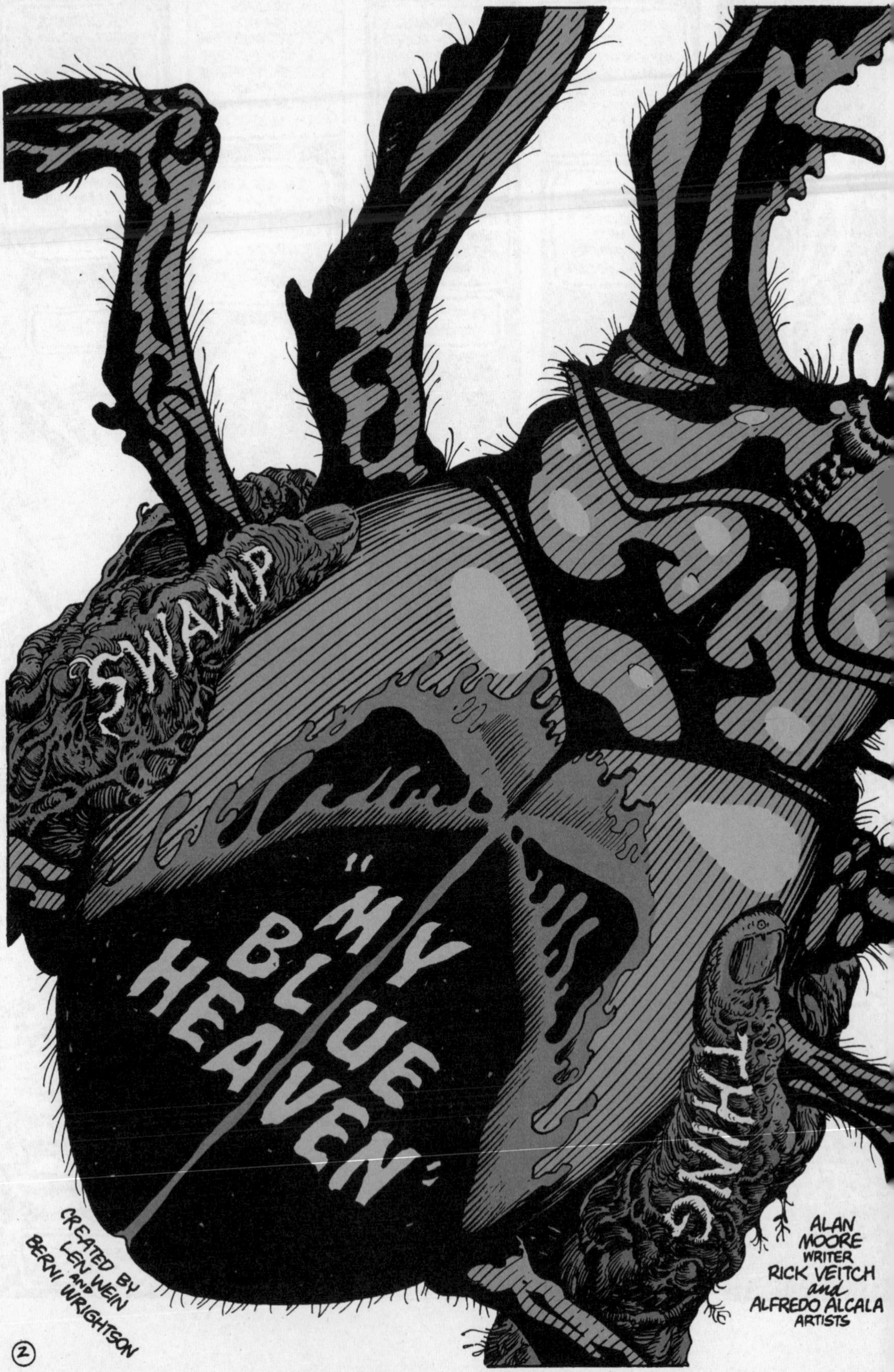
SWAMP
THING
"MY BLUE HEAVEN"
CREATED BY LEN WEIN AND BERNI WRIGHTSON
ALAN MOORE WRITER
RICK VEITCH and ALFREDO ALCALA ARTISTS
2

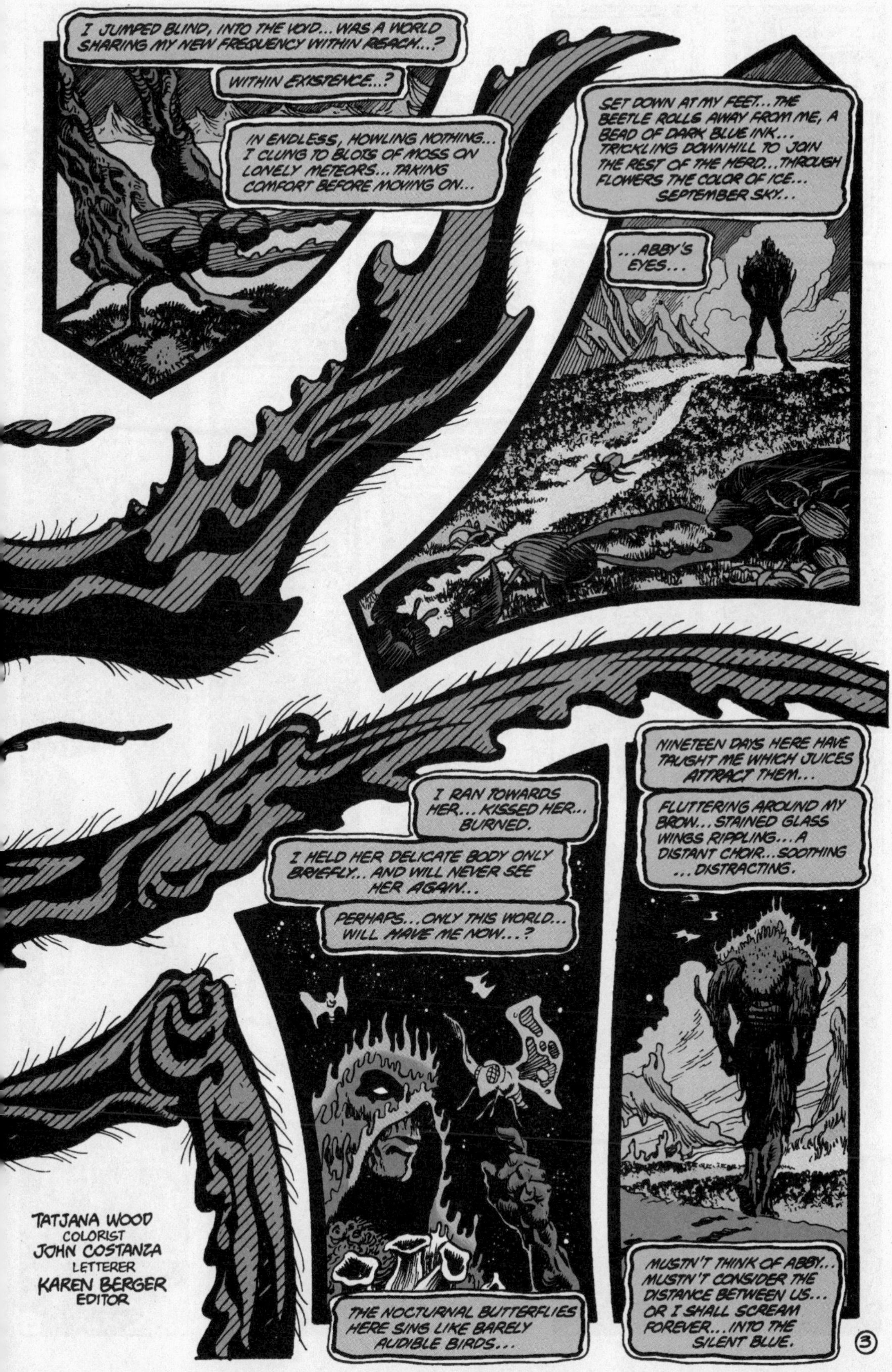
I JUMPED BLIND, INTO THE VOID... WAS A WORLD SHARING MY NEW FREQUENCY WITHIN REACH...?
WITHIN EXISTENCE...?
IN ENDLESS, HOWLING NOTHING... I CLUNG TO BLOTS OF MOSS ON LONELY METEORS... TAKING COMFORT BEFORE MOVING ON...
SET DOWN AT MY FEET... THE BEETLE ROLLS AWAY FROM ME, A BEAD OF DARK BLUE INK... TRICKLING DOWNHILL TO JOIN THE REST OF THE HERD... THROUGH FLOWERS THE COLOR OF ICE... SEPTEMBER SKY...
...ABBY'S EYES...
I RAN TOWARDS HER... KISSED HER... BURNED.
I HELD HER DELICATE BODY ONLY BRIEFLY... AND WILL NEVER SEE HER AGAIN...
PERHAPS... ONLY THIS WORLD... WILL HAVE ME NOW...?
THE NOCTURNAL BUTTERFLIES HERE SING LIKE BARELY AUDIBLE BIRDS...
NINETEEN DAYS HERE HAVE TAUGHT ME WHICH JUICES ATTRACT THEM...
FLUTTERING AROUND MY BROW... STAINED GLASS WINGS RIPPLING... A DISTANT CHOIR... SOOTHING ...DISTRACTING.
MUSTN'T THINK OF ABBY... MUSTN'T CONSIDER THE DISTANCE BETWEEN US... OR I SHALL SCREAM FOREVER... INTO THE SILENT BLUE.
TATJANA WOOD COLORIST
JOHN COSTANZA LETTERER
KAREN BERGER EDITOR
3

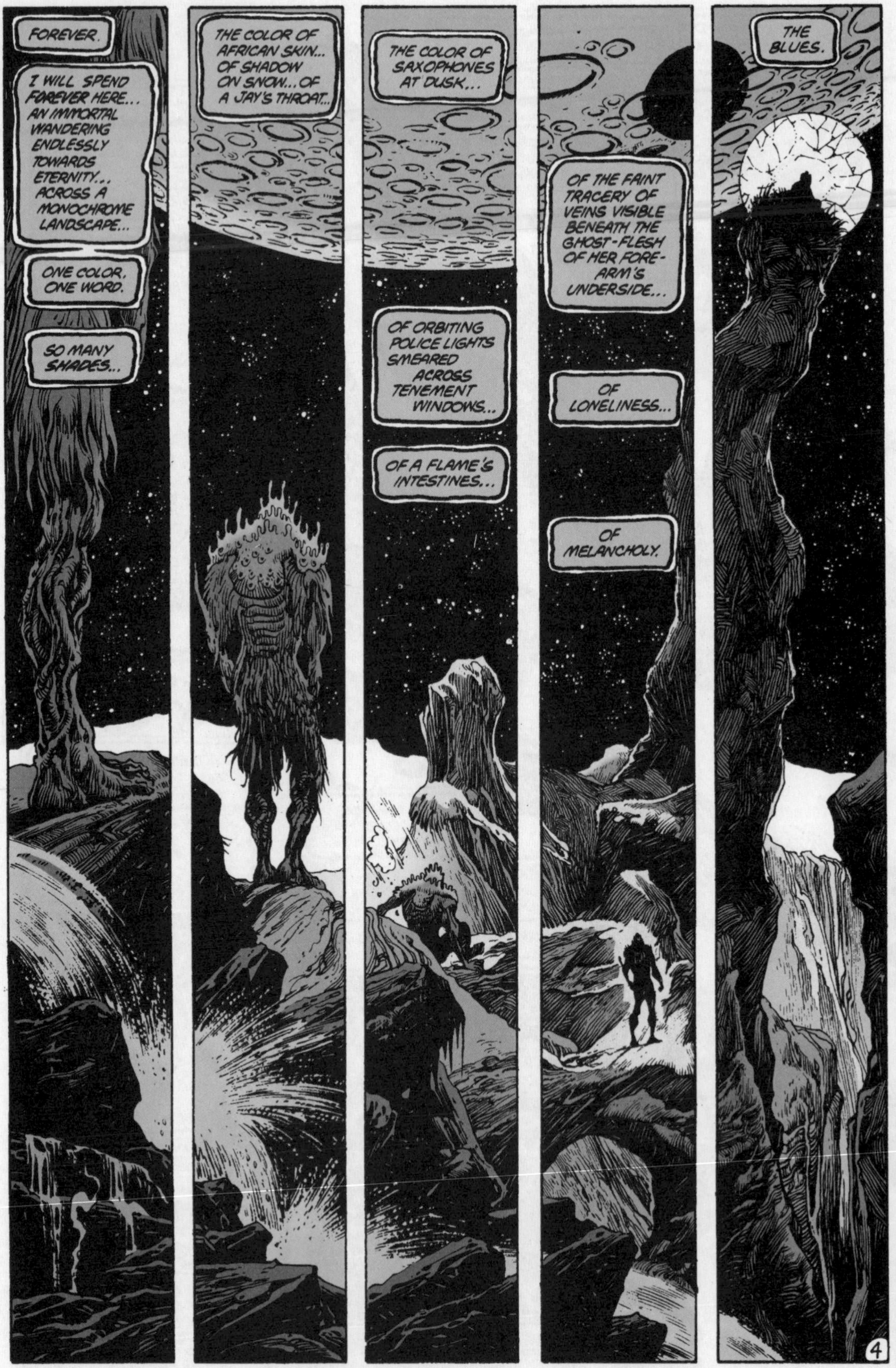
FOREVER.
I WILL SPEND FOREVER HERE... AN IMMORTAL WANDERING ENDLESSLY TOWARDS ETERNITY... ACROSS A MONOCHROME LANDSCAPE...
ONE COLOR. ONE WORD.
SO MANY SHADES...
THE COLOR OF AFRICAN SKIN... OF SHADOW ON SNOW... OF A JAY'S THROAT...
THE COLOR OF SAXOPHONES AT DUSK...
OF ORBITING POLICE LIGHTS SMEARED ACROSS TENEMENT WINDOWS...
OF A FLAME'S INTESTINES...
OF THE FAINT TRACERY OF VEINS VISIBLE BENEATH THE GHOST-FLESH OF HER FORE-ARM'S UNDERSIDE...
OF LONELINESS...
OF MELANCHOLY.
THE BLUES.
4

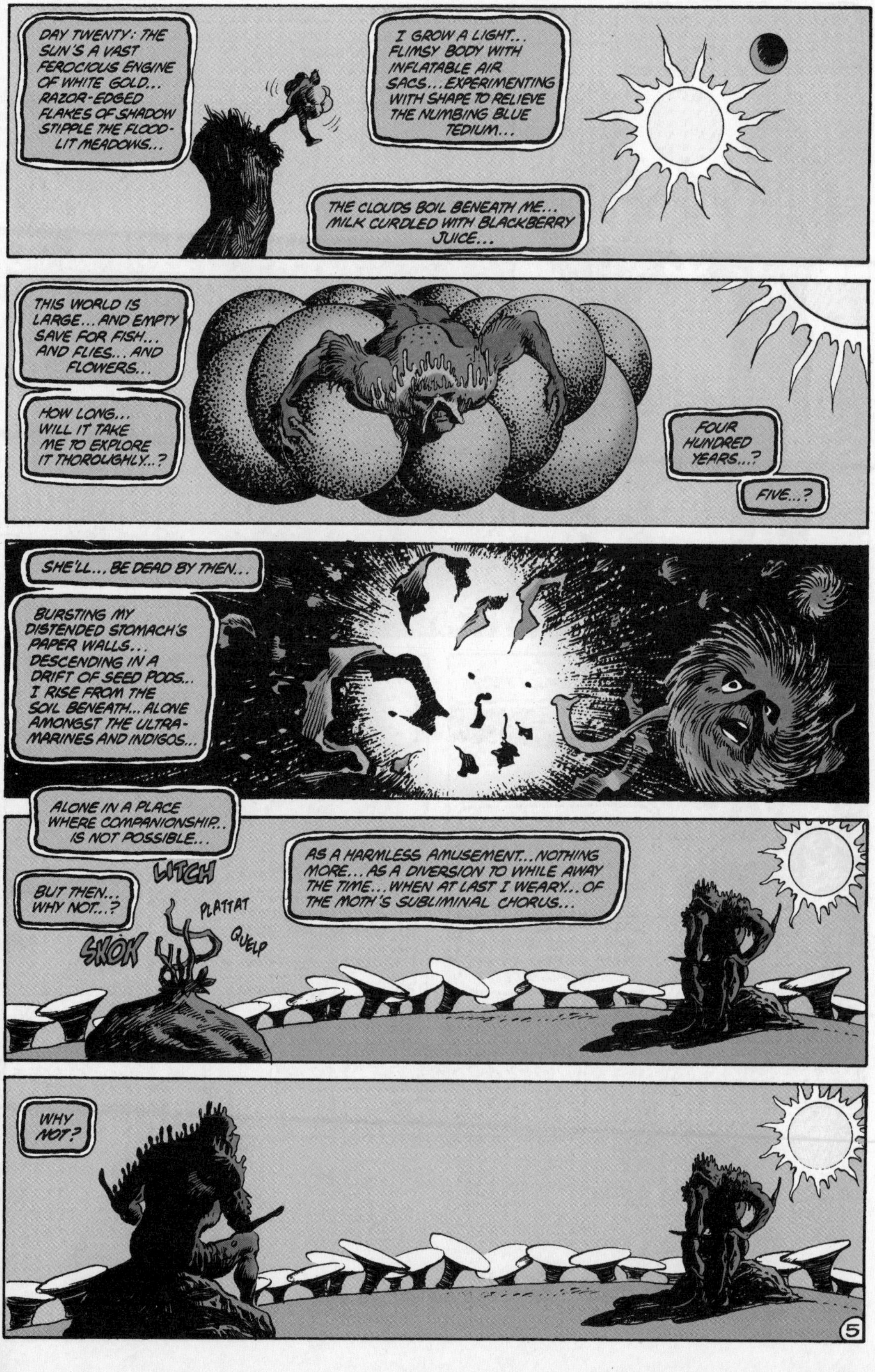
DAY TWENTY: THE SUN'S A VAST FEROCIOUS ENGINE OF WHITE GOLD... RAZOR-EDGED FLAKES OF SHADOW STIPPLE THE FLOOD-LIT MEADOWS...
I GROW A LIGHT... FLIMSY BODY WITH INFLATABLE AIR SACS... EXPERIMENTING WITH SHAPE TO RELIEVE THE NUMBING BLUE TEDIUM...
THE CLOUDS BOIL BENEATH ME... MILK CURDLED WITH BLACKBERRY JUICE...
THIS WORLD IS LARGE... AND EMPTY SAVE FOR FISH... AND FLIES... AND FLOWERS...
HOW LONG... WILL IT TAKE ME TO EXPLORE IT THOROUGHLY...?
FOUR HUNDRED YEARS...?
FIVE...?
SHE'LL... BE DEAD BY THEN...
BURSTING MY DISTENDED STOMACH'S PAPER WALLS... DESCENDING IN A DRIFT OF SEED PODS... I RISE FROM THE SOIL BENEATH... ALONE AMONGST THE ULTRA-MARINES AND INDIGOS...
ALONE IN A PLACE WHERE COMPANIONSHIP... IS NOT POSSIBLE...
BUT THEN... WHY NOT...?
LITCH
PLATTAT
SKOK
QUELP
AS A HARMLESS AMUSEMENT... NOTHING MORE... AS A DIVERSION TO WHILE AWAY THE TIME... WHEN AT LAST I WEARY... OF THE MOTH'S SUBLIMINAL CHORUS...
WHY NOT?
5

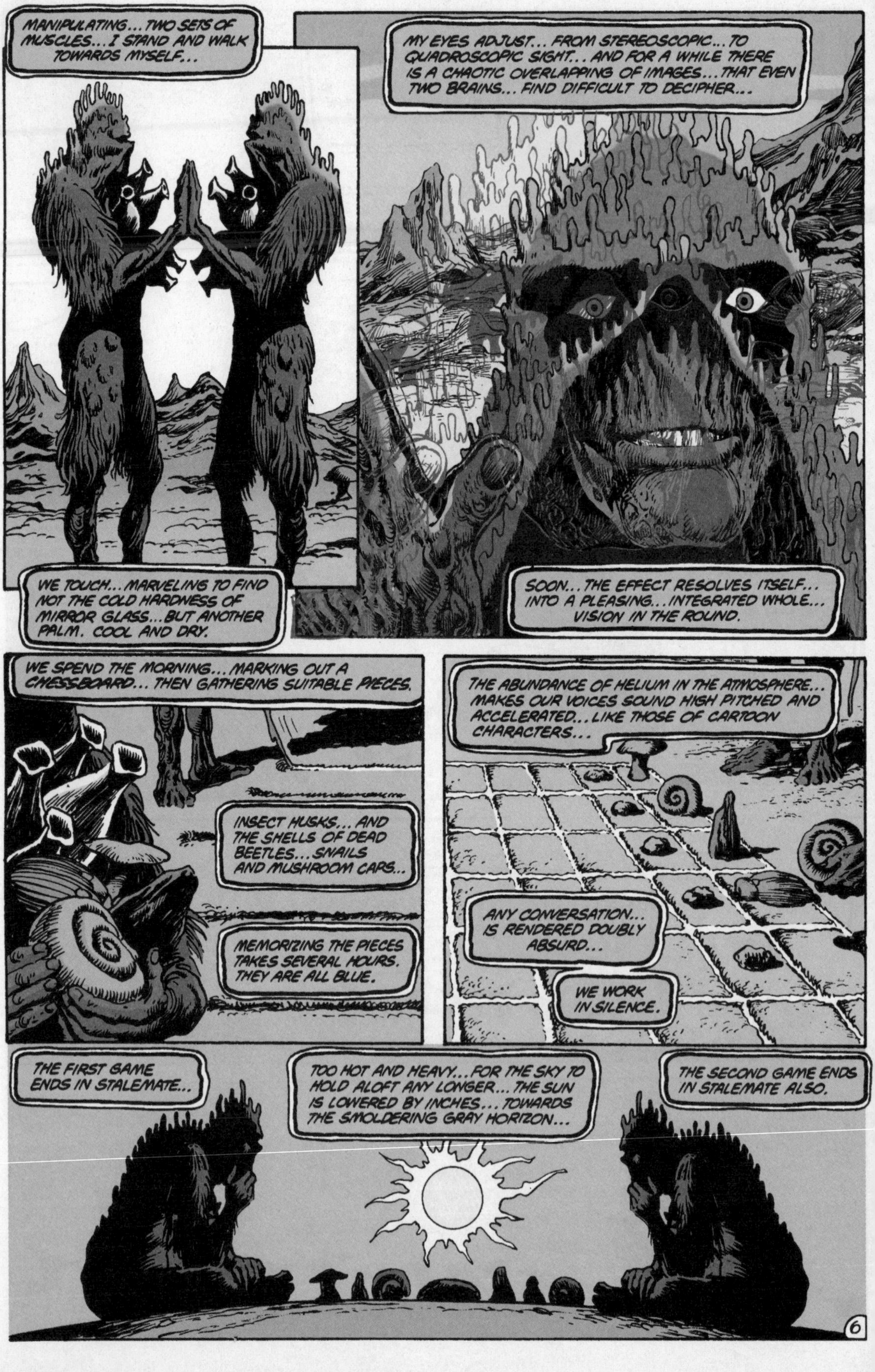
MANIPULATING... TWO SETS OF MUSCLES... I STAND AND WALK TOWARDS MYSELF...
WE TOUCH... MARVELING TO FIND NOT THE COLD HARDNESS OF MIRROR GLASS... BUT ANOTHER PALM. COOL AND DRY.
MY EYES ADJUST... FROM STEREOSCOPIC... TO QUADROSCOPIC SIGHT... AND FOR A WHILE THERE IS A CHAOTIC OVERLAPPING OF IMAGES... THAT EVEN TWO BRAINS... FIND DIFFICULT TO DECIPHER...
SOON... THE EFFECT RESOLVES ITSELF... INTO A PLEASING... INTEGRATED WHOLE... VISION IN THE ROUND.
WE SPEND THE MORNING... MARKING OUT A CHESSBOARD... THEN GATHERING SUITABLE PIECES.
INSECT HUSKS... AND THE SHELLS OF DEAD BEETLES... SNAILS AND MUSHROOM CAPS...
MEMORIZING THE PIECES TAKES SEVERAL HOURS. THEY ARE ALL BLUE.
THE ABUNDANCE OF HELIUM IN THE ATMOSPHERE... MAKES OUR VOICES SOUND HIGH PITCHED AND ACCELERATED... LIKE THOSE OF CARTOON CHARACTERS...
ANY CONVERSATION... IS RENDERED DOUBLY ABSURD...
WE WORK IN SILENCE.
THE FIRST GAME ENDS IN STALEMATE...
TOO HOT AND HEAVY... FOR THE SKY TO HOLD ALOFT ANY LONGER... THE SUN IS LOWERED BY INCHES... TOWARDS THE SMOLDERING GRAY HORIZON...
THE SECOND GAME ENDS IN STALEMATE ALSO.
6

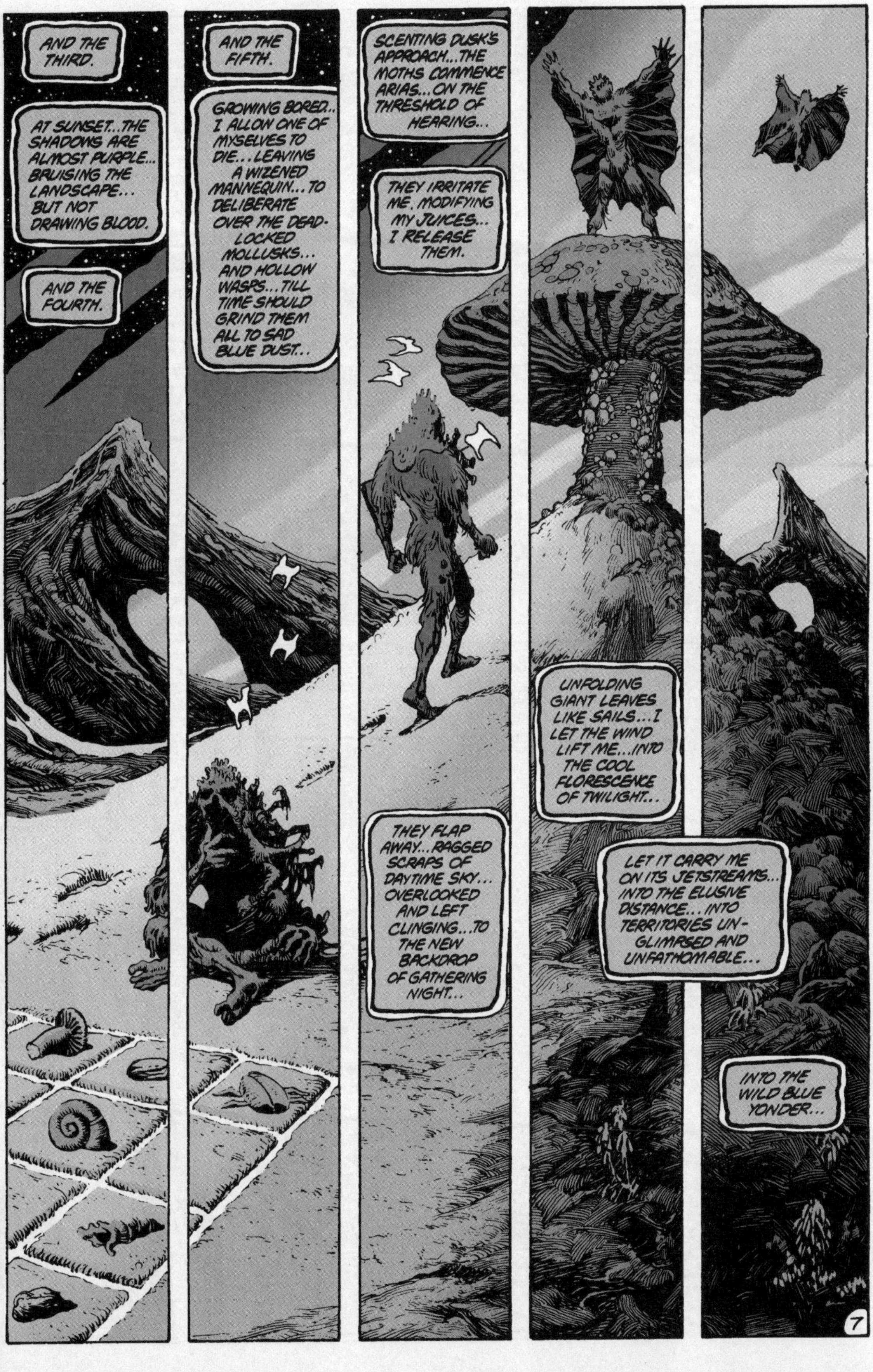
AND THE THIRD.
AT SUNSET...THE SHADOWS ARE ALMOST PURPLE... BRUISING THE LANDSCAPE... BUT NOT DRAWING BLOOD.
AND THE FOURTH.
AND THE FIFTH.
GROWING BORED... I ALLOW ONE OF MYSELVES TO DIE... LEAVING A WIZENED MANNEQUIN... TO DELIBERATE OVER THE DEAD-LOCKED MOLLUSKS... AND HOLLOW WASPS... TILL TIME SHOULD GRIND THEM ALL TO SAD BLUE DUST...
SCENTING DUSK'S APPROACH...THE MOTHS COMMENCE ARIAS...ON THE THRESHOLD OF HEARING...
THEY IRRITATE ME, MODIFYING MY JUICES... I RELEASE THEM.
THEY FLAP AWAY...RAGGED SCRAPS OF DAYTIME SKY... OVERLOOKED AND LEFT CLINGING...TO THE NEW BACKDROP OF GATHERING NIGHT...
UNFOLDING GIANT LEAVES LIKE SAILS...I LET THE WIND LIFT ME...INTO THE COOL FLORESCENCE OF TWILIGHT...
LET IT CARRY ME ON ITS JETSTREAMS... INTO THE ELUSIVE DISTANCE... INTO TERRITORIES UN-GLIMPSED AND UNFATHOMABLE...
INTO THE WILD BLUE YONDER...
7

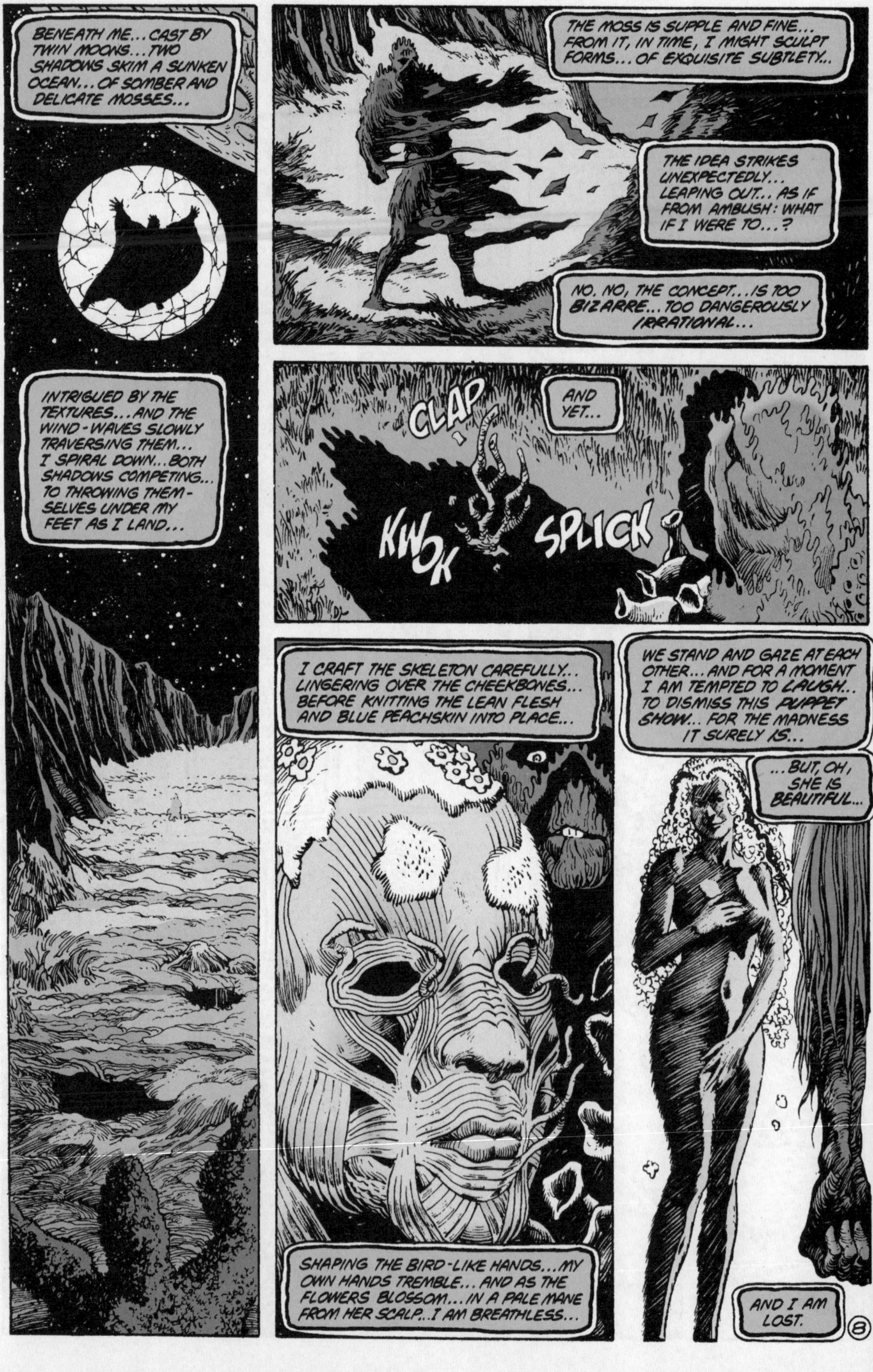
BENEATH ME... CAST BY TWIN MOONS... TWO SHADOWS SKIM A SUNKEN OCEAN... OF SOMBER AND DELICATE MOSSES...
THE MOSS IS SUPPLE AND FINE... FROM IT, IN TIME, I MIGHT SCULPT FORMS... OF EXQUISITE SUBTLETY...
THE IDEA STRIKES UNEXPECTEDLY... LEAPING OUT... AS IF FROM AMBUSH: WHAT IF I WERE TO...?
NO. NO, THE CONCEPT... IS TOO BIZARRE... TOO DANGEROUSLY IRRATIONAL...
INTRIGUED BY THE TEXTURES... AND THE WIND-WAVES SLOWLY TRAVERSING THEM... I SPIRAL DOWN... BOTH SHADOWS COMPETING... TO THROWING THEMSELVES UNDER MY FEET AS I LAND...
CLAP
AND YET...
KWOK
SPLICK
I CRAFT THE SKELETON CAREFULLY... LINGERING OVER THE CHEEKBONES... BEFORE KNITTING THE LEAN FLESH AND BLUE PEACHSKIN INTO PLACE...
SHAPING THE BIRD-LIKE HANDS... MY OWN HANDS TREMBLE... AND AS THE FLOWERS BLOSSOM... IN A PALE MANE FROM HER SCALP... I AM BREATHLESS...
WE STAND AND GAZE AT EACH OTHER... AND FOR A MOMENT I AM TEMPTED TO LAUGH... TO DISMISS THIS PUPPET SHOW... FOR THE MADNESS IT SURELY IS...
...BUT, OH, SHE IS BEAUTIFUL...
AND I AM LOST.
8

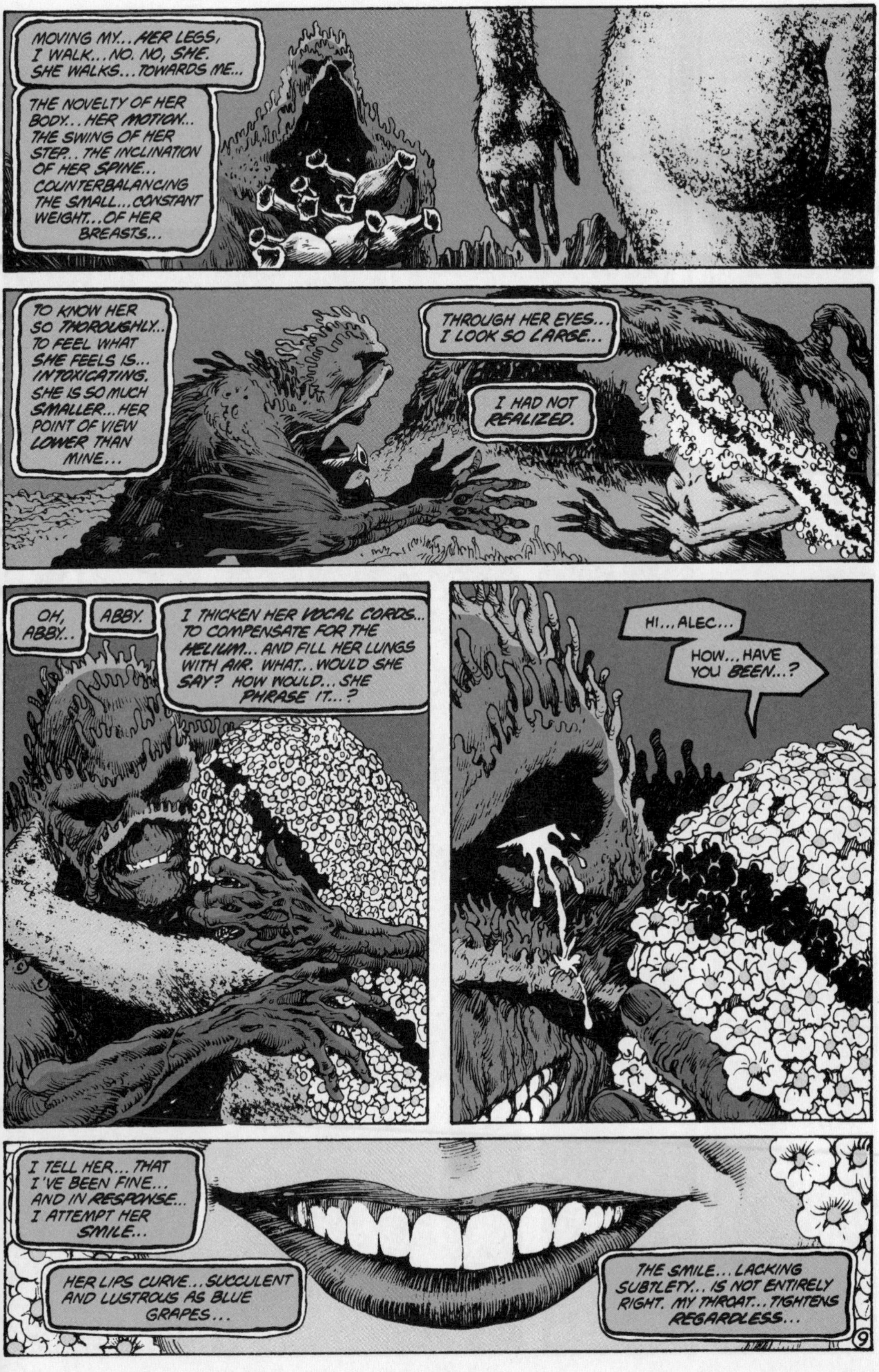
MOVING MY... HER LEGS, I WALK... NO. NO, SHE. SHE WALKS... TOWARDS ME...
THE NOVELTY OF HER BODY... HER MOTION... THE SWING OF HER STEP... THE INCLINATION OF HER SPINE... COUNTERBALANCING THE SMALL... CONSTANT WEIGHT... OF HER BREASTS...
TO KNOW HER SO THOROUGHLY... TO FEEL WHAT SHE FEELS IS... INTOXICATING. SHE IS SO MUCH SMALLER... HER POINT OF VIEW LOWER THAN MINE...
THROUGH HER EYES... I LOOK SO LARGE...
I HAD NOT REALIZED.
OH, ABBY...
ABBY.
I THICKEN HER VOCAL CORDS... TO COMPENSATE FOR THE HELIUM... AND FILL HER LUNGS WITH AIR. WHAT... WOULD SHE SAY? HOW WOULD... SHE PHRASE IT...?
HI... ALEC...
HOW... HAVE YOU BEEN...?
I TELL HER... THAT I'VE BEEN FINE... AND IN RESPONSE... I ATTEMPT HER SMILE...
HER LIPS CURVE... SUCCULENT AND LUSTROUS AS BLUE GRAPES...
THE SMILE... LACKING SUBTLETY... IS NOT ENTIRELY RIGHT. MY THROAT... TIGHTENS REGARDLESS...
9

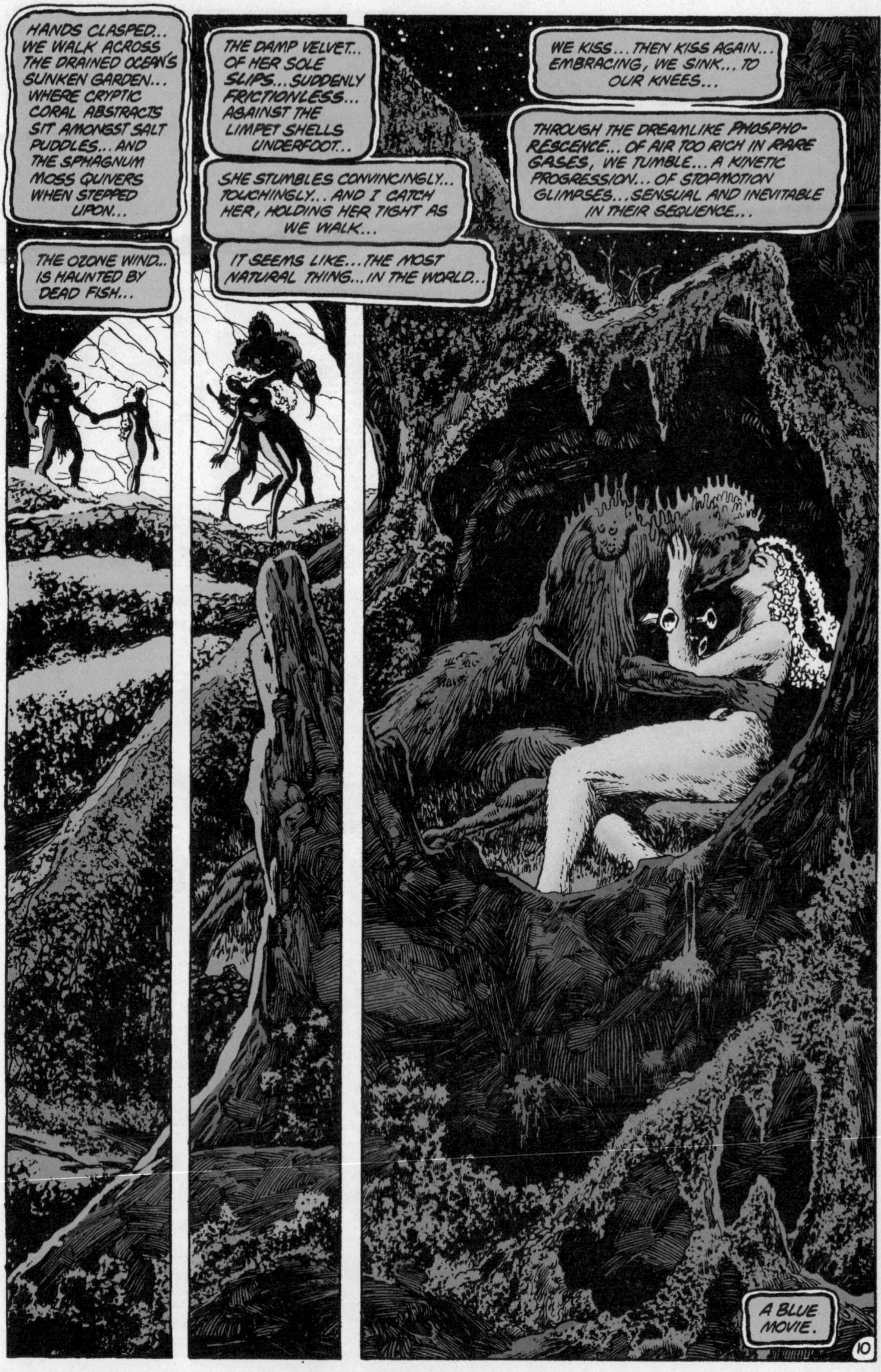
HANDS CLASPED... WE WALK ACROSS THE DRAINED OCEAN'S SUNKEN GARDEN... WHERE CRYPTIC CORAL ABSTRACTS SIT AMONGST SALT PUDDLES... AND THE SPHAGNUM MOSS QUIVERS WHEN STEPPED UPON...
THE OZONE WIND... IS HAUNTED BY DEAD FISH...
THE DAMP VELVET... OF HER SOLE SLIPS... SUDDENLY FRICTIONLESS... AGAINST THE LIMPET SHELLS UNDERFOOT...
SHE STUMBLES CONVINCINGLY... TOUCHINGLY... AND I CATCH HER, HOLDING HER TIGHT AS WE WALK...
IT SEEMS LIKE... THE MOST NATURAL THING... IN THE WORLD...
WE KISS... THEN KISS AGAIN... EMBRACING, WE SINK... TO OUR KNEES...
THROUGH THE DREAMLIKE PHOSPHORESCENCE... OF AIR TOO RICH IN RARE GASES, WE TUMBLE... A KINETIC PROGRESSION... OF STOPMOTION GLIMPSES... SENSUAL AND INEVITABLE IN THEIR SEQUENCE...
A BLUE MOVIE.
10

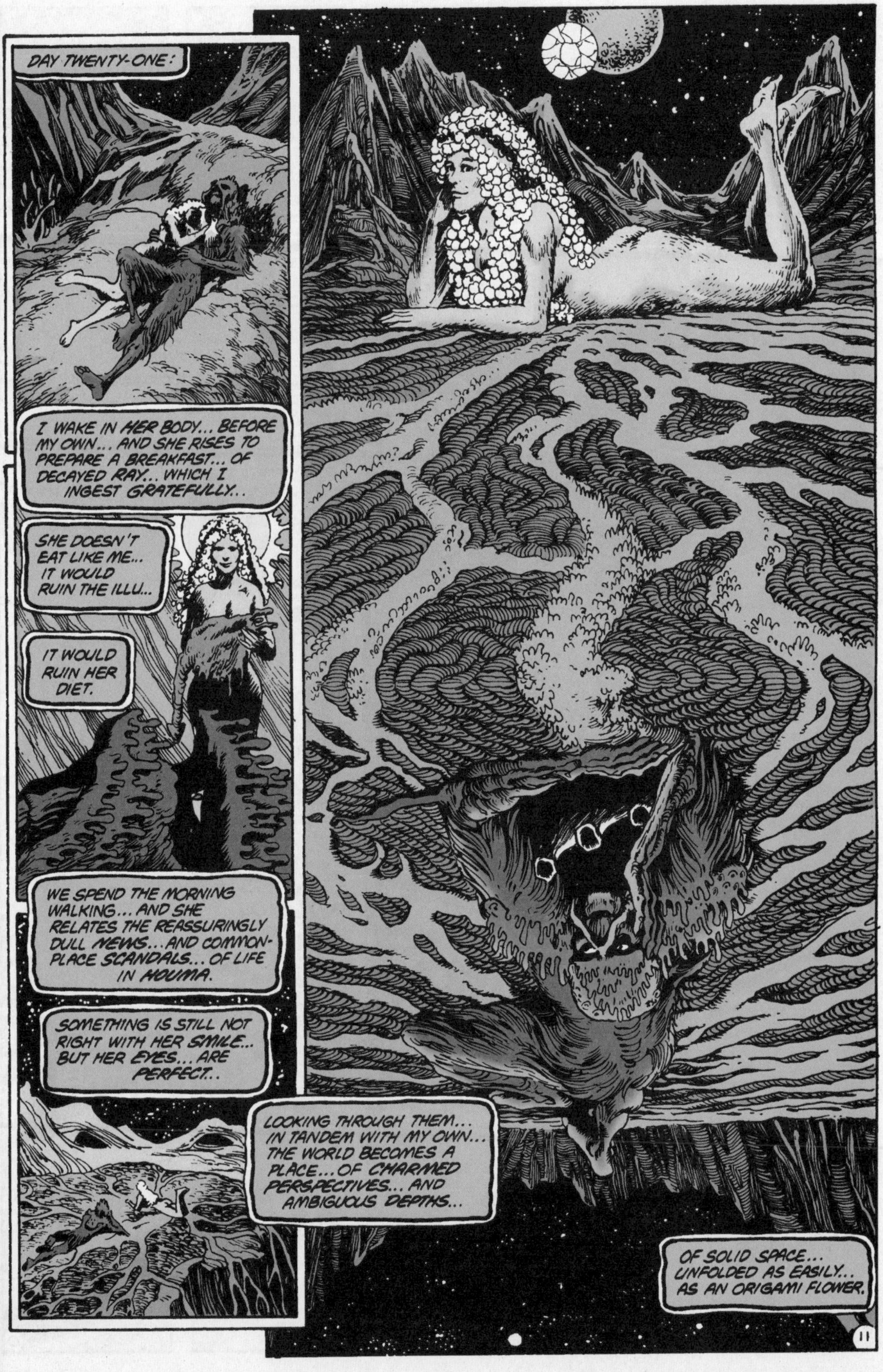
DAY TWENTY-ONE:
I WAKE IN HER BODY... BEFORE MY OWN... AND SHE RISES TO PREPARE A BREAKFAST... OF DECAYED RAY... WHICH I INGEST GRATEFULLY...
SHE DOESN'T EAT LIKE ME... IT WOULD RUIN THE ILLU...
IT WOULD RUIN HER DIET.
WE SPEND THE MORNING WALKING... AND SHE RELATES THE REASSURINGLY DULL NEWS... AND COMMON-PLACE SCANDALS... OF LIFE IN HOUMA.
SOMETHING IS STILL NOT RIGHT WITH HER SMILE... BUT HER EYES... ARE PERFECT...
LOOKING THROUGH THEM... IN TANDEM WITH MY OWN... THE WORLD BECOMES A PLACE... OF CHARMED PERSPECTIVES... AND AMBIGUOUS DEPTHS...
OF SOLID SPACE... UNFOLDED AS EASILY... AS AN ORIGAMI FLOWER.
11

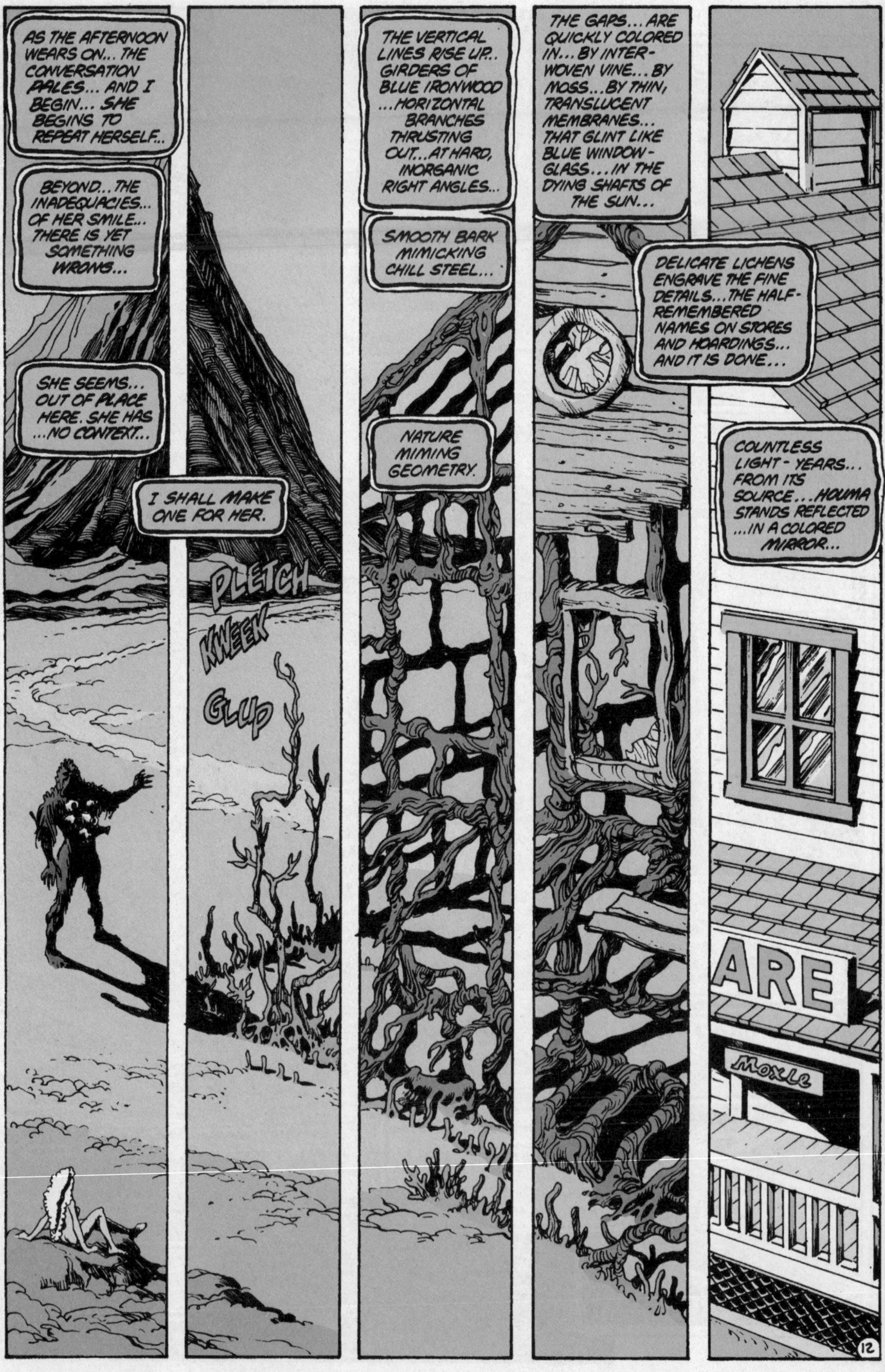
AS THE AFTERNOON WEARS ON... THE CONVERSATION PALES... AND I BEGIN... SHE BEGINS TO REPEAT HERSELF...
BEYOND... THE INADEQUACIES... OF HER SMILE... THERE IS YET SOMETHING WRONG...
SHE SEEMS... OUT OF PLACE HERE. SHE HAS ...NO CONTEXT...
I SHALL MAKE ONE FOR HER.
PLETCH
KWEEK
GLUP
THE VERTICAL LINES RISE UP.. GIRDERS OF BLUE IRONWOOD ...HORIZONTAL BRANCHES THRUSTING OUT...AT HARD, INORGANIC RIGHT ANGLES...
SMOOTH BARK MIMICKING CHILL STEEL...
NATURE MIMING GEOMETRY.
THE GAPS... ARE QUICKLY COLORED IN... BY INTER-WOVEN VINE... BY MOSS... BY THIN, TRANSLUCENT MEMBRANES... THAT GLINT LIKE BLUE WINDOW-GLASS... IN THE DYING SHAFTS OF THE SUN...
DELICATE LICHENS ENGRAVE THE FINE DETAILS...THE HALF-REMEMBERED NAMES ON STORES AND HOARDINGS... AND IT IS DONE...
COUNTLESS LIGHT-YEARS... FROM ITS SOURCE... HOUMA STANDS REFLECTED ...IN A COLORED MIRROR...
ARE
Moxie
12

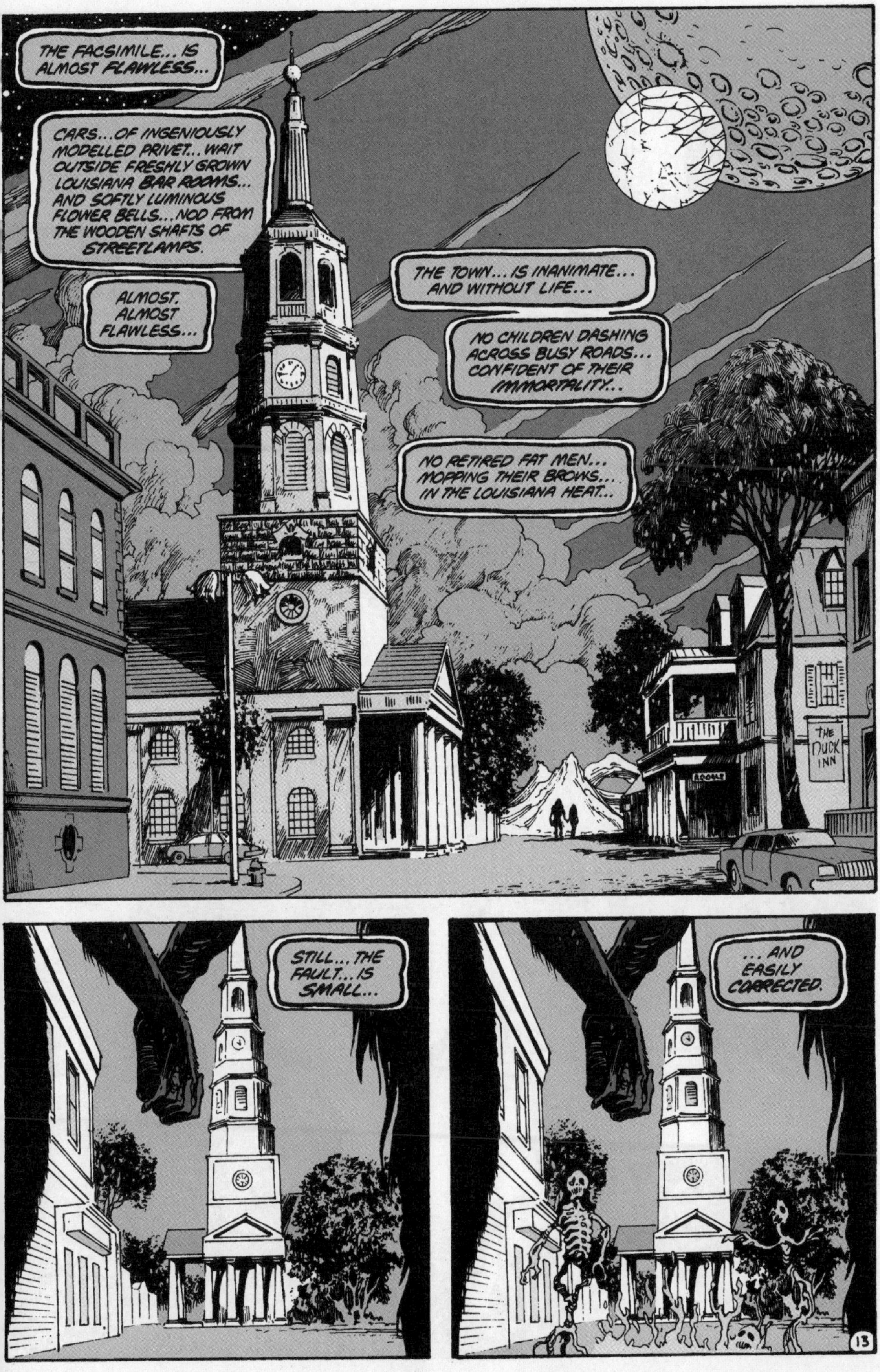
THE FACSIMILE... IS ALMOST FLAWLESS...
CARS...OF INGENIOUSLY MODELLED PRIVET...WAIT OUTSIDE FRESHLY GROWN LOUISIANA BAR ROOMS... AND SOFTLY LUMINOUS FLOWER BELLS...NOD FROM THE WOODEN SHAFTS OF STREETLAMPS.
ALMOST. ALMOST FLAWLESS...
THE TOWN... IS INANIMATE... AND WITHOUT LIFE...
NO CHILDREN DASHING ACROSS BUSY ROADS... CONFIDENT OF THEIR IMMORTALITY...
NO RETIRED FAT MEN... MOPPING THEIR BROWS... IN THE LOUISIANA HEAT...
THE DUCK INN
STILL... THE FAULT... IS SMALL...
... AND EASILY CORRECTED.
13

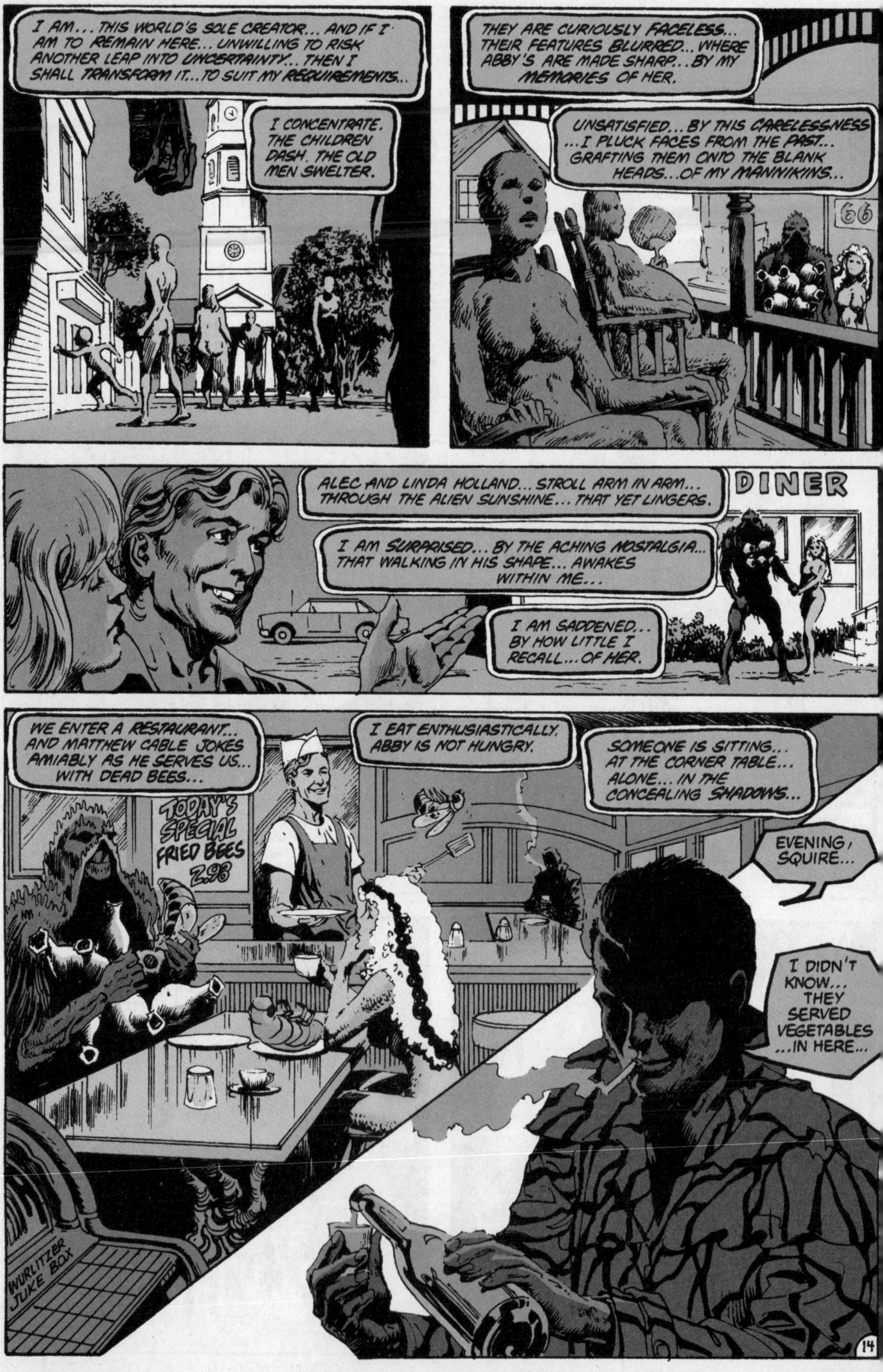
I AM... THIS WORLD'S SOLE CREATOR... AND IF I AM TO REMAIN HERE... UNWILLING TO RISK ANOTHER LEAP INTO UNCERTAINTY... THEN I SHALL TRANSFORM IT... TO SUIT MY REQUIREMENTS...
I CONCENTRATE. THE CHILDREN DASH. THE OLD MEN SWELTER.
THEY ARE CURIOUSLY FACELESS... THEIR FEATURES BLURRED... WHERE ABBY'S ARE MADE SHARP... BY MY MEMORIES OF HER.
UNSATISFIED... BY THIS CARELESSNESS ...I PLUCK FACES FROM THE PAST... GRAFTING THEM ONTO THE BLANK HEADS... OF MY MANNIKINS...
66
ALEC AND LINDA HOLLAND... STROLL ARM IN ARM... THROUGH THE ALIEN SUNSHINE... THAT YET LINGERS.
DINER
I AM SURPRISED... BY THE ACHING NOSTALGIA... THAT WALKING IN HIS SHAPE... AWAKES WITHIN ME...
I AM SADDENED... BY HOW LITTLE I RECALL... OF HER.
WE ENTER A RESTAURANT... AND MATTHEW CABLE JOKES AMIABLY AS HE SERVES US... WITH DEAD BEES...
I EAT ENTHUSIASTICALLY. ABBY IS NOT HUNGRY.
SOMEONE IS SITTING... AT THE CORNER TABLE... ALONE... IN THE CONCEALING SHADOWS...
TODAY'S SPECIAL FRIED BEES 2.98
EVENING, SQUIRE...
I DIDN'T KNOW... THEY SERVED VEGETABLES ...IN HERE...
WURLITZER JUKE BOX
14

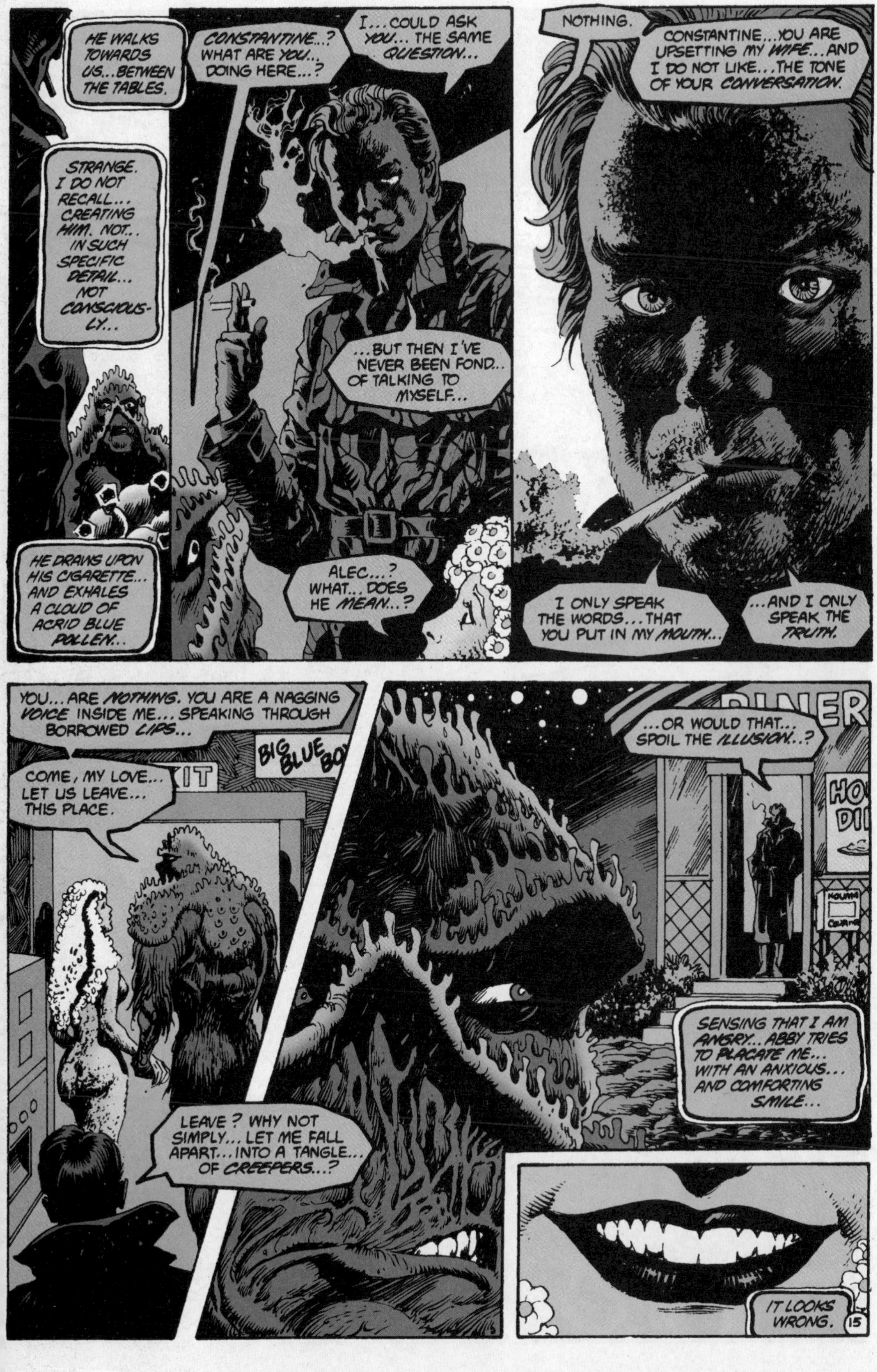
HE WALKS TOWARDS US...BETWEEN THE TABLES.
STRANGE. I DO NOT RECALL... CREATING HIM. NOT... IN SUCH SPECIFIC DETAIL... NOT CONSCIOUSLY...
HE DRAWS UPON HIS CIGARETTE... AND EXHALES A CLOUD OF ACRID BLUE POLLEN...
CONSTANTINE...? WHAT ARE YOU... DOING HERE...?
I...COULD ASK YOU... THE SAME QUESTION...
...BUT THEN I'VE NEVER BEEN FOND... OF TALKING TO MYSELF...
ALEC...? WHAT... DOES HE MEAN...?
NOTHING.
CONSTANTINE...YOU ARE UPSETTING MY WIFE...AND I DO NOT LIKE...THE TONE OF YOUR CONVERSATION.
I ONLY SPEAK THE WORDS...THAT YOU PUT IN MY MOUTH...
...AND I ONLY SPEAK THE TRUTH.
YOU...ARE NOTHING. YOU ARE A NAGGING VOICE INSIDE ME...SPEAKING THROUGH BORROWED LIPS...
BIG BLUE BOX
KIT
COME, MY LOVE... LET US LEAVE... THIS PLACE.
LEAVE? WHY NOT SIMPLY...LET ME FALL APART...INTO A TANGLE... OF CREEPERS...?
DINER
...OR WOULD THAT... SPOIL THE ILLUSION...?
SENSING THAT I AM ANGRY...ABBY TRIES TO PLACATE ME... WITH AN ANXIOUS... AND COMFORTING SMILE...
IT LOOKS WRONG.
15

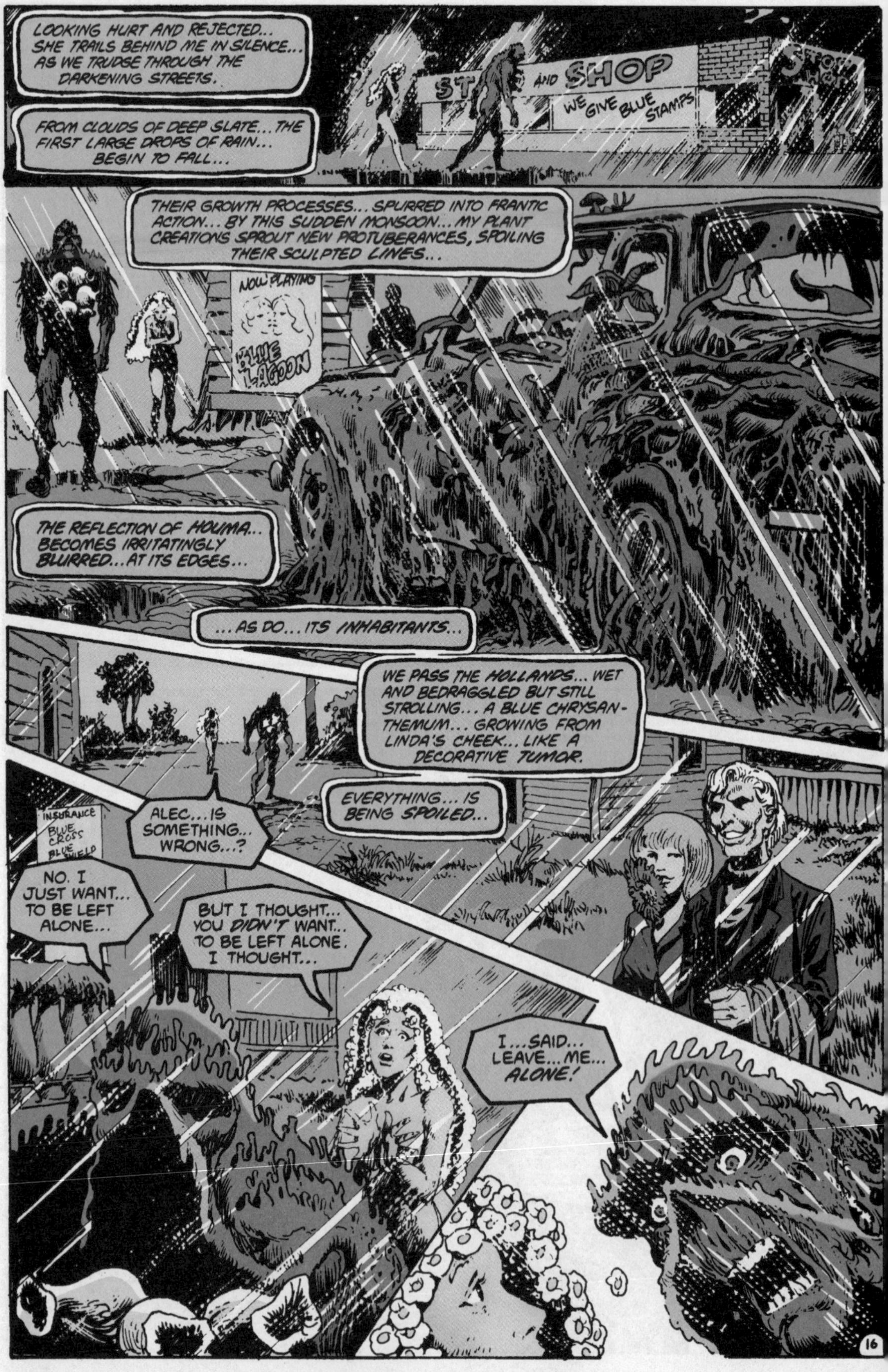
LOOKING HURT AND REJECTED... SHE TRAILS BEHIND ME IN SILENCE... AS WE TRUDGE THROUGH THE DARKENING STREETS.
FROM CLOUDS OF DEEP SLATE... THE FIRST LARGE DROPS OF RAIN... BEGIN TO FALL...
ST
AND SHOP
WE GIVE BLUE STAMPS
THEIR GROWTH PROCESSES... SPURRED INTO FRANTIC ACTION... BY THIS SUDDEN MONSOON... MY PLANT CREATIONS SPROUT NEW PROTUBERANCES, SPOILING THEIR SCULPTED LINES...
NOW PLAYING
BLUE LAGOON
THE REFLECTION OF HOUMA... BECOMES IRRITATINGLY BLURRED... AT ITS EDGES...
... AS DO... ITS INHABITANTS...
WE PASS THE HOLLANDS... WET AND BEDRAGGLED BUT STILL STROLLING... A BLUE CHRYSANTHEMUM... GROWING FROM LINDA'S CHEEK... LIKE A DECORATIVE TUMOR.
EVERYTHING... IS BEING SPOILED...
INSURANCE BLUE CROSS BLUE SHIELD
ALEC... IS SOMETHING... WRONG...?
NO. I JUST WANT... TO BE LEFT ALONE...
BUT I THOUGHT... YOU DIDN'T WANT... TO BE LEFT ALONE. I THOUGHT...
I... SAID... LEAVE... ME... ALONE!
16

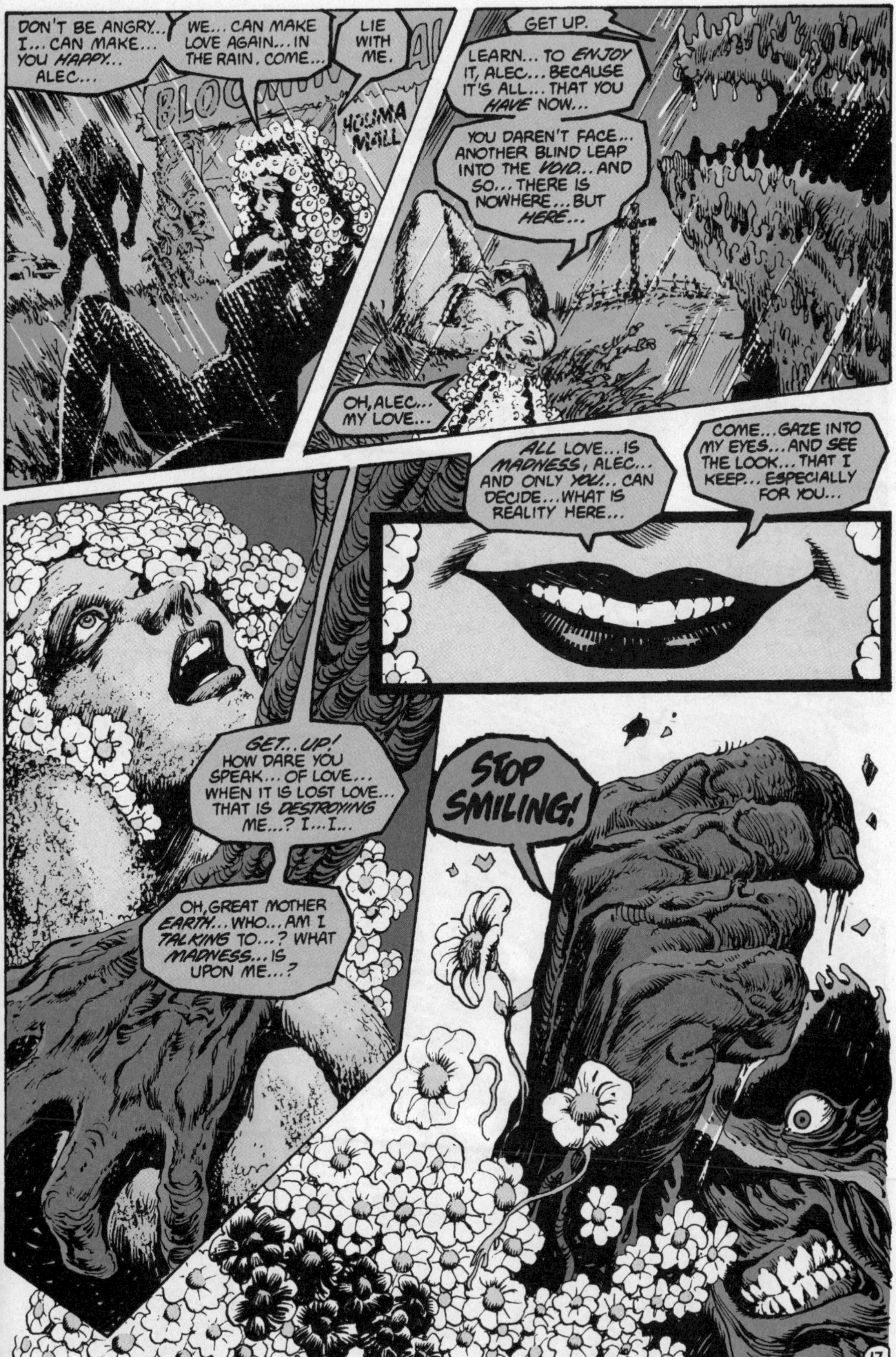
DON'T BE ANGRY... I... CAN MAKE... YOU HAPPY... ALEC...
WE... CAN MAKE LOVE AGAIN... IN THE RAIN. COME...
LIE WITH ME.
HOUMA MALL
GET UP.
LEARN... TO ENJOY IT, ALEC... BECAUSE IT'S ALL... THAT YOU HAVE NOW...
YOU DAREN'T FACE... ANOTHER BLIND LEAP INTO THE VOID... AND SO... THERE IS NOWHERE... BUT HERE...
OH, ALEC... MY LOVE...
ALL LOVE... IS MADNESS, ALEC... AND ONLY YOU... CAN DECIDE... WHAT IS REALITY HERE...
COME... GAZE INTO MY EYES... AND SEE THE LOOK... THAT I KEEP... ESPECIALLY FOR YOU...
GET... UP! HOW DARE YOU SPEAK... OF LOVE... WHEN IT IS LOST LOVE... THAT IS DESTROYING ME...? I... I...
OH, GREAT MOTHER EARTH... WHO... AM I TALKING TO...? WHAT MADNESS... IS UPON ME...?
STOP SMILING!
17

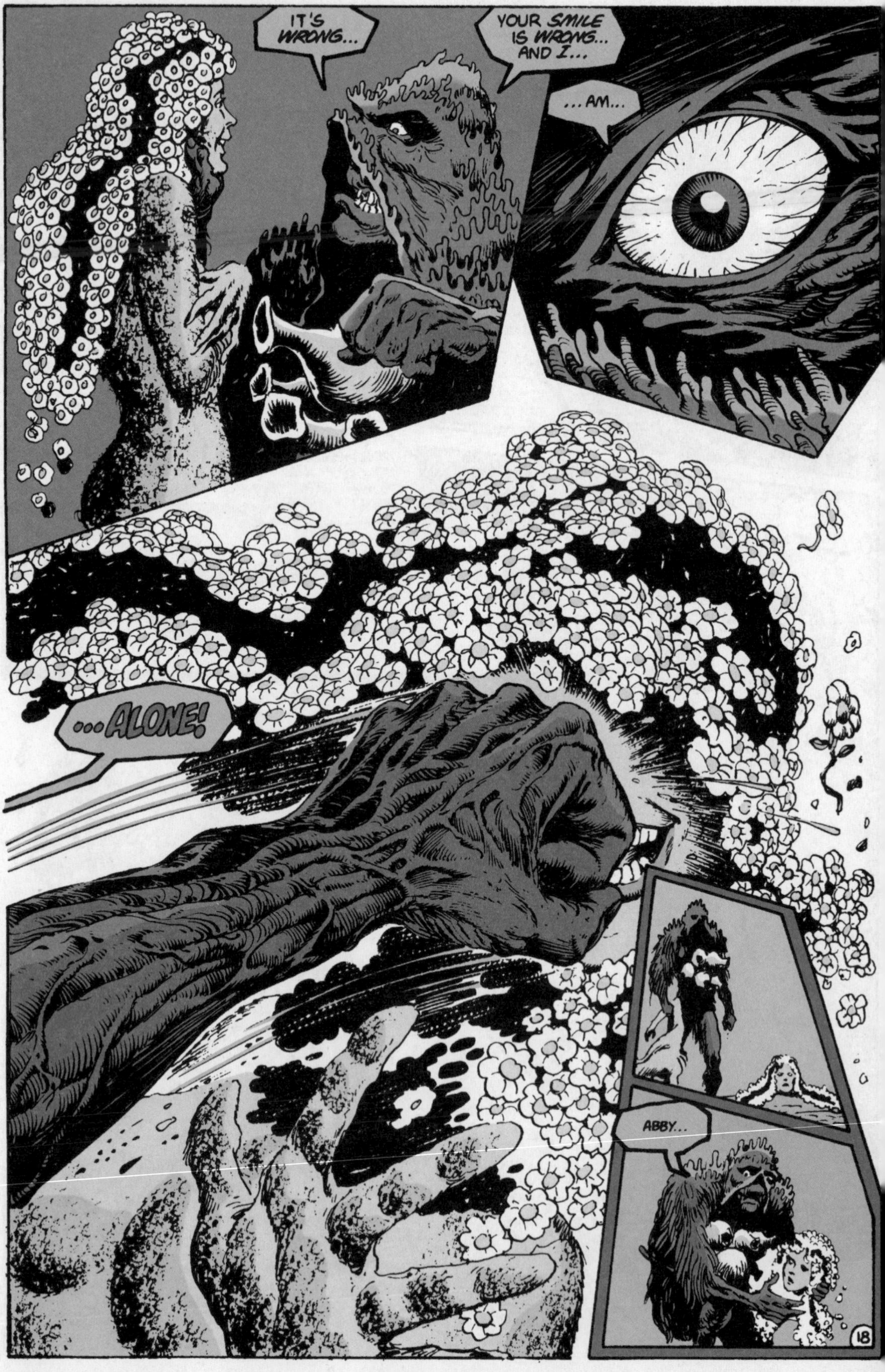
IT'S WRONG...
YOUR SMILE IS WRONG... AND I...
...AM...
...ALONE!
ABBY...
18

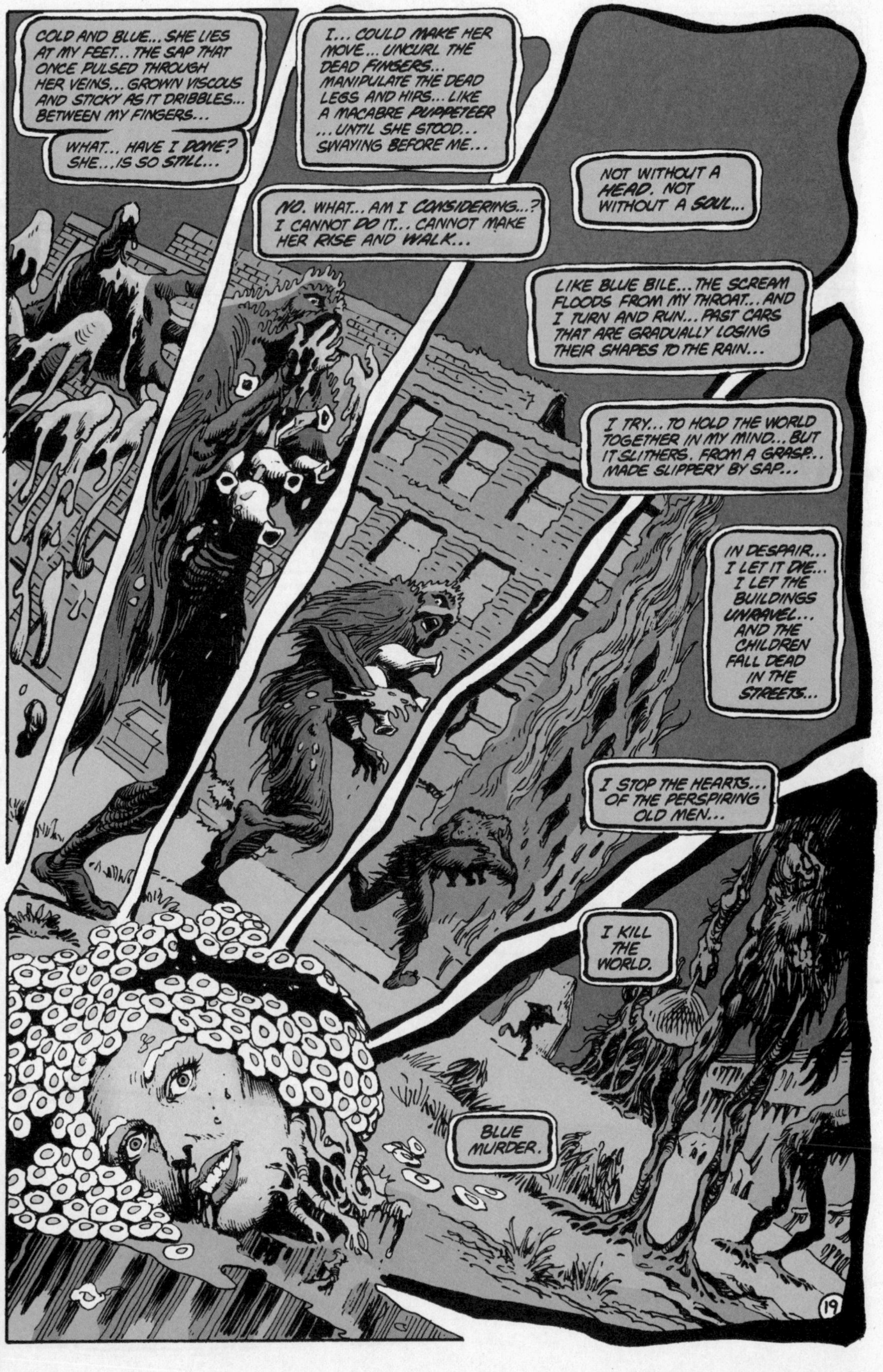
COLD AND BLUE... SHE LIES AT MY FEET... THE SAP THAT ONCE PULSED THROUGH HER VEINS... GROWN VISCOUS AND STICKY AS IT DRIBBLES... BETWEEN MY FINGERS...
WHAT... HAVE I DONE? SHE..., IS SO STILL...
I... COULD MAKE HER MOVE... UNCURL THE DEAD FINGERS... MANIPULATE THE DEAD LEGS AND HIPS... LIKE A MACABRE PUPPETEER ...UNTIL SHE STOOD... SWAYING BEFORE ME...
NO. WHAT... AM I CONSIDERING...? I CANNOT DO IT... CANNOT MAKE HER RISE AND WALK...
NOT WITHOUT A HEAD. NOT WITHOUT A SOUL...
LIKE BLUE BILE... THE SCREAM FLOODS FROM MY THROAT... AND I TURN AND RUN... PAST CARS THAT ARE GRADUALLY LOSING THEIR SHAPES TO THE RAIN...
I TRY... TO HOLD THE WORLD TOGETHER IN MY MIND... BUT IT SLITHERS. FROM A GRASP... MADE SLIPPERY BY SAP...
IN DESPAIR... I LET IT DIE... I LET THE BUILDINGS UNRAVEL... AND THE CHILDREN FALL DEAD IN THE STREETS...
I STOP THE HEARTS... OF THE PERSPIRING OLD MEN...
I KILL THE WORLD.
BLUE MURDER.
19

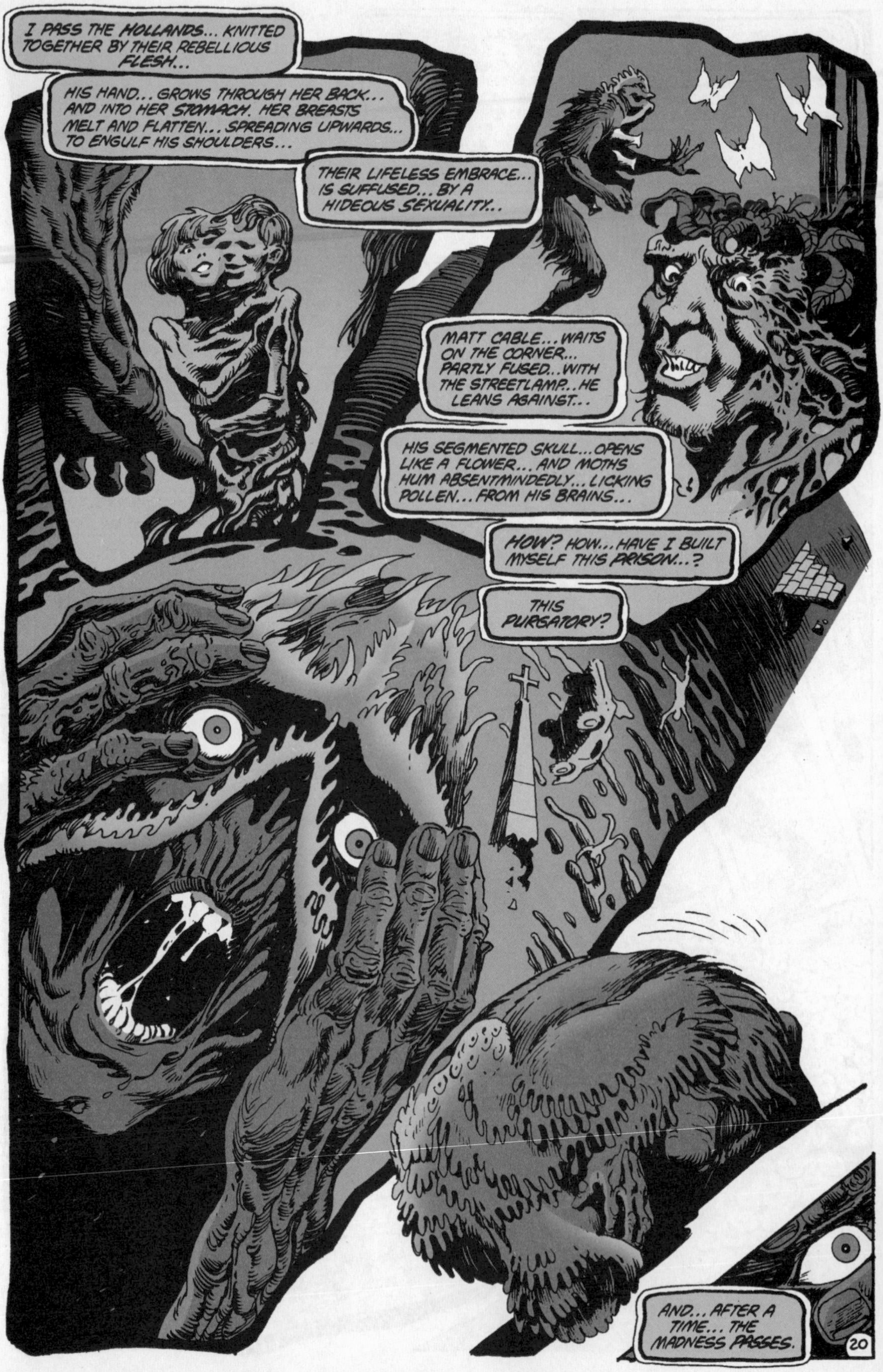
I PASS THE HOLLANDS... KNITTED TOGETHER BY THEIR REBELLIOUS FLESH...
HIS HAND... GROWS THROUGH HER BACK... AND INTO HER STOMACH. HER BREASTS MELT AND FLATTEN... SPREADING UPWARDS... TO ENGULF HIS SHOULDERS...
THEIR LIFELESS EMBRACE... IS SUFFUSED... BY A HIDEOUS SEXUALITY...
MATT CABLE... WAITS ON THE CORNER... PARTLY FUSED... WITH THE STREETLAMP... HE LEANS AGAINST...
HIS SEGMENTED SKULL... OPENS LIKE A FLOWER... AND MOTHS HUM ABSENTMINDEDLY... LICKING POLLEN... FROM HIS BRAINS...
HOW? HOW... HAVE I BUILT MYSELF THIS PRISON...?
THIS PURGATORY?
AND... AFTER A TIME... THE MADNESS PASSES.
20

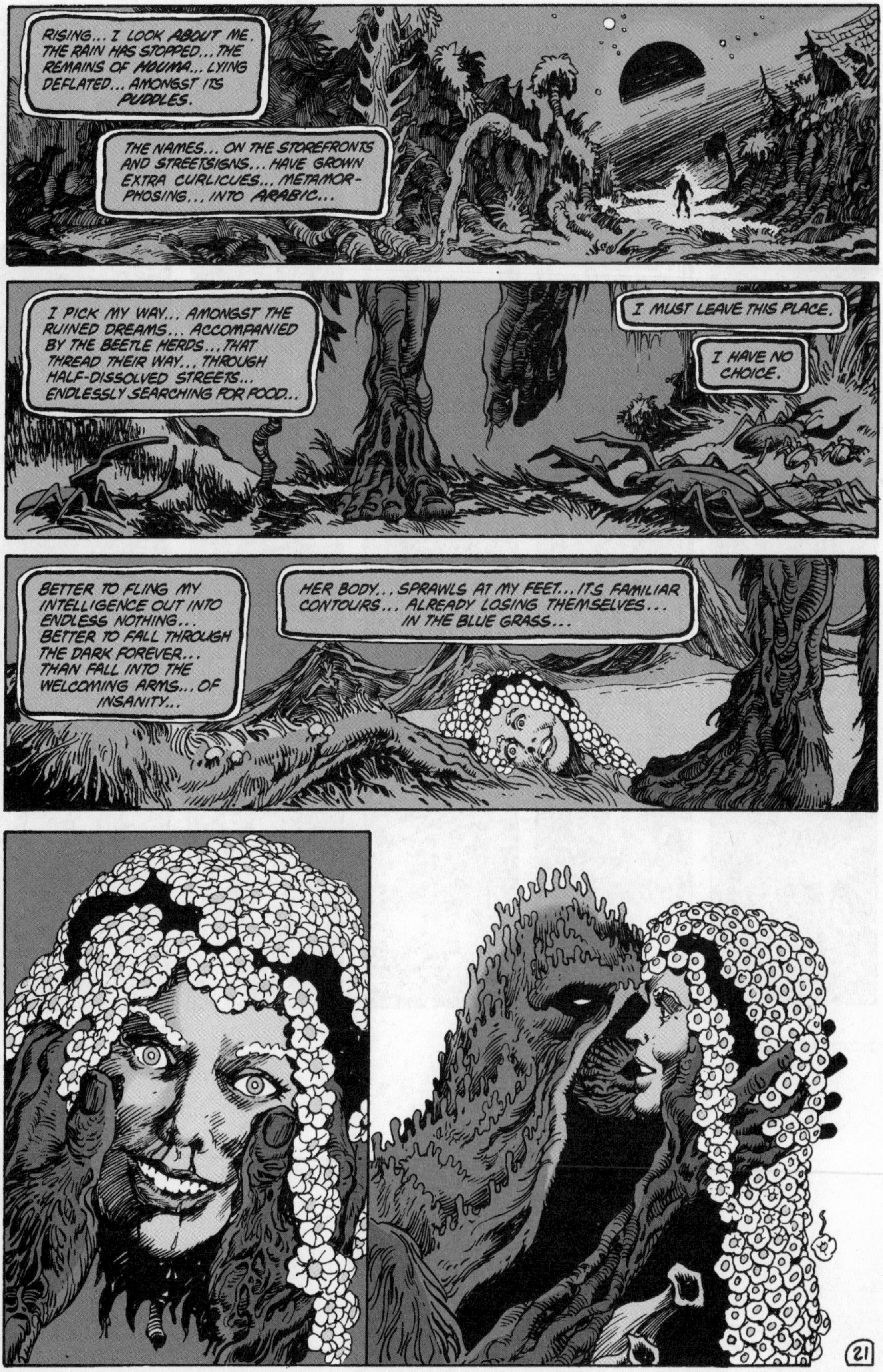
RISING... I LOOK ABOUT ME. THE RAIN HAS STOPPED... THE REMAINS OF HOUMA... LYING DEFLATED... AMONGST ITS PUDDLES.
THE NAMES... ON THE STOREFRONTS AND STREETSIGNS... HAVE GROWN EXTRA CURLICUES... METAMORPHOSING... INTO ARABIC...
I PICK MY WAY... AMONGST THE RUINED DREAMS... ACCOMPANIED BY THE BEETLE HERDS... THAT THREAD THEIR WAY... THROUGH HALF-DISSOLVED STREETS... ENDLESSLY SEARCHING FOR FOOD...
I MUST LEAVE THIS PLACE.
I HAVE NO CHOICE.
BETTER TO FLING MY INTELLIGENCE OUT INTO ENDLESS NOTHING... BETTER TO FALL THROUGH THE DARK FOREVER... THAN FALL INTO THE WELCOMING ARMS... OF INSANITY...
HER BODY... SPRAWLS AT MY FEET... ITS FAMILIAR CONTOURS... ALREADY LOSING THEMSELVES... IN THE BLUE GRASS...
21

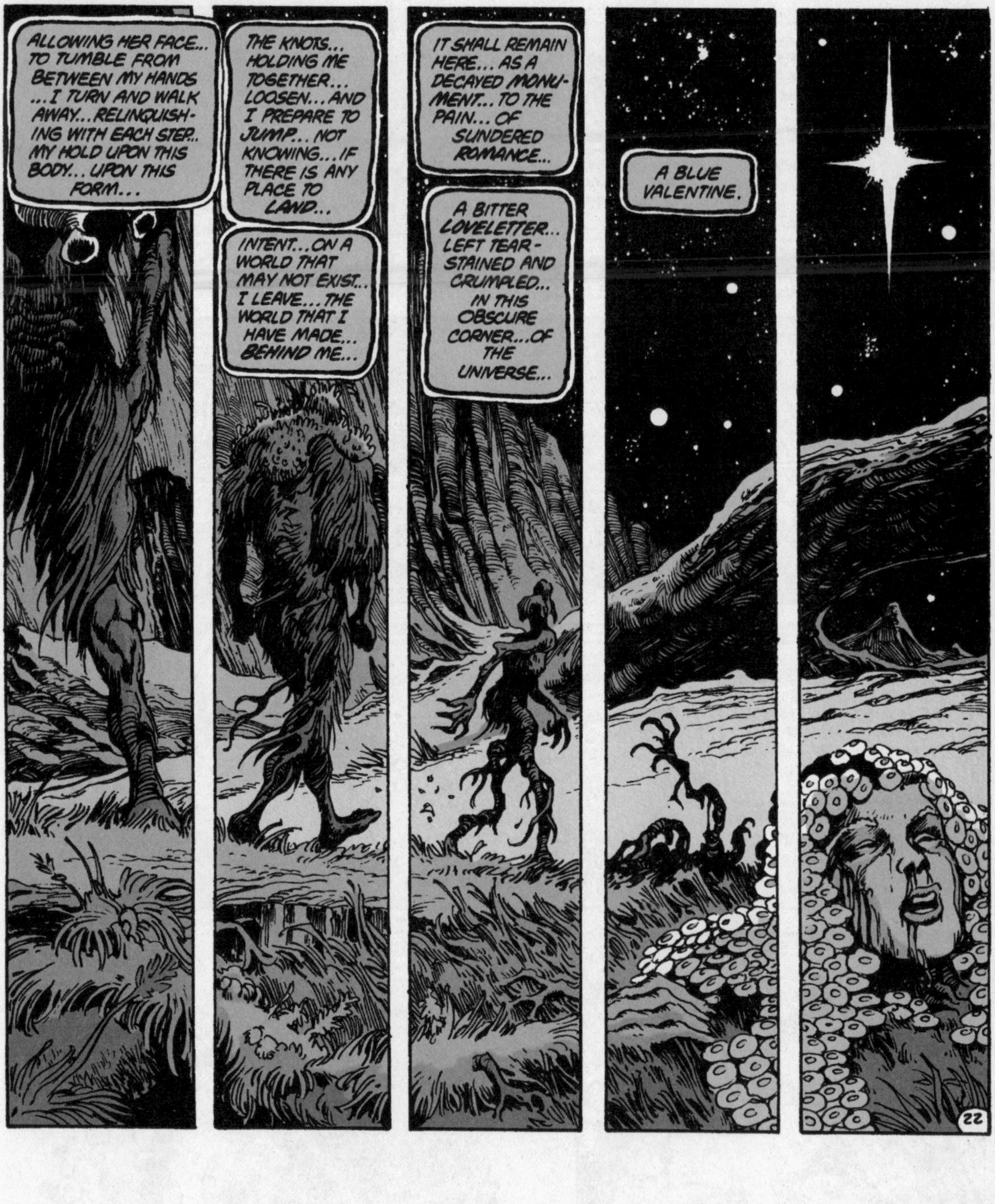
ALLOWING HER FACE... TO TUMBLE FROM BETWEEN MY HANDS ...I TURN AND WALK AWAY...RELINQUISHING WITH EACH STEP.. MY HOLD UPON THIS BODY... UPON THIS FORM...
THE KNOTS... HOLDING ME TOGETHER... LOOSEN... AND I PREPARE TO JUMP... NOT KNOWING... IF THERE IS ANY PLACE TO LAND...
INTENT...ON A WORLD THAT MAY NOT EXIST... I LEAVE... THE WORLD THAT I HAVE MADE... BEHIND ME...
IT SHALL REMAIN HERE... AS A DECAYED MONUMENT... TO THE PAIN... OF SUNDERED ROMANCE...
A BITTER LOVELETTER... LEFT TEAR-STAINED AND CRUMPLED... IN THIS OBSCURE CORNER...OF THE UNIVERSE...
A BLUE VALENTINE.
22

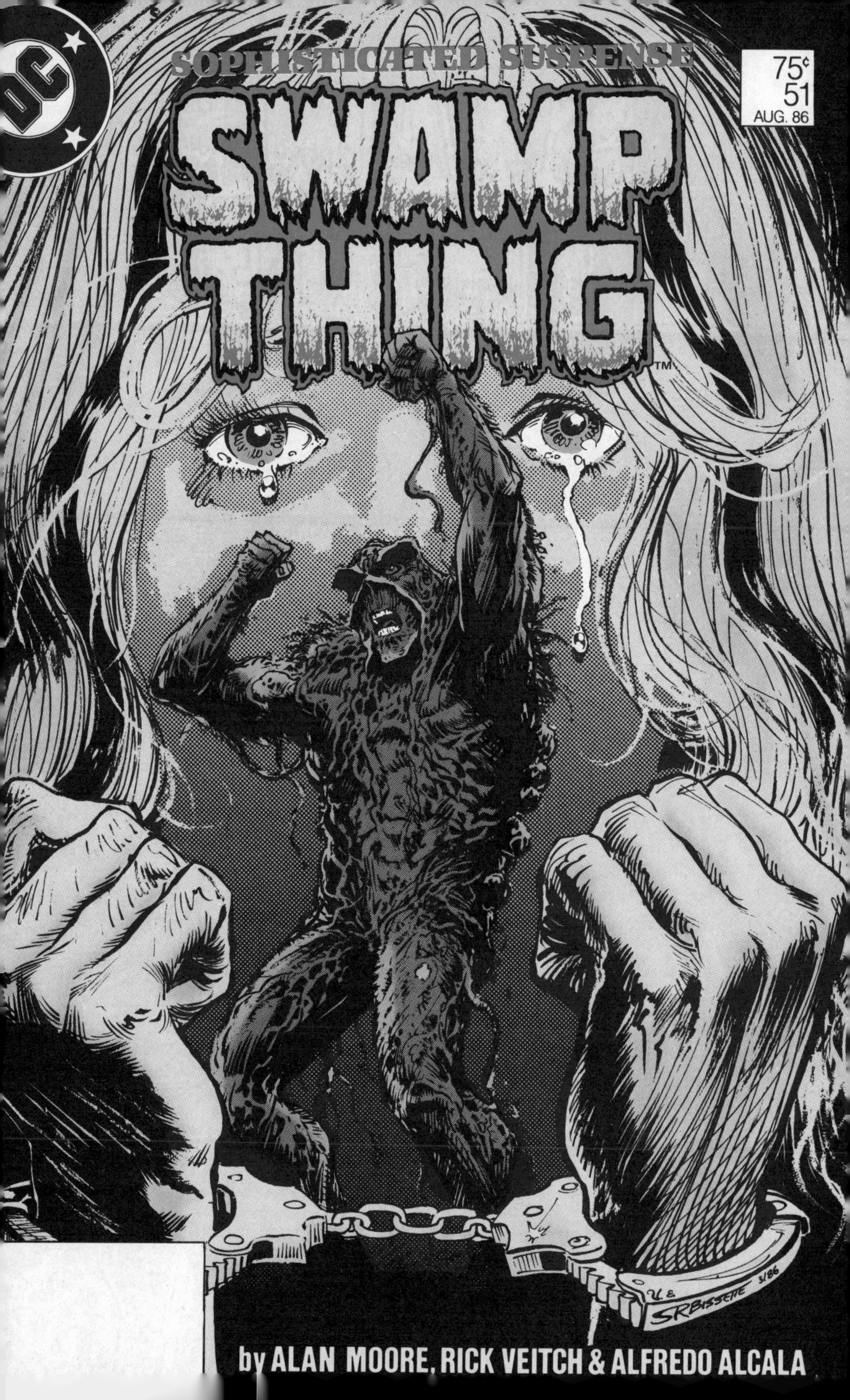
SOPHISTICATED SUSPENSE
SWAMP THING
75¢
51
AUG. 86
by ALAN MOORE, RICK VEITCH & ALFREDO ALCALA

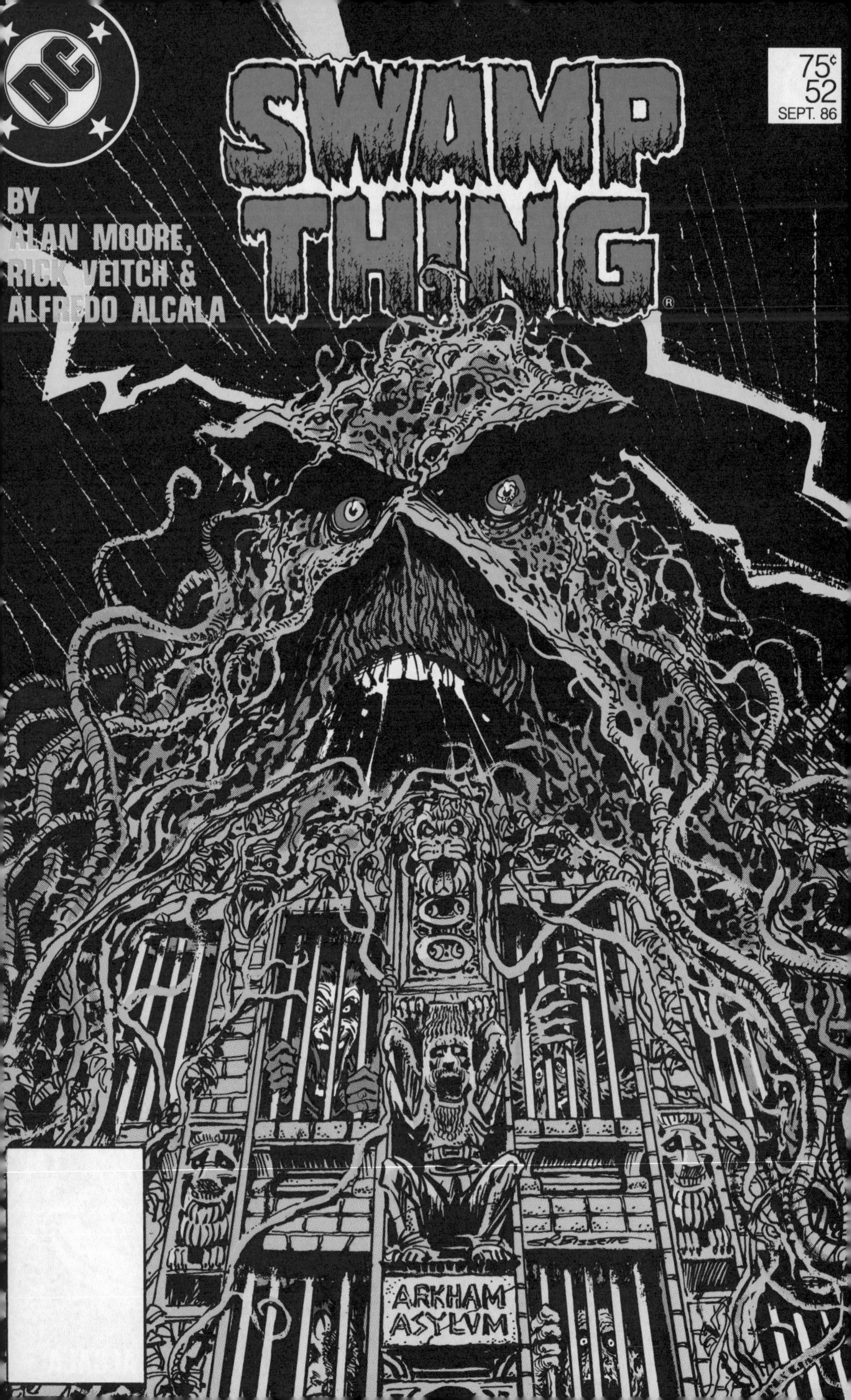

SWAMP THING
75¢
52
SEPT. 86
BY
ALAN MOORE,
RICK VEITCH &
ALFREDO ALCALA
ARKHAM
ASYLUM

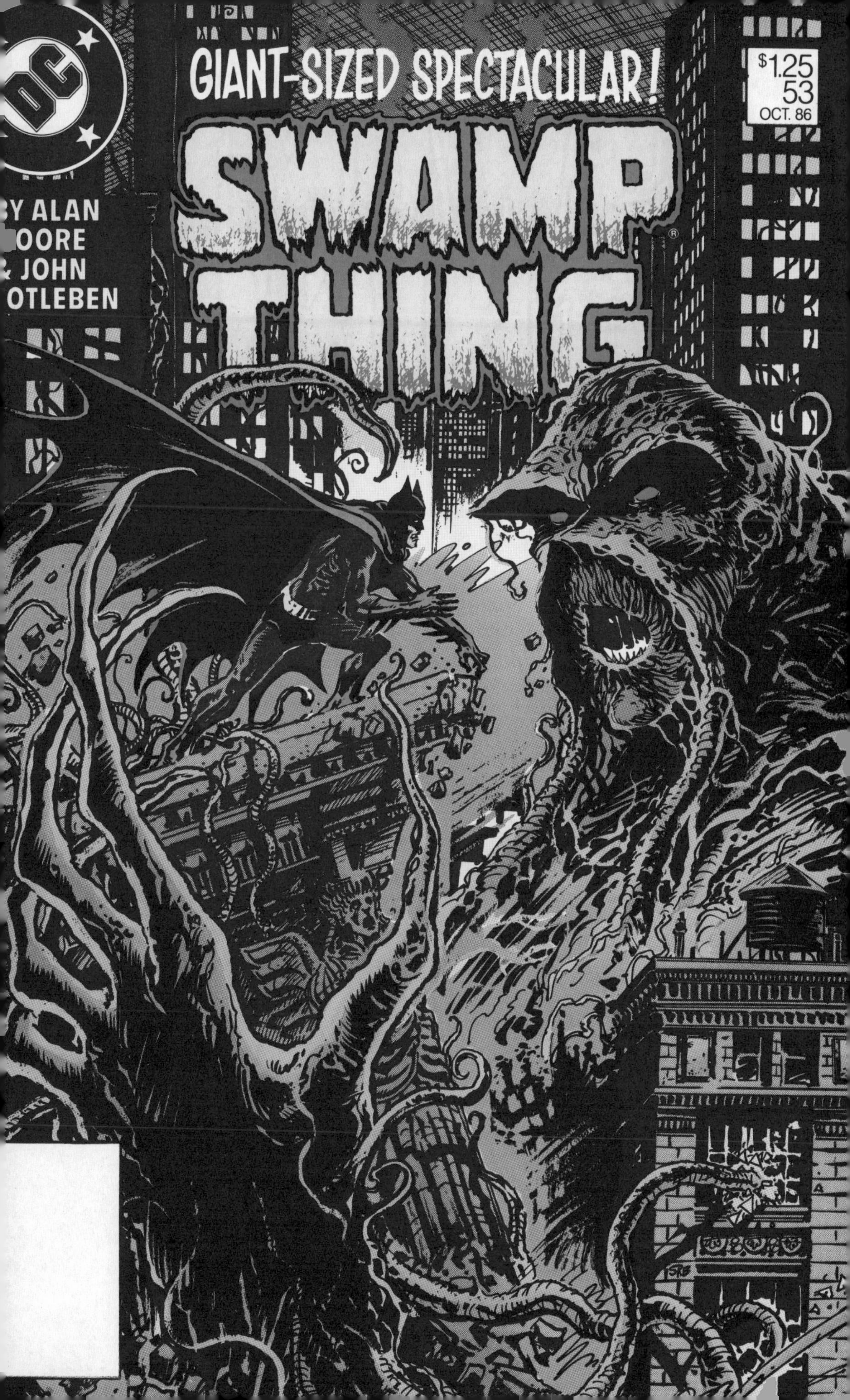

GIANT-SIZED SPECTACULAR!
$1.25
53
OCT. 86
SWAMP THING
Y ALAN
OORE
& JOHN
OTLEBEN

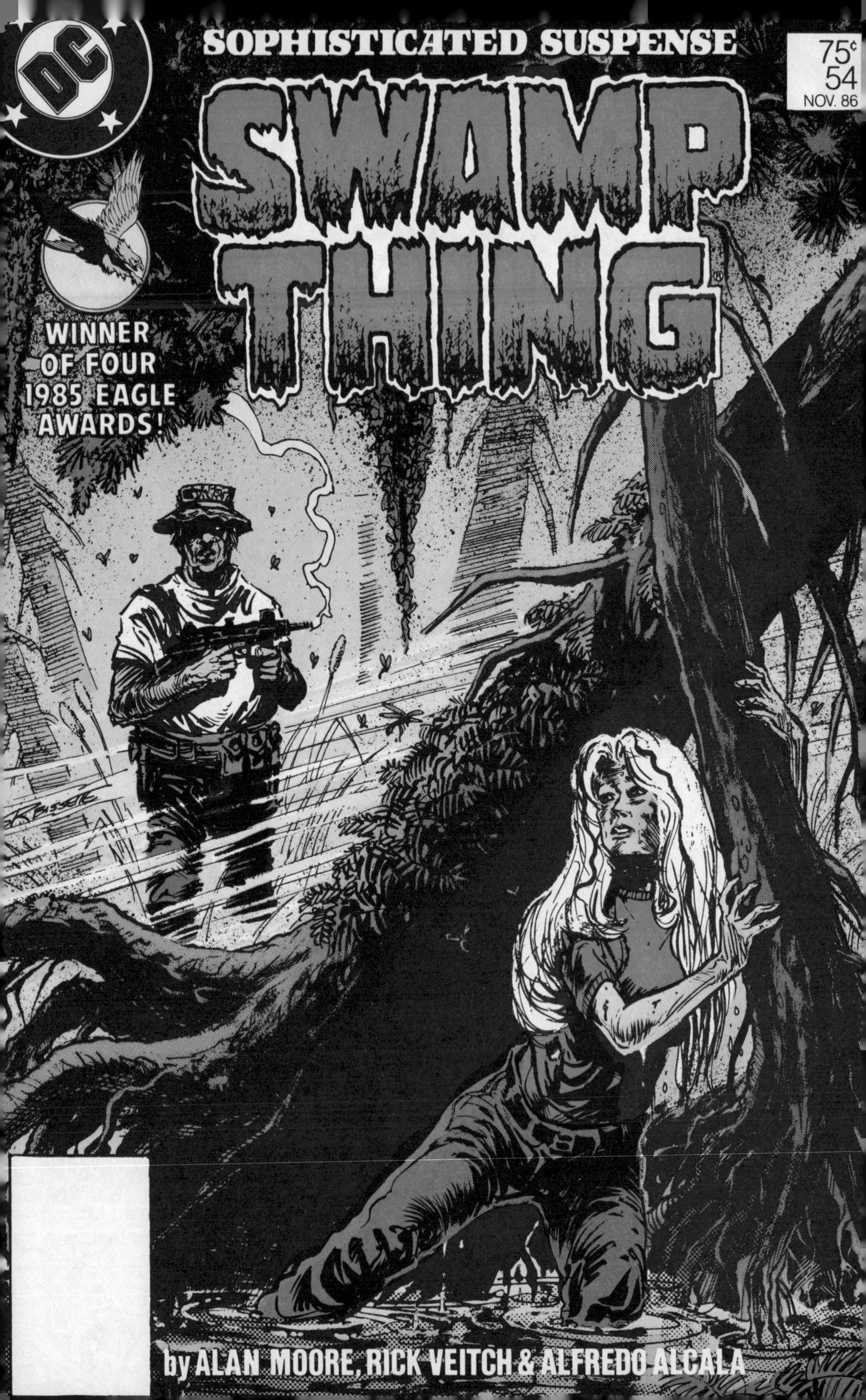
SOPHISTICATED SUSPENSE
75¢
54
NOV. 86
SWAMP THING
WINNER OF FOUR 1985 EAGLE AWARDS!
by ALAN MOORE, RICK VEITCH & ALFREDO ALCALA

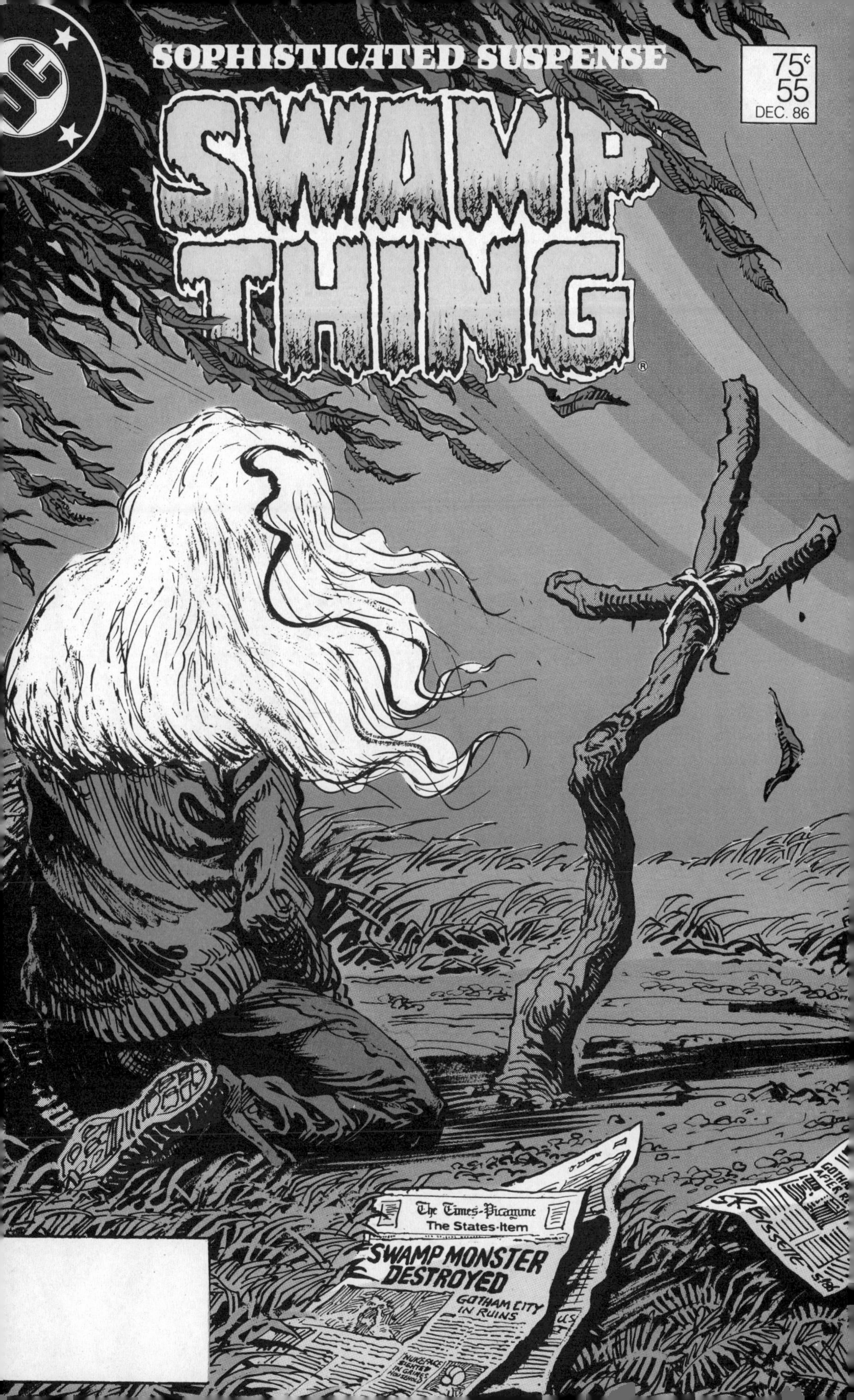
SOPHISTICATED SUSPENSE
75¢
55
DEC. 86
SWAMP THING
The Times-Picayune
The States-Item
SWAMP MONSTER DESTROYED
GOTHAM CITY IN RUINS

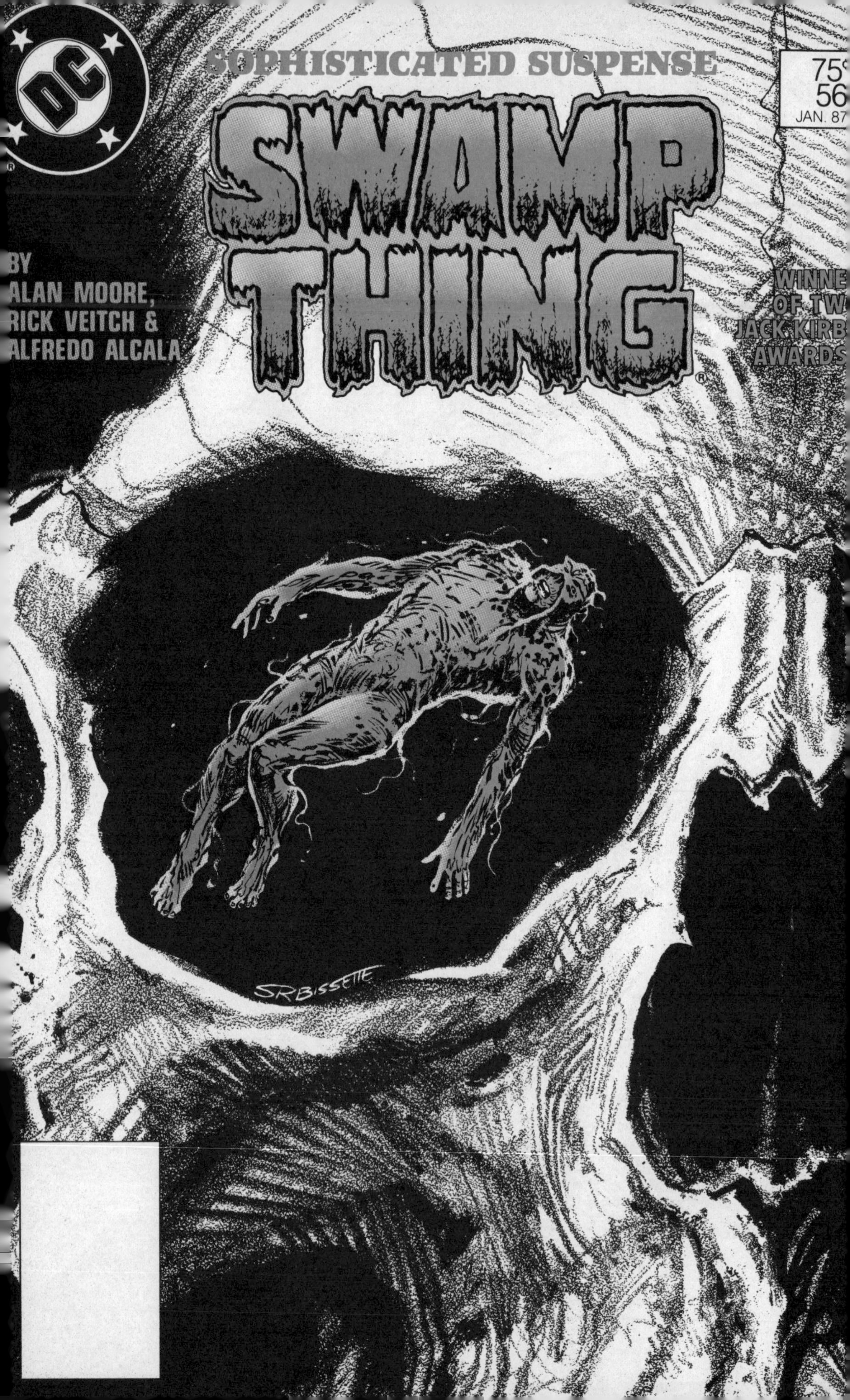

SOPHISTICATED SUSPENSE
75¢
56
JAN. 87
SWAMP THING
BY
ALAN MOORE,
RICK VEITCH &
ALFREDO ALCALA
WINNE
OF TW
JACK KIRB
AWARDS
SRBISSETTE

BIOGRAPHIES

ALAN MOORE

ALAN MOORE began working as a cartoonist in 1979 with several humorous strips in *SOUNDS* music weekly. after a year, he turned to writing, contributing to *DOCTOR WHO weekly* and *2000AD*. this was followed by *MARVELMAN* (published in the united states as *MIRACLEMAN*) and the political thriller *V FOR VENDETTA*, which earned him the british eagle award for best comics writer in 1982 and 1983. his groundbreaking run on *SWAMP THING* revolutionized comics and won him several industry awards. he is also the writer of the hugo award-winning *WATCHMEN*, a landmark series that firmly established him as the most influential writer in contemporary comics. he is currently tirelessly at work writing every comic in the america's best comics line, which he created in 1999.

STEPHEN BISSETTE

best known for his multi-award-winning tenure on *SWAMP THING*, stephen bissette also co-founded, edited, and co-published the eisner award-winning controversial horror anthology *TABOO*, collaborated on *1963*, and wrote, drew, and self-published four issues of *S.R. BISSETTE'S TYRANT*. bissette's film criticism, articles, and short fiction have appeared in over two dozen periodicals and book anthologies, and his original novella *ALIENS: TRIBES* won a bram stoker award in 1993.

JOHN TOTLEBEN

after a childhood in erie, pennsylvania spent consuming a steady diet of comics, monster magazines, and monster movies, john totleben went to the joe kubert school of cartoon and graphic art where he met steve bissette. together they worked on *BIZARRE ADVENTURES* followed by *SWAMP THING*, which they drew for almost three years. totleben is best known for his illustrative work on alan moore's *MIRACLEMAN*. his other credits include *1963*, *VERMILLION* and *THE DREAMING*.

RICK VEITCH

rick veitch worked in the underground comics scene before attending the joe kubert school of cartoon and graphic art. after graduating, he worked with stephen bissette on *BIZARRE ADVENTURES* before creating and illustrating *THE ONE*, the innovative epic comics mini-series. in addition to writing and drawing an acclaimed run on *SWAMP THING*, he is the creator/cartoonist of *BRAT PACK*, *MAXIMORTAL*, and the dream-based *RARE BIT FIENDS*, and a contributing artist on *1963*. currently he is illustrating "grey shirt" in the harvey award-winning *TOMORROW STORIES* from america's best comics.

ALFREDO ALCALA

alfredo alcala's graceful, moody inks helped maintain the style on *SWAMP THING* through many penciller changes. dc first employed alcala's talents in its horror and war comics such as *GHOSTS*, *UNEXPECTED*, and *WEIRD WAR TALES*. later he moved on to titles including *ALL-STAR SQUADRON*, *SAVAGE SWORD OF CONAN*, *BATMAN*, *SWAMP THING* and countless others for both dc and marvel. after a long battle with cancer, alcala passed away in april, 2000.

TATJANA WOOD

tatjana wood switched careers from dressmaking to comics coloring in the late 1960s and quickly established herself as one of the top colorists in the field, winning two shazam awards in the early 1970s. wood continues to color for dc comics.

JOHN COSTANZA

john costanza entered the comics field in the late 1960s, lettering such groundbreaking series as denny o'neil and neal adams's *GREEN LANTERN/GREEN ARROW* and jack kirby's *NEW GODS*. in addition to his lettering work, john is also an accomplished cartoonist.